Guide to the

AUTOMOBILE CERTIFICATION EXAMINATION

Fifth Edition

JAMES G. HUGHES

Automotive Instructor, Rio Hondo College
General Motors Contract Trainer
ASE Certified Master Automobile Technician
ASE Certified Engine Machinist
ASE Certified Engine Performance Specialist
ASE Certified Light Vehicle Compressed Natural Gas Technician
Former Toyota National Training Service Instructor
Member, Automotive Engine Rebuilders Association
Member, Society of Automotive Engineers

Prentice Hall
Upper Saddle River, New Jersey   Columbus, Ohio

Library of Congress Cataloging-in-Publication Data

Hughes, James G.
    Guide to automobile certification examination / James G.
Hughes.—5th ed.
      p.   cm.
    ISBN 0-13-011853-2
    1. Automobiles—Maintenance and repair—Examinations, questions,
etc.
    2. National Institute for Automotive Service Excellence—
Examinations—Study guides. 3. Automobile mechanics—Certification.
    TL152 .H858 2000
    629.28′72′076—dc21   99-31047
                                                      CIP

Cover art: Kevin Hulsey Illustration Inc.
Editor: Ed Francis
Production Editor: Christine M. Buckendahl
Design Coordinator: Karrie Converse-Jones
Cover Designer: Janoski Advertising Design
Production Manager: Patricia A. Tonneman
Marketing Manager: Chris Bracken

This book was set in Century Schoolbook by The Clarinda
Company, and was printed and bound by The Banta Company.
The cover was printed by Phoenix Color Corp.

©2000, 1997, 1993, 1983, 1978 by Prentice-Hall, Inc.
Pearson Education
Upper Saddle River, New Jersey 07458

ISBN: 0-13-011853-2

Prentice-Hall International (UK) Limited, *London*
Prentice-Hall of Australia Pty. Limited, *Sydney*
Prentice-Hall of Canada, Inc., *Toronto*
Prentice-Hall Hispanoamericana, S. A., *Mexico*
Prentice-Hall of India Private Limited, *New Delhi*
Prentice-Hall of Japan, Inc., *Tokyo*
Prentice-Hall (Singapore) Pte. Ltd., *Singapore*
Editora Prentice-Hall do Brasil, Ltda., *Rio de Janeiro*

PREFACE

SOME BRIEF FACTS REGARDING THE AUTOMOBILE CERTIFICATION PROGRAM

The National Institute for Automotive Service Excellence (ASE) is a nonprofit corporation created in 1972 that has been organized to promote and encourage high standards of automotive service and repair. ASE is governed by a Board of Directors. The members represent many different areas of the automotive service industry.

ASE offers tests in eight specific areas of automobile repair and in three specific engine machinist areas. To become certified in a given area, you must pass the related specific test. To become certified as a Master Automobile Technician, you must pass all eight automobile tests. The eight ASE test areas are:

1. Engine Repair (70 questions)
2. Automatic Transmission/Transaxle (50 questions)
3. Manual Drive Train and Axles (40 questions)
4. Suspension and Steering (40 questions)
5. Brakes (55 questions)
6. Electrical/Electronic Systems (50 questions)
7. Heating and Air Conditioning (50 questions)
8. Engine Performance (70 questions)

The three engine machinist test areas are:

1. Cylinder Head Specialist (55 questions)
2. Cylinder Block Specialist (70 questions)
3. Assembly Specialist (60 questions)

An Advanced Engine Performance (L1) Specialist test (45 questions) is part of the ASE program. In order to take this test, you must be currently certified in the regular Automobile Engine Performance (A8) area.

ASE also certifies in medium/heavy truck (including an L2 advanced level), collision repair and refinish, light vehicle CNG (compressed natural gas), and school bus, and in parts specialist areas.

To take the test(s), you must sign up in advance and pay a $25.00 registration fee, plus $20.00 for each test you plan to take. *Exceptions to this are the advanced tests (L1 and L2), which cost $40.00 each to take.* To obtain a registration form, write to ASE and request the free *Bulletin of Information* booklet. The address is:

National Institute for
Automotive Service Excellence
13505 Dulles Technology Drive
Suite 2
Herndon, VA 22071–3421

Tests are conducted in over 600 cities and towns across the nation, as indicated in the *Bulletin of Information*. The tests are normally given twice a year, once in the spring (May) and once in the fall (November).

Certifications are valid for five years. After this time period, you must take a recertification test. Recertification indicates you have kept up with the changing technology.

ACKNOWLEDGMENTS

Specific and grateful acknowledgment is made to the following companies, which provided reference literature used in the preparation of this book:

A-C Delco, General Motors Corporation; A-C Spark Plug Division, General Motors Corporation; All-Test Company; American Honda Motor Company; American Isuzu Motors Inc.; American Motors Corporation; Auto Air Conditioning Parts, Inc.; Automotive Data Systems; Automotive Engine Rebuilders Association; ARA Manufacturing Company; Automotive Services Division/3M Company; Bar's Leak Western, Inc.; Bear Service Equipment, Applied Power, Inc.; Belden Corporation; Bendix Corporation; Buick Motor Division, General Motors Corporation; Cadillac Motor Division, General Motors Corporation; Carter Automotive, A.C.F. Industries, Inc.; C. E. Niehoff and Company, Division of TRW, Inc.; Champion Parts Rebuilders, Inc.; Champion Spark Plug Company; Chevrolet Motor Division, General Motors Corporation; Chrysler Corporation; Clevite Industries Inc.; Dana Corporation, Service Parts Group; Delco-Moraine, Inc.; Delco-Remy Division, General Motors Corporation; Echlin Manufacturing Company, Inc.; Essex International, Inc., Electro-Mechanical Division; Exide Corporation; Federal-Mogul Corporation; Fel-Pro Inc.; Filko Automotive, F & B Manufacturing Company Products Division; FMC Corporation, Automotive Service Equipment Division; Ford Parts and Service Division; Fram Corporation; Garrett Corporation; Gates Rubber Company, Automotive Division; GFI Canada; GM Product Service Training, General Motors Corporation; Hastings Manufacturing Company; Hyundai Motor America; Ignition Manufacturers Institute; Jamco, Inc.; John Fluke Manufacturing Company, Inc.; Kem Manufacturing Company, Inc.; K-Line Industries; Lucas Industries, Inc.; Mazda Motor Corporation; McQuay-Norris Manufacturing Company; Moog Automotive, Inc.; Neway Manufacturing Inc.; Nissan Motors Corporation, USA, Inc.; Oldsmobile Division, General Motors Corporation; Peugeot Motors of America, Inc.; Pontiac Motor Division, General Motors Corporation; Purolator Products, Inc; Raybestos-Manhattan, Inc.; Robert Bosch Sales Corporation; Robinair Automotive Division; Sioux Tools, Inc.; Sun Electric Corporation; Sunnen Products, Inc.; Tomco Inc.; Toyota Motor Sales, USA, Inc.; Trans-Go; Trojan Battery Company; TRW, Inc., Replacement Parts Division; Union Oil Company of California (Western Region); Walker Manufacturing Company; Wells Manufacturing Corporation.

Special thanks are also given to the following certified technicians and friends who assisted in reviewing questions/answers and offered many valuable suggestions:

Pete Blair, Belmont Motor Clinic, Inc.; Sid Burks, Tuneup Masters Inc.; Fred Conners, Toyota Motor Sales; Chris Cottam, General Motors; Phil Fournier, Phil's Auto Clinic; Lorenzo Gameros; Alan Gettman, Drive-in Locksmith Company; Bob Gordon, Fullerton College; Bill Gutzman, B & D Automotive; Lee Haeberlein, Mountain View High School; Mike Hoffman; Glen Hammonds, Rancho Santiago College; John Hoppa, General Motors; Walt Kangas, Southeast Los Angeles County ROP; Arlo (Chip) Lusby, Mt. San Antonio College; Erich Munden, Rio Hondo College; Martin Orozco, Cypress College; Jay Ray; Paul Rudd; Mike Slavich, Rio Hondo College; David Solomon; Quentin Swan, Calif. State Dept. of Education; Mike Vliestra; Steve Vezerian, Steve's Shell Service; Milt Webb; and Artie Wu, Calif. Bureau of Automotive Repair.

CONTENTS

INSTRUCTIONS FOR USING THIS BOOK

This book contains sample certification area pretest exercises. Each pretest contains a large pool of realistic study questions. These questions are not taken from ASE tests, but are similar in content and style to those you will find on actual certification tests. You should also be aware of the fact that the ASE test questions are changed periodically.

The author recommends that you prepare for the ASE tests by doing the following:

1. Find a quiet room where you won't be disturbed.
2. Decide which pretest you want to take.
3. Prepare yourself an answer sheet.
4. Take the pretest that you have selected, grade it, and determine the areas you need to brush up on.
5. Start a study program using your own textbooks or those from a library. Refer to the study outline at the beginning of each pretest.
6. Check with your local schools for training programs and any special refresher courses they may be scheduling.

Here are some additional tips:

1. *Read the study outlines carefully.* Understand all of the terms, repair procedures, and diagnostic methods.
2. *Be aware of question overlap on the actual ASE tests.* For instance, cooling system questions are asked on the Engine Repair test, the Engine Performance test, and the Heating and Air Conditioning test.
3. When studying for the Engine Repair test, refer also to the Engine Performance questions and the Electrical/Electronic Systems questions.
4. When studying for the Engine Performance test, refer also to the Engine Repair questions and the Electrical/Electronic Systems questions.
5. When studying for the Engine Machinist tests, refer also to the Engine Repair questions.
6. When you take the actual ASE tests, an unanswered question counts as a wrong answer. If you are not sure of the correct answer, make the best guess you can.

7. When you take the actual ASE tests, read each question twice. The second time you may notice a key word that you overlooked the first time. Each word in the question is important and may be a clue to the right answer. Each question is of the multiple-choice type with four possible answers. Select the one that is *most* correct.
8. When you take the actual ASE tests, deal only with the information given in the question. Don't be suspicious of being tricked and read hidden meanings into the questions.

Following is a list of the major content areas contained in each ASE Automobile test, in the (L1) test, and in each ASE Engine Machinist test.

Engine Repair (A1)

- General Engine Diagnosis
- Cylinder Head and Valve Train Diagnosis and Repair
- Engine Block Diagnosis and Repair
- Lubrication and Cooling Systems Diagnosis and Repair
- Fuel, Electrical, Ignition, and Exhaust Systems Inspection and Service

Automatic Transmission/Transaxle (A2)

- General Transmission/Transaxle Diagnosis
- Transmission/Transaxle Maintenance and Adjustment
- In-Vehicle Transmission/Transaxle Repair
- Off-Vehicle Transmission/Transaxle Repair

Manual Drive Train and Axles (A3)

- Clutch Diagnosis and Repair
- Transmission Diagnosis and Repair
- Transaxle Diagnosis and Repair
- Drive (Half) Shaft and Universal Joint/Constant Velocity (CV) Joint Diagnosis and Repair (Front and Rear Wheel Drive)
- Rear Axle Diagnosis and Repair
- Four-Wheel Drive Component Diagnosis and Repair

Suspension and Steering (A4)

- Steering Systems Diagnosis and Repair
- Suspension Systems Diagnosis and Repair
- Wheel Alignment Diagnosis, Adjustment and Repair
- Wheel and Tire Diagnosis and Repair

Brakes (A5)

- Hydraulic System Diagnosis and Repair
- Drum Brake Diagnosis and Repair
- Disc Brake Diagnosis and Repair
- Power Assist Units Diagnosis and Repair
- Miscellaneous Diagnosis and Repair
- Anti-Lock Brake System Diagnosis and Repair

Electrical/Electronic Specialist (A6)

- General Electrical/Electronic System Diagnosis
- Battery Diagnosis and Service
- Starting System Diagnosis and Repair
- Charging System Diagnosis and Repair
- Lighting Systems Diagnosis and Repair
- Gauges, Warning Devices, and Driver Information Systems Diagnosis and Repair
- Horn and Wiper/Washer Diagnosis and Repair
- Accessories Diagnosis and Repair

Heating and Air Conditioning (A7)

- A/C System Diagnosis and Repair
- Refrigeration System Component Diagnosis and Repair
- Heating and Engine Cooling Systems Diagnosis and Repair
- Operating Systems and Related Controls Diagnosis and Repair
- Refrigerant Recovery, Recycling, and Handling

Engine Performance (A8)

- General Engine Diagnosis
- Ignition System Diagnosis and Repair
- Fuel, Air Induction, and Exhaust Systems Diagnosis and Repair
- Emissions Control Systems Diagnosis and Repair
- Computerized Engine Controls Diagnosis and Repair

- Engine-Related Service
- Engine Electrical Systems Diagnosis and Repair

Advanced Engine Performance Specialist (L1)

- General Powertrain Diagnosis
- Computerized Powertrain Controls Diagnosis
- Ignition System Diagnosis
- Fuel Systems and Air Induction Systems Diagnosis
- Emissions Control Systems Diagnosis
- I/M Failure Diagnosis

Light Vehicle Compressed Natural Gas (F1)

- Vehicle Compatibility Analysis
- Conversion Parts Fabrication
- Conversion Equipment Installation
- Leak Testing and Repairs
- Conversion Initial Adjustments and Performance Verification
- In-Service System Diagnosis and Repair
- Cylinder Safety

Cylinder Head Specialist

- Cylinder Head Disassembly and Cleaning
- Cylinder Head Crack Repair
- Cylinder Head Inspection and Machining
- Cylinder Head Assembly

Cylinder Block Specialist

- Cylinder Block Disassembly and Cleaning
- Cylinder Block Crack Repair
- Cylinder Block Machining
- Crankshaft Inspection and Machining
- Connecting Rods and Pistons, Inspection and Machining
- Balancing
- Cylinder Block Preparation

Assembly Specialist

- Engine Disassembly, Inspection, and Cleaning
- Engine Preparation
- Short Block Assembly
- Long Block Assembly
- Final Assembly

Section 1

ENGINE REPAIR

STUDY OUTLINE

I. Engine Systems
  A. Four Stroke Cycle
    1. Intake
    2. Compression
    3. Power (combustion)
    4. Exhaust
    5. Cycle completed in two crankshaft revolutions (720°)
  B. Engine Design
    1. Cylinders in-line
    2. V-type
    3. Overhead camshaft(s)
      a. Advantages
      b. How driven? (chain, gears, or belt)
    4. Various valve locations
      a. "I" head most common
      b. Number of valves per cylinder
    5. Valve timing
      a. Opening and closing points with reference to crankpin position
      b. What is valve overlap?
      c. Timing marks
      d. Lobe centerlines
  C. Cylinder Assembly
    1. Crankshafts
      a. Crankpin spacing in degrees
      b. Vibration damper purpose
      c. Flywheel purpose
      d. Internally balanced
      e. Externally balanced
      f. Sludge trap plugs
    2. Pistons and rods
      a. Offset
      b. Assembly markings
      c. Spit-hole
      d. Bleed hole
      e. Valve reliefs
    3. Rings
      a. Compression
      b. Scraper
      c. Oil (3 piece)
      d. Materials
      e. Top-side markings
    4. Cylinder head
      a. Inspection (including cracks and passage condition)
      b. OHC towers
      c. Cam bearings
  D. Valve Train
    1. Camshaft
      a. What speed in relation to crankshaft?
      b. Lift
      c. Duration
      d. Location
      e. Lobe profile nomenclature
      f. Tensioners and guides
    2. Hydraulic valve lifters
      a. Advantages
      b. Operation
      c. Pump-up
      d. Roller-type
      e. Inspection and replacement
    3. Cam drive methods
      a. Gears
      b. Chain and sprockets
      c. Belt
      d. Adjusting belt tension
    4. Push rods (including inspection and replacement)
    5. Rocker arm assembly
      a. Geometry
      b. Inspection and replacement
      c. Shafts
      d. Pivots
      e. Studs
      f. Lubrication holes
      g. End plugs
    6. Valves
      a. Intake
      b. Exhaust
      c. Stem seals
      d. Keepers
      e. Retainers and springs
      f. Buckets and shims
      g. Rotators
      h. Guides
      i. Replacement procedures

E. Lubrication System
   1. API oil classifications
   2. Oil pump
      a. Types
      b. Required clearances
      c. Where are clearances checked?
      d. Wear
      e. Drives
      f. Pressure relief valve
      g. Installation
   3. Full-flow system
      a. Oil filters
      b. Pick-up screen and by-pass hole
      c. Auxiliary coolers
      d. Sending units
   4. Oil pressure light operation
   5. Pre-lubricating engine oiling system prior to starting
   6. Bearings
      a. Rod
      b. Main
      c. Thrust type (flange and separate washers)
      d. Cam
      e. Purpose of crush and spread
      f. Plastigage use
      g. Operating clearances
      h. Replacement procedures
      i. Crown wall measurement procedure
F. Cooling System
   1. Water circulation flow (include heater core)
   2. Radiator
      a. Crossflow design
      b. Downflow design
      c. Expansion tank
      d. Intercooler for ATF
      e. Removal/disassembly
      f. Testing
   3. System deposits
      a. Iron oxide/lime
      b. Electrolysis
      c. Pin-holed front covers
   4. Flushing and refill procedures
   5. Water pumps
      a. Aeration
      b. By-pass
      c. Inspect and replace
   6. Radiator pressure caps
      a. Valves
      b. Collapsed hose
   7. Coolant recovery system (including testing)
   8. Core plugs
   9. Temperature control
      a. Thermostats
      b. Viscous fans
      c. Shrouds
      d. Electric/hydraulic fans
   10. Drive belts (V and V-ribbed types)
      a. Glaze
      b. Fraying
      c. Cracking
      d. Separation
      e. Methods of adjustment
      f. Pulleys
G. Ignition System (Electronic-Type, Hall Effect, and DIS)
   1. Primary and secondary circuit wiring (including by-pass if equipped)
   2. Inspect/test coil(s)
   3. Inspect/test spark plugs and wires
   4. Adjust ignition timing (static and dynamic)
   5. Inspect/test system wiring harness
   6. Inspect/test timing advance devices
H. Battery and Starter System
   1. Slow and fast charge battery
   2. Jump starting
   3. Replace cables
   4. Test relays and solenoids
   5. Battery service
      a. State-of-charge
      b. Built-in specific gravity test indicator
      c. Testing for sulphated condition
   6. Starter problems
I. Intake Manifold System
   1. Improper torque could result in?
   2. Runner layout design/Exhaust cross-over
   3. Warpage
   4. Hot air intake
   5. Gaskets
   6. PCV valve, filter, and hoses
   7. Carburetor or TBI and linkage
   8. Electronic fuel injection
J. Exhaust System
   1. Collapsed exhaust pipe and plugged "cat"
   2. Manifold heat control valve function
   3. Resonators, converters, and mufflers
K. Fuel System
   1. Fuel pumps (electric and mechanical)
   2. Fuel filters
   3. Carburetor and TBI mounting plates
   4. Confirming closed-loop operation
   5. Air cleaner assembly
   6. Turbocharger system inspection
   7. Fuel injectors
II. Engine Service Procedures (Emphasis is placed on the type and use of tools)
A. Be Able to Identify Visually
   1. Micrometers (English and Metric)
   2. Cylinder bore gauges
   3. Cylinder hones
   4. Torque wrenches (click, beam, dial, and electronic types)
   5. Crack detection equipment
   6. Checking warpage with a straightedge and feeler gauge
   7. Dial indicator checks
   8. Hydraulic lifter leak-down test fixture
   9. Ridge reamers
   10. Rod alignment fixture

11. Ring groove cleaning tool
12. Cooling system pressure tester
13. Valve seat concentricity gauge
14. Valve spring tension tester
15. Carbon removing brushes
16. Cylinder block deck plate
17. Torque/angle meter
18. Profilometer

B. Block Assembly
1. Crankshaft measurements
   a. Taper
   b. Out-of-round
   c. End-play
   d. Runout
   e. Fillet radius
2. Cylinder measurements
   a. Taper
   b. Out-of-round
   c. Allowable limits
3. Camshaft measurements
   a. T.I.R. (total indicated runout)
   b. Lift
   c. Base circle runout
   d. End-play
   e. Gear backlash
4. Main bearing bore measurement
   a. Out-of-round
   b. Alignment
   c. Correction
5. Pans, covers, gaskets, and seals
   a. Inspect and replace

C. Heads and Valves
1. Valve and seat refacing
   a. Margin
   b. Seat width and location
   c. Interference angles
   d. "Throating" and "topping"
   e. Concentricity checks
2. Valve guide measurement
3. Valve guide reconditioning methods
4. Head surfacing
   a. Corrective machining on intake manifold
5. Valve spring measurements
   a. Tension
   b. Squareness (slowly rotate spring)
   c. Free length comparison
   d. Installed height (shims)
6. Valve tip height
7. Valve lash adjustment (hydraulic and mechanical lifters)
8. Head installation
   a. Bolt tightening sequence
   b. Torque angle tightening
   c. Torque-to-yield tightening

D. Pistons and Rings
1. Piston design
2. Piston measurements
   a. Where?

3. Ring installation
   a. End-gap measurement and position
   b. Ring side clearance
   c. Ring depth
4. Cylinder wall reconditioning
   a. Washing with soap and water
5. Piston ring groove wear

E. Rods, Pins, and Bearings
1. Rod alignment
   a. Checking piston skirt wear pattern
   b. Big-end wear
2. Piston pin types/installation methods
3. Rod bearing measurements
4. Rod bearing service
5. Determine needed repair

F. Gaskets and Seals
1. RTV silicone rubber
2. Anaerobic compound
3. Installation precautions

G. Replacing Engine (Procedures for Front Wheel Drive Vehicle)

H. Replacing Engine (Procedures for Rear Wheel Drive Vehicle)

III. Engine Problem/Diagnosis

A. Noises
1. Piston slap
2. Piston pin
3. Rod bearings
   a. Wear analysis
4. Main bearings
   a. Wear analysis
5. Crankshaft thrust
6. Valves
   a. Lifters
   b. Rocker arms
   c. Wear analysis
7. Ring "click"
8. Flywheel knock

B. Oil Consumption
1. Rings
2. Valves
3. Guides
4. Leaks
5. Plugged drain holes
6. Defective seals
   a. Internal and external
   b. Black-light detection method
7. Defective intake manifold gaskets
8. Exhaust smoke color
9. Exhaust odor

C. Water Consumption
1. Internal
2. External

D. Low Oil Pressure
1. Worn cam bearings
2. Worn rod bearings

E. Low Compression
  1. Test procedures (including the wet test)
F. Interpretation of Vacuum Gauge Readings
G. Worn Timing Chain Assembly
H. Incorrectly Installed Timing Belt
I. Perform Cylinder Leakage Test
  1. Determine needed repair

J. Perform Cylinder Balance Test (Including on Computer-Controlled Engines)
K. Battery and Starting System Complaints
L. Fuel and Exhaust System Complaints
M. Ignition System Complaints

---

1. An engine has erratic oil pressure and hydraulic valve lifter noise. This occurs only at speeds above 40 mph.

   Technician A says that this could be caused by an air leak.

   Technician B says that this could be caused by an overfilled crankcase.

   Who is right?
   a. A only   c. Both A and B
   b. B only   d. Neither A nor B

2. Due to the configuration of certain engines, air can be trapped in the cylinder head during a coolant drain and refill.

   Technician A says that this can cause a cracked head.

   Technician B says to unscrew the coolant temperature sending unit sufficiently to bleed the air.

   Who is right?
   a. A only   c. Both A and B
   b. B only   d. Neither A nor B

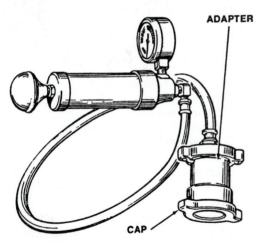

FIGURE 1–1

3. A cooling system is being checked with the tester shown in Figure 1–1. Gauge pressure rises when the engine is started.

   Technician A says that this could be caused by a combustion chamber crack.

   Technician B says that this could be caused by clogged tubes in the radiator core.

   Who is right?
   a. A only   c. Both A and B
   b. B only   d. Neither A nor B

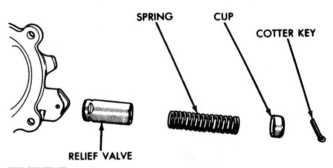

FIGURE 1–2

4. The spring in Figure 1–2 is accidentally left out during an engine repair.

   Technician A says that this will cause a blown oil filter.

   Technician B says that this will cause little or no oil pressure.

   Who is right?
   a. A only   c. Both A and B
   b. B only   d. Neither A nor B

5. A water pump is noisy.

   Technician A says that this could be caused by a corroded bearing.

   Technician B says that this could be caused by a defective seal.

   Who is right?
   a. A only   c. Both A and B
   b. B only   d. Neither A nor B

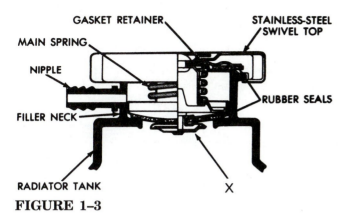

GASKET RETAINER   STAINLESS-STEEL SWIVEL TOP
MAIN SPRING
NIPPLE
FILLER NECK
RUBBER SEALS
RADIATOR TANK   X

FIGURE 1–3

6. Valve X in Figure 1–3 is stuck closed.

Technician A says that this can cause the radiator hoses to collapse on cool-down.

Technician B says that this can prevent coolant return to the radiator on cool-down.

Who is right?

a. A only   **c.** Both A and B

b. B only   **d.** Neither A nor B

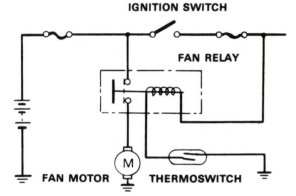

IGNITION SWITCH

FAN RELAY

FAN MOTOR   THERMOSWITCH

FIGURE 1–4

7. The electric fan motor in Figure 1–4 runs continuously.

Technician A says that this could be caused by melted together fan relay contacts.

Technician B says that this could be caused by a defective thermoswitch.

Who is right?

a. A only   **c.** Both A and B

b. B only   **d.** Neither A nor B

8. An engine is being torn down because of a badly spun rod bearing.

Technician A says to flush the oil passages in the block and head.

Technician B says to replace the oil cooler core.

Who is right?

a. A only   **c.** Both A and B

b. B only   **d.** Neither A nor B

9. After each cylinder head on a V-8 OHV engine is surfaced .012″, the intake manifold mounting bolt holes will not line up.

Technician A says to use thicker intake manifold gaskets and extra sealer.

Technician B says to elongate the mounting bolt holes with a file.

Who is right?

a. A only   **c.** Both A and B

b. B only   **d.** Neither A nor B

10. The cylinder heads are being installed on an engine. Some of the mounting bolt holes are "blind" and filled with oil.

Technician A says that failure to clean these holes can result in an erroneous torque reading.

Technician B says that failure to clean these holes can result in a cracked block.

Who is right?

a. A only   **c.** Both A and B

b. B only   **d.** Neither A nor B

FIGURE 1–5

11. Technician A says that noise can result if the check in Figure 1–5 is not according to specifications.

Technician B says that premature bearing wear can result if the check is not according to specifications.

Who is right?

a. A only   **c.** Both A and B

b. B only   **d.** Neither A nor B

12. A valve job is going to be done on a cylinder head.
    Technician A says to resurface the seats before reconditioning the guides.
    Technician B says to check the valve springs for squareness.
    Who is right?
    a. A only   c. Both A and B
    b. B only   d. Neither A nor B

13. Technician A says that a used keeper should not be mated with a new keeper.
    Technician B says that keeper seating should be checked with a hammer.
    Who is right?
    a. A only   c. Both A and B
    b. B only   d. Neither A nor B

FIGURE 1–7

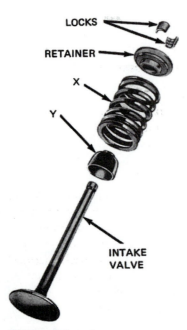

FIGURE 1–6

14. Technician A says that part X in Figure 1–6 can be replaced without removing the cylinder head.
    Technician B says that part Y can be replaced without removing the cylinder head.
    Who is right?
    a. A only   c. Both A and B
    b. B only   d. Neither A nor B

15. What is the technician measuring in Figure 1–7?
    a. Valve face runout   c. Valve margin
    b. Valve lift   d. Valve guide wear

16. Technician A says that an interference angle must be used if the engine burns premium grade fuel.
    Technician B says that an interference angle makes a poor seal when the engine is first started after a valve job.
    Who is right?
    a. A only   c. Both A and B
    b. B only   d. Neither A nor B

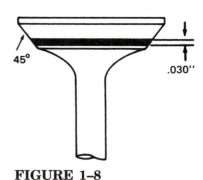

FIGURE 1–8

17. An exhaust valve has a seat contact pattern as shown in Figure 1–8. What needs to be done?
    a. Grind the seat with a 45° stone, and then narrow it by "topping."
    b. Grind the seat with a 45° stone, and then narrow it by "throating."
    c. Widen the seat with a 45° stone.
    d. Nothing

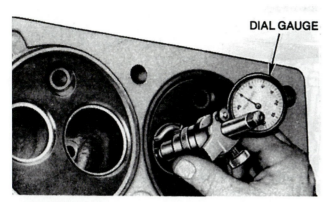

FIGURE 1-9

FIGURE 1-10

18. Technician A says that the dial gauge in Figure 1-9 is measuring valve seat depth.
    Technician B says that the dial gauge is measuring valve seat concentricity.
    Who is right?
    a. A only
    b. B only
    c. Both A and B
    d. Neither A nor B

19. Technician A says that dividers can be used to measure valve spring assembled height.
    Technician B says that a telescoping gauge can be used to measure valve spring assembled height.
    Who is right?
    a. A only   **c.** Both A and B
    b. B only   **d.** Neither A nor B

20. A six-cylinder in-line OHV engine is being assembled. In what direction should the oil feed holes on the rocker arm shaft face?
    a. On the side opposite the pushrods
    b. On the side toward the pushrods
    c. Up
    d. Down

21. All the valve lifters in an engine are cupped (concaved) as shown in Figure 1-10.
    Technician A says to replace the camshaft.
    Technician B says to replace the lifters.
    Who is right?
    a. A only   **c.** Both A and B
    b. B only   **d.** Neither A nor B

22. Technician A says that camshaft wear can cause retarded valve timing.
    Technician B says that camshaft wear can produce a "popping" noise out the top of the carburetor.
    Who is right?
    a. A only
    b. B only
    c. Both A and B
    d. Neither A nor B

23. A car owner complains of excessive exhaust smoke. During a road test the technician verifies the complaint and finds that the automatic transmission shifts rough. Which of these is the MOST LIKELY cause?
    a. Defective vacuum modulator
    b. Cracked flex plate
    c. Rich fuel mixture
    d. Bad intercooler

24. Oil is dripping from the bottom of an engine.
    Technician A says that this could be from a leaky oil gallery plug.
    Technician B says that this could be from a worn rear main bearing.
    Who is right?
    a. A only
    b. B only
    c. Both A and B
    d. Neither A nor B

BUCKET

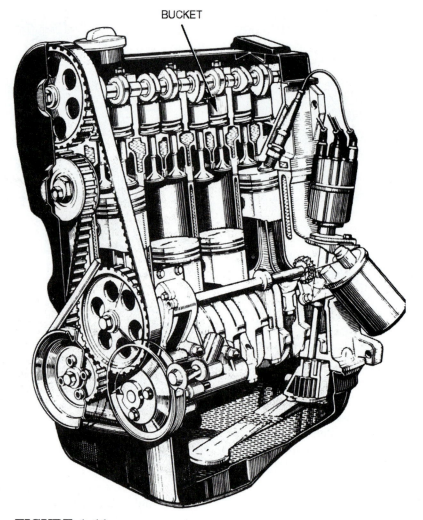

FIGURE 1–11

25. Valve clearance is not correct on the OHC engine in Figure 1–11.

Technician A says to grind the buckets (tappets).

Technician B says to change valve springs.

Who is right?

a. A only   **c.** Both A and B
b. B only   **d.** Neither A nor B

26. A light, double-knocking noise is heard from an idling engine.

Technician A says that this could be from worn rod bearings.

Technician B says that this could be from worn piston pins.

Who is right?

a. A only
b. B only
c. Both A and B
d. Neither A nor B

FIGURE 1–12

27. The bearings in Figure 1–12 are going to be installed in an engine.

Technician A says that alignment must be checked.

Technician B says that clearance must be checked.

Who is right?

a. A only   **c.** Both A and B
b. B only   **d.** Neither A nor B

FIGURE 1–13

FIGURE 1–14

28. Part X shown in Figure 1–13 is left out when replacing a timing chain and cam sprocket on a carburetor-equipped engine.

    Technician A says that fuel pump pressure will be zero.

    Technician B says that camshaft end play will be excessive.

    Who is right?
    a. A only
    b. B only
    c. Both A and B
    d. Neither A nor B

29. Technician A says that camshaft lobe lift is being checked in Figure 1–14.

    Technician B says that valve timing is being checked in Figure 1–14.

    Who is right?
    a. A only
    b. B only
    c. Both A and B
    d. Neither A nor B

30. Technician A says that oil can reach the combustion chamber because of a misaligned intake manifold gasket.

    Technician B says that oil can reach the combustion chamber because of a bad turbo.

    Who is right?
    a. A only
    b. B only
    c. Both A and B
    d. Neither A nor B

31. You are measuring vacuum on an engine at sea level that is in good condition. The MOST NORMAL reading (at idle) would be:
    a. 30″.   b. 17″.   c. 12″.   d. 3″.

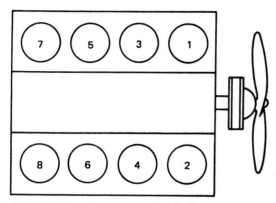

FIGURE 1–15

32. A compression test has been made on the engine in Figure 1–15. Cylinders 4 and 6 have readings of 60 psi. All other cylinders have readings between 130 and 135 psi.

Technician A says that this could be caused by a "loose" timing chain.

Technician B says that this could be caused by a blown head gasket.

Who is right?
a. A only
b. B only
c. Both A and B
d. Neither A nor B

33. A cylinder leakage test shows all cylinders to be okay. Yet the engine just failed a compression test.

Technician A says that slow cranking rpm could be the reason.

Technician B says that an out-of-time camshaft could be the reason.

Who is right?
a. A only
b. B only
c. Both A and B
d. Neither A nor B

34. A transverse mounted engine with front wheel drive must be removed from a car. All of the following is generally recommended EXCEPT:
a. removing the engine and transaxle as a unit.
b. disconnecting the half-shafts.
c. disconnecting the speedometer cable.
d. removing the differential gears.

35. Technician A says to replace an engine mount if the rubber has separated from the metal.

Technician B says to replace an engine mount if it has cracks around a bolt hole.

Who is right?
a. A only
b. B only
c. Both A and B
d. Neither A nor B

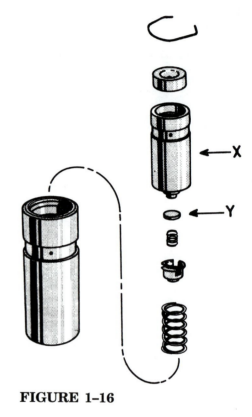

FIGURE 1–16

36. A valve lifter assembly is shown in Figure 1–16.

Technician A says that if part X is "frozen," a loud rapping noise will occur.

Technician B says that if part Y leaks, a moderate clicking noise can occur.

Who is right?
a. A only
b. B only
c. Both A and B
d. Neither A nor B

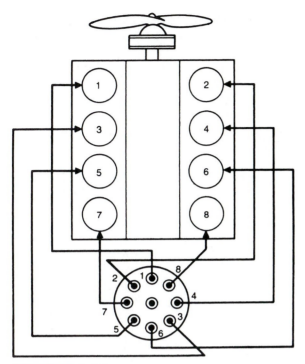

FIGURE 1–17

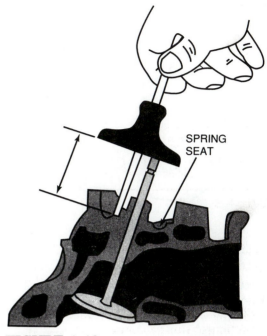

FIGURE 1–18

37. An engine with a firing order of 1, 8, 4, 3, 6, 5, 7, 2 and cc distributor rotation has just had the spark plug wires hooked up as shown in Figure 1–17.

   Technician A says that the wire routing is okay.

   Technician B says that the engine will start, but idle rough.

   Who is right?
   a. A only
   b. B only
   c. Both A and B
   d. Neither A nor B

38. An engine that has electronic ignition will not start (fuel delivery and fuel management systems are good).

   Technician A says that this could be caused by a "punctured" rotor.

   Technician B says that this could be caused by too much pickup coil air gap clearance.

   Who is right?
   a. A only
   b. B only
   c. Both A and B
   d. Neither A nor B

39. Technician A says that the tool in Figure 1–18 is being used to determine combustion chamber depth.

   Technician B says that the tool is being used to determine valve stem installed height.

   Who is right?
   a. A only
   b. B only
   c. Both A and B
   d. Neither A nor B

40. A car equipped with electronic ignition misses intermittently while driving. After the distributor cap, rotor, and spark plug wires are replaced, the problem still exists.

   Technician A says that the cause could be a defective ignition switch.

   Technician B says that the cause could be a poor harness connection at the spark control unit (module).

   Who is right?
   a. A only
   b. B only
   c. Both A and B
   d. Neither A nor B

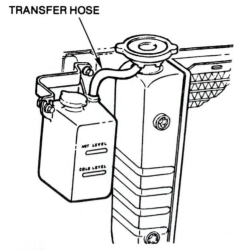

TRANSFER HOSE

FIGURE 1–19

41. A car has a coolant recovery system as shown in Figure 1–19. Coolant does not return to the radiator when the engine cools.

Technician A says that the transfer hose could be plugged.

Technician B says that the filler neck soldered joint could be separated.

Who is right?

a. A only
b. B only
c. Both A and B
d. Neither A nor B

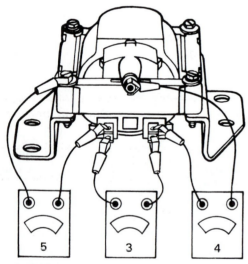

FIGURE 1–20

42. An ohmmeter is being used to test the ignition coil in Figure 1–20.

Technician A says that test point 3 and test point 4 should show continuity.

Technician B says that test point 5 should show infinite resistance.

Who is right?

a. A only
b. B only
c. Both A and B
d. Neither A nor B

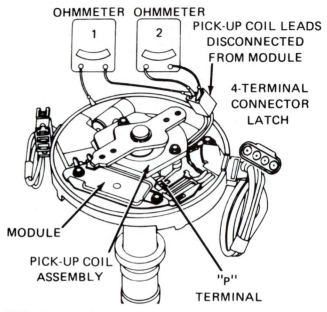

OHMMETER OHMMETER
1   2   PICK-UP COIL LEADS DISCONNECTED FROM MODULE

4-TERMINAL CONNECTOR LATCH

MODULE

PICK-UP COIL ASSEMBLY

"P" TERMINAL

FIGURE 1–21

43. A pickup coil is being tested in Figure 1–21.

Technician A says that ohmmeter 1 should have no reading (infinite).

Technician B says that ohmmeter 2 should have no reading (infinite).

Who is right?

a. A only
b. B only
c. Both A and B
d. Neither A nor B

44. A 4-cylinder engine equipped with port fuel injection is spewing white smoke under all driving conditions.

Technician A says that this could be caused by a cracked throttle body.

Technician B says that this could be caused by a cracked cylinder head.

Who is right?

a. A only
b. B only
c. Both A and B
d. Neither A nor B

FIGURE 1–22

45. Technician A says that the part shown in Figure 1–22 helps reduce valve head heat and increases valve life.

   Technician B says that the part shown in Figure 1–22 helps prevent valve seat recession in lead-free gasoline and liquefied petroleum gas engines.

   Who is right?

   a. A only
   c. Both A and B
   b. B only
   d. Neither A nor B

46. Technician A says that valve lash set too tight will reduce valve overlap.

   Technician B says that valve lash set too tight will cause intake and exhaust valves to open late and close early.

   Who is right?

   a. A only
   b. B only
   c. Both A and B
   d. Neither A nor B

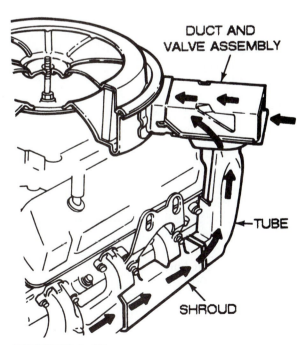

FIGURE 1–23

47. The valve assembly shown in Figure 1–23 is stuck open.

   Technician A says that this will allow exhaust gases to enter the intake manifold.

   Technician B says that this will prevent ignition advance during rapid acceleration.

   Who is right?

   a. A only
   b. B only
   c. Both A and B
   d. Neither A nor B

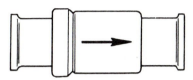

FIGURE 1–24

48. The parts inside the valve shown in Figure 1–24 have broken and fallen out.

   Technician A says that this will cause poor or no engine idle.

   Technician B says that this will cause the oil pan seals to rupture and leak.

   Who is right?

   a. A only
   b. B only
   c. Both A and B
   d. Neither A nor B

49. An engine equipped with a turbocharger has excessive oil consumption and blue exhaust smoke.

   Technician A says that this could be caused by a leaking compressor seal.

   Technician B says that this could be caused by a sludged center housing.

   Who is right?

   a. A only
   b. B only
   c. Both A and B
   d. Neither A nor B

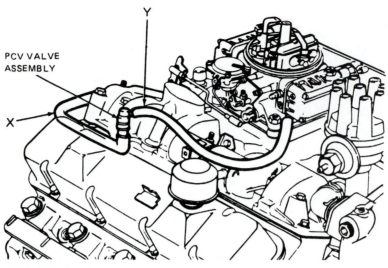

PCV VALVE
ASSEMBLY

Y

X

FIGURE 1–25

50. The engine shown in Figure 1–25 is running at idle speed. When hose X is pinched closed, there is a 50-rpm drop.

Technician A says to replace hose X.
Technician B says to replace hose Y.
Who is right?
a. A only **c.** Both A and B
b. B only **d.** Neither A nor B

51. Spark plugs are being installed in an aluminum cylinder head.

Technician A says that thread damage can be caused by overtorquing.

Technician B says that thread damage can be caused by cross-threading.

Who is right?
a. A only
b. B only
c. Both A and B
d. Neither A nor B

FIGURE 1–26

52. Technician A says that the filter shown in Figure 1–26 (see arrow) is part of the PCV system.

Technician B says that excessive oil consumption can result if this filter becomes clogged.

Who is right?
a. A only
b. B only
c. Both A and B
d. Neither A nor B

53. Technician A says that a crosshatch pattern should be present after using a glaze breaker.

Technician B says to wash the cylinders with solvent after using a glaze breaker.

Who is right?
a. A only
b. B only
c. Both A and B
d. Neither A nor B

54. A press-fit damper has a loose fit on the crank snout.

Technician A says that the problem can be corrected by installing an oversize snout key.

Technician B says that this problem can be corrected by installing a thicker washer behind the snout bolt.

Who is right?
a. A only
b. B only
c. Both A and B
d. Neither A nor B

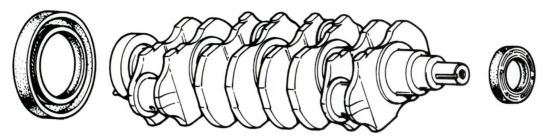

FIGURE 1–27

55. Technician A says that the rear main oil seal in Figure 1–27 is positioned backwards.
Technician B says that the oil seals should be installed dry.
Who is right?
a. A only
b. B only
c. Both A and B
d. Neither A nor B

57. A flywheel ring gear has worn teeth.
Technician A says that this can affect engine balance.
Technician B says that repair can be made by brazing the teeth.
Who is right?
a. A only   **c.** Both A and B
b. B only   **d.** Neither A nor B

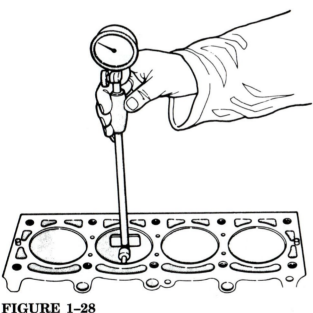

FIGURE 1–28

FIGURE 1–29

56. The gauge pictured in Figure 1–28 checks.
a. bore out-of-roundness.
b. bore taper.
c. Both A and B
d. Neither A nor B

58. The tool in Figure 1–29 is used to:
a. remove cylinder ridges.
b. make a cross-hatch.
c. pull cylinder sleeves.
d. install cylinder liners.

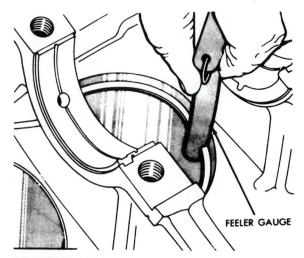

FIGURE 1–30

59. What measurement check is being performed in Figure 1–30?
a. Piston clearance
b. Cylinder out-of-round
c. Cylinder taper
d. Piston ring gap

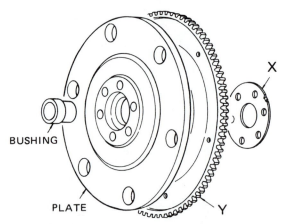

FIGURE 1–31

60. The flywheel in Figure 1–31 has excessive face runout after being installed.

Technician A says that this could be caused by a nick or burr on part X.

Technician B says that this could be caused by uneven wear on part Y.

Who is right?
a. A only
b. B only
c. Both A and B
d. Neither A nor B

61. Technician A says that the bushing shown in Figure 1–31 should fit finger tight in its bore.

Technician B says that it should be lubricated after installing.

Who is right?
a. A only
b. B only
c. Both A and B
d. Neither A nor B

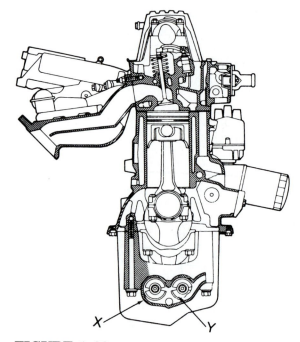

FIGURE 1–32

62. Refer to the engine in Figure 1–32.

Technician A says that shaft X and shaft Y must be timed.

Technician B says that shaft X and shaft Y rotate in opposite directions.

Who is right?
a. A only
b. B only
c. Both A and B
d. Neither A nor B

FIGURE 1–33

63. Technician A says that a broken crankshaft can result if the part in Figure 1–33 is defective.

Technician B says that a sheared woodruff key can result if the part fits loose.

Who is right?
a. A only
b. B only
c. Both A and B
d. Neither A nor B

64. Technician A says that the setup in Figure 1–34 is used to measure thrust wear.

Technician B says that the setup is used to measure the fillet radius.

Who is right?
a. A only
b. B only
c. Both A and B
d. Neither A nor B

65. A dial gauge can be used to check:
a. crankshaft snout trueness.
b. crankshaft end play.
c. Both a and b
d. Neither a nor b

66. A main bearing half shows localized damage near the joint face.

Technician A says that this could be caused by insufficient cap tightening.

Technician B says that this could be caused by insufficient crush.

Who is right?
a. A only
b. B only
c. Both A and B
d. Neither A nor B

67. Technician A says that RTV silicone sealer is often used to secure threaded fasteners.

Technician B says that anaerobic sealer fumes can "poison" an oxygen sensor.

Who is right?
a. A only
b. B only
c. Both A and B
d. Neither A nor B

FIGURE 1–34

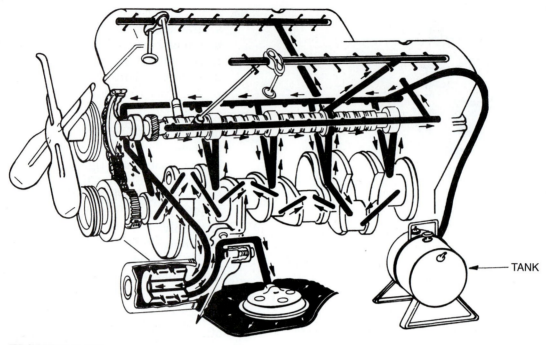

FIGURE 1–35

68. Technician A says that the tank in Figure 1–35 is used to prevent a "dry start" after an engine overhaul.

Technician B says that the tank is used to charge the lubrication system.

Who is right?

a. A only   c. Both A and B
b. B only   d. Neither A nor B

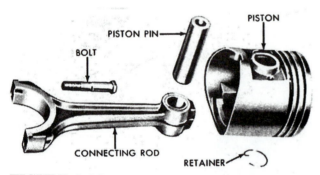

FIGURE 1–36

69. Refer to the illustration in Figure 1–36.

Technician A says that this piston pin is pressed into the connecting rod eye (small end).

Technician B says that this piston pin oscillates in the piston.

Who is right?

a. A only   c. Both A and B
b. B only   d. Neither A nor B

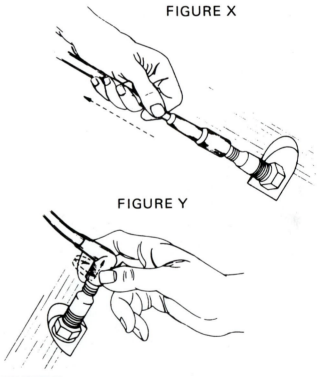

FIGURE X

FIGURE Y

FIGURE 1–37

70. Which figure in Figure 1–37 shows the correct way to disconnect a spark plug cable?

a. X only   c. Both X and Y
b. Y only   d. Neither X nor Y

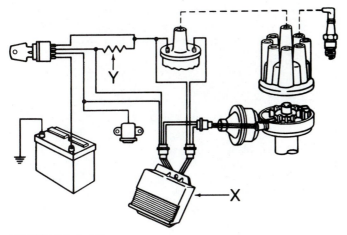

FIGURE 1–38

71. An engine that is equipped with the ignition system in Figure 1–38 will not start (fuel delivery is okay).

Technician A says that part X could be defective.

Technician B says that part Y could be defective.

Who is right?

a. A only
b. B only
c. Both A and B
d. Neither A nor B

FIGURE 1–39

72. Technician A says that the damage shown in Figure 1–39 could have been caused by excessive overrunning after starting.

Technician B says that the damage could have been caused by the driver opening the throttle too wide during starting.

Who is right?

a. A only
b. B only
c. Both A and B
d. Neither A nor B

73. During a cylinder leakage test, the gauge reads 70% and air is heard coming from the exhaust pipe. What is the MOST LIKELY cause?

a. Cracked piston
b. Hole in cylinder wall
c. Burned valve
d. Collapsed lifter

74. Which of the following can cause piston damage?

a. Over-advanced timing
b. Adjusting the distributor by "ear"
c. Cooling system malfunction
d. All of the above

75. A turbocharger is being replaced on an engine.

Technician A says to disconnect the wastegate actuator before starting the engine.

Technician B says to prime the oil feed line with fresh motor oil before starting the engine.

Who is right?

a. A only
b. B only
c. Both A and B
d. Neither A nor B

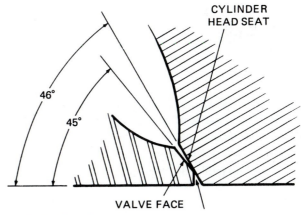

FIGURE 1–40

76. Technician A says that a 3-angle grind is shown in Figure 1–40.

Technician B says that poor valve face-to-valve seat contact is shown in Figure 1–40.

Who is right?

a. A only
b. B only
c. Both A and B
d. Neither A nor B

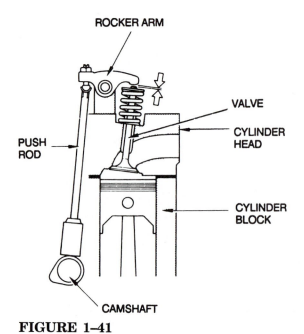

FIGURE 1–41

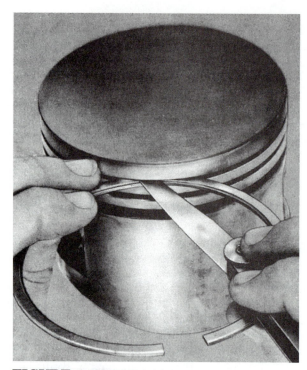

FIGURE 1–42

77. The measurement in Figure 1–41 (see large arrows) has been set incorrectly.

Technician A says that this can cause noise.

Technician B says that this can cause rough idle.

Who is right?
a. A only
b. B only
c. Both A and B
d. Neither A nor B

78. Which of these should be used to clean the cylinder bores after honing?
a. Cleaning solvent
b. Murphy's oil soap
c. Isopropyl alcohol
d. Hot water and soap

79. Refer to the picture in Figure 1–42.

Technician A says to use a new ring when making this check.

Technician B says that a measurement of .020″ would be okay.

Who is right?
a. A only
b. B only
c. Both A and B
d. Neither A nor B

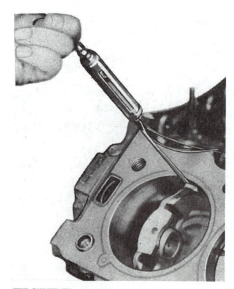

FIGURE 1–43

80. What is being determined in Figure 1–43?
a. Cylinder wall taper
b. Piston clearance
c. Both a and b
d. Neither a nor b

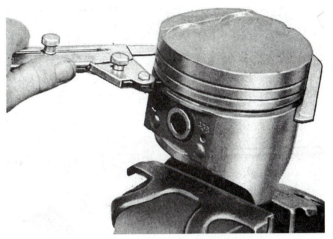

FIGURE 1–44

81. What is being done in Figure 1–44?
    a. Resizing a worn ring groove
    b. Cleaning an oil ring groove
    c. Cleaning a compression ring groove
    d. Measuring ring groove depth

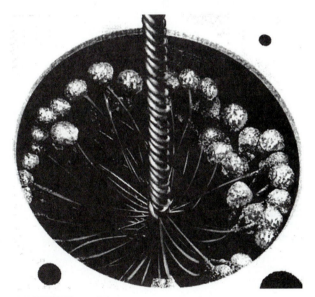

FIGURE 1–45

82. The tool in Figure 1–45 is used for:
    a. boring.   c. ridge reaming.
    b. honing.   d. cleaning.

83. You are going to replace the rod bearings in an engine. Rod journal diameters measure 1.948″. Standard rod journal diameter is 1.9680″ to 1.9690″. What size bearings should be installed?
    a. Undersize .010″   c. Standard
    b. Undersize .020″   d. Oversize .020″

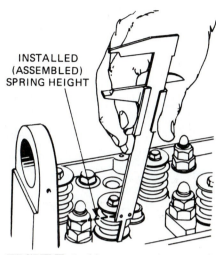

INSTALLED (ASSEMBLED) SPRING HEIGHT

FIGURE 1–46

84. The measurement in Figure 1–46 is .045″ greater than the specification of 1.417″. To correct, what should be done?
    a. Add shims.
    b. Reduce the valve stem height.
    c. Replace the valve spring.
    d. Sink the valve seat.

85. You are overhauling a typical 4-cylinder automobile engine. Which of these would be the MOST NORMAL main bearing clearance specification?
    a. .200″ b. .020″ c. .002″ d. .0002″

86. When making a compression test, a low equal reading is obtained in two adjacent cylinders. This would MOST LIKELY indicate a:
    a. burned valve.
    b. blown head gasket.
    c. leaking intake manifold gasket.
    d. leaking exhaust manifold gasket.

87. A distributor drive gear has badly damaged teeth.
    Technician A says that this could cause hard starting.
    Technician B says that this could cause backfiring.
    Who is right?
    a. A only   c. Both A and B
    b. B only   d. Neither A nor B

88. A piston skirt shows a diagonal wear pattern across its length. This is MOST LIKELY caused by a(n):
    a. twisted rod.
    b. collapsed piston.
    c. worn pin.
    d. out-of-round cylinder.

FIGURE 1–47

89. Technician A says that the damage in Figure 1–47 could have been caused by sharp edges in the combustion chamber.

Technician B says that the damage could have been caused by incandescent carbon particles.

Who is right?
a. A only
b. B only
c. Both A and B
d. Neither A nor B

90. Technician A says that blue-gray exhaust smoke can be caused by piston rings stuck in their grooves.

Technician B says that blue-gray exhaust smoke can be caused by plugged oil return passages in the cylinder head.

Who is right?
a. A only
b. B only
c. Both A and B
d. Neither A nor B

91. An engine equipped with the system in Figure 1–48 has a rough idle.

Technician A says that part X could be defective.

Technician B says that part Y could be defective.

Who is right?
a. A only
b. B only
c. Both A and B
d. Neither A nor B

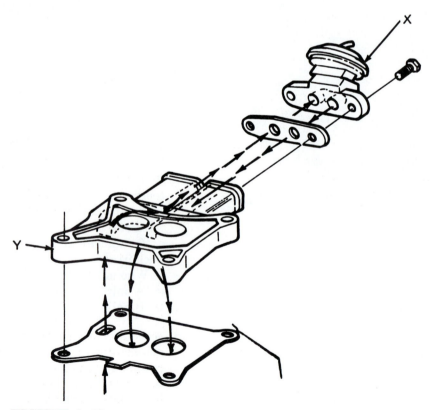

FIGURE 1–48

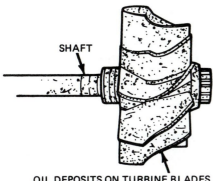

OIL DEPOSITS ON TURBINE BLADES
FIGURE 1–49

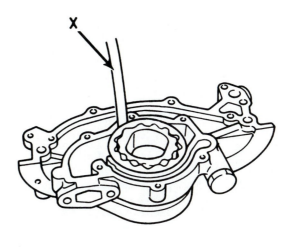

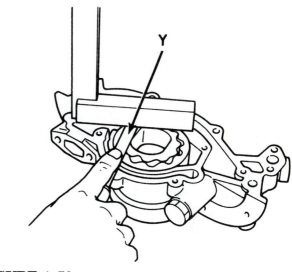

FIGURE 1–50

92. A turbocharger has deposits of burned oil (see Figure 1–49) on the turbine wheel.

Technician A says that this could be caused by a sludged center housing.

Technician B says that this could be caused by a worn shaft assembly.

Who is right?
a. A only
b. B only
c. Both A and B
d. Neither A nor B

93. While driving in stop-and-go city traffic, a car with an electric fan overheats.

Technician A says that this could be caused by a stuck open thermostat.

Technician B says that this could be caused by a bad radiator fan sensor.

Who is right?
a. A only   **c.** Both A and B
b. B only   **d.** Neither A nor B

94. Dull gray vertical scratches are found on the piston rings during an engine teardown. This is MOST LIKELY caused by:
a. using multiviscosity oil.
b. abrasive wear.
c. overrevving.
d. worn ring grooves.

95. An engine has been a "come-back" several times with burned valves.

Technician A says that this could be caused by blocked coolant passages.

Technician B says that this could be caused by using the wrong torque sequence on the head bolts.

Who is right?
a. A only   **c.** Both A and B
b. B only   **d.** Neither A nor B

96. Technician A says that engine oil pressure becomes less as measurement X in Figure 1–50 increases.

Technician B says that engine oil pressure becomes greater as measurement Y increases.

Who is right?
a. A only   **c.** Both A and B
b. B only   **d.** Neither A nor B

97. A valve job has just been completed on a push rod engine that is equipped with nonadjustable hydraulic lifters. The engine will not start. A compression test is made, and all the cylinders read zero. What needs to be done?
a. Surface head(s).
b. Install longer push rods.
c. Install thicker head gasket(s).
d. Grind valve tips.

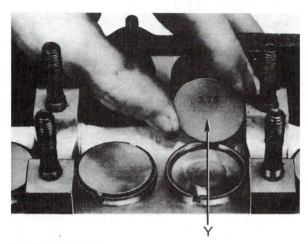

FIGURE 1–51

98. Technician A says that valve adjustment on the engine in Figure 1–51 is made by changing part X.

Technician B says that valve adjustment on the engine is made by changing part Y.

Who is right?
a. A only
b. B only
c. Both A and B
d. Neither A nor B

99. Technician A says to replace the spring retainers when doing a valve job.

Technician B says to replace the stem seals when doing a valve job.

Who is right?
a. A only
b. B only
c. Both A and B
d. Neither A nor B

100. Technician A says that a cracked cylinder head can cause engine overheating.

Technician B says that a cracked cylinder head can cause water to blow out the tailpipe.

Who is right?
a. A only   c. Both A and B
b. B only   d. Neither A nor B

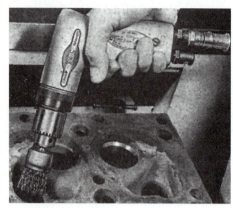

FIGURE 1–52

101. What operation is being performed in Figure 1–52?
a. Cleaning   c. Peening
b. Knurling   d. Honing

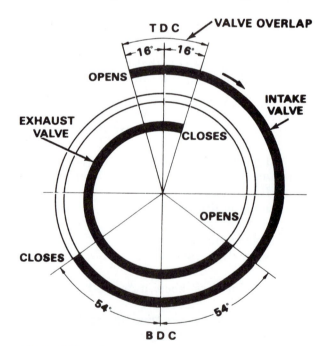

FIGURE 1–53

102. Refer to the valve timing diagram in Figure 1–53. The exhaust valve is off its seat for how many degrees of crankshaft rotation?
a. 32°   b. 108°   c. 140°   d. 250°

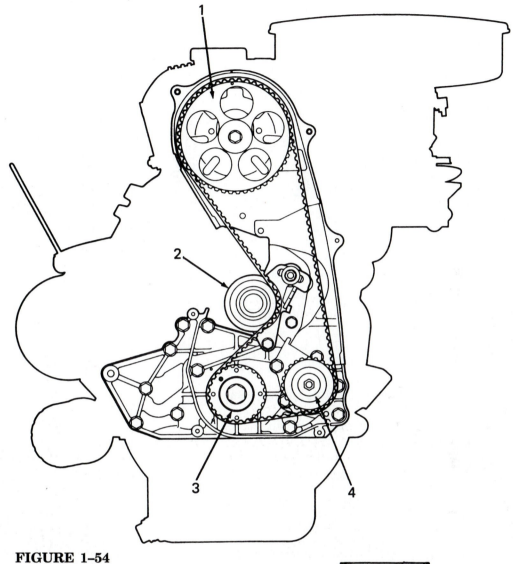

FIGURE 1–54

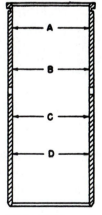

FIGURE 1–55

103. At which location is timing belt tension adjusted on the engine in Figure 1–54?
a. #1 **b.** #2 **c.** #3 **d.** #4

104. Main bearing bores in a block are stretched (out-of-round).

Technician A says that this problem can be corrected by filing the caps.

Technician B says that this problem can be corrected by replacing the caps.

Who is right?

a. A only
b. B only
c. Both A and B
d. Neither A nor B

105. Refer to the cylinder liner cross-section in Figure 1–55. The greatest wear will generally occur across which point?
a. A **b.** B **c.** C **d.** D

106. Technician A says that valve burning is often caused by too thin a margin.

Technician B says that valve burning is often caused by too wide a seat.

Who is right?
   a. A only
   b. B only
   c. Both A and B
   d. Neither A nor B

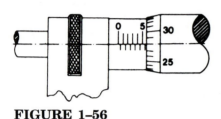

FIGURE 1–56

107. What is the reading on the micrometer in Figure 1–56?
   a. 6.28 mm   **c.** 5.53 mm
   b. 5.78 mm   **d.** 5.28 mm

108. The exhaust manifold heat control valve on an engine is stuck open.

Technician A says that this could cause low cranking rpm.

Technician B says that this could cause hesitation during cold driveaway.

Who is right?
   a. A only   **c.** Both A and B
   b. B only   **d.** Neither A nor B

109. An engine idles rough, but runs smooth above 2,500 rpm.

Technician A says that this could be caused by a burned valve.

Technician B says that this could be caused by a warped intake manifold.

Who is right?
   a. A only   **c.** Both A and B
   b. B only   **d.** Neither A nor B

110. A technician removes the spark plugs from an engine. All the firing ends are coated with dry, fluffy carbon deposits.

Technician A says that this could be caused by worn piston rings.

Technician B says that this could be caused by a vacuum leak.

Who is right?
   a. A only   **c.** Both A and B
   b. B only   **d.** Neither A nor B

111. The rod bearing journals in an engine are .005″ out-of-round. Which of the following would be the correct procedure?
   a. Grind the journals and install thicker bearings.
   b. Grind the journals and install thinner bearings.
   c. Polish the journals.
   d. Shim the bearings.

112. Technician A says to span the full width of the bearing when using Plastigage®.

Technician B says to slowly turn the crankshaft a full revolution when using Plastigage®.

Who is right?
   a. A only
   b. B only
   c. Both A and B
   d. Neither A nor B

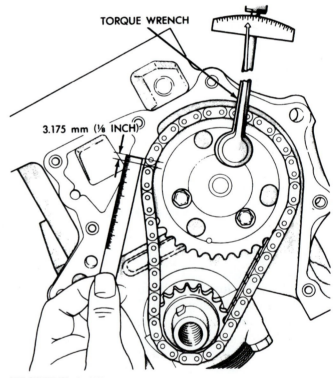

FIGURE 1–57

113. What procedure is being performed in Figure 1–57?
   a. Setting cam timing
   b. Locating exact TDC
   c. Measuring timing chain wear and stretch
   d. None of the above

114. After a recent engine overhaul, the oil consumption has greatly increased.

Technician A says that this could be caused by installing the rings into worn grooves.

Technician B says that this could be caused by installing the rings upside down.

Who is right?
a. A only
b. B only
c. Both A and B
d. Neither A nor B

115. An engine runs, but the oil warning light stays on.

Technician A says that this could be caused by too much cam bearing clearance.

Technician B says that this could be caused by a ground in the warning light circuit.

Who is right?
a. A only   **c.** Both A and B
b. B only   **d.** Neither A nor B

116. A 4-cylinder engine has compression readings of 135, 70, 130, 75. Which of the following is the MOST LIKELY cause?
a. Burned valves
b. Broken valve springs
c. Incorrect valve timing
d. Missing stem seals

117. Compression readings of 130, 135, 130, 140, 15, and 135 could be caused by:
a. a hole in a piston.
b. a broken exhaust valve push rod.
c. Both a and b
d. Neither a nor b

118. A computer-controlled engine has a lean condition. Which of the following is the MOST LIKELY cause?
a. A bad PCV system
b. A bad vehicle speed sensor (VSS)
c. A bad cat
d. A stuck closed EGR valve

119. During a power balance test, a V-8 engine has two cylinders on opposite corners of the block that do not show any drop in engine rpm. The MOST LIKELY cause would be:
a. a bad head gasket.
b. a leaking throttle body base gasket.
c. a distributor cap cracked between two terminals.
d. switched spark plug wires.

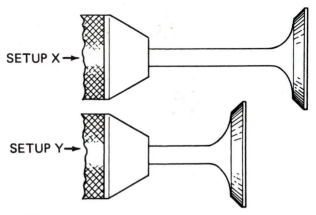

SETUP X →

SETUP Y →

FIGURE 1–58

120. A valve is going to be refaced in a valve grinding machine in Figure 1–58.

Technician A says that setup X is OK.

Technician B says that setup Y is OK.

Who is right?
a. A only
b. B only
c. Both A and B
d. Neither A nor B

121. Technician A says that battery cable diameter affects cranking ability of the starter.

Technician B says that battery cable length affects cranking ability of the starter.

Who is right?
a. A only
b. B only
c. Both A and B
d. Neither A nor B

122. Which of the following would be the MOST LIKELY cause of an engine "pinging" complaint?
a. Defective catalytic converter
b. Fuel octane too high
c. Bad EGR valve
d. Bad vapor canister

123. A power balance test is being performed on a computer-controlled engine.

Technician A says to disconnect the check engine light.

Technician B says to disconnect the computer power supply.

Who is right?
a. A only
b. B only
c. Both A and B
d. Neither A nor B

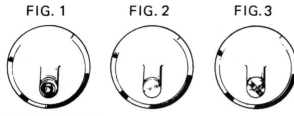

FIG. 1   FIG. 2   FIG. 3

FIGURE 1–59

124. An engine is equipped with valve rotators. Which wear pattern shown in Figure 1–59 indicates that the rotator is functioning properly?
   a. Figure 1
   b. Figure 2
   c. Figure 3
   d. None of the above

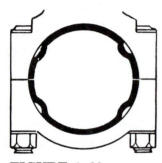

FIGURE 1–60

125. What could cause a connecting rod bearing assembly to buckle as pictured in Figure 1–60?
   a. Excessive crush
   b. Overtightening the cap
   c. Both a and b
   d. Neither a nor b

126. A vehicle comes into the shop for a ring job. The cylinders measure from 4.006″ to 4.018″ directly under the ridge in the thrust direction. Original equipment (OE) bore size is 4.000″.
   Technician A recommends honing the cylinders and expanding the old pistons.
   Technician B recommends boring the cylinders and installing new pistons.
   Who is right?
   a. A only
   b. B only
   c. Both A and B
   d. Neither A nor B

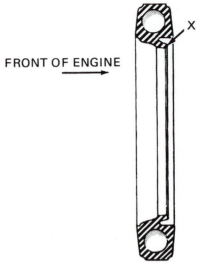

FRONT OF ENGINE →   X

FIGURE 1–61

127. The seal in Figure 1–61 is being installed in an engine.
   Technician A says that lip X must face the flywheel.
   Technician B says to trim lip X with a razor blade.
   Who is right?
   a. A only   **c.** Both A and B
   b. B only   **d.** Neither A nor B

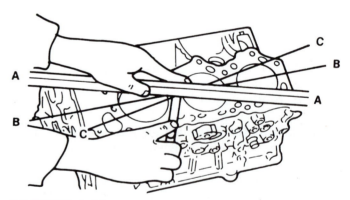

FIGURE 1–62

128. A .015″ (.40mm) feeler gauge leaf can be inserted while making the check in Figure 1–62. What should be done?
   a. Install a thicker head gasket with special sealer.
   b. Deck the block.
   c. Both a and b
   d. Neither a nor b

129. An engine has lifter noise.
    Technician A says that this could be caused by a flat cam.
    Technician B says that this could be caused by a dented oil pan.
    Who is right?
    a. A only
    b. B only
    c. Both A and B
    d. Neither A nor B

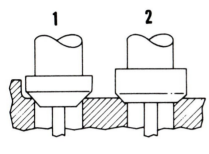
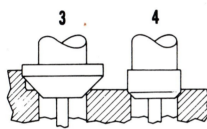

FIGURE 1–63

130. Which one of the valve grinding stones shown in Figure 1–63 fits the seat correctly and should be used?
    a. Stone 1
    b. Stone 2
    c. Stone 3
    d. Stone 4

131. An engine runs at a higher than normal temperature. This could be caused by all of the following EXCEPT:
    a. a plugged cat.
    b. a defective thermostat.
    c. a loose fan belt.
    d. a bad baro sensor.

132. All of the compression readings on a 6-cylinder engine are higher than normal.
    Technician A says that this can be caused by a stretched timing belt.
    Technician B says that this can be caused by excessive head milling.
    Who is right?
    a. A only
    b. B only
    c. Both A and B
    d. Neither A nor B

133. An idling engine makes a hollow, muffled, bell-like sound when cold. After the engine is warm, the noise disappears.
    Technician A says that this could be a valve sticking.
    Technician B says that this could be piston slap.
    Who is right?
    a. A only
    b. B only
    c. Both A and B
    d. Neither A nor B

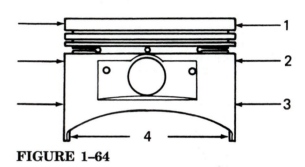

FIGURE 1–64

134. Refer to Figure 1–64. Across which point is piston diameter generally measured?
    a. #1   b. #2   c. #3   d. #4

135. As an engine cools off, the upper radiator hose collapses.
    Technician A says that this could be caused by a defective thermostat.
    Technician B says that this could be caused by a loose hose clamp.
    Who is right?
    a. A only
    b. B only
    c. Both A and B
    d. Neither A nor B

136. Technician A says that a defective head gasket can cause rust to form in the cooling system.
    Technician B says that a defective water pump can cause rust to form in the cooling system.
    Who is right?
    a. A only
    b. B only
    c. Both A and B
    d. Neither A nor B

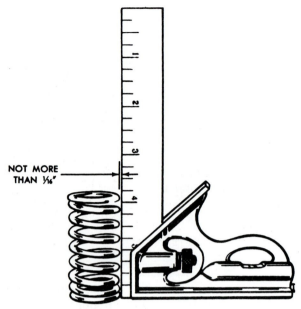

FIGURE 1–65

137. What is being measured in Figure 1–65?
   a. Tension   c. Coil clearance
   b. Working height   d. Squareness

138. A crankshaft journal is being measured in the same direction at opposite ends. This is done when measuring for:
   a. taper.
   b. out-of-roundness.
   c. Both a and b
   d. Neither a nor b

OIL INLET HOLE CLOSED

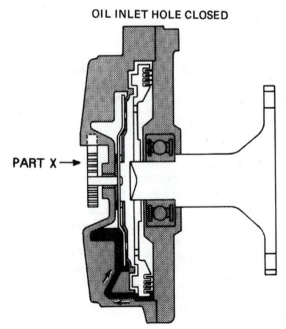

PART X →

FIGURE 1–66

139. A fluid fan drive assembly is pictured in Figure 1–66.
   Technician A says that part X senses air temperature.
   Technician B says that overheating can result if part X is broken.
   Who is right?
   a. A only   c. Both A and B
   b. B only   d. Neither A nor B

140. A "reground" cam has just been installed in an engine and the valves won't stay adjusted (they continue to become loose).
   Technician A says that the cam could be going flat.
   Technician B says that the rocker studs could be pulling out.
   Who is right?
   a. A only   c. Both A and B
   b. B only   d. Neither A nor B

141. An engine overheats only during high speed driving.
   Technician A says that this could be caused by a missing spring in the lower radiator hose.
   Technician B says that this could be caused by a bad water pump.
   Who is right?
   a. A only   c. Both A and B
   b. B only   d. Neither A nor B

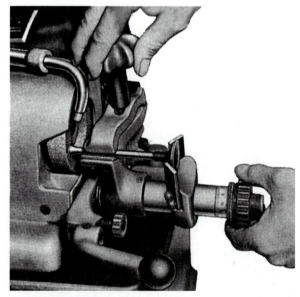

FIGURE 1–67

142. What is the technician doing in Figure 1–67?
   a. Putting new finish on valve end
   b. Grinding tip length
   c. Both a and b
   d. Neither a nor b

143. Technician A says that some engines use head bolts that are designed to "stretch."

Technician B says that some engines use head bolts that must not be reused.

Who is right?

a. A only
b. B only
c. Both A and B
d. Neither A nor B

144. An engine oil light "flickers" while driving. Also, a knock can be heard when the engine is cold. This could be caused by:

a. worn bearings.
b. wrong viscosity oil.
c. Both a and b
d. Neither a nor b

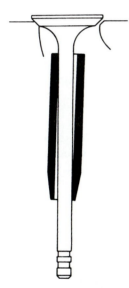

FIGURE 1–68

145. Technician A says that excessive stem-to-guide clearance is shown in Figure 1–68.

Technician B says that valve leakage is shown in Figure 1–68.

Who is right?

a. A only
b. B only
c. Both A and B
d. Neither A nor B

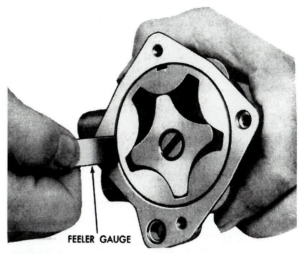

FEELER GAUGE

FIGURE 1–69

146. The clearance measurement in Figure 1–69 is excessive. What should be done?

Technician A says to add shims.

Technician B says to install oversize rotors.

Who is right?

a. A only c. Both A and B
b. B only d. Neither A nor B

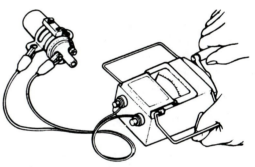

FIGURE 1–70

147. What is being tested in Figure 1–70?

a. Primary winding resistance
b. Secondary winding resistance
c. Coil capacitance
d. None of the above

148. An engine will not start after being rebuilt.

Technician A says that this could be caused by incorrect valve adjustment.

Technician B says that this could be caused by incorrect camshaft timing.

Who is right?

a. A only
b. B only
c. Both A and B
d. Neither A nor B

149. A starter spins and makes a grinding noise, but does not crank the engine.
    Technician A says that this could be caused by a worn crankshaft thrust bearing.
    Technician B says that this could be caused by a worn flywheel ring gear.
    Who is right?
    a. A only
    b. B only
    c. Both A and B
    d. Neither A nor B

150. An engine cranks very slowly and will not start. Also, the headlights dim considerably during cranking.
    Technician A says that this could be caused by a "spun" connecting rod bearing.
    Technician B says that this could be caused by a weak battery.
    Who is right?
    a. A only
    b. B only
    c. Both A and B
    d. Neither A nor B

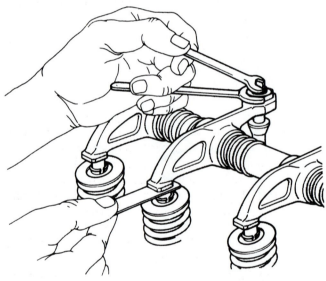

FIGURE 1–71

151. The adjustment in Figure 1–71 is set too wide.
    Technician A says that this will retard valve timing.
    Technician B says that this will reduce valve overlap.
    Who is right?
    a. A only
    b. B only
    c. Both A and B
    d. Neither A nor B

152. An engine runs on (diesels) when shut off at operating temperature.
    Technician A says that this can be caused by an improperly adjusted throttle stop.
    Technician B says that this can be caused by low heat range spark plugs.
    Who is right?
    a. A only
    b. B only
    c. Both A and B
    d. Neither A nor B

153. An engine is using too much oil. This could be caused by:
    a. wrist pins fitted too tightly.
    b. tapered cylinder walls.
    c. Both a and b
    d. Neither a nor b

154. A 6-cylinder engine has a loose intake manifold. This would MOST LIKELY cause:
    a. rough idle.
    b. overheating.
    c. spark plug fouling.
    d. loss of power.

155. Technician A says that resistor-type spark plug cables reduce fouling of the spark plugs.
    Technician B says that resistor-type spark plug cables reduce the likelihood of being damaged when removing and installing.
    Who is right?
    a. A only
    b. B only
    c. Both A and B
    d. Neither A nor B

156. A car is towed into the shop with a burst oil filter. What MOST LIKELY caused this?
    a. Using too low viscosity oil
    b. Using too high viscosity oil
    c. Oil pump pressure relief valve stuck open
    d. Oil pump pressure relief valve stuck closed

157. After sitting overnight, an engine has lifter noise that goes away after running for a short period of time. The MOST LIKELY cause is:
    a. low oil pressure.
    b. low oil level.
    c. a worn lifter bottom.
    d. excessive lifter leakdown.

158. An engine has excessive oil consumption. Wet and dry compression tests both are acceptable.

Technician A says that there could be a problem with the PCV system.

Technician B says that there could be a problem with the valve guide seals.

Who is right?

a. A only   **c.** Both A and B
b. B only   **d.** Neither A nor B

TOOL X

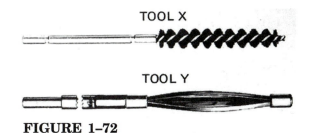

TOOL Y

FIGURE 1–72

159. Refer to the tools in Figure 1–72.

Technician A says that tool X is used to clean valve guides.

Technician B says that tool Y is used to ream valve guides.

Who is right?

a. A only   **c.** Both A and B
b. B only   **d.** Neither A nor B

160. An exhaust system has a crimp in the tailpipe.

Technician A says that this can cause loss of engine power.

Technician B says that this can cause engine overheating.

Who is right?

a. A only   **c.** Both A and B
b. B only   **d.** Neither A nor B

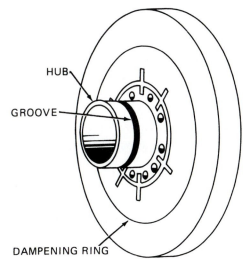

HUB

GROOVE

DAMPENING RING

FIGURE 1–73

161. The part in Figure 1–73 has a groove worn into its hub.

Technician A says that this can cause an oil leak.

Technician B says that repair sleeves are available.

Who is right?

a. A only
b. B only
c. Both A and B
d. Neither A nor B

162. You are replacing a radiator hose (for the third time in a month) that is torn. What could be the possible cause?

a. A loose mounted radiator
b. A loose radiator shroud
c. A defective radiator cap
d. Damaged motor mount(s)

163. A computer-controlled engine won't go into closed loop.

Technician A says that the oxygen sensor could be coated with carbon.

Technician B says that the thermostat could be missing.

Who is right?

a. A only
b. B only
c. Both A and B
d. Neither A nor B

164. You are going to install new piston rings in an engine. If the ring ridge is not removed:

a. the piston will be hard to install.
b. the cylinder walls will be distorted.
c. the top ring and piston land can be broken.
d. the rings will not seat properly.

165. The electric cooling fan on a front-wheel drive vehicle is inoperative.

Technician A says that this could be due to a bad ground to the fan motor.

Technician B says that this could be due to a melted wire to the fan relay.

Who is right?

a. A only
b. B only
c. Both A and B
d. Neither A nor B

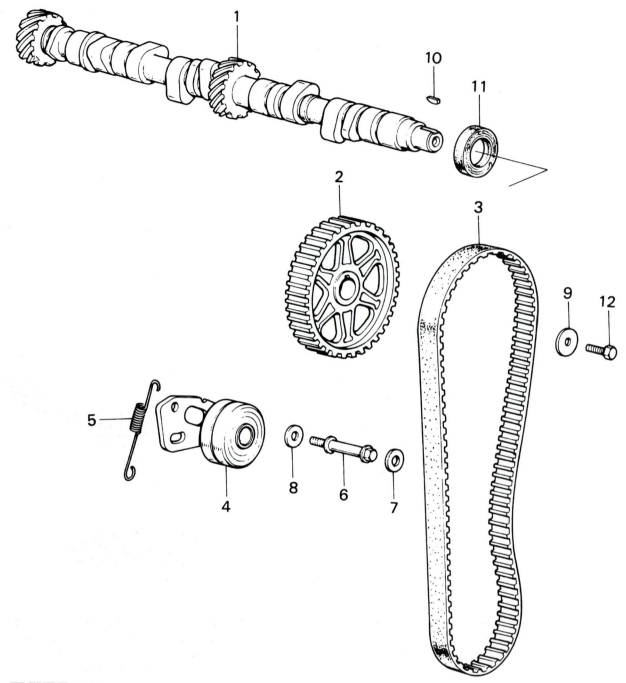

FIGURE 1–74

166. The timing belt pictured in Figure 1–74 is being replaced.

Technician A says that part 10 should be replaced.

Technician B says that part 4 should be coated with grease.

Who is right?

a. A only
c. Both A and B
b. B only
d. Neither A nor B

167. An engine has a knocking noise on medium to hard acceleration. Which of these would be the MOST LIKELY cause?

a. Ignition pickup (trigger) coil shorted
b. Vacuum advance diaphragm leaking
c. Fuel mixture too rich
d. EGR passage restricted

168. Spark timing is being set on an older engine. When the technician revs up the engine, the timing marks do not move. Which of these could be the reason?
a. Punctured vacuum advance diaphragm
b. Worn distributor shaft upper bushing
c. Stuck mechanical advance weights
d. All of the above

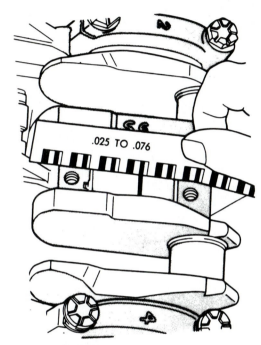

FIGURE 1–75

169. What is the technician doing in the picture in Figure 1–75?
a. Measuring rod bearing clearance
b. Measuring main bearing clearance
c. Determining crankshaft thrust wear
d. Checking crankshaft journal indexing

170. When removing the intake valves from a cylinder head, hard carbon deposits under the valve heads are noticed. Which of these is the MOST LIKELY cause?
a. Cracked intake manifold
b. Malfunctioning heat riser
c. Worn valve guides
d. Worn camshaft lobes

171. All of the connecting rod bearing backs from an engine have a shiny mirrorlike appearance.
   Technician A says that .001″ or .002″ oversize bearings should have been installed.
   Technician B says that shim stock should have been installed behind the bearings.
   Who is right?
a. A only
b. B only
c. Both A and B
d. Neither A nor B

FIGURE 1–76

172. Which of these would be the MOST LIKELY cause of the damage in Figure 1–76?
a. Excessive valve clearance
b. Worn camshaft lobes
c. Incorrect ignition timing
d. Broken timing belt

173. A turbocharged engine lacks power and is emitting black smoke.
   Technician A says that this could be caused by a dirty air cleaner.
   Technician B says that this could be caused by loose ducting connections.
   Who is right?
a. A only   c. Both A and B
b. B only   d. Neither A nor B

174. Belt timing is off one cog on an OHC engine.

  Technician A says to turn the engine backwards until the marks line up.

  Technician B says to turn the camshaft sprocket with a chain wrench.

  Who is right?
  a. A only
  b. B only
  c. Both A and B
  d. Neither A nor B

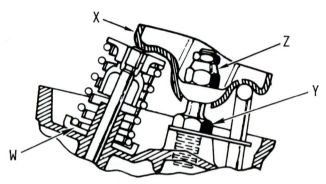

FIGURE 1–77

175. How is valve lash adjusted on the valve train in Figure 1–77?
  a. Add shims at point W.
  b. Grind material from part X.
  c. Turn nut Y.
  d. Turn nut Z.

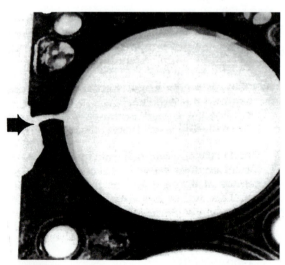

FIGURE 1–78

176. The gasket in Figure 1–78 has failed three times in the same place (see arrow).

  Technician A says that this could be caused by improper torque.

  Technician B says that this could be caused by incorrect tightening sequence.

  Who is right?
  a. A only   **c.** Both A and B
  b. B only   **d.** Neither A nor B

177. A FWD car with a transverse mounted engine overheats.

  Technician A says that this could be caused by the cooling fan belt soaked with oil.

  Technician B says that this could be caused by a bad thermostatic fan clutch.

  Who is right?
  a. A only   **c.** Both A and B
  b. B only   **d.** Neither A nor B

178. An engine starts and idles, but will not run at higher speeds. Which of these is the MOST LIKELY cause?
  a. Bad fuel pump
  b. Bad crank sensor
  c. Dirty injectors
  d. Pinched gas line

179. Technician A says that too much turbo boost can cause a ruptured wastegate diaphragm.

  Technician B says that too much turbo boost can cause bent compressor wheel blades.

  Who is right?
  a. A only   **c.** Both A and B
  b. B only   **d.** Neither A nor B

FIGURE 1–79

180. With the engine at idling speed, the pointer in Figure 1–79 is floating between 15 and 20. The MOST LIKELY cause would be:
  a. retarded timing.
  b. advanced timing.
  c. a stuck EGR valve.
  d. a too lean idle mixture.

181. When installing a cylinder head, where does the tightening sequence usually start?
   a. At the ends
   b. In the middle
   c. At the bolts closest to the exhaust manifold
   d. At the bolts closest to the intake manifold

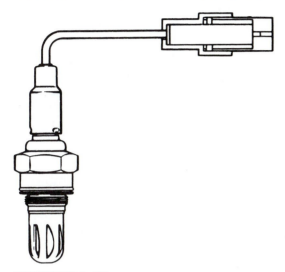

FIGURE 1–80

182. The zirconia-type device in Figure 1–80 shows a fixed voltage reading of 1.0 V during engine idle.
   Technician A says that this indicates a lean air-fuel ratio.
   Technician B says that this indicates the absence of oxygen in the exhaust gas.
   Who is right?
   a. A only   **c.** Both A and B
   b. B only   **d.** Neither A nor B

183. The cams on a radiator filler neck are badly worn.
   Technician A says that this will cause the radiator cap to seal at a higher pressure.
   Technician B says that this will affect compression of the radiator cap pressure relief valve spring.
   Who is right?
   a. A only   **c.** Both A and B
   b. B only   **d.** Neither A nor B

184. A technician is going to adjust valves without running the engine. Which of the following statements is correct?
   a. Each valve is adjusted during the exhaust stroke.
   b. All the valves can be adjusted during two crankshaft revolutions.
   c. Both a and b
   d. Neither a nor b

185. No fuel squirts into the carburetor when the throttle is jabbed. All of these could be the cause EXCEPT:
   a. a plugged pump nozzle.
   b. a damaged main jet.
   c. hard pump plunger rubber.
   d. disconnected linkage.

186. A vehicle has a ruptured oil filter.
   Technician A says that this usually happens when the filter in a full-flow system clogs up.
   Technician B says that pieces of nylon from a worn timing gear may have entered into the pressure relief valve of the oil pump, causing extreme high pressure.
   Who is right?
   a. A only
   b. B only
   c. Both A and B
   d. Neither A nor B

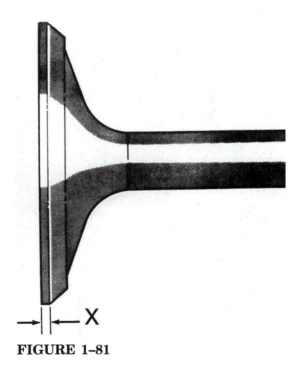

FIGURE 1–81

187. What is dimension X as shown in Figure 1–81?
   a. Margin
   b. Rim overlap
   c. Seat width
   d. Head thickness

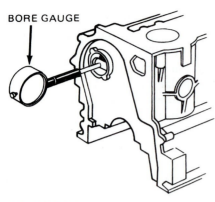

FIGURE 1–82

188. The measurement in Figure 1–82 indicates bearing out-of-roundness. This could cause:
  a. low oil pressure.
  b. A blinking oil light.
  c. Both a and b
  d. Neither a nor b

FIGURE 1–83

189. The picture in Figure 1–83 shows a vibration damper (harmonic balancer) being removed.
  Technician A says that this type of puller will damage the damper.
  Technician B says to pull on the damper rim with a 3-jaw puller.
  Who is right?
  a. A only
  b. B only
  c. Both A and B
  d. Neither A nor B

190. Technician A says that the oil control ring has oil return slots or holes.
  Technician B says that on a 3-ring piston, the oil control ring is installed in the bottom groove.
  Who is right?
  a. A only   **c.** Both A and B
  b. B only   **d.** Neither A nor B

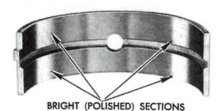

BRIGHT (POLISHED) SECTIONS

FIGURE 1–84

191. What does the bearing wear pattern shown in Figure 1–84 indicate?
  a. Improper seating
  b. Lack of lubrication
  c. Too much clearance
  d. Overloading

192. The bearing in Figure 1–85 shows wear near the edge on one side of its centerline. What does this indicate?
  a. Insufficient lubrication
  b. Radius ride
  c. Fatigue failure
  d. A twisted connecting rod

WEAR

FIGURE 1–85

193. Technician A says that worn piston rings can cause excessive crankcase blow-by.
  Technician B says that a collapsed piston can cause excessive crankcase blow-by.
  Who is right?
  a. A only
  b. B only
  c. Both A and B
  d. Neither A nor B

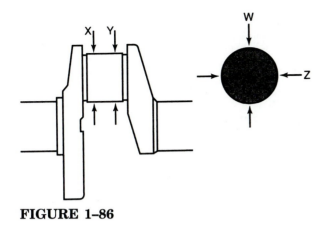

FIGURE 1–86

194. Refer to Figure 1–86.
Technician A says that the difference between X and Y is the amount of journal taper.
Technician B says that the difference between W and Z is the amount of journal clearance.
Who is right?
a. A only
b. B only
c. Both A and B
d. Neither A nor B

195. All of the following procedures are used to correct valve assembly height EXCEPT:
a. shimming the springs.
b. installing new valves.
c. butt grinding valve ends.
d. installing new retainers.

196. A fully warmed up engine backfires through the exhuast during deceleration. All of the following could be a cause EXCEPT:
a. an exhaut leak.
b. a vacuum leak.
c. a bad decel valve.
d. a bad diverter valve.

197. Intake valves removed from a cylinder head have wet oily deposits on them.
Technician A says that this could be caused by bad rings.
Technician B says this could be caused by bad seals
Who is right?
a. A only
b. B only
c. Both A and B
d. Neither A nor B

NOTE: Refer to the Engine Performance Test, Electrical/Electronic Systems Test, and Engine Machinist Test questions in this book. Some of these questions are applicable for use on the Engine Repair Test.

Section 2

AUTOMATIC TRANSMISSION/TRANSAXLE

STUDY OUTLINE

I. Basic Gear Systems
   A. Speed versus Torque
   B. Gear Ratios

II. Planetary Gear Systems
   A. Construction
   B. Principles of Operation
      1. Rules of planetary gears
      2. Typical transmission power flow
      3. How various ratios can be obtained (including overdrive)
         a. Hold one member
         b. Drive two members
         c. Neutral
      4. Compound Planetary (Simpson and Ravigneaux)
         a. Used in pairs or as a multiple unit
         b. Operation

III. Friction Elements
   A. Basic Principles of Hydraulics
   B. Hydraulic System Components (Identification of Parts and Operation)
      1. Reservoir (sump)
      2. Pump
      3. Valving
         a. Pressure regulator
         b. Manual valve
         c. Governor valve
         d. Shift valve
         e. Throttle modulator valve
         f. Down-shift valve (detent)
         g. Scheduling valve
         h. Orifice control valve
         i. Cut-back valve
         j. Relief valve
         k. Accumulator valve
         l. Non-return valve (ball)
         m. Converter check valve
   C. Torque Converters
      1. Elements of the converter
      2. Principles of converter operation
      3. Stator
      4. Converter hydraulic circuit
      5. Lock-up (be familiar with various methods)
   D. Fluids
      1. General Motors
      2. Ford
      3. Others
   E. Bands, Clutches, One-way Clutches
   F. Servos

IV. Transmission/Transaxle Light Duty Service
   A. Oil Level and Condition (Draining and Refilling)
   B. Linkage Adjustments
      1. Manual
      2. Throttle, kickdown, and accelerator pedal
      3. Neutral start systems
      4. Cable for throttle valve (TV) kickdown and pedal
   C. Vacuum Modulators ("Weighing" and Adjustment)
   D. Leaks (Seal and Gasket Replacement)
   E. Fluid/Filter
   F. Band Adjustment
   G. Adjust/Repair Electrical Kickdown Switch and Circuit
   H. Inspect/Adjust/Replace Electronic Sensors

V. Transmission/Transaxle Repair Procedures (In-Car and Off-Car)
   A. Required End-Play and Clearance Checks
   B. Inspection/Assembly of Components
      1. Foreign material in pan
      2. Gears (sun, ring, and carrier assembly)
      3. Pumps (including housings)
      4. Bands and clutches
      5. Machined surfaces
      6. Control valves
      7. Converter assembly (including bolts and pilot area)
      8. Turbine shaft
      9. Flex plate
      10. Parking pawl, shaft, spring, and retainer
      11. Accumulator
      12. Extension housing, case, and slip yoke
      13. Governor cover, valve, weights, and gears
      14. Seal ring grooves

15. Servo (including bore, piston, seal, pin, spring, and retainers)
16. Clutch drum, piston, check balls, springs, and pressure plates
17. Roller and sprag clutches
18. Vents
19. Transaxle drive chains and sprockets

C. Seals (Including How to Check Fit)
1. Metal clad
2. Lip
3. Flat and o-ring
4. Metal seal rings
5. Plastic
6. Teflon

D. Bushings
1. Installation/tools

E. Thrust Washers
1. Torrington
2. Plastic
3. Phenolic resin

F. Assembly of Components (Be Familiar with the Following Procedures)
1. Clutch soak
2. Converter flush/test for leaks
3. Install valve body following torque specifications
4. Indexing the manual shift valve
5. Clearance checks/end play/preload
6. Lubing the convertor hub
7. Converter drive lug installation position
8. Flushing cooler lines
9. Inspect oil delivery seal rings
10. Speedometer gear installation
11. Valve body surface and bore measurement/repair
12. Inspecting, testing, adjusting or replacing electrical/electronic computers, solenoids, sensor, relays, and switches

VI. Problem/Diagnosis
A. No Drive
B. Drive in One Range Only
C. Moves in Range Other Than One Selected
1. Bad mounts/proper alignment
2. Bent linkage/frozen cables
3. Linkage adjustment (cable and hard rods)

D. Noises/Problems
1. Pump
2. Friction plates/bands
3. Lock-up shudder
4. Gears
5. Roller and sprag clutches

E. Vacuum Modulators
1. Late shift
2. Early shift
3. Rough downshift
4. Rough upshift
5. Checking vacuum
6. Exhaust smoke

F. Shifting Late and Early
G. Rough Shifting (Upshifts/Downshifts)
H. Vehicle Does Not Hold in "P"
I. Slip on Upshifts
J. Harsh Engagement in Any Gear
K. No Downshift
L. Leaks
M. "Hunting" Gear Selection
1. External
2. Internal

N. Fluid Usage
O. Vibration (Including Flex Plate and Converter as a Cause)
P. Converter
1. Stall testing procedures
2. Slipping one-way clutch/frozen stator
3. Overheating

Q. Tests
1. Road testing (determine shift points)
2. Pressure (test plug location)
3. Vacuum
4. Air (clutch pack and servo operation)
5. Determine needed repairs
6. Lock-up converter (electronic, mechanical, and vacuum control system tests)
7. Pulling trouble codes
8. Scan tool diagnostics/DVOM usage

VII. Transmission/Transaxle Unit Removal and Replacement Procedures (Be Familiar With)

---

1. An automatic transaxle equipped vehicle creeps forward in neutral. This could be caused by:
   a. insufficient clutch plate clearance.
   b. incorrect cable adjustment.
   c. Both a and b.
   d. Neither a nor b.

2. A car has a no-drive-forward condition. This could be caused by:
   a. broken input shaft seal rings.
   b. valve body leakage.
   c. Both a and b
   d. Neither a nor b

3. Technician A says that a bad front clutch can cause no drive in reverse.
   Technician B says that a bad servo can cause no drive in reverse.
   Who is right?
   a. A only   c. Both A and B
   b. B only   d. Neither A nor B

4. All of these can cause an automatic transmission to slip, EXCEPT:
   a. a clogged oil filter.
   b. a faulty one-way clutch.
   c. hardened seals in servos.
   d. worn planetary gears.

5. When checking a front pump, the technician finds the front cover hub (stator support) seal badly worn with evidence of leaking. This could be caused by:
   a. excess oil pressure.
   b. excess crankshaft end play.
   c. worn converter one-way clutch.
   d. None of the above

6. An automatic transaxle does not work right. To find the cause, which of these should the technician do first?
   a. Adjust the bands
   b. Make a pressure test
   c. Check the engine vacuum
   d. Check the transmission fluid

7. Technician A says that some ATF is designed for transmissions having low friction, soft shift qualities.
   Technician B says that some ATF is a high friction, firm shift oil.
   Who is right?
   a. A only   c. Both A and B
   b. B only   d. Neither A nor B

8. Which component of the torque converter is attached to the transmission input shaft?
   a. Turbine   c. Pump
   b. Impeller   d. Stator

9. Technician A says that the stator is used when the vehicle is taking off from a standstill.
   Technician B says that the torque is multiplied in a torque converter because the stator blades redirect fluid back to the impeller.
   Who is right?
   a. A only   c. Both A and B
   b. B only   d. Neither A nor B

10. During conditions of high vortex:
    a. the one-way clutch is locked up.
    b. the one-way clutch is unlocked.
    c. fluid is redirected to the turbine.
    d. None of the above

11. When checking voltage drop in a transmission ground circuit, an acceptable value would be:
    a. zero volts only.
    b. less than .1 volt.
    c. less than 1 volt.
    d. Doesn't matter because it's ground

12. The sun gear is being held in a simple planetary gear set. The ring gear is the driver, and the carrier is driven. What would be the result?
    a. Forward gear reduction
    b. Forward speed increase
    c. Reverse gear
    d. Direct drive

13. Which of the following is a planetary gearbox holding device?
    a. Multiple disc clutch
    b. Double- or single-wrapped band and servo
    c. One-way clutch
    d. All of the above

FIGURE 2–1

14. Technician A says that the automatic transmission component in Figure 2–1 is a sprag clutch.
    Technician B says that it is a one-way clutch.
    Who is right?
    a. A only   c. Both A and B
    b. B only   d. Neither A nor B

15. With the transmission oil pan removed, the best way to pinpoint an oil pressure leak is to:
    a. check hydraulic pressures.
    b. take a pump pressure reading.
    c. remove and examine the valve body.
    d. perform air pressure tests.

16. Technician A says that a porous automatic transmission modulator diaphragm can cause an engine to produce blue-gray smoke.

Technician B says that a porous automatic transmission modulator diaphragm can be diagnosed with a Mityvac® pump.

Who is right?
a. A only
b. B only
c. Both A and B
d. Neither A nor B

17. A car owner says that his automatic transmission is not shifting right. During a road test the technician finds all upshifts are very late under light throttle pressure. What could be the problem?
a. Excessive modulator pressure
b. A faulty governor
c. Both a and b
d. Neither a nor b

18. Stall test rpm is below specifications in D, 2, and 1 driving ranges.

Technician A says that the stator in the converter is possibly not locking.

Technician B says that the engine could be in need of a tune-up.

Who is right?
a. A only
b. B only
c. Both A and B
d. Neither A nor B

19. Technician A says that rancid smelling ATF (like burned popcorn) indicates prolonged fluid overheating.

Technician B says that this indicates antifreeze has found its way into the transmission.

Who is right?
a. A only
b. B only
c. Both A and B
d. Neither A nor B

20. Technician A says that overfilling an automatic transmission can result in slipping.

Technician B says that overfilling can cause fluid aeration.

Who is right?
a. A only
b. B only
c. Both A and B
d. Neither A nor B

21. Figure 2–2 shows a technician checking a front pump for:
a. cover warpage.
b. crescent tip clearance.
c. body face to drive gear face clearance.
d. body face to driven gear face clearance.

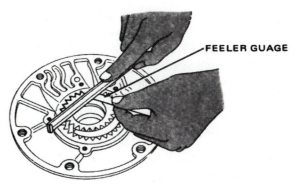

FEELER GUAGE

FIGURE 2–2

SLIDE HAMMER

FIGURE 2–3

22. What is being done in Figure 2–3?
a. Aligning the stator support
b. Installing the planetary carrier
c. Removing the governor body support
d. Removing the front oil pump

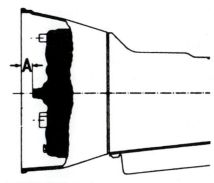

FIGURE 2–4

23. Technician A says that the correct measurement in Figure 2–4 will ensure that the converter hub is fully engaged in the pump gear.

Technician B says that the dimension in Figure 2–4 is a converter end play measurement.

Who is right?
a. A only
b. B only
c. Both A and B
d. Neither A nor B

24. An engine starts with the automatic transmission gear selector in any position. What is the MOST LIKELY reason?
    a. A shorted neutral safety switch
    b. An open neutral safety switch
    c. A grounded transmission regulated spark switch
    d. A shorted ignition switch

25. A very common cause of "stop sign crawling" in a car equipped with an automatic transmission is:
    a. the ATF level is too high.
    b. a defective governor.
    c. multiple clutch disc wear.
    d. an incorrect idle speed adjustment.

26. When does the stator overrunning clutch unlock?
    a. Under acceleration
    b. During stall
    c. In passing gear
    d. At coupling speed

27. Technician A says that the throttle valve in some automatic transmissions is activated by mechanical linkage.
    Technician B says that the throttle valve in some automatic transmissions is activated by a vacuum diaphragm.
    Who is right?
    a. A only   c. Both A and B
    b. B only   d. Neither A nor B

28. Technician A says that a stall test is performed on an automatic transmission to determine if the converter sprag assembly is slipping.
    Technician B says that a stall test is performed to determine if the bands and clutches are holding.
    Who is right?
    a. A only   c. Both A and B
    b. B only   d. Neither A nor B

29. Technician A says that sagging engine mounts can alter the TV rod adjustment.
    Technician B says that sagging engine mounts can alter the downshift cable adjustment.
    Who is right?
    a. A only   c. Both A and B
    b. B only   d. Neither A nor B

30. Technician A says that a vacuum modulator is used on automatic transmissions to regulate pressure to the governor.
    Technician B says that a vacuum modulator is used to sense any change in the torque input to the transmission.
    Who is right?
    a. A only   c. Both A and B
    b. B only   d. Neither A nor B

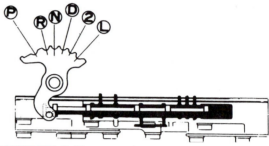

FIGURE 2–5

31. The spool valve in Figure 2–5 is a(n):
    a. pressure regulator valve.
    b. sequence valve.
    c. accumulator valve.
    d. manual valve.

32. Technician A says that automatic transmission shift valves are operated by governor pressure.
    Technician B says that shift valves are operated by main control pressure.
    Who is right?
    a. A only   c. Both A and B
    b. B only   d. Neither A nor B

33. Technician A says that automatic transmission multiple disc clutches are generally engaged by spring pressure and disengaged by a hydraulic piston.
    Technician B says that shift valves are operated by line pressure.
    Who is right?
    a. A only   c. Both A and B
    b. B only   d. Neither A nor B

34. An automatic transmission shift valve:
    a. is a pressure regulating valve.
    b. must be manually present.
    c. is a diaphragm type valve.
    d. is a control valve operated by oil pressure.

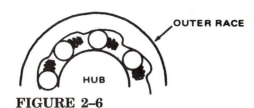

FIGURE 2–6

35. The illustration in Figure 2–6 shows an overrunning clutch.

Technician A says that if the hub is held, the outer race can turn clockwise.

Technician B says that if the outer race is held, the hub can turn counterclockwise.

Who is right?
a. A only
b. B only
c. Both A and B
d. Neither A nor B

36. A low automatic transmission oil pressure reading could be caused by:
a. a stuck pressure regulating valve.
b. a worn pump.
c. low fluid level.
d. All of the above.

37. A car with a lock-up converter slips in reverse.

Technician A says that the planetary gear set could be worn.

Technician B says that the lock-up converter could be worn.

Who is right?
a. A only
b. B only
c. Both A and B
d. Neither A nor B

38. All shifts are higher than normal with a computer-controlled automatic transmission. The downshifts are also high. Which of these is the MOST LIKELY cause?
a. High line pressure adjustment
b. Incorrect ATF level
c. Open speed sensor circuit
d. Misadjusted throttle position switch

39. The lock-up converter clutch facing is being replaced because of wear. What else should be done at this time?
a. Increase throttle pressure
b. Flush the oil cooler
c. Both a and b
d. Neither a nor b

40. Which of these would be the MOST LIKELY reason for a leak at the rear of an automatic transmission?
a. Too much output shaft end play
b. An out-of-round slip yoke
c. Too high of a fluid level
d. A worn extension housing bushing

41. An automatic transmission was just bolted up to the engine and the converter won't turn.

Technician A says that the converter lugs could be misaligned with the pump.

Technician B says that the front pump drive gear could be installed wrong.

Who is right?
a. A only   **c.** Both A and B
b. B only   **d.** Neither A nor B

42. If the pressure regulator valve spring tension were increased:
a. the system pressure would decrease.
b. more pump pressure would be required to move the valve into the bleed-off position.
c. Both a and b
d. Neither a nor b

43. If an automatic transmission vehicle does not have a rear pump:
a. it cannot be push-started.
b. oil will not be circulated through the transmission, unless the engine is running.
c. Both a and b
d. Neither a nor b

44. Technician A says that engine speed should change when the hose is pulled off the vacuum modulator.

Technician B says that a slight amount of transmission fluid should be present at the vacuum side of the modulator.

Who is right?
a. A only
b. B only
c. Both A and B
d. Neither A nor B

45. Which of the following statements is true?
a. Automatic transmissions must be in "D" range for an accurate fluid level check.
b. The dipstick "add" mark indicates that the fluid level is generally one quart low.
c. Many late model automatic transmissions do not have a fluid drain plug in the pan.
d. All of the above

Cope Chisel

FIGURE 2–7

46. What is the technician removing in Figure 2–7?
   a. The stator support bushing
   b. The high clutch hub bushing
   c. The center support sleeve
   d. The sun gear input shell

47. Technician A says that as a vehicle gets older, the engine vacuum drops and a lower modulator pressure results.

   Technician B says that the higher the engine vacuum, the higher the modulator pressure.
   Who is right?
   a. A only
   b. B only
   c. Both A and B
   d. Neither A nor B

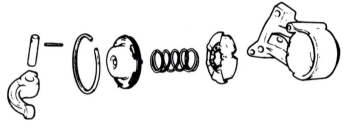

FIGURE 2–8

48. The automatic transmission part shown in Figure 2–8:
   a. is hydraulically actuated.
   b. actuates a band.
   c. Both a and b
   d. Neither a nor b

49. Technician A says that the automatic transmission front pump operates when the engine is cranking.

   Technician B says that the front pump is driven by drive lugs (dogs) on the end of the torque converter housing.
   Who is right?
   a. A only   **c.** Both A and B
   b. B only   **d.** Neither A nor B

50. The governor valve:
   a. is located on the output shaft.
   b. senses road speed.
   c. nearly closes off the exhaust as vehicle speed increases.
   d. All of the above

51. A vehicle has a slight flare between upshifts. What would be the first thing to check?
   a. Governor
   b. Valve body
   c. Intermediate servo
   d. Fluid level

52. You are servicing a valve body.
   Technician A says that a magnet can be used to remove any sticking valves.
   Technician B says that a plastic stick should be used to poke out sticking valves.
   Who is right?
   a. A only   **c.** Both A and B
   b. B only   **d.** Neither A nor B

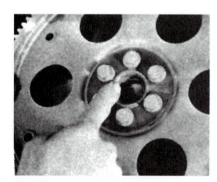

FIGURE 2–9

53. You are installing an automatic transmission. What type of lubricant should you apply to the pilot hole in the drive plate (see Figure 2–9)?
   a. Petroleum jelly
   b. ATF
   c. Wheel bearing grease
   d. No lubricant

54. The automatic transmission fluid in a vehicle looks like a strawberry milkshake.

Technician A says that rain water may have entered because the dipstick was not pushed down all the way.

Technician B says that a broken heat exchanger in the radiator may be the problem.

Who is right?
a. A only
b. B only
c. Both A and B
d. Neither A nor B

55. When new composition clutch plates are used, Technician A says to soak the plates in ATF for a minimum of 15 minutes before they are installed.

Technician B says to coat the friction surfaces with vaseline prior to installation.

Who is right?
a. A only
b. B only
c. Both A and B
d. Neither A nor B

56. A car equipped with a computer-controlled automatic transmission starts off in high gear. This could be caused by:
a. a slipping one-way clutch.
b. a bad transmission control computer.
c. a bad coolant temperature sensor.
d. a low ATF level.

57. A front-wheel drive 3-speed automatic transmission has slipping bands and clutches during acceleration.

Technician A says that this could be caused by low throttle pressure.

Technician B says that this could be caused by low line pressure.

Who is right?
a. A only   **c.** Both A and B
b. B only   **d.** Neither A nor B

58. Technician A says that in modern day automatic transmissions the clutch apply pistons are generally released by spring pressure.

Technician B says that in modern day automatic transmissions the clutch apply pistons are generally applied by oil pressure.

Who is right?
a. A only   **c.** Both A and B
b. B only   **d.** Neither A nor B

59. The fluid level in an automatic transmission drops 1 quart in 1,000 miles of driving.

Technician A says to check for fluid in the modulator vacuum line.

Technician B says to check the modulator to see if it holds 18″ of vacuum.

Who is right?
a. A only
b. B only
c. Both A and B
d. Neither A nor B

60. Technician A says that a double wrap band has better holding ability than a single wrap band.

Technician B says that a double wrap band requires more servo force to create the same holding effort as a single wrap band.

Who is right?
a. A only
b. B only
c. Both A and B
d. Neither A nor B

61. When an automatic transmission is in high gear (direct drive), the power flow is generally through:
a. multiple disc clutches.
b. one-way clutches.
c. bands.
d. servos.

62. Technician A says that band adjustment is made to be sure the band does not drag on the drum in the release position.

Technician B says that band adjustment is made to keep the servo from bottoming as it is applied.

Who is right?
a. A only
b. B only
c. Both A and B
d. Neither A nor B

63. A vehicle is making a forced downshift for acceleration. Which of the following is true?
a. The detent valve controls the shift
b. The governor pressure is overcome
c. Both a and b
d. Neither a nor b

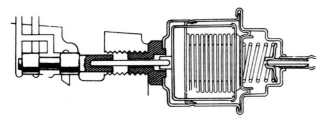

FIGURE 2–10

64. What statement is true with reference to Figure 2–10?
   a. The diaphragm is altitude compensated.
   b. Control pressure is increased by turning the adjusting screw counterclockwise.
   c. Both a and b
   d. Neither a nor b

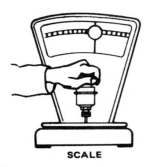

SCALE

FIGURE 2–11

65. The technician in Figure 2–11 is:
   a. checking for ruptured bellows.
   b. checking the modulator setting by "weighing."
   c. Both a and b
   d. Neither a nor b

FIGURE 2–12

66. Figure 2–12 shows:
   a. installation of the rear pump seal.
   b. installation of the extension housing seal.
   c. installation of the rear bushing.
   d. None of the above

67. Slight burrs and nicks can be removed from valve body valves by using:
   a. a file.   c. crocus cloth.
   b. emery paper.   d. a wire wheel.

68. Technician A says that a chipped planetary gear tooth would cause transmission noise in any forward gear.
   Technician B says that a damaged speedometer drive gear would cause noise in all drive gears.
   Who is right?
   a. A only   c. Both A and B
   b. B only   d. Neither A nor B

69. A vehicle has no engine braking in manual second gear. What could be the cause of this problem?
   a. Linkage
   b. Band adjustment
   c. Both a and b
   d. Neither a nor b

70. Technician A says that accelerator (throttle) linkage should be adjusted before the kickdown or downshift linkage is set.
   Technician B says that accelerator (throttle) linkage should be adjusted before manual (shift) linkage is set.
   Who is right?
   a. A only   c. Both A and B
   b. B only   d. Neither A nor B

71. An automatic transmission shifts directly from 1 to 3 in drive range. What could be the cause of this problem?
   a. The intermediate band adjustment
   b. The governor
   c. Both a and b
   d. Neither a nor b

72. Endwise (thrust) movement of automatic transmission shafts and drums is controlled by:
   a. Torrington needle bearings.
   b. phenolic resin thrust washers.
   c. nylon thrust washers.
   d. All of the above

73. Technician A says that clutch pack plates are stacked alternately when assembled (steel, lined, steel, etc.).
   Technician B says that plates are generally dished when new.
   Who is right?
   a. A only
   b. B only
   c. Both A and B
   d. Neither A nor B

74. Internal leakage in an automatic transmission is controlled by:
  a. cast iron seals.
  b. o-ring seals.
  c. lip type seals.
  d. All of the above

77. The arrow in Figure 2–14 is pointing to:
  a. the parking gear.
  b. the low-reverse clutch hub.
  c. the governor valve.
  d. the stator support.

FIGURE 2–13

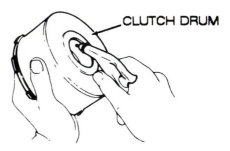

FIGURE 2–15

75. The technician in Figure 2–13 is:
  a. measuring snap ring to plate clearance.
  b. installing the multiple disc square-cut seal.
  c. removing the clutch drum retaining plate.
  d. None of the above

76. An automatic transmission has returned to the shop three times in 300 miles with the front seal leaking badly, even though it has been replaced each time.
  Technician A says that this could be caused by too much converter hub runout.
  Technician B says that this could be caused by a blocked seal drainback hole.
  Who is right?
  a. A only
  b. B only
  c. Both A and B
  d. Neither A nor B

78. What is being done in Figure 2–15?
  a. Popping out the sun gear snap ring
  b. Blowing out the clutch piston
  c. Removing stuck one-way clutch rollers
  d. None of the above

79. A vehicle does not move in any gear range.
  Technician A says that clutch and band material clogging the oil screen could be the reason.
  Technician B says the oil pump internal leakage could be the reason.
  Who is right?
  a. A only
  b. B only
  c. Both A and B
  d. Neither A nor B

80. An automatic transmission has a clunk noise during a 2–3 upshift.
  Technician A says that this can be caused by using the wrong type fluid.
  Technician B says that this can be caused by a defective accumulator.
  Who is right?
  a. A only
  b. B only
  c. Both A and B
  d. Neither A nor B

FIGURE 2–14

FIGURE 2–16

81. If the hub on the component in Figure 2–16 is lightly scored:
    a. install a new converter.
    b. polish the hub with 600 grit crocus cloth.
    c. have the hub turned down on a lathe.
    d. dress the scored surface with a mill smooth file.

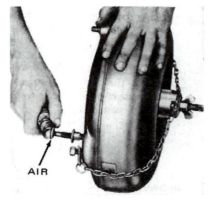

FIGURE 2–17

82. Figure 2–17 shows:
    a. the converter being flushed.
    b. a converter leakage test.
    c. the stator clutch being tested for lock-up.
    d. None of the above

83. Technician A says that overtightening the valve body can jam valves.
    Technician B says that a loose valve body can reduce line pressure.
    Who is right?
    a. A only
    b. B only
    c. Both A and B
    d. Neither A nor B

84. Technician A says that planetary gear teeth should have sharp edges.
    Technician B says that the front pump crescent should have a sharp edge.
    Who is right?
    a. A only
    b. B only
    c. Both A and B
    d. Neither A nor B

85. When stall testing an automatic transmission:
    a. accelerate to wide open throttle for approximately five seconds.
    b. check motor mounts beforehand.
    c. set the hand brake.
    d. All of the above

86. An automatic transmission has a noise in all gears that sounds like a rod knock. The MOST LIKELY cause is:
    a. a cracked flex plate.
    b. the oil pump driven gear installed upside down.
    c. bent linkage.
    d. excessive input shaft end play.

87. Pepper-colored flake material is discovered in the transmission pan during a fluid change and filter screen replacement. What does this indicate?
    a. Band and clutch wear
    b. Bearing wear
    c. Valve body wear
    d. None of the above

88. How often should the automatic transmission cooler and lines be flushed?
    a. Every two years
    b. Every 24,000 miles
    c. Every fluid drain
    d. Whenever rebuilding

89. Technician A says that a stuck governor can cause a car to start from a stop in second or third gear.
    Technician B says that a stuck shift valve can cause a car to start from a stop in second or third gear.
    Who is right?
    a. A only
    b. B only
    c. Both A and B
    d. Neither A nor B

FIGURE 2–18

90. With regard to the grooves in Figure 2–18:
   a. they should be tapered.
   b. metal rings often fit into them.
   c. Both a and b
   d. Neither a nor b

91. A car accelerates okay, but seems to "drag" at cruise speed.
   Technician A says that this could be caused by a locked converter stator.
   Technician B says that this could be caused by a clogged transmission filter.
   Who is right?
   a. A only
   b. B only
   c. Both A and B
   d. Neither A nor B

92. An automatic transmission in a rear wheel drive car hunts from 3–4 and from 4–3. It also clunks on downshifts. The MOST LIKELY cause would be:
   a. a misadjusted governor.
   b. misadjusted throttle pressure.
   c. incorrect fluid level.
   d. a plugged oil screen.

93. In an automatic transmission, the shift valves are moved to the upshift position by:
   a. line pressure.
   b. governor pressure.
   c. throttle (modulator) pressure.
   d. compensator pressure.

94. Which of these could be the cause of a converter drainback problem?
   a. Worn pump bushing
   b. Worn input shaft bushing
   c. Both a and b
   d. Neither a nor b

95. Technician A says that a bad transaxle mount can cause a FWD vehicle to pull to the right on acceleration.
   Technician B says that a bad transaxle mount can cause a FWD vehicle to "shudder" on acceleration.
   Who is right?
   a. A only
   b. B only
   c. Both A and B
   d. Neither A nor B

FIGURE 2–19

96. What is the technician doing in Figure 2–19?
   a. Pulling the secondary sun gear
   b. Pulling the rear pump drive
   c. Installing the reverse ring gear
   d. Removing the speedometer drive gear

FIGURE 2–20

97. Figure 2–20 shows the technician:
   a. removing the front pump seal.
   b. removing the front pump.
   c. removing the pump housing bushing.
   d. None of the above

98. A car owner complains of harsh, late shifts. This could result from:
   a. a broken diaphragm in the vacuum modulator.
   b. a lack of vacuum at the vacuum modulator.
   c. Both a and b
   d. Neither a nor b

99. Your car has a 3.22 top gear ratio. When pulling away from a stop sign under light throttle, at what speed should the 1–2 shift occur? Refer to Figure 2–21.
   a. 13–16 mph
   b. 17–21 mph
   c. 24–27 mph
   d. 34–42 mph

100. When a "Simpson" gear train is operating in *first* ratio:
   a. the front unit ring gear and the long sun gear are the driving members.
   b. the reverse unit carrier is the stationary member.
   c. Both a and b
   d. Neither a nor b

101. Technician A says that a "hissing" sound under the hood with the engine running could indicate a vacuum leak.
   Technician B says that a "whining" noise coming from the front pump area could indicate a clogged filter.
   Who is right?
   a. A only
   b. B only
   c. Both A and B
   d. Neither A nor B

102. A transmission is hard to fill because of oil blowing out of the filler tube. This condition could be caused by:
   a. a damaged radiator intercooler.
   b. a clogged breather.
   c. worn input shaft seal rings.
   d. All of the above

AUTOMATIC SHIFT SPEEDS AND GOVERNOR PRESSURE CHART
(APPROXIMATE MILES AND KILOMETERS PER HOUR AT ROAD LOAD)

Overall Top Gear Ratio*	2.78		3.22		3.02 (except turbocharged)		3.02 (turbocharged)	
	mph	km/h	mph	km/h	mph	km/h	mph	km/h
Throttle Minimum								
1-2 Upshift	13-16	21-27	13-16	21-26	13-17	21-27	15-19	24-31
2-3 Upshift	17-21	27-34	17-21	27-34	18-22	29-35	20-25	32-40
3-1 Downshift	12-15	19-24	12-15	19-24	13-16	21-26	15-19	24-31
Throttle Wide Open								
1-2 Upshift	35-42	56-68	34-42	55-68	36-44	58-71	38-42	61-68
2-3 Upshift	61-68	98-103	59-66	95-106	63-71	101-114	70-80	113-129
Kickdown Limit								
3-2 WOT Downshift	56-64	90-103	55-62	89-100	58-66	93-106	64-74	103-119
3-2 Part Throttle Downshift	44-52	71-84	44-51	71-82	46-54	74-87	48-59	77-95
3-1 WOT Downshift	31-38	50-61	30-37	48-60	32-39	51-63	37-40	60-64
Governor Pressure**								
15 psi	23-25	37-40	24-27	39-43	24-27	39-43	28-31	45-50
50 psi	59-65	95-105	56-63	92-101	61-68	98-109	69-76	111-122

*See "Specification" for details.
**Governor pressure should be from zero to 3 psi at standstill or downshift may not occur.
Changes in tire size or tire pressure will cause shift points to occur at corresponding higher or lower vehicle speeds.
Km/h = Kilometers per hour.

FIGURE 2–21

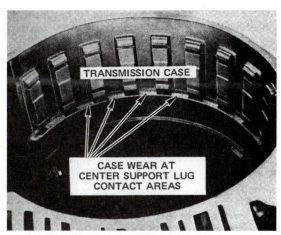

FIGURE 2–22

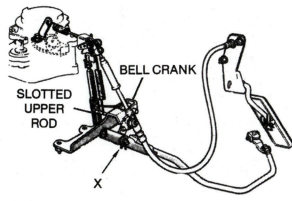

FIGURE 2–23

103. An automatic transmission has case wear at the center support (see Figure 2–22).

Technician A says that this can cause front planetary noise.

Technician B says that this can cause high gear to disengage when hot.

Who is right?

a. A only **c.** Both A and B
b. B only **d.** Neither A nor B

104. A vehicle is very sluggish on take-off. Yet the engine is properly tuned and acceleration is normal above 35 mph.

Technician A says that this could be caused by a defective torque converter.

Technician B says that this could be caused by a worn front pump.

Who is right?

a. A only **c.** Both A and B
b. B only **d.** Neither A nor B

105. A car owner complains of no passing gear. This could be caused by:

a. a sticking governor valve.
b. incorrect accelerator pedal height.
c. Both a and b
d. Neither a nor b

106. A FWD vehicle has a severe vibration in all gears.

Technician A says that this could be caused by an out-of-balance torque converter.

Technician B says that this could be caused by out-of-balance planet gears.

Who is right?

a. A only **c.** Both A and B
b. B only **d.** Neither A nor B

107. What would happen if the linkage in Figure 2–23 became accidentally disconnected at point X?

a. The vehicle would not upshift properly
b. The vehicle would not downshift properly
c. Both a and b
d. Neither a nor b

108. A transmission won't hold in park. This could be caused by:

a. a faulty servo.
b. a broken pawl.
c. Both a and b
d. Neither a nor b

FIGURE 2–24

109. What measurement is being performed in Figure 2–24?

a. Output shaft end play
b. Front clutch drum end play
c. Oil pump cover clearance
d. None of the above

110. Refer to Figure 2–24. How is this measurement generally adjusted?
    a. By turning the servo piston stem
    b. By selecting different thickness washers
    c. By removing or adding clutch plates
    d. None of the above

111. The governor bore in a transmission is worn out-of-round. This can cause:
    a. low line pressure.
    b. slipping when starting off in low or drive when hot.
    c. Both a and b
    d. Neither a nor b

112. What could cause a vehicle to move forward while the transmission is in neutral?
    a. Incorrect manual valve indexing
    b. The shift control linkage out-of-adjustment
    c. Both a and b
    d. Neither a nor b

113. Two technicians are discussing a vacuum modulated automatic transmission.
    Technician A says that low vacuum causes higher shift point speeds.
    Technician B says that with the engine idling in drive, there should be no vacuum at the modulator.
    Who is right?
    a. A only
    b. B only
    c. Both A and B
    d. Neither A nor B

114. A car's speedometer needle fluctuates badly.
    Technician A says that this could be caused by a bad head.
    Technician B says that this could be caused by a kinked cable.
    Who is right?
    a. A only
    b. B only
    c. Both A and B
    d. Neither A nor B

115. When installing the parts in Figure 2–25, what should the technician put on the mating surfaces?
    a. Nothing, leave dry
    b. Hardening sealer
    c. Nonhardening sealer
    d. White grease

FIGURE 2–25

116. Air can enter into the main hydraulic control system of an automatic transmission whenever:
    a. the fluid level becomes too low or too high in the sump.
    b. the filter screen becomes clogged with foreign material.
    c. Both a and b
    d. Neither a nor b

117. When an engine is operating, all delivery lines and passages in an automatic transmission are:
    a. kept full of fluid.
    b. not always under pressure.
    c. Both a and b
    d. Neither a nor b

118. Moving the shift valves into position automatically is the job of:
    a. the governor.
    b. the modulator.
    c. main line pressure.
    d. Both a and b

119. An automatic transmission valve body is being discussed.

Technician A says that all the fluid entering the valve body must pass through the pressure regulator valve.

Technician B says that the shift valve directs fluid to a clutch or band.

Who is right?

a. A only   **c.** Both A and B
b. B only   **d.** Neither A nor B

FIGURE 2–26

120. A vacuum gauge is hooked up according to the setup in Figure 2–26. The vacuum reading is zero at 1,500 rpm. What does this indicate?

a. The presence of moisture
b. A restriction
c. Both a and b
d. Neither a nor b

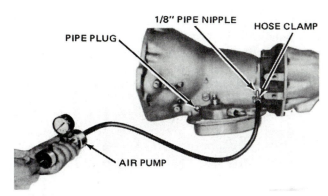

FIGURE 2–27

121. What is the mechanic testing for in Figure 2–27?

a. Case porosity
b. Pump housing leaks
c. Gasket leaks
d. All of the above

122. A sectional view of an automatic transmission is pictured in Figure 2–28. Engine power is transmitted to the transmission input shaft by the:

a. ring gear.   **c.** flex plate.
b. drive pinion gear.   **d.** chain.

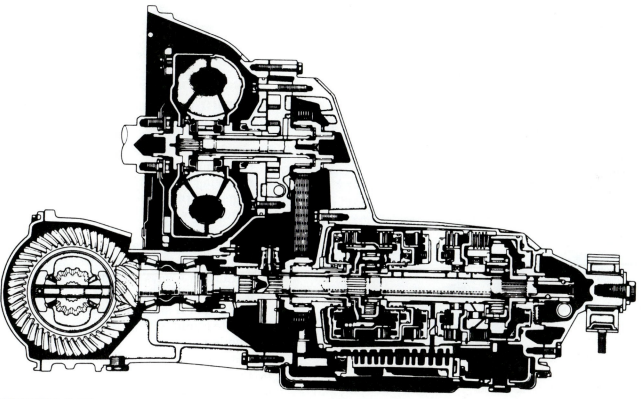

FIGURE 2–28

123. Technician A says that metal sealing rings used in servos and accumulators do not rotate.

Technician B says that Teflon sealing rings are highly resistant to scratching and impregnation by metal particles.

Who is right?
a. A only
b. B only
c. Both A and B
d. Neither A nor B

124. The converter hub is badly scored and it is being replaced along with the front seal. What else should be replaced at this time?
a. Stator support bushing
b. Converter flex plate
c. Pump body bushing
d. Input shaft

125. Incorrect throttle linkage adjustment can cause:
a. early upshifts.
b. delayed upshifts.
c. Both a and b
d. Neither a nor b

126. After rebuilding, an automatic transmission does not work right. Teardown inspection reveals that the disc (diaphragm) spring in the clutch pack has turned inside out. What rebuilding operation was done wrong?
a. Adjustment of mainshaft clearance
b. Adjustment of band clearance
c. Adjustment of clutch pack clearance
d. Installation of clutch piston seal

FIGURE 2–29

127. The assembly in Figure 2–29 can be air tested to check for:
a. clutch pack clearance.
b. piston seal condition.
c. Both a and b
d. Neither a nor b

128. Technician A says that clutch pack clearance in some transmissions is changed by using a different thickness snap ring.

Technician B says that clutch pack clearance in some transmissions is changed by using a different thickness pressure plate.

Who is right?
a. A only   c. Both A and B
b. B only   d. Neither A nor B

FIGURE 2–30

129. Figure 2–30 shows the technician:
a. removing the clutch sprag.
b. removing the clutch piston retainer.
c. removing the dished plate.
d. None of the above

130. It takes a moment for a vehicle to move forward after the selector has been placed in drive.

Technician A says that this could be caused by a partially plugged screen.

Technician B says that this could be caused by aerated fluid.

Who is right?
a. A only
b. B only
c. Both A and B
d. Neither A nor B

CLUTCH AND BAND APPLICATION CHART

LOW (D) (Breakaway)	LOW (1) (Manual)	SECOND	DIRECT	REVERSE
REAR CLUTCH	REAR CLUTCH	REAR CLUTCH	REAR CLUTCH	FRONT CLUTCH
OVERRUNNING CLUTCH	LOW AND REVERSE BAND	KICKDOWN BAND	FRONT CLUTCH	LOW AND REVERSE BAND

FIGURE 2–31

131. Low and second gear in a transmission operate okay, but there's slippage in direct drive. What could be the problem according to the chart in Figure 2–31?
  a. Failing overrunning clutch
  b. Burned-out kickdown band
  c. Loose low and reverse band
  d. Defective front clutch

132. An automatic transmission won't shift down into first gear when coming to a stop sign. Which of these is the MOST LIKELY cause?
  a. Sticking governor
  b. Glazed band
  c. Worn one-way clutch
  d. Damaged servo

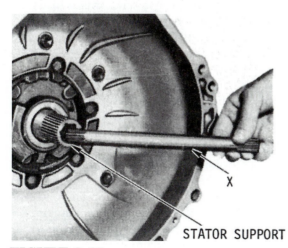

FIGURE 2–32

133. Part X shown in Figure 2–32 is:
  a. the stator shaft.
  b. the input shaft.
  c. the direct drive shaft.
  d. None of the above

134. ATF is dripping from the bottom of a bell housing. This could be caused by all of the following EXCEPT:
  a. front pump housing porosity.
  b. the front seal wearing out.
  c. a cut clutch seal lip.
  d. a loose converter drain plug.

135. An automatic transaxle "clunks" going into reverse.
  Technician A says that this could be caused by the engine idle speed being too high.
  Technician B says that this could be caused by the hydraulic pressure being too high.
  Who is right?
  a. A only
  b. B only
  c. Both A and B
  d. Neither A nor B

136. A car equipped with a torque converter clutch (TCC) has poor acceleration from a standstill. At speeds above 30–35 mph, the car acts normally.
  Technician A says that the engine exhaust system may be blocked.
  Technician B says that the transmission may not be in first gear when starting out.
  Who is right?
  a. A only
  b. B only
  c. Both A and B
  d. Neither A nor B

Lever Position	Start Safety	Parking Sprag	Clutches			Bands	
			Front	Rear	Over-running	(Kickdown) Front	(Low-Rev.) Rear
P—Park	X	X					
R—REVERSE			X				X
N—NEUTRAL	X						
D—DRIVE:							
First				X	X		
Second				X		X	
Third			X	X			
2—SECOND:							
First				X	X		
Second				X		X	
1—LOW (First)				X			X

FIGURE 2–33

137. Refer to the transaxle "element in use" chart in Figure 2–33.

Technician A says that if the transaxle slips in "D" range first gear but does not slip in "1" first gear, the overrunning clutch is probably bad.

Technician B says that if the transaxle slips in any two forward gears, the rear clutch is probably bad.

Who is right?

a. A only
b. B only
c. Both A and B
d. Neither A nor B

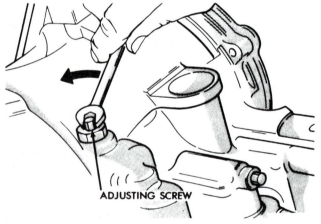

FIGURE 2–34

138. Technician A says that a charred and cracked band can result if the adjustment in Figure 2–34 is wrong.

Technician B says that an overheated transaxle can result if the adjustment in Figure 2–34 is wrong.

Who is right?

a. A only
b. B only
c. Both A and B
d. Neither A nor B

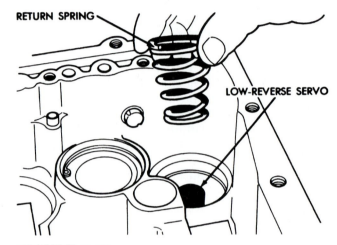

FIGURE 2–35

139. The spring in Figure 2–35 is weaker than it should be.

Technician A says that this will cause the servo to apply slower.

Technician B says that this will cause the servo to apply softer.

Who is right?

a. A only
b. B only
c. Both A and B
d. Neither A nor B

140. Two technicians are discussing the functional checking of a typical TCC system.

Technician A says that while maintaining a 50–55 mph light road load, lightly touch the brake pedal. There should be a slight bump.

Technician B says that a tachometer can be used to check converter clutch release. There should be a slight rpm gain.

Who is right?

a. A only
b. B only
c. Both A and B
d. Neither A nor B

FIGURE 2–36

141. What is being checked in Figure 2–36?
a. Converter end play
b. One-way clutch operation
c. Both a and b
d. Neither a nor b

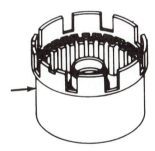

FIGURE 2–37

142. Technician A says that if the part in Figure 2–37 is too rough at the point of the arrow, the clutch seal can be damaged.

Technician B says that if the part in Figure 2–37 is slightly dished at the point of the arrow, this is okay.

Who is right?
a. A only   c. Both A and B
b. B only   d. Neither A nor B

143. Technician A says that no converter clutch apply can be caused by a shorted solenoid wire.

Technician B says that no converter clutch release can be caused by a stuck apply valve.

Who is right?
a. A only
b. B only
c. Both A and B
d. Neither A nor B

144. A typical TCC system would include which of these components?
a. Throttle position sensor
b. Vehicle speed sensor
c. Electronic control module
d. All of the above

FIGURE 2–38

145. Technician A says that a stall test is being performed in Figure 2–38.

Technician B says that a leak test is being performed in Figure 2–38.

Who is right?
a. A only
b. B only
c. Both A and B
d. Neither A nor B

146. Technician A says that the check ball located in a multiple disc clutch allows air to be vented during application.

Technician B says that the check ball prevents too much hydraulic pressure buildup during application.

Who is right?
a. A only   c. Both A and B
b. B only   d. Neither A nor B

147. Technician A says that burned ATF means that the cooler is defective.

Technician B says that "rancid" smelling ATF means that the transmission must be rebuilt.

Who is right?
a. A only   c. Both A and B
b. B only   d. Neither A nor B

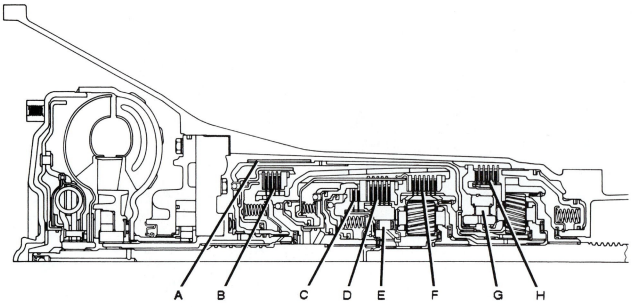

FIGURE 2–39

148. Refer to Figure 2–39. Which of these statements is correct?
  a. Part A is a band; Part B is an overrunning clutch.
  b. Part C is an overrunning clutch; Part D is a multiple disc clutch.
  c. Part E is a multiple disc clutch; Part F is a sprag clutch.
  d. Part G is a multiple disc clutch; Part H is a roller clutch.

149. Refer to the illustration for question 148.
  Technician A says that this transmission has two planetary gear sets.
  Technician B says that this transmission provides 3 forward gear ranges and a reverse.
  Who is right?
  a. A only
  b. B only
  c. Both A and B
  d. Neither A nor B

150. Technician A says that when rebuilding an automatic transmission, thrust washers can be held in place with petroleum jelly.
  Technician B says that when rebuilding an automatic transmission, all plastic thrust washers should be replaced with steel ones.
  Who is right?
  a. A only
  b. B only
  c. Both A and B
  d. Neither A nor B

FIGURE 2–40

151. An "applecored" wear condition is shown on the governor driven gear in Figure 2–40.
  Technician A says that this wear condition can cause an erratic upshift condition.
  Technician B says that this wear condition has been a problem on low fiberglass content driven gears.
  Who is right?
  a. A only   **c.** Both A and B
  b. B only   **d.** Neither A nor B

152. Technician A says that a misadjusted TV cable can cause high oil pressure.
  Technician B says that a misadjusted TV cable can cause low oil pressure.
  Who is right?
  a. A only   **c.** Both A and B
  b. B only   **d.** Neither A nor B

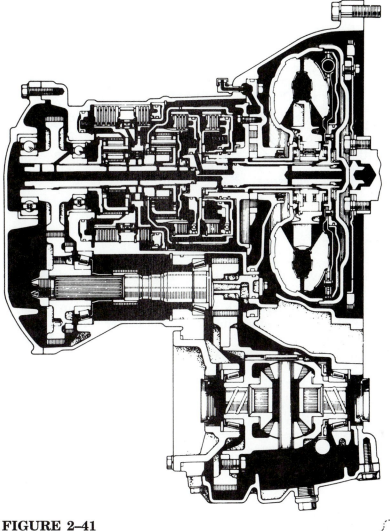

FIGURE 2–41

153. An automatic transaxle sectional view is shown in Figure 2–41.

Technician A says that the preload on the differential side bearings is adjusted with shims.

Technician B says that the backlash between the drive pinion and ring gear is adjusted with shims.

Who is right?

a. A only   **c.** Both A and B
b. B only   **d.** Neither A nor B

154. Technician A says that bad motor mounts can cause a "clunk" noise during a stall test.

Technician B says that bad motor mounts can cause a distributor cap to crack.

Who is right?

a. A only
b. B only
c. Both A and B
d. Neither A nor B

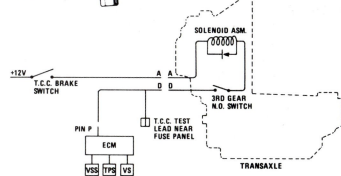

FIGURE 2–42

155. A torque converter clutch (TCC) wiring diagram is shown in Figure 2–42.

Technician A says that the solenoid is energized when a certain speed is reached.

Technician B says that the converter clutch is released when the brakes are applied in order to avoid stalling the engine.

Who is right?

a. A only   **c.** Both A and B
b. B only   **d.** Neither A nor B

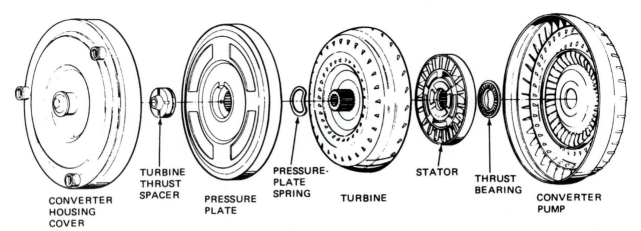

TURBINE THRUST SPACER

CONVERTER HOUSING COVER

PRESSURE PLATE

PRESSURE-PLATE SPRING

TURBINE

STATOR

THRUST BEARING

CONVERTER PUMP

FIGURE 2–43

156. A disassembled torque converter clutch assembly is shown in Figure 2–43.

Technician A says that when the clutch is engaged, the pressure plate is forced against the converter housing cover.

Technician B says that the pressure plate is splined to the turbine shaft.

Who is right?

a. A only
b. B only
c. Both A and B
d. Neither A nor B

157. An engine has poor performance. This could cause:

a. harsh shifts.
b. delayed shifts.
c. Both a and b
d. Neither a nor b

158. Technician A says to disconnect the battery when removing the converter from a car.

Technician B says to unbolt the flex plate from the engine when removing the converter from a car.

Who is right?

a. A only
b. B only
c. Both A and B
d. Neither A nor B

159. Technician A says that in order for a shift valve to move, throttle pressure must be overcome.

Technician B says that in order for a shift valve to move, spring pressure must be overcome.

Who is right?

a. A only
b. B only
c. Both A and B
d. Neither A nor B

160. Fluid level rises in a transmission when the engine is not running.

Technician A says that fluid in the converter could be draining back.

Technician B says that the oil cooler could be bad.

Who is right?

a. A only
b. B only
c. Both A and B
d. Neither A nor B

161. Technician A says that a "snapped-off" converter hub can cause a no-drive condition.

Technician B says that a clogged oil screen can cause a no-drive condition.

Who is right?

a. A only
b. B only
c. Both A and B
d. Neither A nor B

162. Technician A says that the throttle valve is moved by linkage connected to the shift quadrant.

Technician B says that the manual valve is moved by linkage connected to the accelerator pedal.

Who is right?

a. A only
b. B only
c. Both A and B
d. Neither A nor B

163. Technician A says that low line pressure in all shift selector positions could be caused by a stuck pressure regulator valve.

Technician B says that low throttle pressure can cause engine runaway on shifts.

Who is right?

a. A only
b. B only
c. Both A and B
d. Neither A nor B

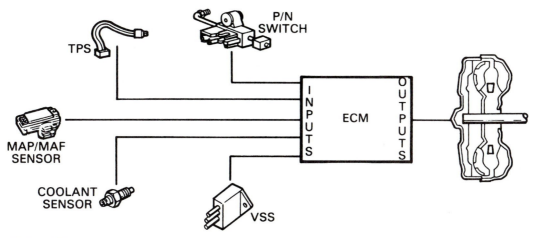

FIGURE 2–44

164. An automatic transmission equipped vehicle has sensor inputs for the TCC as shown in Figure 2–44.

Technician A says that a bad coolant sensor can cause no TCC.

Technician B says that a bad VSS can cause no TCC.

Who is right?
a. A only   c. Both A and B
b. B only   d. Neither A nor B

165. A TV cable that is kinked or binding can cause:
a. chatters on takeoff.
b. intermittent second gear starts.
c. Both a and b
d. Neither a nor b

166. Technician A says that a cracked spark plug can affect automatic transaxle performance.

Technician B says that dirty fuel injectors can affect automatic transaxle performance.

Who is right?
a. A only   c. Both A and B
b. B only   d. Neither A nor B

167. Plugged orifices in a valve-body spacer plate can cause:
a. low oil pressure.
b. first speed only, and no 1–2 upshift.
c. no-drive.
d. All of the above

168. Technician A says that excessive input shaft end play can be caused by a worn case.

Technician B says that excessive input shaft end play can be caused by the wrong washers.

Who is right?
a. A only   c. Both A and B
b. B only   d. Neither A nor B

169. Technician A says that TCC apply shudder can be caused by the converter damper plate not being parallel.

Technician B says that TCC apply shudder can be caused by lining damage from coolant.

Who is right?
a. A only
b. B only
c. Both A and B
d. Neither A nor B

170. A "scan" tool is being used to diagnose an automatic transmission problem.

Technician A says that voltage should not change when the gear shift selector is moved from neutral to drive.

Technician B says that voltage should not change when the throttle is moved from closed position to wide open position.

Who is right?
a. A only
b. B only
c. Both A and B
d. Neither A nor B

171. The internal TCC circuitry of an automatic transaxle is being checked.

Technician A says to test the apply solenoid by touching the leads to an automotive battery.

Technician B says to test the apply solenoid by using an analog-type ohmmeter.

Who is right?
a. A only
b. B only
c. Both A and B
d. Neither A nor B

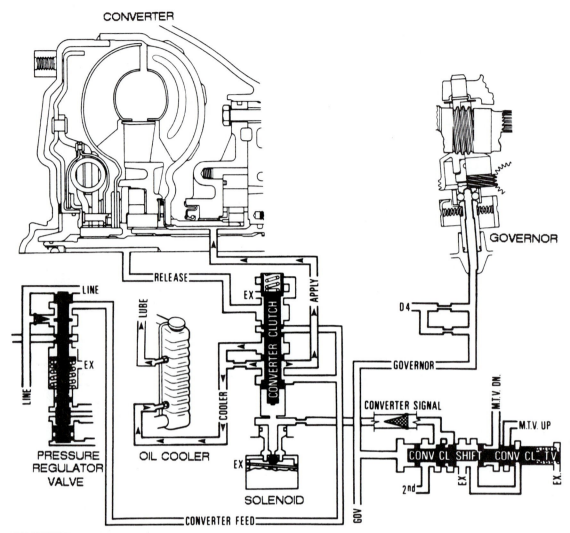

FIGURE 2–45

172. Refer to the hydraulic circuit in Figure 2–45.

Technician A says that oil flow to the cooler and lube system is provided through an orifice in the apply line to cooler passage.

Technician B says that when the solenoid is not energized, converter clutch oil is exhausted and the TCC will stay released.

Who is right?

a. A only
b. B only
c. Both A and B
d. Neither A nor B

173. A transmission has just been overhauled and will not upshift. With the brakes applied, line pressure in neutral at 1,000 rpm is 160 psi (specs. are 55–70). This problem could be caused by:

a. a vacuum leak.
b. case porosity.
c. an incorrect pressure regulator spring.
d. All of the above

174. Burned forward clutch plates could be caused by:

a. a missing check ball.
b. low line pressure.
c. broken pump cover oil seal rings.
d. All of the above

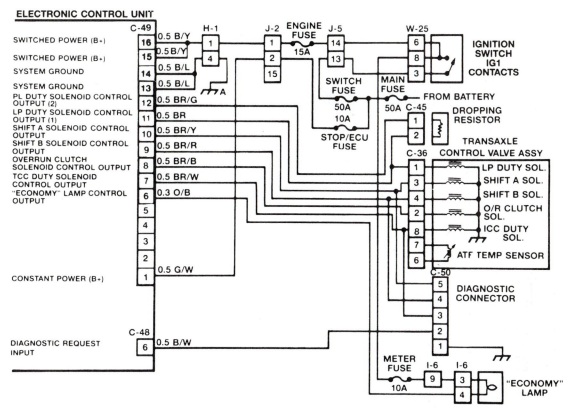

FIGURE 2–46

175. An output control diagram for a 4-speed electronically controlled automatic transaxle is pictured in Figure 2–46.

Technician A says that the ECU controls line pressure.

Technician B says that the ECU controls upshift timing.

Who is right?

a. A only
b. B only
c. Both A and B
d. Neither A nor B

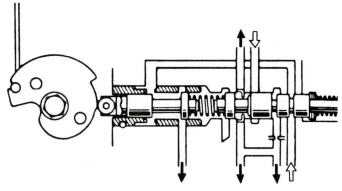

FIGURE 2–47

176. Technician A says that a throttle valve is pictured in Figure 2–47.

Technician B says that a governor valve is pictured.

Who is right?

a. A only
b. B only
c. Both A and B
d. Neither A nor B

177. A vehicle has a binding slip yoke. This could cause:

a. thrust washer wear.
b. "clunking" noise.
c. Both a and b
d. Neither a nor b

178. Technician A says that it's okay to install a transmission in a vehicle as long as one dowel pin is present on the back of the engine block.

Technician B says that the weights on some converters are used to balance the engine crankshaft.

Who is right?

a. A only   **c.** Both A and B
b. B only   **d.** Neither A nor B

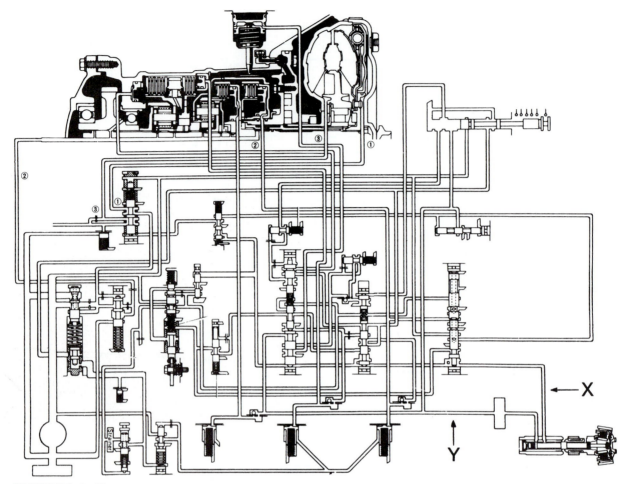

FIGURE 2–48

179. Technician A says that oil line X shown in Figure 2–48 is for line pressure.

Technician B says that oil line Y shown in Figure 2–48 is for governor pressure.

Who is right?

a. A only
b. B only
c. Both A and B
d. Neither A nor B

180. An automatic transaxle has a broken case due to a driving accident.

Technician A says that good components from the broken case can be installed into a new case.

Technician B says that it is not necessary to check endplay if a new case is being used.

Who is right?

a. A only
b. B only
c. Both A and B
d. Neither A nor B

181. Technician A says that oil pressure tests are seldom useful for diagnosis on newer transmissions.

Technician B says that a "scan" tool is useful for diagnosis on newer transmissions.

Who is right?

a. A only
b. B only
c. Both A and B
d. Neither A nor B

182. A lock-up transmission comes to your shop for an overhaul. The transmission is burned up, and the torque converter has turned blue.

Which of these is the MOST LIKELY cause?

a. Seized governor valve
b. Restricted oil cooler
c. Slipping kickdown band
d. Defective low sprag

183. Technician A says that when changing a leaking rear seal on a transmission, it is usually recommended that a new rear bushing be installed also.

Technician B says that it is a good idea to install another ground strap on vehicles with cable operated linkage.

Who is right?
a. A only
b. B only
c. Both A and B
d. Neither A nor B

184. Technician A says that what feels like lock-up shudder is often an engine problem.

Technician B says that monitoring the oxygen sensor is a way to diagnose whether a lock-up shudder is an engine or transmission problem.

Who is right?
a. A only
b. B only
c. Both A and B
d. Neither A nor B

185. Technician A says that a bad EGR valve will have no effect on transmission performance.

Technician B says that a bad engine thermostat can cause a lock-up problem.

Who is right?
a. A only
b. B only
c. Both A and B
d. Neither A nor B

186. Technician A says that a digital multimeter is safer on electronics than an analog meter.

Technician B says that when checking voltage on a car battery, the reading must be at least 11.8 volts.

Who is right?
a. A only
b. B only
c. Both A and B
d. Neither A nor B

187. Technician A says that an ammeter is an effective tool to pinpoint high resistance problems.

Technician B says that if voltage remains the same, an increase in current will also cause an increase in resistance.

Who is right?
a. A only
b. B only
c. Both A and B
d. Neither A nor B

FIGURE 2–49

188. Intermediate clutch clearance is being measured in the transmission in Figure 2–49. The depth mike reads 1.730″. The specs are 1.634 to 1.646″. Which of the following selective size outer plates should be used for correction?
a. .071″ **b.** .081″ **c.** .091″ **d.** .101″

FIGURE 2–50

189. A clutch piston lip seal cross-section is shown in Figure 2–50.

Technician A says that the seal lip shows wear caused by poor drum finish.

Technician B says that the seal lip shows wear caused by poor piston groove finish.

Who is right?
a. A only   **c.** Both A and B
b. B only   **d.** Neither A nor B

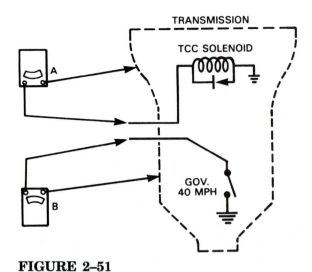

FIGURE 2–51

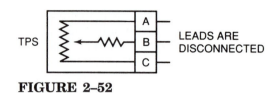

FIGURE 2–52

191. An ohmmeter is connected between A and B in Figure 2–52.

Technician A says that different resistance values will be displayed as the throttle is depressed.

Technician B says that only a high impedance meter can be used.

Who is right?

a. A only   c. Both A and B
b. B only   d. Neither A nor B

190. Refer to the ohmmeter hookup shown in Figure 2–51.

Technician A says that meter B should change from infinity to near zero when the governor switch closes.

Technician B says that power from meter A will destroy the diode.

Who is right?

a. A only   c. Both A and B
b. B only   d. Neither A nor B

Section 3

MANUAL DRIVE TRAIN AND AXLES

STUDY OUTLINE

I. Clutch Assembly
  A. Components
    1. Flywheel—purpose
    2. Pilot bushing (bearing)
    3. Friction disc—construction
    4. Ring gear for starter (removal and replacement)
      a. Torsional springs or rubber inserts
      b. Cushion springs
      c. Hub
    5. Pressure plate (diaphragm and coil-spring type)
    6. Clutch cover
    7. Throwout bearing (include self-centering type)
    8. Release levers (include adjustable type)
  B. Adjustments
    1. Free-play clearance
    2. Over-center spring
    3. Automatic adjuster mechanisms
    4. Align mounts
  C. Measurements
    1. Flywheel-to-block runout
    2. Bell housing bore-to-crankshaft runout
    3. Crankshaft end play
    4. Flywheel runout
    5. Friction disc runout
    6. Crankshaft flange runout
  D. Problem/Diagnosis
    1. Does not engage
    2. Does not release
    3. Noises
      a. Pedal depressed
      b. Pedal released
    4. Pulsating pedal
    5. Chatter
    6. Slipping
    7. Binding
    8. Shudder in reverse
    9. Grab
  E. Replacement Procedures/Tools
    1. Aligning mandrels
    2. Guide pins
    3. Hydraulic clutch slave and master cylinder (bleeding)/lines/hoses
    4. Pilot bearing pullers
    5. Pedal linkage, brackets, bushings, and pivots

II. Manual Transmission/Transaxle
  A. Power Flow (3-speed, 4-speed, and 5-speed)
  B. Components (Identification and Replacement)
    1. Shafts and retainers
    2. Gears—nomenclature
    3. Bearings, bores, and bushings
    4. Thrust washers and thrust bearings
    5. Synchromesh devices—operation
    6. Shift levers, cables, and guides
    7. Interlock mechanisms (detent)
    8. Speedometer drive gear and driven gear
    9. Extension housing and/or case
    10. Gaskets and seals (include sealants)
    11. Mounts/dampers
    12. Column and floor shifter mechanisms
    13. Vents
    14. Shift cover, grommets, and linkage (hard rods)
    15. Lubrication devices
  C. Rebuilding Procedures/Clearance Checks/Adjustments/Cleaning
    1. Shim/spacer selection
    2. End play/preload
    3. Shrink fit gear and bearing race installation
  D. Problem/Diagnosis
    1. Noises
    2. Jumping out of gear
    3. Gears do not engage
    4. Backlash or end-play
    5. Stays locked in gear
    6. Leaks
    7. Hard shifting
    8. Premature bearing failure

III. Drive Line
  A. Type of Drive
    1. Hotchkiss
    2. Four wheel
    3. Front wheel drive half shafts
      a. Diagnose noise and vibration
      b. Replace shaft, boots, and universal joints
  B. Types of Universal Joints
    1. Cross/Yoke
    2. Constant velocity
      a. No speed fluctuation

3. Half shaft inboard and outboard joints
4. Service procedures
   a. Grease fitting direction
   b. Relieving in order to prevent bind
   c. "Burping" the boot

C. Shaft Design
1. Tube
2. Solid
3. Two-piece/Three-piece
   a. Phasing
   b. Checking stub shaft runout
   c. Working angle limits
   d. "Odd" joint assemblies
4. Damper rings
5. Balance weights

D. Drive Shaft
1. Lateral runout
2. Companion flange runout
3. Bend

E. Problem/Diagnosis
1. Noise
   a. Acceleration rumble (launch shudder)
   b. Deceleration clunk or rattle
   c. Squeaking/drone
   d. Steer torque
   e. Correction procedures
2. Vibrations
   a. Drive line angle (measure and adjust)
   b. Checking balance with hose clamps
   c. First and second order
   d. Pressure in ears
   e. Correction procedures
3. Backlash clunk (excessive play)

F. U-Joint Wear Patterns
1. Brinelling
2. Trunion end-galling

G. Inspect/Service/Replace Center Support Bearings

IV. Differential and Axle Assembly

A. Types
1. Full floating axles
2. Semi-floating axles
3. Hypoid gear design
4. Timed gear sets
5. Transaxle
6. Gear ratio calculation

B. Construction and Components (Be Able to Identify Visually)
1. Carrier and bearings
2. Axle (side) gears
3. Thrust washers
4. Shafts and retainers
5. Ring gear/case
6. Drive pinion gear
7. Drive pinion bearings
8. Pinion (differential or "spider") gears
9. Axle shaft and bearings
   a. End-play

   b. Removal
   c. Inspection
10. Seals (direction of lip faces grease)
11. Vents (remote)
12. Gear housing

V. Differential Service/Adjustments

A. Terms
1. Preload (how measured)
2. Backlash (how measured)
3. Depth
4. Pattern

B. Drive Pinion Preload Adjustment
1. Crush sleeve (purpose)
2. Shims (location)
3. New bearings versus used bearings

C. Drive Pinion Depth Setting
1. Shims (location)
2. Thickness and effect of change
3. Depth markings
4. Depth setting tools
5. Gear marking compound

D. Carrier Bearing Preload
1. Shims
2. Threaded adjusters

E. Ring Gear Backlash
1. Effected by movement of carrier
2. Shims
3. Threaded adjusters
4. Specifications

F. Ring Gear Runout

G. Differential Case Runout

H. Tooth Contact Patterns
1. Coast side
2. Drive side
3. Toe contact heavy
4. Heel contact heavy
5. Face contact high
6. Flank contact low
7. Determine correction needed

I. Rebuilding Procedures
1. Visual checks
2. Housing spreader (using in conjunction with dial indicator)
3. Clutch (cone/plate) pack replacement and adjustment

J. Replacement
1. Companion flange (may or may not have attached weight)
2. Ring and pinion (as a matched set)
3. Case assembly
   a. "Spiders"
   b. Shaft
   c. Side gears
   d. Thrust washers
   e. Case
4. Pinion seal

K. Problem/Diagnosis
  1. Noises
    a. Coast
    b. Drive
    c. Float
    d. On turns
    e. Chatter
    f. Seal fit
    g. Clunks
    h. Improper lubricant (limited slip differential)
    i. Limited slip differential operational test
    j. Vibration
    k. Fluid leaks
    l. Axle shaft/flange runout
    m. Bearing wear
    n. Whine

VI. Four-Wheel Drive Component Diagnosis and Repair
  A. Diagnose
    1. Noise
    2. Vibration
    3. Hard shifting
    4. Steering problems
  B. Inspect, Adjust, and/or Repair
    1. Transfer case shifting mechanisms
    2. Front wheel bearings and locking hubs
    3. Seals and remote vents
    4. Axle knuckles and driving shafts
    5. Front-drive propeller shafts and universal joints
    6. Lube level

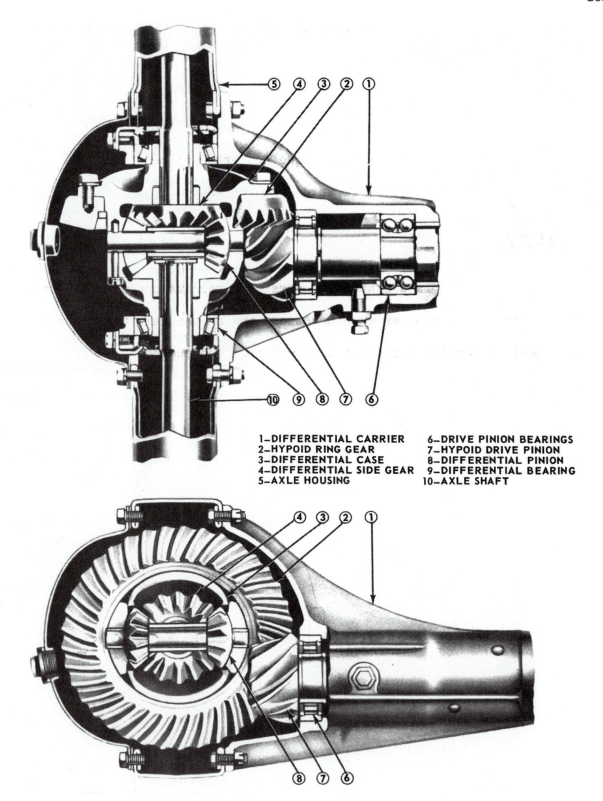

1—DIFFERENTIAL CARRIER   6—DRIVE PINION BEARINGS
2—HYPOID RING GEAR   7—HYPOID DRIVE PINION
3—DIFFERENTIAL CASE   8—DIFFERENTIAL PINION
4—DIFFERENTIAL SIDE GEAR   9—DIFFERENTIAL BEARING
5—AXLE HOUSING   10—AXLE SHAFT

Part names used in questions for this section.

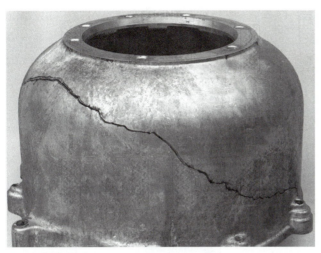

FIGURE 3–1

FIGURE 3–2

1. The part in Figure 3–1 is badly cracked.

   Technician A says that this could cause the transmission to shift hard.

   Technician B says that this could cause the transmission to slip out of gear.

   Who is right?
   a. A only
   b. B only
   c. Both A and B
   d. Neither A nor B

2. New blocker rings are being installed in a transaxle assembly.

   Technician A says that the inside surface should be polished with crocus cloth.

   Technician B says that the inside surface should be lightly sanded with #400 grit paper.

   Who is right?
   a. A only
   b. B only
   c. Both A and B
   d. Neither A nor B

3. A car with a 4-speed manual transmission has the shift lever touching the front edge of the floor console.

   Technician A says that this condition means that all three linkage rods must be adjusted.

   Technician B says that this condition can cause the transmission to jump out of gear.

   Who is right?
   a. A only
   b. B only
   c. Both A and B
   d. Neither A nor B

4. A manual transaxle has a slight vibration during turns only. Which of these would be the MOST LIKELY cause?
   a. Worn inner axle u-joint
   b. Loose differential case assembly
   c. Out-of-balance half shaft
   d. Worn outer axle u-joint

5. The transmission in Figure 3–2 is in what gear?
   a. Neutral
   b. Third
   c. Fourth
   d. Fifth (overdrive)

6. What is NOT true about using sealants to assemble a transmission?
   a. Sealing surfaces should be free from grease and oil.
   b. Sealing surfaces should be examined for damage before assembly.
   c. Sealant should be oxygen sensor safe.
   d. Sealant should be allowed to cure completely before assembly.

7. Upon draining a transmission, brass colored dust is found in the old lubricant.

   Technician A says that this could be caused by a worn counter gear.

   Technician B says that this could be caused by a worn synchro assembly.

   Who is right?
   a. A only
   b. B only
   c. Both A and B
   d. Neither A nor B

8. A transmission comes out of first gear while decelerating down a hill.

   Technician A says that this could be caused by a worn shift fork.

   Technician B says that this could be caused by a broken detent spring.

   Who is right?
   a. A only
   b. B only
   c. Both A and B
   d. Neither A nor B

9. A transmission has very bad bearing noise in all forward gears except fourth. The noise is also quite noticeable in reverse. Which of these is the MOST LIKELY cause?
   a. Rough countershaft bearings
   b. Chipped reverse idler
   c. Worn main shaft rear bearing
   d. Dry pilot bearing

FIGURE 3–3

10. The transaxle in Figure 3–3 is engaged in what gear?
    a. First
    b. Second
    c. Third
    d. Fourth

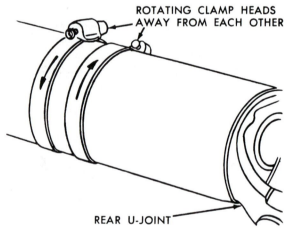

ROTATING CLAMP HEADS AWAY FROM EACH OTHER

REAR U-JOINT

FIGURE 3–4

11. What procedure is being performed on the drive shaft in Figure 3–4?
    a. Balancing
    b. Noise dampening
    c. U-joint operating angle check
    d. Yoke alignment check

12. Driveline vibration occurs around 50 mph. What should you check?
    a. Driveshaft runout
    b. Driveshaft balance
    c. Both a and b
    d. Neither a nor b

13. A transaxle shifts hard. This could be caused by all of the following EXCEPT:
    a. improper lubricant.
    b. loose engine mounts.
    c. broken final drive teeth.
    d. damaged synchro sleeves.

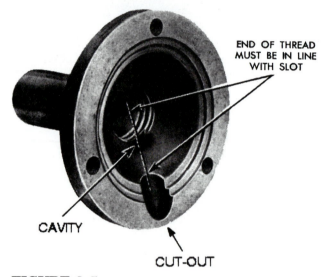

END OF THREAD MUST BE IN LINE WITH SLOT

CAVITY

CUT-OUT

FIGURE 3–5

14. The transmission bearing retainer in Figure 3–5 is being installed.
    Technician A says that the bearing snap ring gap must line up at the cut-out.
    Technician B says that the retainer gasket cut-out must line up at the cut-out.
    Who is right?
    a. A only
    b. B only
    c. Both A and B
    d. Neither A nor B

15. Technician A says that speedometer error can result by changing rear tire size.
    Technician B says that speedometer error can result by changing rear axle ratio.
    Who is right?
    a. A only
    b. B only
    c. Both A and B
    d. Neither A nor B

16. Excessive counter gear (cluster) end play can cause:
  a. noise in all reduction gears.
  b. excessive backlash in all reduction gears.
  c. Both a and b
  d. Neither a nor b

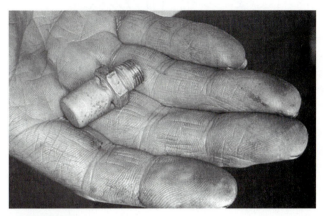

FIGURE 3–6

17. The differential part in Figure 3–6 becomes clogged with mud.
    Technician A says that this could cause a pressure buildup inside the carrier.
    Technician B says that this could cause an oil leak at the pinion seal.
    Who is right?
  a. A only   **c.** Both A and B
  b. B only   **d.** Neither A nor B

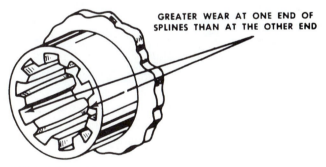

FIGURE 3–7

18. The splines on the clutch disc hub in Figure 3–7 show greater wear on the ends than in the middle.
    Technician A says that this could be caused by dirt, chips, or burrs between the transmission case and the bell-housing.
    Technician B says that this could be caused by lack of lubricant on the input shaft.
    Who is right?
  a. A only   **c.** Both A and B
  b. B only   **d.** Neither A nor B

FIGURE 3–8

19. Technician A says that clutch noise is often caused by the part in Figure 3–8.
    Technician B says that a slipping clutch is often caused by the part in Figure 3–8.
    Who is right?
  a. A only
  b. B only
  c. Both A and B
  d. Neither A nor B

20. A new clutch plate is being installed in a vehicle.
    Technician A says to compress the pressure plate springs.
    Technician B says to use an aligning tool.
    Who is right?
  a. A only   **c.** Both A and B
  b. B only   **d.** Neither A nor B

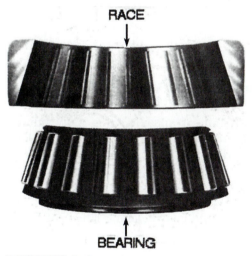

FIGURE 3–9

21. What is indicated by the wear pattern in Figure 3–9?
  a. Lack of lubrication
  b. Impact loading
  c. Spalling
  d. Fretting

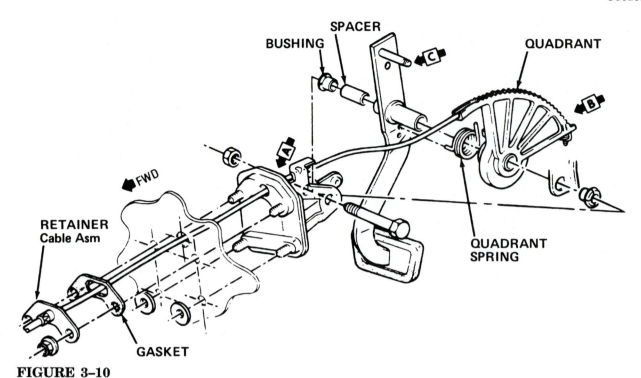

FIGURE 3–10

22. A front wheel drive car with a transverse mounted engine has a self-adjusting cable operated clutch (see Figure 3–10).

Technician A says that adjustment is automatically made as the clutch pedal returns to the full-up position.

Technician B says that the pressure plate fingers constantly contact the throwout bearing.

Who is right?

a. A only
c. Both A and B
b. B only
d. Neither A nor B

23. A manual transaxle shifts okay, but slips out of second gear. Which of these parts is the MOST LIKELY cause?
a. Input (clutch) shaft bearing
b. Counter (cluster) gear bearing
c. Second gear
d. Second gear blocking ring

24. A rear axle bearing (sealed ball bearing type) is being pressed onto the axle shaft.

Technician A says to apply pressure on the outer race.

Technician B says to apply pressure on the inner race.

Who is right?

a. A only
c. Both A and B
b. B only
d. Neither A nor B

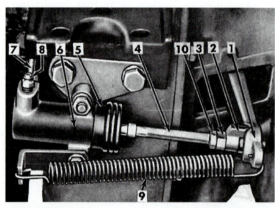

FIGURE 3–11

25. A vehicle is equipped with the clutch system in Figure 3–11. After the pedal is engaged, the clutch slowly releases. This could be caused by:
a. a worn cup inside part 6.
b. part 9 being too weak.
c. part 4 being adjusted wrong.
d. All of the above

26. A 4WD transfer case jumps out of gear.

Technician A says that this could be caused by dry front and rear driveshaft slip yokes.

Technician B says that this could be caused by different size tires.

Who is right?

a. A only
c. Both A and B
b. B only
d. Neither A nor B

FIGURE 3–12

27. What is being adjusted in Figure 3–12?
    a. Rear axle universal joint angle
    b. Rear wheel caster
    c. Spring rate
    d. Tracking

28. A 4WD vehicle steers hard. With the front end raised, each wheel is rotated on its spindle while turning from stop to stop. What is true if one wheel becomes hard to rotate as it nears its stop?
    a. Locking hub is bad.
    b. U-joint is bad.
    c. Both a and b
    d. Neither a nor b

29. A 4WD vehicle has a vibration in 2WD with the hubs locked. Which of these is the MOST LIKELY cause?
    a. Bad front wheel bearing
    b. Bad front half-shaft u-joints
    c. Loose transfer case mounts
    d. Bad transfer case bearings

30. The transfer case in a full-time 4WD vehicle shifts hard.
    Technician A says that the shifter assembly could be clogged with mud or dirt.
    Technician B says that the shifting linkage could be corroded.
    Who is right?
    a. A only
    b. B only
    c. Both A and B
    d. Neither A nor B

31. All of the following should be done when disconnecting the front driveshaft on a full-time 4WD vehicle, EXCEPT:
    a. supporting transfer case.
    b. supporting front axle.
    c. replacing transfer case seal.
    d. checking yokes for phasing.

32. What factor can be said to affect driveline angle?
    a. Wheel diameter
    b. Suspension height
    c. Both a and b
    d. Neither a nor b

33. A lift kit is used to raise a 4WD vehicle. This will affect which of these items?
    a. Brake hose length
    b. Driveshaft length
    c. Handling characteristics
    d. All of the above

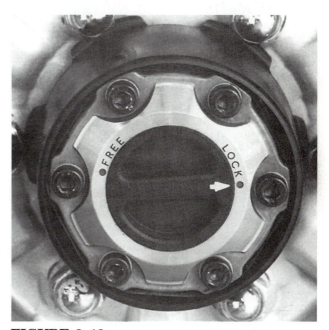

FIGURE 3–13

34. Technician A says that the device in Figure 3–13 is engaged by using special pliers.
    Technician B says that the device is set to disengage the front axle.
    Who is right?
    a. A only
    b. B only
    c. Both A and B
    d. Neither A nor B

35. A transaxle has a rattle with the clutch engaged, but it disappears as the pedal is pushed in.

   Technician A says that this could be caused by a bad throwout bearing.

   Technician B says that this could be caused by bad damper springs in the clutch disc.

   Who is right?
   a. A only
   b. B only
   c. Both A and B
   d. Neither A nor B

36. On a light truck equipped with automatic locking hubs, the hubs will not disengage.

   Technician A says that this could be caused by incorrect shifting procedure.

   Technician B says that this could be caused by the wrong locking washer behind the wheel bearing lock nut.

   Who is right?
   a. A only   c. Both A and B
   b. B only   d. Neither A nor B

37. Technician A says that air in the clutch hydraulic system can cause gear grind when shifting.

   Technician B says that fluid leaks in the clutch hydraulic system can cause gear grind when shifting.

   Who is right?
   a. A only   c. Both A and B
   b. B only   d. Neither A nor B

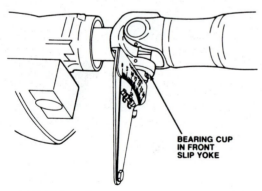

BEARING CUP
IN FRONT
SLIP YOKE

FIGURE 3–14

38. What is being checked in Figure 3–14?
   a. Driveshaft runout
   b. U-joint phase
   c. Both a and b
   d. Neither a nor b

39. A front wheel drive car traveling on a level road pulls to the right during heavy throttle application.

   Which of these is the LEAST LIKELY cause?
   a. Improper tire pressure
   b. Unequal drive axle lengths
   c. Unequal front tire diameters
   d. Improper engine/transaxle assembly alignment

40. Technician A says that shimming a transverse engine mount can affect steer torque.

   Technician B says that shimming a transverse engine mount can affect outer CV joint angle.

   Who is right?
   a. A only
   b. B only
   c. Both A and B
   d. Neither A nor B

41. A manual transaxle has had a torn outer CV joint boot for 2,000 miles.

   Technician A says to inspect the CV joint and replace the boot.

   Technician B says to "burp" the new boot.

   Who is right?
   a. A only
   b. B only
   c. Both A and B
   d. Neither A nor B

42. Pilot or guide pins should be used in transmission installation to prevent damage to the:
   a. friction disc.
   b. clutch shaft.
   c. main drive bearing.
   d. shift linkage.

43. A car owner complains of a chattering clutch.

   Technician A says that oil on the disc facing can be the problem.

   Technician B says that worn motor mounts can be the problem.

   Who is right?
   a. A only
   b. B only
   c. Both A and B
   d. Neither A nor B

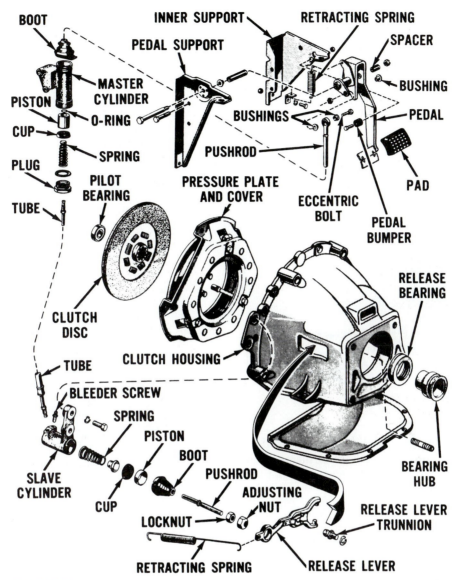

FIGURE 3–15

44. The clutch assembly in Figure 3–15 has too much free pedal travel.

Technician A says that this could be caused by a misadjusted pushrod.

Technician B says that this could be caused by low fluid.

Who is right?
a. A only
b. B only
c. Both A and B
d. Neither A nor B

45. What can cause a clutch to slip?
a. Sticking release levers
b. Oil-soaked disc
c. Weak pressure plate springs
d. All of the above

46. Technician A says that the clutch cover bolts should be released one at a time.

Technician B says that the clutch cover bolts should be released in a certain order.

Who is right?
a. A only
b. B only
c. Both A and B
d. Neither A nor B

47. A transmission mainshaft rear bearing is being inspected by spin testing.

    Technician A says to lubricate the bearing raceways lightly with oil after cleaning and drying.

    Technician B says to take off the outer snap ring and spin the outer bearing race using compressed air.

    Who is right?
    a. A only
    b. B only
    c. Both A and B
    d. Neither A nor B

FIGURE 3–16

48. Which of the following is the MOST LIKELY cause for the evenly spaced indentations on the bearing race in Figure 3–16?
    a. Fine dirt
    b. Chips
    c. Improper seating
    d. Forcing the bearing off with a hammer and chisel

49. These parts should not be washed in cleaning solvent EXCEPT the:
    a. friction disc and clutch cover.
    b. release levers and pressure plate.
    c. friction disc and throwout bearing.
    d. clutch cover and throwout bearing.

50. Whenever replacing the drive pinion gear, always replace the:
    a. differential pinion gears.
    b. side bearings.
    c. side gears.
    d. ring gear.

51. A car has a high-pitched "whine" noise similar to a whistle. The noise occurs at all driving speeds and seems to come from the rear end.

    Technician A says that the drive pinion front bearing could be bad.

    Technician B says that the differential could need lubricant.

    Who is right?
    a. A only   c. Both A and B
    b. B only   d. Neither A nor B

52. A "dummy" shaft is often used when working on manual transmissions. This is done to help the installation of what part?
    a. Counter gear
    b. Shift rail(s)
    c. Extension housing
    d. Input shaft retainer

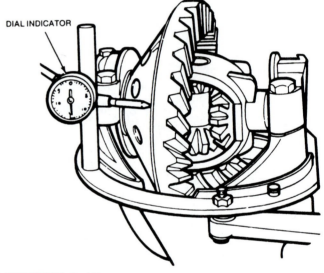

DIAL INDICATOR

FIGURE 3–17

53. The set up shown in Figure 3–17 is used to check:
    a. ring gear runout.
    b. ring gear backlash.
    c. differential case clearance.
    d. None of the above

54. A rear end is being overhauled. What is normally the order of adjustment?
    a. Drive pinion preload, backlash, carrier bearing preload
    b. Drive pinion preload, carrier bearing preload, backlash
    c. Carrier bearing preload, backlash, drive pinion preload
    d. Backlash, carrier bearing preload, drive pinion preload

55. Technician A says that rear axle noise can be caused by worn keyways.
    Technician B says that rear axle noise can be caused by brinelled wheel bearings.
    Who is right?
    a. A only
    b. B only
    c. Both A and B
    d. Neither A nor B

56. Vibration in a rear wheel drive vehicle equipped with CV u-joints can be caused by:
    a. worn center support bearings.
    b. bent centering ball stud.
    c. distorted pinion flange.
    d. All of the above

57. A leaking pinion seal on a crush sleeve type differential needs to be replaced.
    Technician A says that the entire rear axle carrier will have to be disassembled.
    Technician B says that a new crush sleeve is recommended.
    Who is right?
    a. A only
    b. B only
    c. Both A and B
    d. Neither A nor B

58. A transmission is hard to shift.
    Technician A says that this can be caused by worn blocker rings.
    Technician B says that this can be caused by linkage out-of-adjustment.
    Who is right?
    a. A only
    b. B only
    c. Both A and B
    d. Neither A nor B

59. A transaxle "walks" out of gear.
    Technician A says that this could be caused by broken engine mounts.
    Technician B says that this could be caused by an improperly installed boot.
    Who is right?
    a. A only
    b. B only
    c. Both A and B
    d. Neither A nor B

60. Technician A says that the part in Figure 3–18 permits the driveshaft to change effective length.
    Technician B says that the part shows wear at point X.
    Who is right?
    a. A only
    b. B only
    c. Both A and B
    d. Neither A nor B

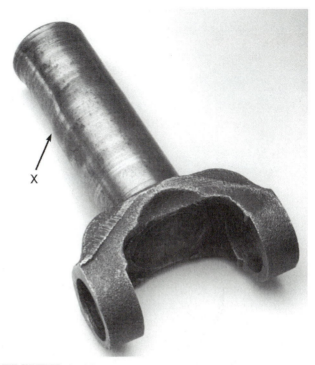

FIGURE 3–18

FIGURE 3–19

61. Technician A says that the parts in Figure 3–19 are used when setting side bearing preload.
    Technician B says that the parts are used when setting drive pinion preload.
    Who is right?
    a. A only
    b. B only
    c. Both A and B
    d. Neither A nor B

FIGURE 3–20

62. Technician A says that the damage in Figure 3–20 could have been caused by driver abuse.

Technician B says that the damage could have been caused by overloading.

Who is right?
a. A only
b. B only
c. Both A and B
d. Neither A nor B

63. If the tooth contact pattern is too close to the heel on the drive side of the ring gear, the drive pinion should be:
a. moved farther from the ring gear.
b. moved closer to the ring gear.
c. replaced.
d. adjusted for more preload.

64. Technician A says that manual transaxles use automatic transmission fluid for lubricant.

Technician B says that manual transaxles use 5W-30 oil for lubricant.

Who is right?
a. A only
b. B only
c. Both A and B
d. Neither A nor B

65. A transaxle will not shift into one certain gear, yet all other gears shift okay. Which of the following is the MOST LIKELY cause?
a. Low lubricant level
b. Damaged external shift mechanism
c. Loose cylinder block bolts
d. Clutch disc installed backwards

FIGURE 3–21

66. What usually causes the bearing damage shown in Figure 3–21?
a. Fatigue
b. Overheating
c. Wear
d. Improper handling

FIGURE 3–22

67. Which of the following is the MOST LIKELY cause for the wear pattern on the u-joint cup in Figure 3–22?
a. Brinelling
b. Corrosion
c. Etching
d. Improperly grounded are welder

68. A car owner complains of vehicle vibration. A check shows that the rear universal joint operating angle is not correct.

Technician A says that on some cars this angle is changed by inserting tapered shims between the rear leaf springs and axle housing.

Technician B says that on some cars this angle is changed by tilting the axle housing.

Who is right?
a. A only
b. B only
c. Both A and B
d. Neither A nor B

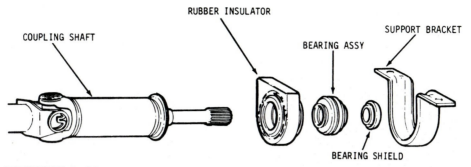

FIGURE 3-23

69. A coupling shaft/center bearing assembly is shown in Figure 3–23.

Technician A says that excessive compression of the rubber insulator may cause vibration.

Technician B says that shimming the support bracket may eliminate driveaway (launch) shudder.

Who is right?

a. A only **c.** Both A and B
b. B only **d.** Neither A nor B

70. The main reason for making a rear end gear tooth contact pattern is to check:
a. carrier end play.
b. carrier bearing preload.
c. axle gear clearance.
d. pinion depth.

71. Refer to the differential assembly in Figure 3–24.

Technician A says that the cones slip when the car turns a corner.

Technician B says that the cones transfer torque when the car wheels are on snow.

Who is right?

a. A only
b. B only
c. Both A and B
d. Neither A nor B

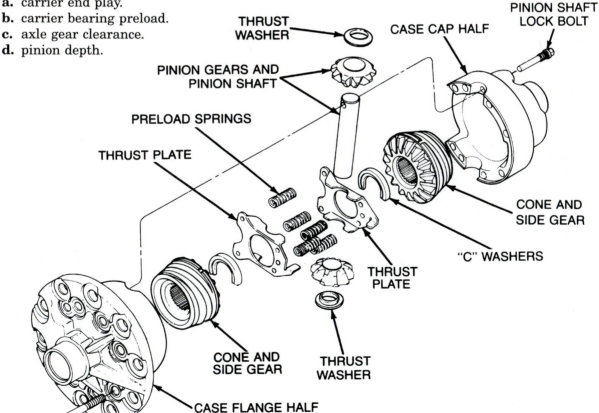

FIGURE 3-24

72. When installing a rear axle bearing seal:
   a. apply sealer to the outside diameter of the seal.
   b. the seal lip should face toward the differential.
   c. Both a and b
   d. Neither a nor b

73. A car owner says that when she releases the accelerator pedal and coasts, there is a siren noise coming from the rear end. Which of these is the MOST LIKELY cause?
   a. Badly worn u-joints
   b. Scored spider gears
   c. Incorrect side gear end play
   d. Incorrect ring gear backlash

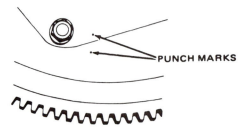

FIGURE 3–25

74. Why would a technician center punch mark the clutch cover and flywheel as shown in Figure 3–25?
   a. To prevent cover warpage
   b. To maintain assembly balance
   c. To maintain correct release lever height
   d. All of the above

FIGURE 3–26

75. Technician A says that the springs in Figure 3–26 prevent clutch drag when shifting.
   Technician B says that the springs dampen engine firing impulses.
   Who is right?
   a. A only   **c.** Both A and B
   b. B only   **d.** Neither A nor B

76. A broken right side motor mount could cause which of the following?
   a. Shudder in reverse
   b. Broken distributor cap
   c. Torn radiator hose
   d. All of the above

77. When replacing a leaky drive pinion seal, what is one of the first things a technician should do?
   a. Check the yoke surface.
   b. Install a new spacer and shims.
   c. Install a new oil slinger.
   d. Solvent flush the axle housing tubes.

78. A transmission is low on lubricant. Which of the following would be the LEAST LIKELY to fail?
   a. Mainshaft
   b. Countershaft bearings
   c. Synchronizer assemblies
   d. Clutch (input) shaft bearing

79. A car has chronic clutch failure. Complete breakage of the hub from the clutch plate occurs every 500–600 miles.
   Technician A says that elongated bolt holes connecting the bell-housing to the engine could be the cause.
   Technician B says that a badly worn pilot bushing could be the cause.
   Who is right?
   a. A only   **c.** Both A and B
   b. B only   **d.** Neither A nor B

80. What procedure is being performed in Figure 3–27?
   a. Installing the pilot bearing
   b. Aligning the release levers
   c. Aligning the clutch disc
   d. Aligning the pressure plate

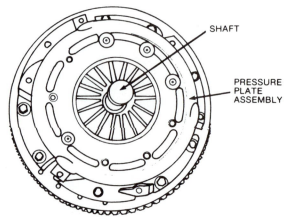

FIGURE 3–27

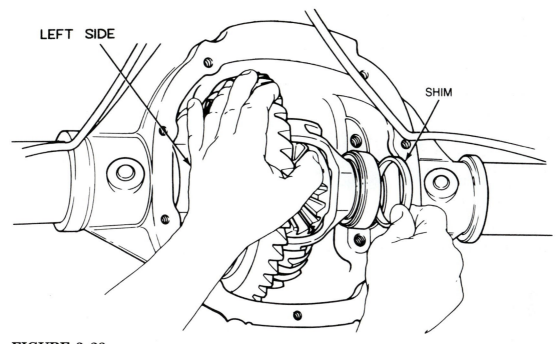

LEFT SIDE

SHIM

FIGURE 3-28

81. When measuring pinion bearing preload, which tool below is recommended?
   a. Click-type torque wrench
   b. Dial-type torque wrench
   c. Depth micrometer
   d. Dial indicator

82. Refer to Figure 3–28. What will happen when a shim is removed from the right side, and shifted to the left side?
   a. Backlash will increase.
   b. Backlash will decrease.
   c. Preload will decrease.
   d. Preload will increase.

FIGURE 3-29

83. What is the "+2" marking on the gear in Figure 3–29?
   a. Depth shim reference number
   b. Gear set number
   c. Preload setting number
   d. Backlash variance number

84. All of the bearings in a rear axle assembly are badly worn and discolored a dark blue.
   Technician A says that this could be caused by excessive heat.
   Technician B says that this could be caused by water in the lubricant.
   Who is right?
   a. A only
   b. B only
   c. Both A and B
   d. Neither A nor B

85. After installing a pair of new FWD axles, the inboard boot on one side is stretched and torn. The inboard boot on the other side is compressed. What is the MOST LIKELY reason?
   a. Half-shafts installed backwards
   b. Bad CV joints
   c. Bad motor mounts
   d. Misaligned cradle

FIGURE 3–30

86. The kit in Figure 3–30 is going to be installed.
Technician A says that part X must be fully seated.
Technician B says that part Y must face the proper direction.
Who is right?
a. A only
b. B only
c. Both A and B
d. Neither A nor B

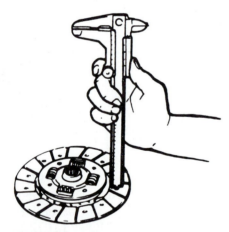

FIGURE 3–31

87. Technician A says that the tool in Figure 3–31 is being used to measure clutch hub height.
Technician B says that the tool is being used to measure clutch disc thickness.
Who is right?
a. A only
b. B only
c. Both A and B
d. Neither A nor B

88. You are making the check shown in Figure 3–32. Which figure would you consider to be the MOST NORMAL?
a. .0005″ to .0015″
b. .008″ to .012″
c. .030″ to .040″
d. .080″ to .110″

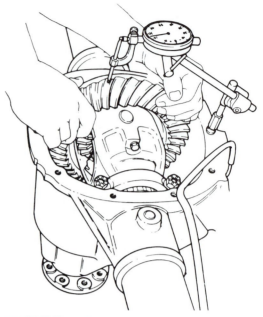

FIGURE 3–32

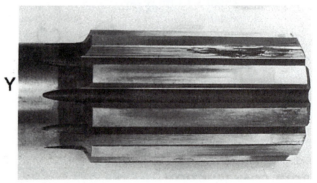

FIGURE 3–33

89. Technician A says that part X shown in Figure 3–33 indicates a lubrication failure.
Technician B says that part Y indicates a brinelling failure.
Who is right?
a. A only
b. B only
c. Both A and B
d. Neither A nor B

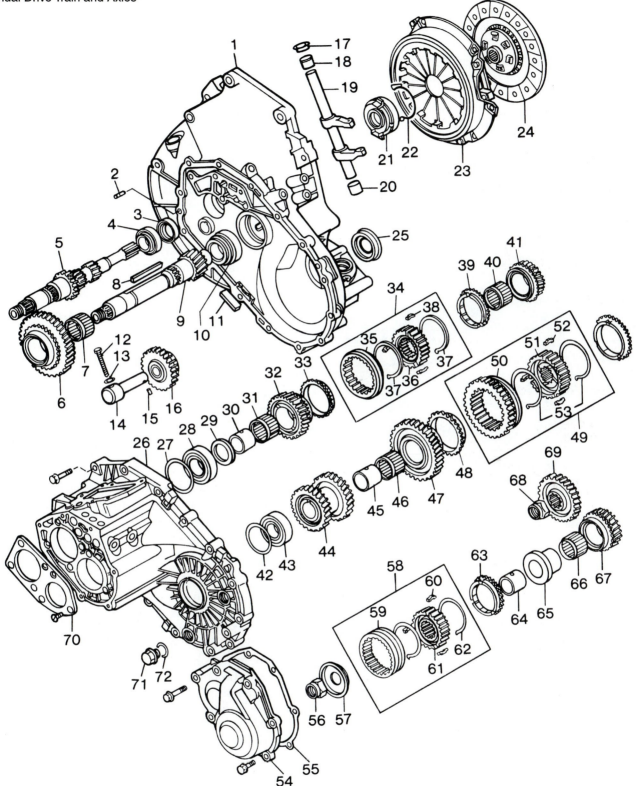

FIGURE 3–34

90. Figure 3–34 shows a manual transaxle in disassembled form.

Technician A says that part 5 is the output shaft.

Technician B says that part 42 is the output shaft bearing shim.

Who is right?

a. A only
b. B only
c. Both A and B
d. Neither A nor B

91. Different height tires are installed on each side of a drive axle.

Technician A says that this can cause the differential pinion (spider) gear shaft to wear suddenly.

Technician B says that this can cause the ring gear to wear suddenly.

Who is right?

a. A only
b. B only
c. Both A and B
d. Neither A nor B

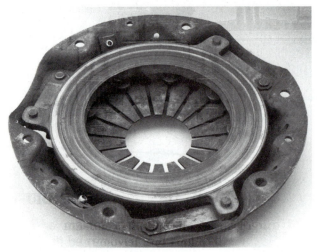

FIGURE 3–35

92. The part in Figure 3–35 needs to be replaced.
Technician A says to replace the clutch disc.
Technician B says to inspect the flywheel.
Who is right?

a. A only
b. B only
c. Both A and B
d. Neither A nor B

93. As the clutch pedal is pressed down, the release levers will move the pressure plate away from the:

a. throwout bearing.
b. clutch disc.
c. clutch cover.
d. apply springs.

94. A differential makes noise on turns only. The MOST LIKELY cause would be:

a. worn drive pinion bearings.
b. worn carrier bearings.
c. worn differential pinion gears.
d. a bad axle bearing.

95. A car vibrates and chatters when turning.

Technician A says that in limited slip differentials, this could be caused by the wrong lubricant.

Technician B says that in conventional differentials, this could be caused by too many differential pinion thrust washers.

Who is right?

a. A only
b. B only
c. Both A and B
d. Neither A nor B

96. On a FWD car, grease is dripping on the ground between the front wheels.

Technician A says that a CV joint boot could be torn.

Technician B says that this condition requires immediate attention.

Who is right?

a. A only
b. B only
c. Both A and B
d. Neither A nor B

97. Excessive end play of the engine crankshaft can cause:

a. clutch slippage.
b. premature throwout bearing failure.
c. Both a and b
d. Neither a nor b

98. A front wheel drive car has a shudder during acceleration.

Technician A says that this could be caused by a sticking inboard CV joint assembly.

Technician B says that this could be caused by an excessive CV joint angle.

Who is right?

a. A only
b. B only
c. Both A and B
d. Neither A nor B

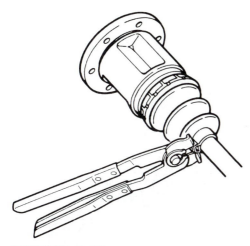

FIGURE 3–36

99. Refer to Figure 3–36.

Technician A says that a boot clamp is being removed.

Technician B says that an eared clamp tool is being used.

Who is right?

a. A only   **c.** Both A and B
b. B only   **d.** Neither A nor B

100. What is the reason for having the drive pinion bearings properly preloaded?
a. To prevent the pinion gear from moving away from the ring gear under load
b. To prevent bearing looseness under all driving conditions
c. Both a and b
d. Neither a nor b

FIGURE 3–37

101. The setup in Figure 3–37 is for:
a. spreading the differential housing.
b. checking axle housing alignment.
c. straightening the axle tubes.
d. timing the gearset.

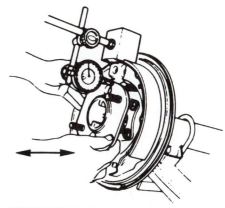

FIGURE 3–38

102. What is being checked in Figure 3–38?
a. Axle end play
b. Flange runout
c. Wheel bearing looseness
d. Axle runout

FEELER GAUGE
FIGURE 3–39

103. What check is being made in Figure 3–39?
a. Counter gear end play
b. Reverse idler washer wear
c. Bias mechanism operation
d. None of the above

104. A 5-speed manual transmission is noisy in neutral with the engine running (clutch engaged). This could be caused by:
a. bad input shaft bearing.
b. bad speed gear bearing.
c. Both a and b
d. Neither a nor b

105. A speedometer needle jumps back and forth. Which of these is the MOST LIKELY reason?
a. Bad head
b. Kinked cable
c. Broken speedometer gear housing
d. Broken speedometer gear tooth

106. A thinner than specified clutch disc results in shorter facing life and:
  a. more apply pressure.
  b. less apply pressure.
  c. increased torque capacity.
  d. no change in apply pressure.

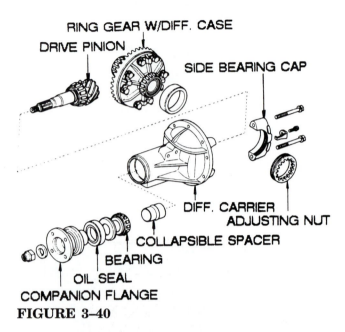

FIGURE 3–40

107. Which used parts are generally replaced when disassembling a differential (refer to Figure 3–40)?
  a. Collapsible spacer
  b. Oil seal
  c. Both a and b
  d. Neither a nor b

FIGURE 3–41

108. Technician A says that the picture in Figure 3–41 shows the disc being test fitted.
  Technician B says that the picture shows the disc reversed.
  Who is right?
  a. A only   **c.** Both A and B
  b. B only   **d.** Neither A nor B

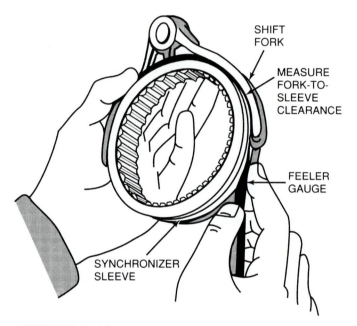

FIGURE 3–42

109. The clearance shown being measured in Figure 3–42 is excessive.
  Technician A says that this can cause gear clash when shifting.
  Technician B says that this could be caused by missing nylon inserts.
  Who is right?
  a. A only   **c.** Both A and B
  b. B only   **d.** Neither A nor B

110. A clutch pedal stays on the floor. This could be caused by a:
  a. broken cable.
  b. worn release bearing.
  c. Both a and b
  d. Neither a nor b

111. A transaxle equipped vehicle has a "clicking" noise during turns. This could be caused by:
  a. a worn outboard drive axle joint.
  b. worn differential pinions.
  c. Both a and b
  d. Neither a nor b

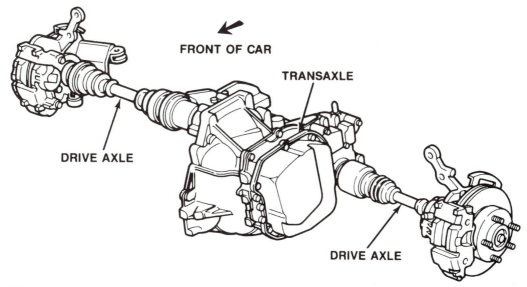

FIGURE 3–43

112. Which of the following is LEAST LIKELY to cause clutch slippage?
   a. Incorrect linkage adjustment
   b. Excessive free play
   c. Weak pressure plate springs
   d. Binding linkage

113. Technician A says that the FWD assembly in Figure 3–43 uses nonconstant velocity universal joints.
   Technician B says that the FWD assembly uses a longitudinally mounted engine.
   Who is right?
   a. A only
   b. B only
   c. Both A and B
   d. Neither A nor B

114. Refer to Figure 3–44. This differential has too much side gear clearance.
   Technician A says to remove shims.
   Technician B says to tighten threaded adjuster nuts.
   Who is right?
   a. A only   **c.** Both A and B
   b. B only   **d.** Neither A nor B

115. A transaxle has a clunk in reverse. This could be caused by a:
   a. worn or damaged reverse idler gear.
   b. loose engine mount.
   c. Both a and b
   d. Neither a nor b

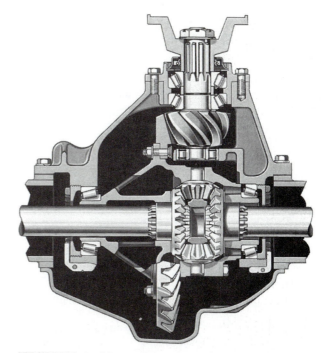

FIGURE 3–44

116. The differential shown in Figure 3–44 is being disassembled.
   Technician A says that the bearing caps are interchangeable.
   Technician B says that the bearing cups (races) are interchangeable.
   Who is right?
   a. A only
   b. B only
   c. Both A and B
   d. Neither A nor B

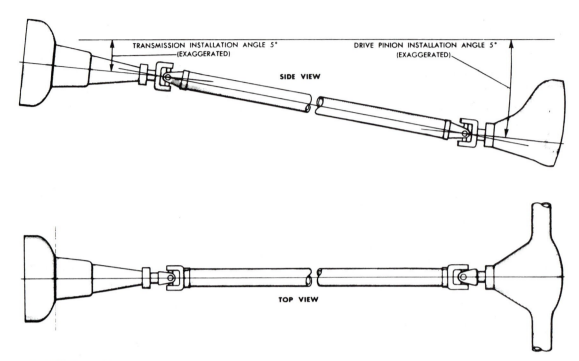

FIGURE 3–45

117. Technician A says that pedal free play will increase as the friction disc wears.

    Technician B says that slippage can occur if pedal free play is NOT correct.

    Who is right?

  a. A only   **c.** Both A and B

  b. B only   **d.** Neither A nor B

118. Technician A says that the yokes shown in Figure 3–45 are "in phase."

    Technician B says that the front and rear installation angles shown are acceptable.

    Who is right?

  a. A only   **c.** Both A and B

  b. B only   **d.** Neither A nor B

119. A drive pinion bearing cup is spinning in the differential carrier.

    Technician A says to shim the cup.

    Technician B says to stake the cup.

    Who is right?

  a. A only   **c.** Both A and B

  b. B only   **d.** Neither A nor B

120. What is the purpose of a transmission interlock?

  a. To prevent accidentally engaging reverse while driving forward

  b. To prevent being in two forward speeds at the same time

  c. Both a and b

  d. Neither a nor b

FIGURE 3–46

121. The gear in Figure 3–46 (see arrow) is seized to its shaft.

    Technician A says that this can be caused by spinning the tires excessively when stuck in mud.

    Technician B says that this can be caused by continued driving with the "space-saver" spare tire installed.

    Who is right?

  a. A only   **c.** Both A and B

  b. B only   **d.** Neither A nor B

122. A transaxle has a noise in neutral while the engine is running with the clutch engaged. The MOST LIKELY cause is:
   a. bad input shaft bearings.
   b. bad input shaft gears.
   c. bad output shaft gears.
   d. bad output shaft bearings.

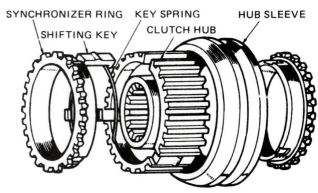

FIGURE 3-48

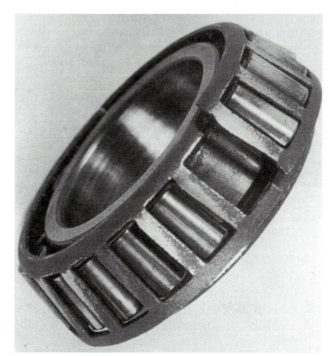

FIGURE 3-47

125. A transmission equipped with the mechanism in Figure 3-48 pops out of reverse
   Technician A says that this could be caused by worn shifting keys.
   Technician B says that this could be caused by a cracked synchronizer ring.
   Who is right?
   a. A only
   b. B only
   c. Both A and B
   d. Neither A nor B

FIGURE 3-49

123. Technician A says that the part in Figure 3-47 is damaged and needs to be replaced.
   Technician B says that the race for the part should be replaced.
   Who is right?
   a. A only
   b. B only
   c. Both A and B
   d. Neither A nor B

124. A car makes noise while in gear with the clutch disengaged. However, there is no noise in neutral with the clutch engaged. Which of these is the MOST LIKELY cause?
   a. Dry pilot bushing
   b. Worn 1-2 synchro splines
   c. Worn transmission bearings
   d. Bad throwout bearing

126. Technician A says that a transmission can jump out of gear if the measurement in Figure 3-49 is excessive.
   Technician B says that the above measurement limit is generally considered to be 0.100″.
   Who is right?
   a. A only   **c.** Both A and B
   b. B only   **d.** Neither A nor B

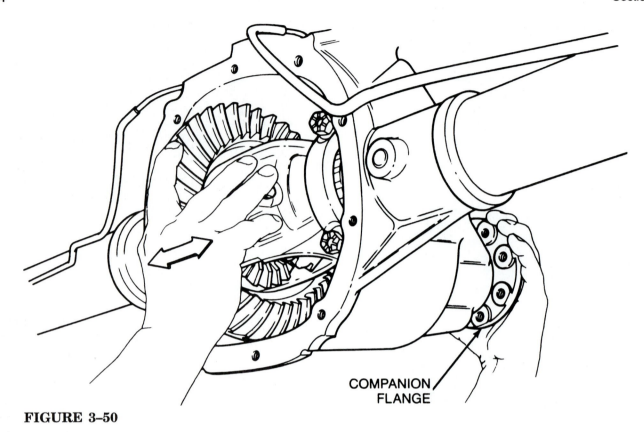

COMPANION
FLANGE

FIGURE 3–50

127. A standard transmission has no power coming out of it.

Technician A says that this could be caused by a frozen pilot bearing.

Technician B says that this could be caused by a torn-out clutch hub.

Who is right?
a. A only
b. B only
c. Both A and B
d. Neither A nor B

128. The differential in Figure 3–50 has excessive back-and-forth movement (note arrow).

Technician A says that this could be caused by incorrect preload.

Technician B says that this could be caused by incorrect backlash.

Who is right?
a. A only
b. B only
c. Both A and B
d. Neither A nor B

129. A differential is being rebuilt. The technician tightens the companion flange nut too much when setting "crush." What should be done?
a. Back off the flange nut.
b. Loosen the cap adjusters.
c. Replace the flange.
d. Replace the collapsible spacer.

130. A pickup truck has a 2-piece driveshaft connecting the transfer case to the front drive axle that must be removed for service.

Technician A says that vibration can result if the u-joints are assembled out of phase.

Technician B says that vibration can result if the driveshaft is dented.

Who is right?
a. A only
b. B only
c. Both A and B
d. Neither A nor B

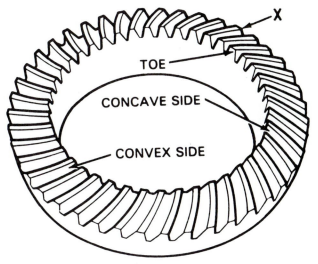

FIGURE 3–51

FIGURE 3–53

131. Refer to Figure 3–51.

Technician A says that the concave side of the gear tooth is the drive side.

Technician B says that point X is the heel part of the gear tooth.

Who is right?

a. A only   **c.** Both A and B

b. B only   **d.** Neither A nor B

133. A differential assembly is being overhauled. What would you consider to be maximum when making the measurement in Figure 3–53?

a. .002″   **b.** 1/64″   **c.** .020″   **d.** 1/32″

134. A 4-wheel drive vehicle is operated for extended periods on hard, dry surface (paved) roads in the 4H mode.

Technician A says that this can cause abnormal tire wear.

Technician B says that this can cause difficult transfer case shifting.

Who is right?

a. A only   **c.** Both A and B

b. B only   **d.** Neither A nor B

132. Shims can be installed at points A, B, C, and D in Figure 3–52 to correct for:

a. bell-housing face alignment.

b. block squareness.

c. Both a and b

d. Neither a nor b

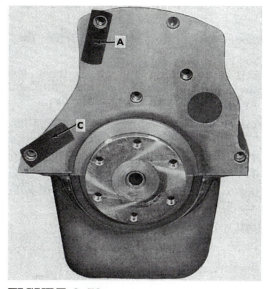

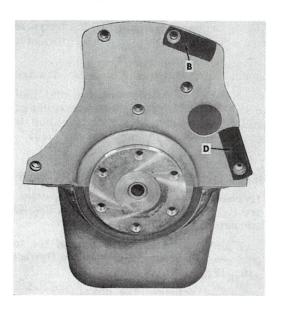

FIGURE 3–52

135. When a transaxle equipped car accelerates from a stop, a single loud clunk can be heard.

Technician A says that this could be caused by excessive main gear backlash.

Technician B says that this could be chipped input gear teeth.

Who is right?

a. A only   **c.** Both A and B
b. B only   **d.** Neither A nor B

136. Technician A says that clutch slippage can be caused by the pressure plate release lever adjusting bolts set too low.

Technician B says that clutch pedal "fluttering" can be caused by the pressure plate release lever adjusting bolts set at different heights.

Who is right?

a. A only   **c.** Both A and B
b. B only   **d.** Neither A nor B

137. Study the wheel arrangement in Figure 3–54.

Technician A says that a full-floating axle shaft is used.

Technician B says that the axle shaft carries all the vehicle weight.

Who is right?

a. A only
b. B only
c. Both A and B
d. Neither A nor B

138. What is the ratio of a differential which has 39 teeth on the ring gear and 11 teeth on the drive pinion gear?

a. 4.11 to 1   **c.** 3.54 to 1
b. 3.78 to 1   **d.** None of the above

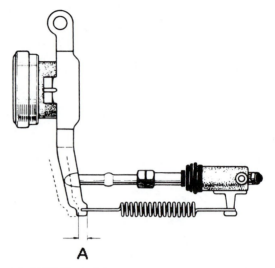

A

FIGURE 3–55

139. Dimension A shown in Figure 3–55 sets:

a. clutch pedal height.
b. clutch pedal free play.
c. Both a and b
d. Neither a nor b

140. While checking a car equipped with a locking differential, a technician is able to hold one wheel stationary and rotate the other wheel slowly with even pressure. This means the differential is:

a. capable of locking.
b. worn in the clutch plate area.
c. worn in the case.
d. binding.

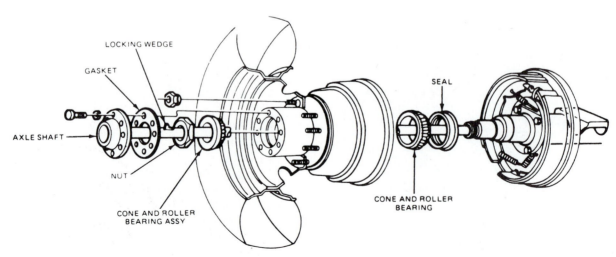

FIGURE 3–54

141. How is end play adjusted on the axle shaft pictured in Figure 3–54?
    a. By placing metal shims behind the gasket
    b. By tightening the axle shaft nut
    c. Both a and b
    d. Neither a nor b

142. The transmission in Figure 3–56 has a heavy device attached to its extension housing. This device:
    a. reduces gear noise.
    b. reduces vibration.
    c. dampens driveshaft whirl noise.
    d. controls driveshaft whip.

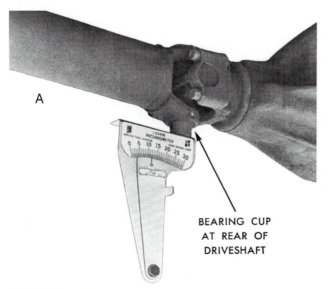

FIGURE 3–56

FIGURE 3–58

143. Technician A says that driveshaft vibration can occur if measurement A (shown in Figure 3–57) is excessive.
    Technician B says that driveshaft vibration can occur if measurement B is excessive.
    Who is right?
    a. A only
    b. B only
    c. Both A and B
    d. Neither A nor B

144. Technician A says that the flywheel in Figure 3–58 is grooved and hard spotted.
    Technician B says that the flywheel can be hand sanded and reused.
    Who is right?
    a. A only
    b. B only
    c. Both A and B
    d. Neither A nor B

BEARING CUP
AT REAR OF
DRIVESHAFT

FIGURE 3–57

145. Semi-centrifugal clutch weights are sometimes located on the:
a. flywheel.
b. pressure plate springs.
c. clutch shaft.
d. release levers.

FIGURE 3–59

146. The universal joint in Figure 3–59:
a. is a constant velocity (CV) joint.
b. does not transfer motion at uniform speed.
c. is a double Cardan u-joint.
d. Both a and c

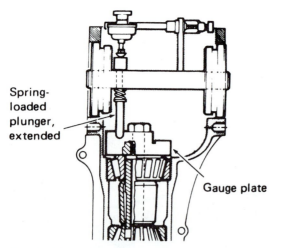

FIGURE 3–60

147. What check is being performed in the picture in Figure 3–60?
a. Carrier distortion
b. Crush sleeve size
c. Drive pinion end play
d. Drive pinion depth

FIGURE 3–61

148. On a rear axle assembly that uses nut locks (see Figure 3–61), what tool is generally used to set carrier bearing preload?
a. Spanner wrench
b. Torque wrench
c. Spring scale
d. Dial indicator

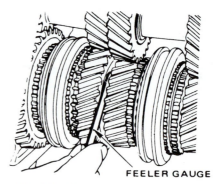

FIGURE 3–62

149. What check is being performed in Figure 3–62?
a. Synchronizer clearance
b. Cluster gear lash
c. Speed gear end play
d. Mainshaft clearance

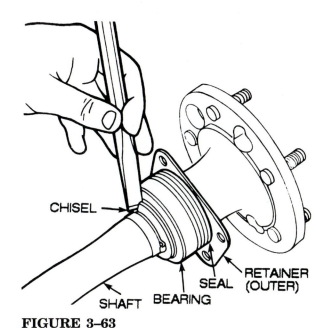

FIGURE 3–63

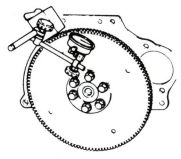

FIGURE 3–64

150. The technician shown in Figure 3–63 is:
   a. removing the axle shaft grease seal.
   b. distorting the wheel bearing retainer ring.
   c. safety staking the axle retainer.
   d. adjusting bearing preload.

151. The measurement in Figure 3–64 is not within specifications. What could be the result?
   a. Shifts hard in all gears
   b. Jumps out of gear
   c. Pedal pulsation
   d. All of the above

152. When removing the half shafts on certain transaxles, a tool must be installed in the differential to prevent the:
   a. differential case from dropping into the transaxle housing.
   b. drive pinion and differential drive gear from falling out of time.
   c. pinion shaft from falling out of place.
   d. differential pinion gears (spiders) from falling out of place.

153. Drive pinion preload is NOT enough on the differential assembly in Figure 3–65. What needs to be done?
   a. Decrease the shims.
   b. Increase the shims.
   c. Remove the shims and install an O/S spacer.
   d. Install the next thickness adjusting washer.

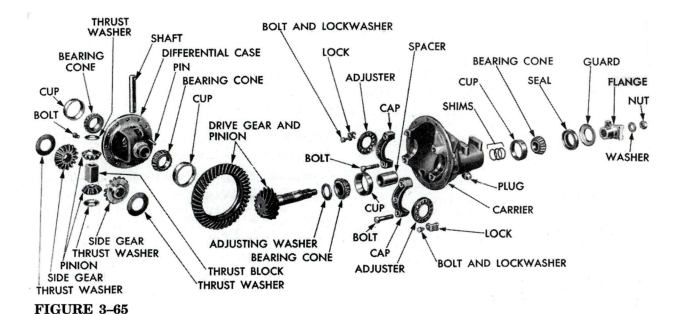

FIGURE 3–65

154. You are installing a new flywheel ring gear that requires a shrink fit. To avoid softening the gear teeth, do NOT heat above:
a. 200°F. **b.** 450°F. **c.** 650°F. **d.** 900°F.

155. What is the purpose of the shifting keys (inserts) in a synchronizer assembly?
a. To push the blocker ring against the cone clutch
b. To prevent gear lock-up
c. To block the shift until speeds synchronize
d. To allow for gear disengagement

156. An engine has a noise similar to a main bearing knock. A loose flywheel is suspected.

Technician A says that flywheel knock can be diagnosed by turning the ignition off, and then on, just as the engine is about to stop turning.

Technician B says that flywheel knock will generally NOT change when spark plugs are individually shorted out.

Who is right?
a. A only
b. B only
c. Both A and B
d. Neither A nor B

157. The engine flywheel:
a. is an inertia wheel.
b. absorbs power from the engine.
c. provides a mounting surface.
d. All of the above

158. What could cause noise to come from the bellhousing when the clutch pedal is released?
a. Bad pilot bearing
b. Loose friction disc hub
c. Worn main drive gear bearings
d. All of the above

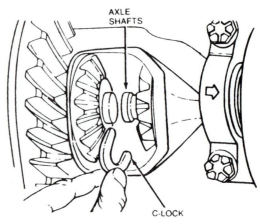

FIGURE 3–66

159. The c-lock shown in Figure 3–66 must be taken out prior to:
a. removing the pinion shaft.
b. removing the axle shaft.
c. Both a and b
d. Neither a nor b

160. Refer to Figure 3–67.

Technician A says that part X helps prevent the front pinion bearing cone from spinning on the drive pinion.

Technician B says that part X helps maintain pinion bearing preload.

Who is right?
a. A only
b. B only
c. Both A and B
d. Neither A nor B

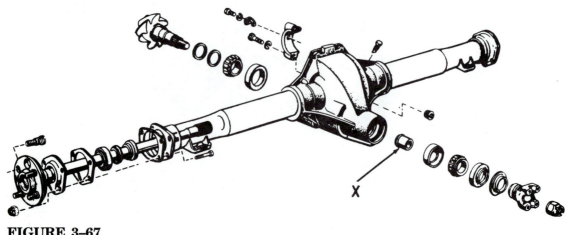

FIGURE 3–67

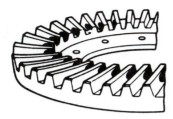

FIGURE 3–68

161. The gear tooth pattern in Figure 3–68 shows:
a. heavy flank contact.
b. heavy toe contact.
c. correct coast side contact.
d. correct drive side contact.

162. When shifting from third to fourth speed, the 3–4 synchronizer assembly:
a. speeds up the mainshaft.
b. speeds up the countershaft gear.
c. Both a and b
d. Neither a nor b

163. A 4-speed fully-synchronized transmission makes noise only in first and reverse. This could be caused by a:
a. broken main drive gear tooth.
b. broken cluster gear tooth.
c. Both a and b
d. Neither a nor b

164. Technician A says that a worn rear transmission bearing CANNOT be heard when the clutch is disengaged.
Technician B says that a worn rear transmission bearing CANNOT be heard when the vehicle is coasting in neutral.
Who is right?
a. A only
b. B only
c. Both A and B
d. Neither A nor B

165. A rear tire on a car shows uneven tread wear. This could be caused by:
a. a bent axle.
b. a bad wheel bearing.
c. Both a and b
d. Neither a nor b

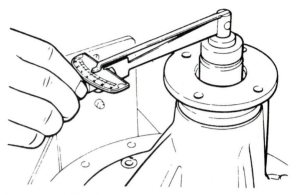

FIGURE 3–69

166. Technician A says that the setup in Figure 3–69 is measuring pinion bearing preload.
Technician B says that the setup above is measuring pinion seal drag.
Who is right?
a. A only
b. B only
c. Both A and B
d. Neither A nor B

167. Direct drive (high gear) in the transmission in Figure 3–70 is accomplished by:
a. moving part B to the right.
b. moving part C to the left.
c. moving part A to the left.
d. moving part D to the right.

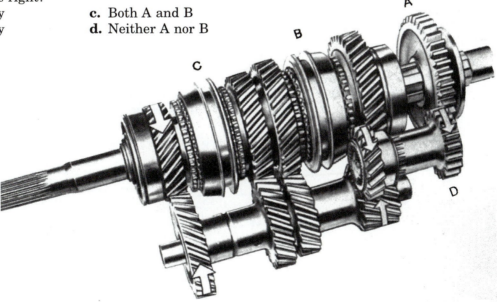

FIGURE 3–70

FIGURE 3–71

168. The cable in Figure 3–71 needs to be lubricated.

Technician A says that it is necessary to pull out the entire length of cable.

Technician B says that it is necessary to coat the entire length of cable with graphite.

Who is right?

a. A only
b. B only
c. Both A and B
d. Neither A nor B

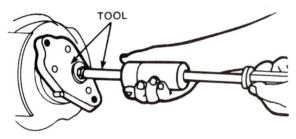

FIGURE 3–72

169. Figure 3–72 shows:
a. installing a rear wheel bearing.
b. installing a rear wheel bearing oil seal.
c. removing an axle shaft.
d. None of the above

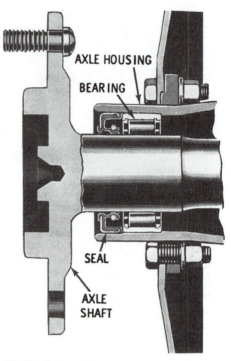

FIGURE 3–73

170. The seal in Figure 3–73 is leaking and needs to be replaced.

Technician A says to apply sealer to the inside edge of the lip on the new seal.

Technician B says to hit the outside of the new seal with a punch in order to fully seat it.

Who is right?

a. A only   **c.** Both A and B
b. B only   **d.** Neither A nor B

171. A car equipped with the 2-piece driveshaft in Figure 3–74 has a vibration on acceleration. This could be caused by:
a. a dry centering ball.
b. missing bolts at center bearing support to frame crossmember.
c. Both a and b
d. Neither a nor b

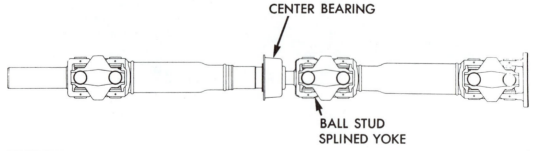

FIGURE 3–74

172. A manual transmission slips out of high gear. This can be caused by:
  a. the transmission being loose on the bell-housing.
  b. the shift rods interfering with the clutch throwout lever.
  c. Both a and b
  d. Neither a nor b

FIGURE 3–75

173. If several teeth were broken off the gear in Figure 3–75 (indicated by the arrow), the result would be noise in:
  a. first gear.
  b. second gear.
  c. reverse gear.
  d. All of the above

174. What is a hypoid gear set?
  a. Where the pinion engages the ring gear at the center line
  b. Where the pinion engages the ring gear below the center line
  c. Where the small end of the pinion is supported by a bearing
  d. Where a thrust block is used to control ring gear deflection

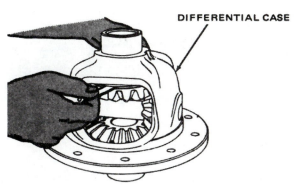

FIGURE 3–76

175. What is the technician doing in Figure 3–76?
  a. Checking backlash between the side gear and the differential pinion shaft
  b. Checking clearance between the spider gear and the differential case
  c. Checking clearance between the side gear and thrust washer
  d. None of the above

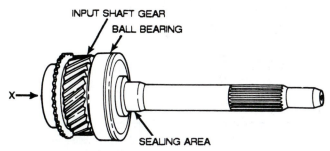

FIGURE 3–77

176. What part of the shaft in Figure 3–77 is arrow X pointing to?
  a. Cone clutch surface
  b. Main drive bearing
  c. Synchronizer hub
  d. Blocking ring

177. An overdrive manual transmission provides for:
  a. increased fuel economy.
  b. less engine wear.
  c. reduced tailpipe emissions.
  d. All of the above

FIGURE 3–78

178. What can be said about the differential assembly in Figure 3–78?
   a. This type of differential requires a special lubricant additive.
   b. Torque is always equally divided to each wheel.
   c. Both a and b
   d. Neither a nor b

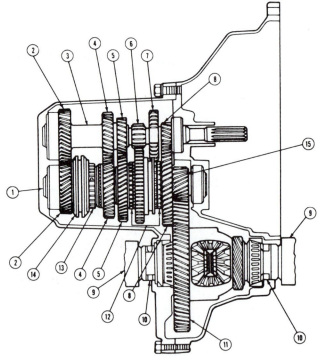

FIGURE 3–79

179. The transaxle in Figure 3–79 has a noise that occurs only in reverse. This could be caused by:
   a. gear 7.   **c.** Both a and b
   b. gear 5.   **d.** Neither a nor b

180. Refer to the picture shown for question 179.
   Technician A says that the speedometer gear is NOT numbered.
   Technician B says that backlash for the final drive ring gear is adjusted by shims.
   Who is right?
   a. A only   **c.** Both A and B
   b. B only   **d.** Neither A nor B

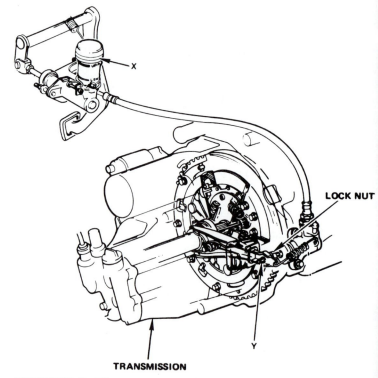

FIGURE 3–80

181. A car is equipped with the clutch system in Figure 3–80.
   Technician A says that the slave cylinder is located at point X.
   Technician B says that release bearing clearance is adjusted at point Y.
   Who is right?
   a. A only   **c.** Both A and B
   b. B only   **d.** Neither A nor B

182. The transmission shown in question 181 shifts hard.
   Technician A says that this could be caused by missing detent springs.
   Technician B says that this could be caused by a bent fork.
   Who is right?
   a. A only   **c.** Both A and B
   b. B only   **d.** Neither A nor B

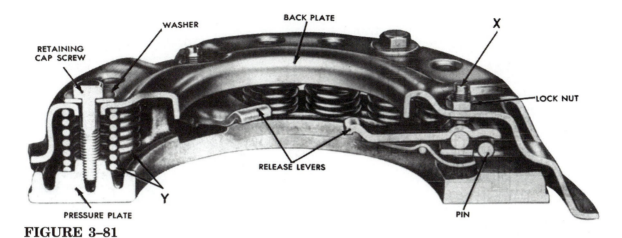

FIGURE 3–81

183. Technician A says that part X shown in Figure 3–81 is used to adjust pressure on the friction disc as it wears.

Technician B says that part Y is used to provide tension between the friction disc and the pressure plate.

Who is right?

a. A only   **c.** Both A and B

b. B only   **d.** Neither A nor B

FIGURE 3–83

185. The arrow in Figure 3–83 is pointing to the:

a. output shaft oil slinger.

b. reverse idler gear.

c. overdrive gear.

d. speedometer drive gear.

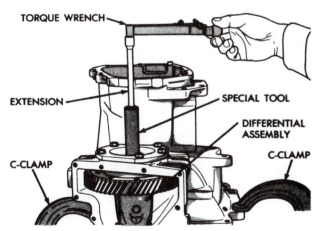

FIGURE 3–82

184. A transaxle is being checked as shown in Figure 3–82.

Technician A says that bearing preload is being measured.

Technician B says that adjustment is made by using selective sized shims.

Who is right?

a. A only

b. B only

c. Both A and B

d. Neither A nor B

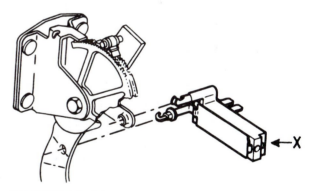

FIGURE 3–84

186. Part X shown in Figure 3–84:

a. is a neutral start switch.

b. can be checked with a jumper wire.

c. Both a and b

d. Neither a nor b

187. Proper matching of the drive gear, driven gear, tire diameter, and rear axle ratio are important when checking the speedometer/odometer for:

a. surging.

b. accuracy.

c. noise.

d. inoperation.

188. Refer to Figure 3–85.

Technician A says that a full-time transfer case is shown.

Technician B says that in the 4H shift position, there is power to the front and rear axles at reduced speed.

Who is right?

a. A only   **c.** Both A and B

b. B only   **d.** Neither A nor B

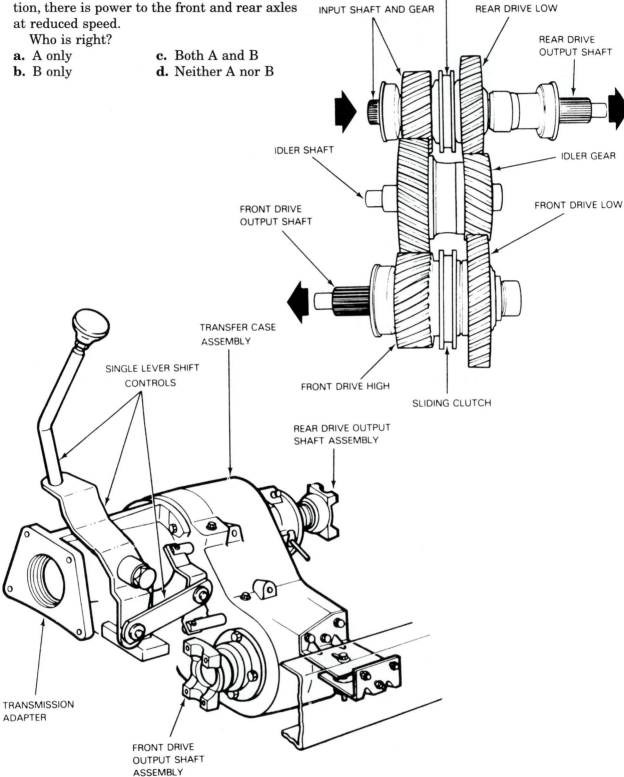

FIGURE 3–85

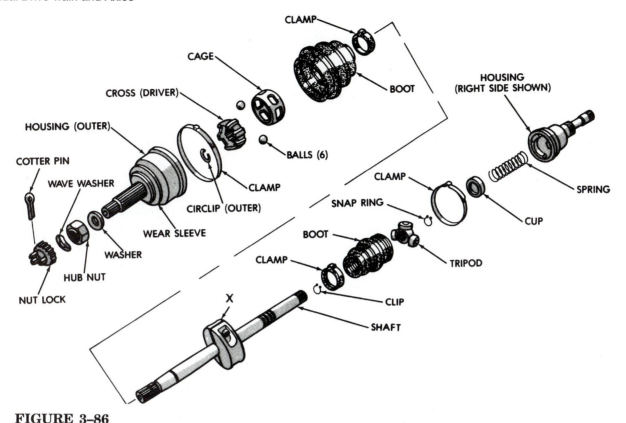

FIGURE 3–86

189. The axle shaft in Figure 3–86 has a split-ring installed near the middle (see arrow X). This device:
- **a.** keeps axle speed constant.
- **b.** eliminates axle "wind-up."
- **c.** Both a and b
- **d.** Neither a nor b

190. Technician A says that in order for the device in Figure 3–87 to be set, the driver is required to get out of the vehicle.

Technician B says that the device is used on 4-wheel drive vehicles.

Who is right?
- **a.** A only
- **b.** B only
- **c.** Both A and B
- **d.** Neither A nor B

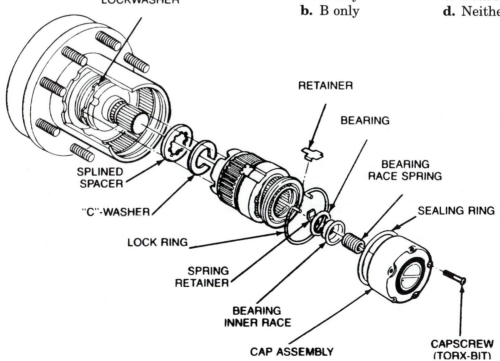

FIGURE 3–87

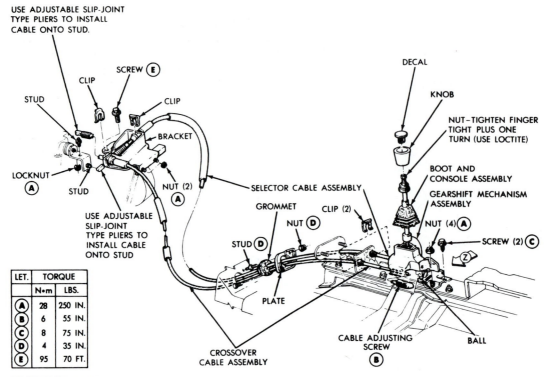

FIGURE 3–88

191. Refer to Figure 3–88.

Technician A says that the selector cable adjusting screw should be torqued to 55 inch pounds.

Technician B says that the cable bracket nuts do NOT have a torque spec.

Who is right?

a. A only
b. B only
c. Both A and B
d. Neither A nor B

192. The linkage rods on the transmission in Figure 3–89 need adjusting.

Technician A says to place the transmission shift levers in neutral (middle detent) position.

Technician B says to adjust the shift rod swivels so the linkage rods will install freely into levers.

Who is right?

a. A only
b. B only
c. Both A and B
d. Neither A nor B

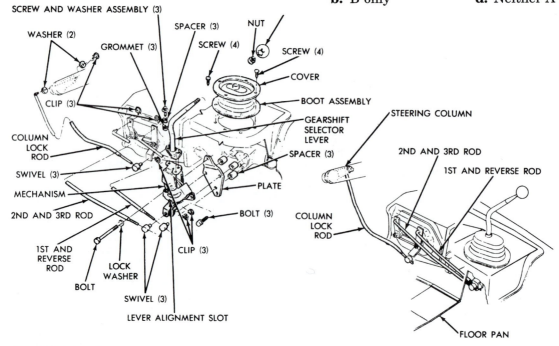

FIGURE 3–89

193. A vehicle has transfer case shudder at low speed. This is MOST LIKELY caused by a:
- **a.** damaged planetary gear set.
- **b.** loose drive chain.
- **c.** spalled set of support bearings.
- **d.** bad viscous coupling.

194. Technician A says that the best way to remove differential bearings is to use a rawhide hammer.

Technician B says that the best way to remove transmission bearings is to use a wax temperature stick and a toaster oven.

Who is right?
- **a.** A only
- **b.** B only
- **c.** Both A and B
- **d.** Neither A nor B

195. Technician A recommends replacing the throwout bearing when replacing a clutch disc.

Technician B recommends surface grinding the pressure plate when replacing a clutch disc.

Who is right?
- **a.** A only
- **b.** B only
- **c.** Both A and B
- **d.** Neither A nor B

Section 4

SUSPENSION AND STEERING

STUDY OUTLINE

I. Front End Types and Construction
- A. Solid Axle Front End
  1. King pin and steering knuckle
  2. Linkage component identification
- B. Independent Front Suspension
  1. Lower coil spring mount
  2. Upper coil spring mount
  3. Torsion bar
  4. Nomenclature of parts
- C. MacPherson Strut Suspension
- D. Twin I-Beam Design

II. Types of Springs
- A. Leaf
  1. Rebound clip
  2. Center bolt
  3. Tapered single leaf
- B. Coil
  1. Should be replaced in pairs
  2. Importance of proper ride height
- C. Torsion Bar
  1. Adjustable
  2. Left and Right
- D. Controlling Spring Oscillation
  1. Function of shock absorber
- E. Computer-controlled air springs

III. Alignment Factors
- A. Caster
- B. Camber
- C. Toe
- D. Steering Axis Inclination (S.A.I.)
- E. Toe-out on Turns (Turning Radius)
- F. Included Angle
- G. Steering Wheel Centering
- H. Point of Intersection
- I. Riding Height/Frame Angle
- J. Thrust Angle
- K. Setback
- L. Scrub Radius

IV. Alignment Angle Effects
- A. Caster
  1. Positive or negative
  2. A directional control angle
  3. Wander and weave
  4. Stability
  5. Turning effort
  6. Returnability
  7. Road crown pull
  8. Can cause outside shoulder "chew" if excessive
- B. Camber
  1. Positive or negative
  2. Is a tire wearing angle
  3. Pulling
  4. Provides for easy steering
  5. Brings road contact point of tire more nearly under point of load
- C. Toe
  1. Purpose
  2. Tire wear (feather edge or saw tooth wear)
  3. Toe wear can look like a camber problem
  4. Stability
- D. Steering Axis Inclination
  1. Provides a pivot point to produce easier steering
  2. Reduces need for excessive camber
  3. Effect on wheel bearings
  4. Non-adjustable
- E. "Included" Angle
  1. Can help determine a bent spindle or strut
- F. Toe-out on Turns
  1. Built-in design angle (steering arms)
  2. Purpose
  3. Greater angle on inside wheel
  4. Oversteering and understeering
  5. Tire wear (scuffing)
- G. Determine Needed Repairs

V. Rear Suspension Systems
- A. Function of Components
  1. "U" Bolts
  2. Control arms
  3. Stabilizer bar
  4. Controlling "wrap-up"
  5. Shackles, brackets and mounts
  6. Springs
  7. Transverse links
- B. Rear Wheel Alignment
  1. Dog tracking

110

2. Tram gauges
3. Setting camber (positive or negative)
4. Checking axle housing bend
5. Setting toe (positive or negative)
6. Full-circle shims
7. Track/thrust line
C. Replace Components (Procedures)
VI. Front Suspension Service
A. Inspection
  1. Ball joints
    a. Load carrying (on short and long-type suspension)
    b. Follower
    c. Compression
    d. Tension
    e. Jacking points
    f. Wear indicator type joint
    g. Axial and radial movement
    h. Checking MacPherson strut ball joints
  2. Idler arms
    a. Types
    b. Installation (wheels straight ahead)
    c. Acceptable looseness
    d. Adjustment
  3. Control arm bushings
  4. Pivot shaft (cross shaft)
  5. Tie rod ends/sleeves/clamps
  6. Relay rod (center link)
  7. Pitman arm and sector shaft
  8. King pins/bushings/knuckle
  9. Twin I-beam axle bushings and radius arms
  10. Shock absorbers
    a. Conventional
    b. Air
    c. Strut cartridge installation
    d. Computer actuated motors
  11. Rebound bumpers
  12. Torsion bars
  13. Steering knuckle assemblies
  14. Sway bar and linkage
  15. Strut rod bushings
  16. Wheel bearings/adjustments
  17. Steering damper
  18. Rack mounting bushings and brackets
  19. Spring insulators
B. Determine Needed Repairs
C. Replace Components (Procedures)
  1. Tool identification
    a. Spring compressors/clips
    b. Ball joint press
D. Alignment (Including Prealignment Inspection)
  1. Sequence procedure for alignment (2-wheel, 4-wheel, and electronic systems)
  2. Method of adjustment for caster and camber
    a. Shims (understand adjustment location)
    b. Eccentrics
    c. Serrated/slotted cross shaft

    d. Strut rods
    e. Cold bending
  3. Toe
    a. Scribing the tire
    b. Adjusting sleeve tool
    c. Left-hand and right-hand threads
    d. Centering steering wheel
    e. Shims
  4. MacPherson strut adjustment(s)
  5. Toe-out on turns
    a. Left (outside wheel) turn in 20°
    b. Right (inside wheel) should read?
    c. Checks for a bent steering arm
  6. 4-wheel drive vehicle adjustment(s)
  7. Equipment identification and use
    a. Magnetic gauge
    b. Radius plate
    c. Brake pedal jack
    d. Toe gauge
    e. Steering wheel holder
    f. Wheel runout gauge
    g. Scuff gauge
    h. Tire scribe
    i. Wheel clamp adapter
    j. Pit rack
    k. Fixed/power rack
    l. Hoist rack
    m. Mechanical balancer head
E. Problem/Diagnosis
  1. Noise
  2. Sway
  3. Uneven riding height
  4. Torque steer/memory steer
  5. Cradle misalignment
VII. Wheels and Tires
A. Runout
  1. Radial/lateral
  2. Match mounting
  3. Specifications
B. Effects of Wheels and Tires Not Within Specifications
C. Tire Tread Wear Patterns and Causes
D. Wheel Balance (On-Car and Off-Car)
  1. Static
  2. Dynamic
  3. Tramp (pounding)
  4. Shimmy
E. Tire Rotation Patterns
  1. Bias-belted
  2. Radial (modified "X" method)
F. Check Tire Pressure
G. Radial Force Variation
  1. Tire "buffing"
H. Lateral Force Variation
I. Stud Circle Runout
J. Axle Flange/Rotor Hub Runout

VIII. Problem/Diagnosis
    A. Idler Arm Wear
    B. Control Arm Bushing Wear
    C. Ball Joint Wear
    D. Pulling
    E. Wheel Shimmy
    F. Wheel Tramp
    G. First- and Second-Order Vibrations
    H. Conicity
    I. Handling Characteristics Poor
        1. Interpreting wheel alignment readings and charts

IX. Steering Gears
    A. Manual
        1. Types
        2. Adjustments
            a. Lash
            b. Preload
        3. Inspect and replace steering shaft u-joint(s)
        4. Inspect and replace flexible coupling ("rag" joint)
        5. Diagnosis
            a. Hard steering
            b. Looseness
            c. Roughness
            d. Binding through the center of travel
            e. Column noise (including tilt mechanisms)
    B. Power
        1. Types (including variable assist)
        2. Inspect and check system
        3. Replace components (procedures)
        4. Bleeding

        5. Diagnosis
            a. Hard steering (reduced assist)
            b. Loss of fluid (leakage points)
            c. Checking procedures
            d. Noises
            e. Checking pump pressures
            f. Pull
            g. Poor returnability out of a turn
            h. Wrong fluid used (seal swelling)
        6. Adjustments
            a. Worm bearing preload (torsion bar feel)
            b. Sector (ball nut) mesh
            c. Centering shims (spool valve)
            d. Pump belt tension
         7. Steering pump overhaul procedures
            a. Vane and rotor/cam ring kit
            b. Seal kit
    C. Rack and Pinion (Center and End Takeoff Types)
        1. Components
        2. Diagnosis
            a. Noise
            b. Vibration
            c. Looseness
            d. Hard steering
            e. Bump or orbital steer
            f. Poor assist when cold
            g. Poor returnability
            h. Fluid in bellows boots
            i. Momentary loss of assist
        3. Adjustments
        4. Mounting levelness/bump steer
        5. Seal replacement procedures
        6. Hose replacement procedures
        7. System flushing/filter installation
        8. Short rack replacement

---

1. When driving over railroad tracks, the front end of a car shimmys. Which of these would be the MOST LIKELY cause?
    a. Weak coil springs
    b. Broken sway bar link
    c. Bad wheel alignment
    d. Bad idler arm

2. A car equipped with rack and pinion steering wanders on a straight level road. This could be caused by:
    a. loose steering gear mounting bolts.
    b. excessive lash in the steering gear.
    c. Both a and b
    d. Neither a nor b

3. A vehicle pulls to the right when braking. This could be caused by:
    a. a bent right wheel.
    b. worn strut rod bushings.
    c. Both a and b
    d. Neither a nor b

4. A car with manual rack and pinion steering has poor returnability to the straight ahead position after turning. Which of these is the MOST LIKELY reason?
    a. Rusted u-bolts on the steering column
    b. Worn inner tie rod ends
    c. Incorrect wheel alignment
    d. Incorrect steering gear lash

5. A car with MacPherson front suspension sways too much when cornering. The MOST LIKELY cause would be:
   a. uneven camber settings.
   b. uneven caster settings.
   c. loose strut rod mounts.
   d. loose stabilizer bar links.

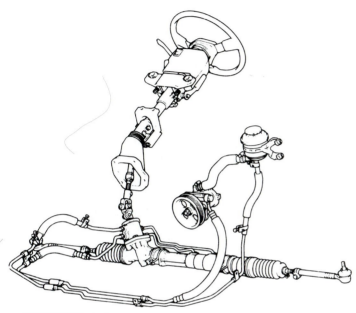

FIGURE 4–1

6. The owner of a vehicle equipped with the steering system in Figure 4–1 comments about hearing a "suction-type sound" at times. At what location in the hydraulic system would an obstruction cause this condition?
   a. The reservoir passage to the pump intake
   b. The reservoir passage to the rack gear
   c. The pressure line fitting
   d. The pump outlet union fitting

7. Which of the following is not generally considered a tire wearing angle?
   a. Caster
   b. Camber
   c. Toe-in
   d. Turning radius

8. A car turns a corner. Which of the following is true?
   a. The inside wheel turns at a greater angle.
   b. The outside wheel turns at a greater angle.
   c. Both wheels turn at equal angles.
   d. None of the above

9. What can be the effect of the toe not being set correctly?
   a. A little too much toe-in can result in wear on the outside shoulder of the right front tire.
   b. A little too much toe-out can result in wear on the inside shoulder of the left front tire.
   c. Toe-in wear can result in a feather edge on the tire tread.
   d. All of the above

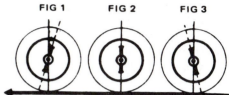

FRONT OF CAR

FIGURE 4–2

10. Refer to Figure 4–2. Which of the following statements is correct?
    a. Figure 1 shows negative caster.
    b. Figure 2 shows zero caster.
    c. Figure 3 shows positive caster.
    d. None of the above

11. A customer complains of front wheel shimmy. This could be caused by:
    a. dynamic imbalance.
    b. static imbalance.
    c. Both a and b
    d. Neither a nor b

12. Which of the following would be a cause of wheel tramp?
    a. Dynamic imbalance
    b. Static imbalance
    c. Both a and b
    d. Neither a nor b

13. The purpose of S.A.I. is:
    a. to help offset road crown pull.
    b. to help reduce the need for excessive camber.
    c. to keep the camber and caster angles constant when the vehicle is in motion.
    d. All of the above

14. When correcting for static inbalance, the total amount of required weight is generally divided equally between the inside and outside of the rim. This is done to:
    a. help prevent vertical shake.
    b. help prevent wheel tramp.
    c. help prevent the creation of dynamic imbalance (shimmy)
    d. All of the above

15. A customer wants the wheels balanced on his 4-wheel drive vehicle.

     Technician A says that the recommended procedure is to use an off-car balancer.

     Technician B says that the recommended procedure is to use an electronic on-car balancer.

     Who is right?
     a. A only
     b. B only
     c. Both A and B
     d. Neither A nor B

16. You are installing an idler arm with compressed rubber (molded) bushings. Where should the wheels be positioned during installation?
     a. To the left and off the ground
     b. To the right and off the ground
     c. Straight ahead
     d. Either left or right and touching the ground

17. You pass your hand across a tire from the inside to the outside. You feel a sharp and ragged feather edge. This condition is caused by:
     a. excessive toe-in.
     b. excessive toe-out.
     c. Both a and b
     d. Neither a nor b

18. Technician A says that too much negative caster can cause wander, weave, and instability at high speeds.

     Technician B says that too much positive caster can cause hard steering, excessive road shock, and shimmy.

     Who is right?
     a. A only
     b. B only
     c. Both A and B
     d. Neither A nor B

19. You have just aligned the front end of a car equipped with a short-long-arm (S.L.A.) suspension system. The owner weighs 250 lbs. When he sits down behind the steering wheel:
     a. camber on the left wheel will increase toward positive.
     b. camber on the right wheel will increase toward positive.
     c. camber on both wheels becomes more positive.
     d. camber on both wheels becomes more negative.

20. A very heavy load is placed in the trunk of a car equipped with a short-long-arm (S.L.A.) suspension system.

     Technician A says that the front wheel caster will increase toward positive.

     Technician B says that camber of both front wheels will decrease toward negative.

     Who is right?
     a. A only
     b. B only
     c. Both A and B
     d. Neither A nor B

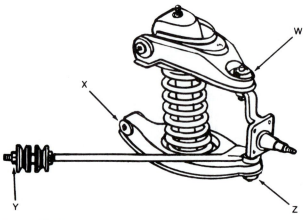

FIGURE 4–3

21. Refer to Figure 4–3. Where is the caster adjustment usually made on this type of suspension system?
     a. Point W
     b. Point X
     c. Point Y
     d. Point Z

22. Which of the following is true of the conventional shock absorber?
     a. A slight leakage film is considered normal.
     b. A worn or leaky shock will not cause a car to lean.
     c. Purge air from new shocks before installing.
     d. All of the above

23. Standing height (curb height) on a non-torsion bar car should be equal on both sides within:
     a. 1/16″ b. 1/2″ c. 1″ d. 2″

FIGURE 4–4

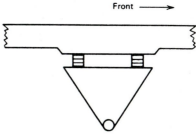

FIGURE 4–5

24. Refer to Figure 4–4. Which of the following statements is true?
   a. Figure 1 shows negative camber.
   b. Figure 2 shows positive camber.
   c. Figure 1 and 2 show negative camber.
   d. None of the above

25. Technician A says that a vehicle will have a tendency to pull to the side having the most positive camber.
   Technician B says it will tend to pull to the side having the most negative caster.
   Who is right?
   a. A only
   b. B only
   c. Both A and B
   d. Neither A nor B

26. Inspection reveals a weak front coil spring. What would be the recommended service procedure?
   Technician A says to replace both front springs.
   Technician B says to install spacers in the weak spring.
   Who is right?
   a. A only
   b. B only
   c. Both A and B
   d. Neither A nor B

27. Technician A says that incorrect negative camber will produce outside tire tread wear.
   Technician B says that excessive unequal camber between wheels will cause a pull to one side.
   Who is right?
   a. A only
   b. B only
   c. Both A and B
   d. Neither A nor B

28. A right front upper control arm is shown in Figure 4–5. What would the technician do to change camber to a more positive angle without changing caster?
   a. Remove an equal thickness of shim from the front and the rear shim pack.
   b. Add an equal thickness of shims to the front and the rear shim pack.
   c. Add shims to the rear shim pack only.
   d. Remove shims from the front shim pack, and add an equal thickness to the rear shim pack.

29. A car is equipped with power steering. The owner complains of a pull to the right side. What could be the cause?
   a. Improper wheel alignment
   b. Internal leakage in the steering gear control valve
   c. Both a and b
   d. Neither a nor b

30. Which one of the following items is NOT a means of adjusting camber on a vehicle?
   a. A cam-bolt assembly
   b. A strut rod
   c. A sliding control arm shaft
   d. Shims

31. Technician A says that sagged steering linkage can cause hidden toe change when the vehicle is in motion.
   Technician B says that the toe setting is the most critical tire wearing angle.
   Who is right?
   a. A only   c. Both A and B
   b. B only   d. Neither A nor B

32. One rear wheel of a vehicle is 2″ behind the other side (leaf spring type). This would be MOST LIKELY caused by a:
   a. worn spring eye bushing.
   b. worn control arm bushing.
   c. broken shock mount.
   d. broken center bolt.

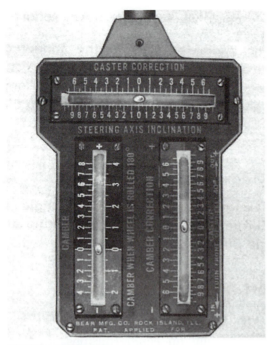

FIGURE 4–6

33. When taking a caster reading with the type gauge in Figure 4–6, the wheel is:
   a. turned through a 40° arc.
   b. locked in a straight-ahead position.
   c. turned through a 20° arc.
   d. rolled 180°.

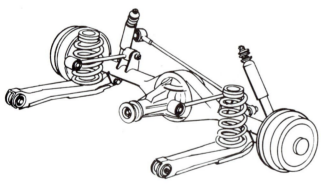

FIGURE 4–7

34. Rear axle housing "wrap-up" on the type of suspension system in Figure 4–7 is controlled by:
   a. the coil springs.
   b. the rebound clips.
   c. the control arms.
   d. the shock absorbers.

35. The caster on the left front wheel has been set at 1 3/4 degrees negative. The right front wheel caster has been set at 1/8 degree negative. What would be the MOST LIKELY result?
   a. The car would pull to the right.
   b. The car would pull to the left.
   c. The car would travel straight ahead.
   d. The left tire would show second rib wear.

36. The idler arm is loose on a car with a conventional short-long-arm front end.
   Technician A says that this could cause the camber to increase when the vehicle is driven.
   Technician B says that this could cause the caster to increase when the vehicle is driven.
   Who is right?
   a. A only
   c. Both A and B
   b. B only
   d. Neither A nor B

37. Even after removing all the shims from an upper control arm, the camber is still too negative.
   Technician A says that this could be caused by a bent steering knuckle (spindle).
   Technician B says that this could be caused by a sagged front cross-member.
   Who is right?
   a. A only
   c. Both A and B
   b. B only
   d. Neither A nor B

38. The front springs were replaced, but the vehicle still sags to the left.
   Technician A says that this could be caused by a worn left front shock absorber.
   Technician B says that this could be caused by a worn left rear spring.
   Who is right?
   a. A only
   c. Both A and B
   b. B only
   d. Neither A nor B

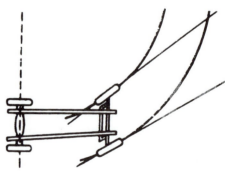

FIGURE 4–8

39. Figure 4–8 illustrates a vehicle making a left turn. The left wheel is turning at a 20° angle. Which angle below would the right wheel MOST LIKELY be turning at?
   a. 17°   b. 20°   c. 23°   d. 30°

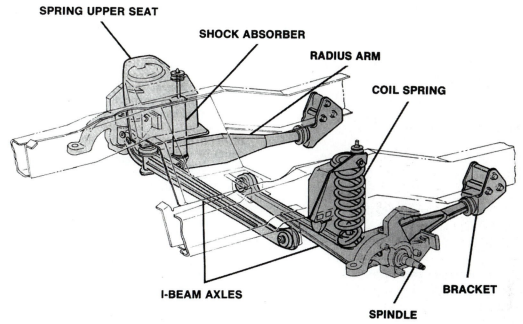

SPRING UPPER SEAT

SHOCK ABSORBER

RADIUS ARM

COIL SPRING

I-BEAM AXLES

SPINDLE

BRACKET

FIGURE 4–9

40. Camber can be adjusted on the front suspension assembly in Figure 4–9 by:
   a. turning the nut on the end of the radius arm.
   b. cold bending the axle.
   c. heating the axle with a torch and bending.
   d. repositioning the upper spring seat.

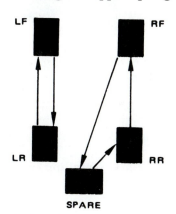

LF   RF

LR   RR

SPARE

FIGURE 4–10

41. The tire rotation pattern in Figure 4–10 is often used for:
   a. bias tires.
   b. bias-belted tires.
   c. radial tires.
   d. nylon tires.

42. When performing a front wheel alignment, which adjustment is generally made first?
   a. Toe-in   **c.** Caster
   b. Camber   **d.** Turning radius

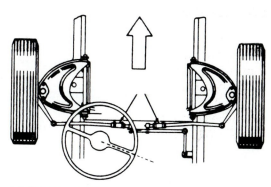

FIGURE 4–11

43. The steering wheel spoke in Figure 4–11 is low on the right side. If the toe-in is correct, what is required to center the wheel?
   a. Shorten the right tie rod.
   b. Lengthen the left tie rod.
   c. Lengthen the left tie rod and shorten the right tie rod.
   d. Shorten the left tie rod and lengthen the right tie rod.

44. Technician A says that the "included" angle is a diagnostic angle for bent parts.
   Technician B says that the purpose of the "included" angle is to reduce tire scuffing during cornering.
   Who is right?
   a. A only
   b. B only
   c. Both A and B
   d. Neither A nor B

45. Technician A says that the measurement of turning radius checks the accuracy of the caster and toe adjustment.

Technician B says that this measurement checks for bent, damaged, or worn steering components.

Who is right?
a. A only
b. B only
c. Both A and B
d. Neither A nor B

46. A car owner has 3″ longer shackles installed on the rear of his car.

Technician A says that this will change toe-out on turns.

Technician B says that this will change camber on the front tires.

Who is right?
a. A only
b. B only
c. Both A and B
d. Neither A nor B

47. A rim-mounted caster/camber gauge is going to be used on a car.

Technician A says to check the wheel runout and compensate.

Technician B says to check the wheel bearing adjustment beforehand.

Who is right?
a. A only
b. B only
c. Both A and B
d. Neither A nor B

48. Which one of the following would you consider to be a typical automobile front end camber specification?
a. −4 1/4° **b.** +6° **c.** 1/8″ **d.** +1/4°

49. When rear axle misalignment on a rear wheel drive (RWD) vehicle is suspected, you can check rear wheel camber and toe-in. Which of the following would indicate factory original settings on the rear of most RWD vehicles?
a. Camber +1/4; toe-in 3/16 inch
b. Camber 0; toe-in 1/8 inch
c. Camber 0; toe-in 0 inch
d. Camber +1/4; toe-in 0 inch

RUNOUT GUAGE

FIGURE 4–12

50. When performing the runout check in Figure 4–12, what is generally considered the maximum allowed?
a. 1/16″ **b.** .040″ **c.** .1875″ **d.** 1/4″

FIGURE 4–13

51. The tool in Figure 4–13 is used for:
a. setting torsion bar height.
b. removing and installing control arm bushings.
c. removing and installing press fit-type ball joints.
d. compressing the strut.

52. The front tires on a car wear out too fast and squeal on turns. This could be caused by:
a. the wrong toe setting.
b. incorrect toe-out on turns.
c. Both a and b
d. Neither a nor b

53. A car with power rack and pinion has poor assist. This could be caused by:
a. low pump output.
b. a loose pinion bearing.
c. Both a and b
d. Neither a nor b

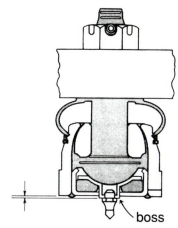

FIGURE 4–14

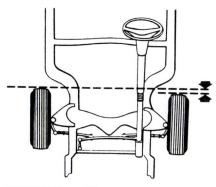

FIGURE 4–15

54. On the wear indicator-type ball joint shown in Figure 4–14, replace the joint when:
   a. the grease fitting boss projects .050″ from the base plate.
   b. the boss becomes flush with the base plate.
   c. the boss is recessed into the base plate.
   d. Both b and c

55. Technician A says that ball joints are threaded into the control arms.
   Technician B says that ball joints are pressed into the control arms.
   Who is right?
   a. A only
   b. B only
   c. Both A and B
   d. Neither A nor B

56. On a P195/75R14 tire, what does the "75" indicate?
   a. The approximate tire section width in millimeters
   b. The aspect ratio
   c. The tire traction rating
   d. The load range rating

57. If the upper ball joints are positioned ahead of the lower ball joints, the tires have:
   a. negative camber.
   b. positive camber.
   c. negative caster.
   d. positive caster.

58. An independent rear suspension (IRS) car comes into the shop for a 4-wheel alignment.
   Technician A says that shims are sometimes used to adjust toe and track.
   Technician B says that tie bars are sometimes used to adjust toe and track.
   Who is right?
   a. A only
   b. B only
   c. Both A and B
   d. Neither A nor B

59. Figure 4–15 shows a _____ condition.
   a. scrub radius
   b. set back
   c. camber roll
   d. lateral runout

60. A front wheel drive (FWD) car equipped with a rigid rear axle drives into the shop. Both rear tires show shoulder wear, yet there is no built-in factory provision for rear wheel alignment.
   Technician A says that shims can be placed between the spindle and the axle.
   Technician B says that shims can be used to adjust both camber and toe.
   Who is right?
   a. A only
   b. B only
   c. Both A and B
   d. Neither A nor B

61. A car equipped with MacPherson struts has camber wear on the front tires. This could be caused by:
   a. weak front springs.
   b. bent parts.
   c. Both a and b
   d. Neither a nor b

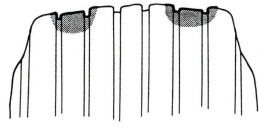

FIGURE 4–16

62. Technician A says that the tread wear problem in Figure 4–16 can be reduced by rotating the tires.
   Technician B says that the above tread wear problem can be considered normal for many bias-ply tires.
   Who is right?
   a. A only
   b. B only
   c. Both A and B
   d. Neither A nor B

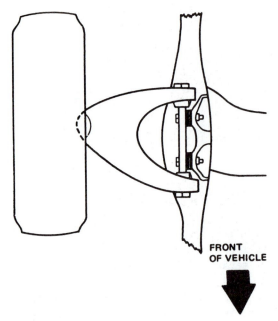

FIGURE 4–17

63. Refer to Figure 4–17. Two shims are removed from the front pivot shaft bolt.

Technician A says that this will change caster only.

Technician B says that this will change camber only.

Who is right?
a. A only
b. B only
c. Both A and B
d. Neither A nor B

64. When the rear of the front tires are closer together than at the front, the tires have:
a. negative camber.
b. positive camber.
c. toe-in.
d. toe-out.

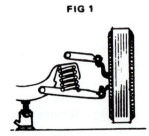
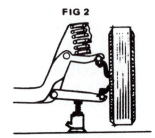

FIGURE 4–18

65. To check for the ball joint wear on some vehicles, they must be lifted a certain way. Which statement is true regarding the illustrations in Figure 4–18?
a. Figures 1 and 2 show correct procedure.
b. Figures 1 and 2 show incorrect procedure.
c. Only Figure 1 is correct.
d. Only Figure 2 is correct.

FIGURE 4–19

66. Which tie rod clamp in Figure 4–19 shows correct position?
a. Figure 1 only
b. Figure 2 only
c. Both Figures 1 and 2
d. Neither Figure 1 nor 2

67. Refer to Figure 4–23. What is the name of the part to which arrow Y points?
a. Relay rod
b. Torsion bar
c. Strut rod
d. Stabilizer bar

68. The axial wear measurement of a ball joint is the movement:
a. up and down.
b. sideways.
c. in a horizontal direction.
d. in a lateral direction.

69. The center bolt:
a. holds the leaf spring to the axle housing.
b. holds the leaf spring together.
c. holds the leaf spring together and locates the spring.
d. positions the shackle assembly in the spring eye bushing.

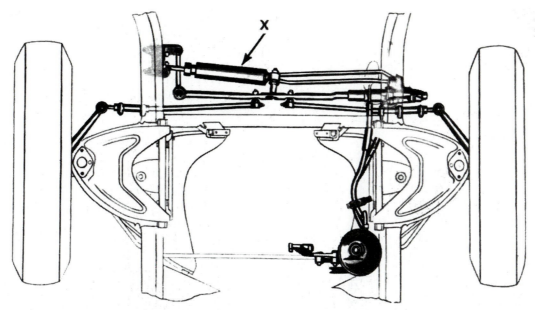

FIGURE 4–20

70. What is the name of part X shown in Figure 4–20?
   a. Steering linkage stabilizer
   b. Steering damper
   c. Power cylinder
   d. Power steering control valve

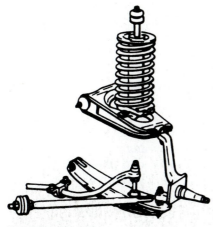

FIGURE 4–21

71. You are checking the load carrying ball joint for wear on the suspension system in Figure 4–21.

   Technician A says to place a jack under the frame.

   Technician B says to place a wedge between the frame and upper control arm.

   Who is right?
   a. A only
   b. B only
   c. Both A and B
   d. Neither A nor B

72. Unsprung weight refers to:
   a. the GVW rating.
   b. weight not supported by the springs.
   c. weight not attached to the springs.
   d. weight supported by the springs.

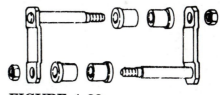

FIGURE 4–22

73. What is the purpose of the parts assembly in Figure 4–22?
   a. To dampen vibration and noise
   b. To compensate for spring length changes
   c. To minimize body roll
   d. To limit jounce and rebound

74. A rack and pinion steering system turns hard in both directions. This could be caused by all of the following EXCEPT:
   a. reversed hoses.
   b. tight tie-rod ends.
   c. a bad pump.
   d. low tire pressure.

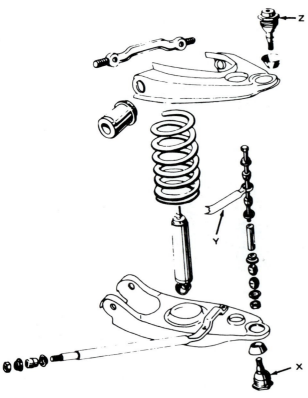

FIGURE 4–23

75. Technician A says that the follower (guide) ball joint in the type of suspension in Figure 4–23 is located at point X.

Technician B says it is located at point Z. Who is right?

a. A only   c. Both A and B
b. B only   d. Neither A nor B

76. To counteract the pulling effect of road crown, most manufacturers recommend that the left front wheel be adjusted to have:

a. less positive caster than the right front wheel.
b. more negative camber than the right front wheel.
c. more toe-in than the right front wheel.
d. less toe-in than the right front wheel.

77. In the linkage type power steering system, which statement below is true?

a. The end of the pitman arm actuates a spool valve.
b. The control valve is built into the steering gearbox.
c. The assist cylinder is built into the steering gearbox.
d. All of the above

78. A customer complains of poor steering wheel return when going around a corner.

Technician A says that underinflated tires could be the cause.

Technician B says that incorrect alignment angles could be the cause.

Who is right?

a. A only
b. B only
c. Both A and B
d. Neither A nor B

79. A power steering equipped car makes a squealing noise (particularly when parking).

Technician A says that underinflated tires could be the cause.

Technician B says that incorrect alignment angles could be the cause.

Who is right?

a. A only
b. B only
c. Both A and B
d. Neither A nor B

80. A "binding" is felt when the steering wheel is turned through the center position. What adjustment is wrong?

a. Cross shaft end play
b. Worm shaft end play
c. Hi-point
d. Worm bearing preload

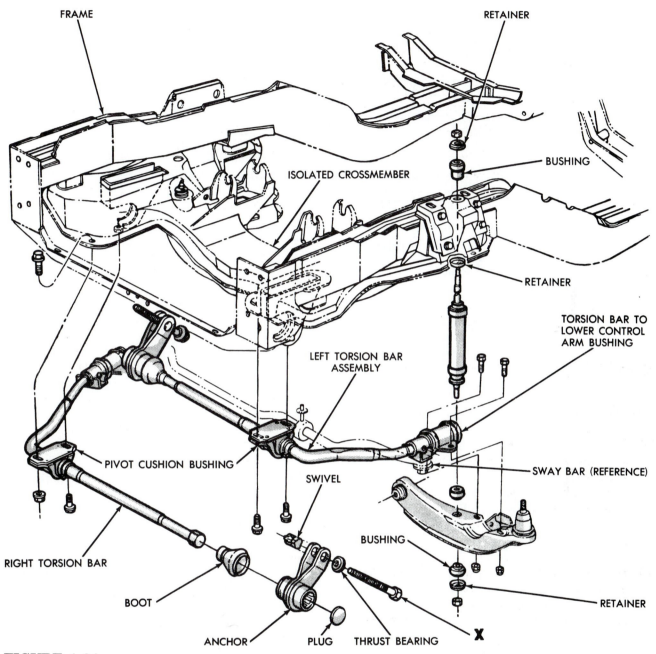

FRAME

RETAINER

ISOLATED CROSSMEMBER

BUSHING

RETAINER

TORSION BAR TO LOWER CONTROL ARM BUSHING

LEFT TORSION BAR ASSEMBLY

PIVOT CUSHION BUSHING

SWIVEL

SWAY BAR (REFERENCE)

BUSHING

RIGHT TORSION BAR

BOOT

ANCHOR   PLUG   THRUST BEARING

RETAINER

X

FIGURE 4–24

81. Refer to the front suspension system pictured in Figure 4–24.

Technician A says that bolt X must be removed before the lower left control arm is removed.

Technician B says that bolt X is used to adjust ride height.

Who is right?

a. A only **c.** Both A and B
b. B only **d.** Neither A nor B

82. A vehicle is equipped with an integral power steering system. The owner complains of hard steering. A pressure gauge hooked into the system reads 250 psi when the hand valve is closed.

Technician A says that the problem is in the pump.

Technician B says that the problem is in the steering gearbox.

Who is right?

a. A only **c.** Both A and B
b. B only **d.** Neither A nor B

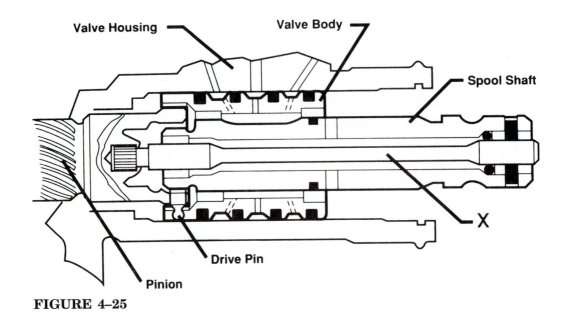

Valve Housing **Valve Body** **Spool Shaft** **Drive Pin** **Pinion** X

FIGURE 4–25

83. The purpose of part X in Figure 4–25 is to:
    a. provide "feel" for the driver.
    b. help absorb road shock.
    c. give maximum steering assist when required.
    d. maintain preload on the worm bearing race.

84. Bleeding a power steering system is generally accomplished by:
    a. opening a bleeder valve.
    b. removing the pressure line.
    c. removing the return line.
    d. turning the steering wheel.

85. A vehicle with a power rack and pinion steering system has a center take-off (CTO) gear that has a loose mounting. Which sound would this condition MOST LIKELY produce?
    a. Squeak   b. Rattle   c. Hiss   d. Pop

86. The front tires on a car are bubble balanced. However, the owner says that there is still a shimmy.
    Technician A says that a bent rim could be the cause.
    Technician B says that dynamic imbalance could be the cause.
    Who is right?
    a. A only
    b. B only
    c. Both A and B
    d. Neither A nor B

87. New cartridges are being installed on a MacPherson strut system vehicle. The technician pours a slight amount of oil into the strut. This is done in order to:
    a. dissipate heat.
    b. lubricate the upper bearing.
    c. Both a and b
    d. Neither a nor b

88. A power rack and pinion equipped car has no assist. This could be caused by:
    a. a damaged center seal.
    b. torn bellows.
    c. Both a and b
    d. Neither a nor b

89. Technician A says that rear tire wear can be caused by a broken shock.
    Technician B says that rear tire wear can be caused by a bent axle flange.
    Who is right?
    a. A only   c. Both A and B
    b. B only   d. Neither A nor B

90. A heavy-duty front stabilizer bar is installed on a car.
    Technician A says that this will change chassis height.
    Technician B says that this will change toe-out on turns.
    Who is right?
    a. A only   c. Both A and B
    b. B only   d. Neither A nor B

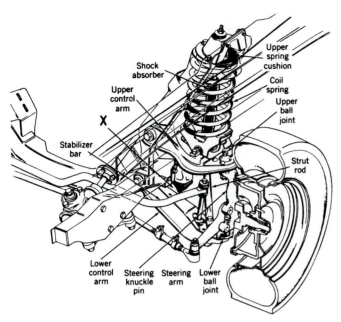

FIGURE 4–26

91. Part X shown in Figure 4–26 is badly battered on a car. This could be caused by all of the following EXCEPT:
a. a weak coil spring.
b. a weak shock absorber.
c. driving on rough roads.
d. panic stops.

92. The owner of a vehicle equipped with power steering comments about poor assist. What would be the first step in diagnosing this problem?
a. Hook up pressure gauge
b. Inspect relief valve
c. Inspect flow control valve
d. Check fluid

93. A car has excessive lean (body roll) when cornering. This could be caused by:
a. worn links.
b. bad shocks.
c. Both a and b
d. Neither a nor b

94. You are aligning a RWD vehicle that has front and rear radial tires. It was originally equipped with non-radial tires. What front wheel settings are generally recommended in this situation?
a. Minimum toe-in setting as specified by vehicle manufacturer
b. Maximum positive caster as specified
c. Minimum camber setting as specified
d. All of the above

95. You are pressure testing a unitized (integral) power steering system. The engine is idling and the gauge hand valve is open. The steering wheel is turned from extreme left to extreme right. The pressure readings obtained at each extreme are different.
　Technician A says that a seal could be leaking within the gearbox unit.
　Technician B says that the pump flow control valve could be sticking open.
　Who is right?
a. A only　　　　**c.** Both A and B
b. B only　　　　**d.** Neither A nor B

96. Technician A says that the purpose of camber is to provide easy steering by having the vehicle weight supported by the inner wheel bearing.
　Technician B says that the purpose of camber is to bring the road contact of the tire more nearly under the point of load.
　Who is right?
a. A only　　　　**c.** Both A and B
b. B only　　　　**d.** Neither A nor B

97. If the steering wheel spoke is in correct position, how should toe-in be adjusted?
a. At the right tie rod sleeve
b. At the left tie rod sleeve
c. Lengthen or shorten both tie rods equally.
d. Both a and b

98. Technician A says that cupped tires can be caused by faulty shock absorbers.
　Technician B says that wheels or tires out-of-balance can be a cause of tire cupping.
　Who is right?
a. A only　　　　**c.** Both A and B
b. B only　　　　**d.** Neither A nor B

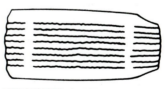

FIGURE 4–27

99. What does the tire wear pattern in Figure 4–27 indicate?
a. Overinflation wear
b. Underinflation wear
c. Cornering wear
d. The tread depth is approximately 1/16″ and the tire is unsafe.

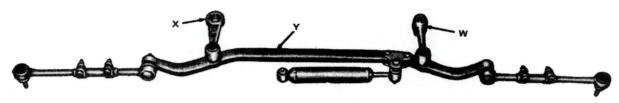

FIGURE 4–28

100. Refer to the illustrated steering linkage in Figure 4–28. Which statement is correct?
    a. The pitman arm is located at point W.
    b. The idler arm is located at point X.
    c. The center link is located at point Y.
    d. All of the above

101. In order to accurately inspect an idler arm:
    a. grasp the center link near the idler and shake it up and down.
    b. squeeze the idler pivot point with grease cap pliers and observe for internal looseness.
    c. measure the clearance between the frame and idler bracket.
    d. compare the left and right side included angle.

102. Technician A says that incorrect chassis height can affect camber.
    Technician B says that worn stabilizer links can cause incorrect chassis height.
    Who is right?
    a. A only
    b. B only
    c. Both A and B
    d. Neither A nor B

103. A car has a strut rod from the front of the frame to the lower control arm.
    Technician A says that increasing the rod length will change caster.
    Technician B says that the rod nut should be torqued with the full-car weight on the tires.
    Who is right?
    a. A only
    b. B only
    c. Both A and B
    d. Neither A nor B

104. All of the following describe a conventional shock absorber, EXCEPT:
    a. Has a damping function.
    b. Holds the vehicle up.
    c. Aids in handling and stability.
    d. Aids in holding the tire down.

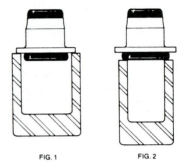

FIG. 1   FIG. 2

FIGURE 4–29

105. A new control arm bushing is being installed with a hammer and driver. Which driver position in Figure 4–29 is correct?
    a. Figure 1 only
    b. Figure 2 only
    c. Both Figures 1 and Figure 2
    d. Neither Figure 1 nor Figure 2

106. Technician A says that the follower (non-load carrying) ball joint should be replaced when any perceptible looseness exists.
    Technician B says that the follower ball joint should be replaced when the load carrying joint is replaced.
    Who is right?
    a. A only   c. Both A and B
    b. B only   d. Neither A nor B

107. Which of the following conditions is the LEAST LIKELY to indicate a worn control arm bushing?
    a. Pivot shaft off-center in bushing
    b. Rubber portion of bushing cracked
    c. Squeaking noise
    d. Ball joint looseness

108. Technician A says that torsion bars are interchangeable side-to-side on like vehicles.
    Technician B says that torsion bars can be adjusted to change chassis height.
    Who is right?
    a. A only   c. Both A and B
    b. B only   d. Neither A nor B

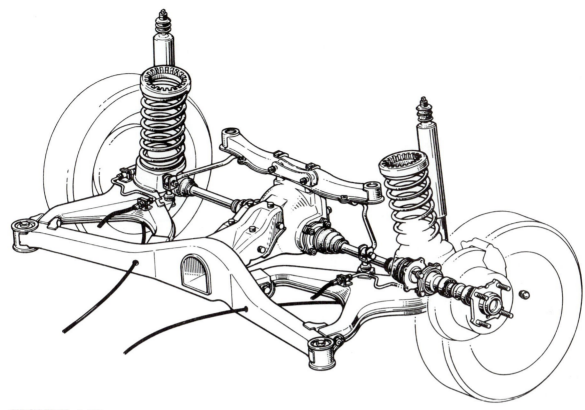

FIGURE 4–30

109. The wheels on the rear suspension system shown in Figure 4–30 need aligning.

Technician A says that vehicle height must be checked.

Technician B says that toe-in must be checked.

Who is right?
a. A only
b. B only
c. Both A and B
d. Neither A nor B

110. Which of the following would indicate a worn shock?
a. Sway on turns
b. More than two cycles when vehicle is bounced
c. Both a and b
d. Neither a nor b

111. When installing a ball joint in a knuckle that has an "out-of-round" taper:
a. torque the stud nut 25 ft. lbs. more than specifications require.
b. use shim stock to take up looseness.
c. ream the taper.
d. you run the risk of the ball joint stud breaking off; the knuckle should be replaced.

112. Wear indicator load carrying ball joints should be:
a. checked only on a frame contact hoist.
b. unloaded when inspected.
c. checked using a pry bar and dial gauge.
d. loaded when inspected.

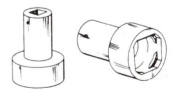

FIGURE 4–31

113. The tool pictured in Figure 4–31 is used when:
a. replacing coil springs mounted on the upper control arm.
b. replacing coil springs mounted on the lower control arm.
c. replacing strut cartridges.
d. installing ball joints.

114. For cars with _____ on the rear wheels, the wheel should be supported when removing the shocks.
a. leaf springs
b. coil springs
c. torsion bars
d. traction bars

115. Two technicians are discussing how to correctly center the steering wheel on a car.

Technician A says to remove the wheel and reposition it on the steering shaft.

Technician B says to adjust the length of the tie rods and reset toe-in.

Who is right?
a. A only
b. B only
c. Both A and B
d. Neither A nor B

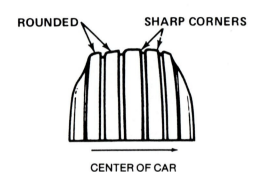

ROUNDED   SHARP CORNERS

CENTER OF CAR

FIGURE 4–32

116. Both front tires on a car have the wear pattern in Figure 4–32. This indicates too much:
a. negative camber.
b. positive camber.
c. toe-out.
d. toe-in.

117. A steering wheel fails to return to top tilt position. This could be caused by:
a. a defective tilt spring.
b. the turn signal switch wires being too tight.
c. Both a and b
d. Neither a nor b

118. A tire has too much radial (up and down) runout.

Technician A says that this is often corrected by rotating the wheel and tire on the drum or rotor.

Technician B says that this is often corrected by rotating the tire on the wheel.

Who is right?
a. A only
b. B only
c. Both A and B
d. Neither A nor B

119. The camber on a left front wheel is set at 3/4° positive. The right wheel camber is set at 1 1/2° negative. Caster is set a 0° on both wheels.

Technician A says that these settings will cause a pull to the right.

Technician B says that these settings will cause right tire wear on the outside.

Who is right?
a. A only   **c.** Both A and B
b. B only   **d.** Neither A nor B

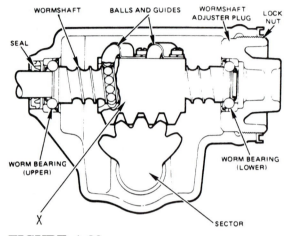

FIGURE 4–33

120. What is the name of part X in Figure 4–33?
a. Ball nut
b. Pitman gear
c. Steering gear
d. Main drive gear

121. Technician A says that when installing a sector shaft seal, the lip of the seal must face outward.

Technician B says that when the steering wheel is turned, the sector shaft should move.

Who is right?
a. A only   **c.** Both A and B
b. B only   **d.** Neither A nor B

122. A power steering pump is damaged inside and needs to be replaced.

Technician A says to disconnect the return hose and flush the system before installing the new pump.

Technician B says to remove the air by turning the wheel back and forth after installing the new pump.

Who is right?
a. A only   **c.** Both A and B
b. B only   **d.** Neither A nor B

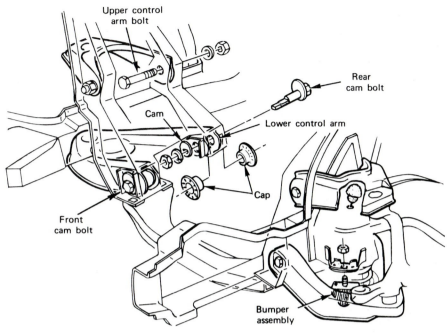

FIGURE 4–34

123. The suspension system in Figure 4–34 uses cam bolts at the lower control arms.

Technician A says that the rear cam bolt is used when adjusting caster.

Technician B says that the front cam bolt is used when adjusting camber.

Who is right?

a. A only   **c.** Both A and B
b. B only   **d.** Neither A nor B

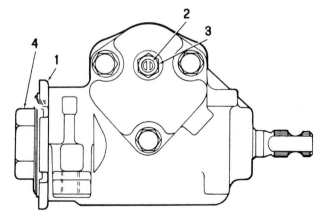

FIGURE 4–35

124. Refer to the steering gear in Figure 4–35.

Technician A says that part 1 should be loosened before part 2 is turned.

Technician B says that part 3 should be loosened before part 4 is turned.

Who is right?

a. A only   **c.** Both A and B
b. B only   **d.** Neither A nor B

125. When removing a rack and pinion steering assembly from a car that uses an end take-off (ETO) gear, do all the following, EXCEPT:

a. disconnecting the flexible coupling.
b. removing the bellows clamps.
c. breaking the taper at the tie-rods.
d. removing the support bolts.

126. A front inner wheel bearing has failed and is being replaced for the third time in several months.

Technician A says that this could be caused by a bad spindle.

Technician B says that this could be caused by a leaky seal.

Who is right?

a. A only
b. B only
c. Both A and B
d. Neither A nor B

127. There is excessive side-to-side rock in a steering wheel.

Technician A says that this could be caused by a bad upper bearing in the column.

Technician B says that this could be caused by the wrong worm bearing adjustment.

Who is right?

a. A only
b. B only
c. Both A and B
d. Neither A nor B

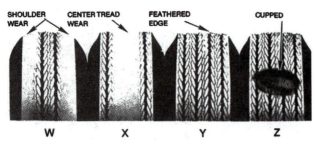

FIGURE 4–36

128. What tire wear pattern in Figure 4–36 would be MOST LIKELY caused by worn suspension parts?
   a. Pattern W
   b. Pattern X
   c. Pattern Y
   d. Pattern Z

129. Technician A says that a misaligned flexible coupling can cause excessive steering effort.
   Technician B says that a fractured flexible coupling can cause loose steering.
   Who is right?
   a. A only
   b. B only
   c. Both A and B
   d. Neither A nor B

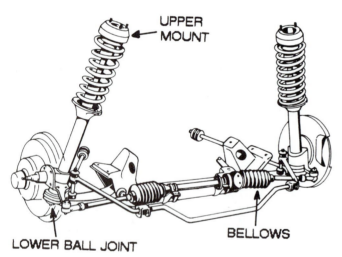

FIGURE 4–37

130. Which of the following statements is true regarding the suspension system shown in Figure 4–37?
   a. A strut plunger is inside the bellows.
   b. The lower ball joints carry the weight of the vehicle.
   c. A thrust bearing or bushing is built into the upper mount.
   d. All of the above

131. How is camber usually set on the suspension system shown in Figure 4–37?
   a. By rotating lower ball joint
   b. By sliding upper mount toward the front or rear of car
   c. By turning strut plunger
   d. None of the above

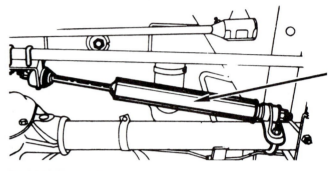

FIGURE 4–38

132. An owner installs the aftermarket part in Figure 4–38 (see arrow) on his 4-wheel drive pickup.
   Technician A says that this part is a steering damper.
   Technician B says that this part is designed to eliminate front wheel shimmy.
   Who is right?
   a. A only   **c.** Both A and B
   b. B only   **d.** Neither A nor B

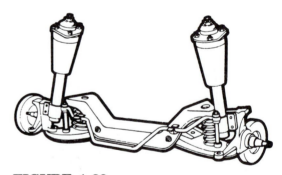

FIGURE 4–39

133. Refer to the modified MacPherson strut suspension system shown in Figure 4–39.
   Technician A says that the lower ball joints are load carrying.
   Technician B says that the shock absorbers are mounted inside the coil springs.
   Who is right?
   a. A only
   b. B only
   c. Both A and B
   d. Neither A nor B

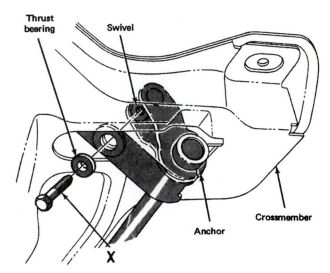

FIGURE 4–40

134. Bolt X in Figure 4–40 is used for:
  a. adjusting turning radius.
  b. adjusting caster.
  c. adjusting camber.
  d. None of the above

135. When on-car spin balancing rear wheels on a car equipped with a conventional differential:
  a. block the wheel opposite the wheel being balanced.
  b. the speedometer will indicate one-half wheel speed.
  c. Both a and b
  d. Neither a nor b

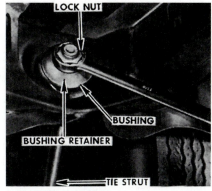

FIGURE 4–41

136. What is being adjusted in Figure 4–41?
  a. Toe
  b. Caster
  c. Camber
  d. Turning radius

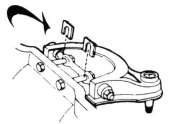

FIGURE 4–42

137. The illustration shown in Figure 4–42 shows a right front upper control arm mounting. One shim is removed as shown.
  Technician A says that the camber will be changed to a more negative angle.
  Technician B says that the caster will be changed to a more negative angle.
  Who is right?
  a. A only   **c.** Both A and B
  b. B only   **d.** Neither A nor B

138. When aligning a front end, the mechanic finds that toe-out on turns is not within specifications. The MOST LIKELY cause is:
  a. a bent control arm.
  b. a bent steering arm.
  c. the steering wheel is not centered.
  d. worn tie-rod ends.

139. Technician A says that a sheared center bolt can cause "dog tracking."
  Technician B says that a sheared center bolt can cause a vehicle to steer (pull) to one side.
  Who is right?
  a. A only
  b. B only
  c. Both A and B
  d. Neither A nor B

140. An integral power steering gearbox has a leak at the sector shaft. What is the MOST LIKELY cause?
  a. Bad bushing
  b. Damaged control valve
  c. Scored piston bore
  d. Flex coupling bottoming

141. All of the following must be checked before aligning a front end EXCEPT:
  a. tire pressure.
  b. wheel bearing adjustment.
  c. curb height (chassis height).
  d. wheel balance.

142. Which statement below is correct?
   a. Collapse in the front main cross-member can affect camber.
   b. A vehicle will always steer (pull) to the side having the shortest wheelbase.
   c. Both a and b
   d. Neither a nor b

143. Which of these will MOST LIKELY happen if there is too much negative caster on the left front wheel?
   a. A pull to the left
   b. A pull to the right
   c. Left tire wear on the inside edge
   d. Left tire wear on the outside edge

FIGURE 4-43

144. The tool in Figure 4–43 is used for:
   a. bending the strut.
   b. compressing the strut spring.
   c. aligning the cartridge.
   d. None of the above

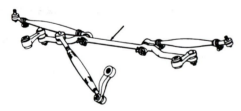

FIGURE 4-44

145. The part in Figure 4–44 (see arrow) is being replaced on a van. What alignment angle will MOST LIKELY be changed?
   a. Toe-out on turns
   b. Turning radius
   c. Tracking
   d. Toe-in

146. A vehicle with an integral power steering system has no assist to the right.
   Technician A says that this could be caused by an incorrectly installed torsion (steering shaft) bar.
   Technician B says that this could be caused by a defective seal.
   Who is right?
   a. A only
   b. B only
   c. Both A and B
   d. Neither A nor B

147. New king pins have just been installed on a light truck. The technician finds too much side-to-side movement. What should be done?
   a. Weld the axle.
   b. Weld the steering knuckle.
   c. Weld the axle and steering knuckle.
   d. None of the above.

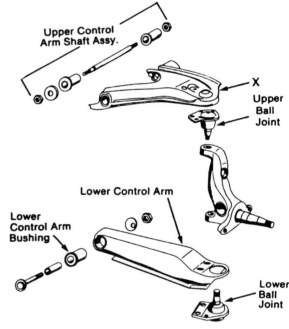

FIGURE 4-45

148. Part X in Figure 4–45 is replaced.
   Technician A says that camber should be checked.
   Technician B says that this will change steering axis inclination.
   Who is right?
   a. A only
   b. B only
   c. Both A and B
   d. Neither A nor B

149. To properly adjust a steering gear, the first adjustment must be:
- **a.** sector mesh.
- **b.** worm bearing preload.
- **c.** cross shaft end play.
- **d.** backlash.

150. A vehicle with a linkage power steering system steers hard.

Technician A says that the box and column could be out of alignment.

Technician B says that the flex coupling could be rubbing.

Who is right?
- **a.** A only
- **b.** B only
- **c.** Both A and B
- **d.** Neither A nor B

151. The caster specifications for a vehicle with manual steering is 0°. If both tires were set at positive 3°, what would be the MOST LIKELY result?
- **a.** Hard steering
- **b.** Easy steering
- **c.** Tire wear
- **d.** Wander and weave

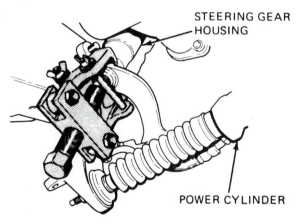

STEERING GEAR HOUSING

POWER CYLINDER

FIGURE 4–46

152. Figure 4–46 shows:
- **a.** the removal of the idler arm.
- **b.** the removal of the pitman arm.
- **c.** the removal of the control arm.
- **d.** the installation of the sector shaft bushing.

153. The drive pulley on the power steering pump in Figure 4–47 must be removed.

Technician A says to use a hammer and punch.

Technician B says to use a puller.

Who is right?
- **a.** A only
- **b.** B only
- **c.** Both A and B
- **d.** Neither A nor B

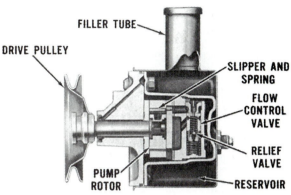

FILLER TUBE

DRIVE PULLEY

SLIPPER AND SPRING

FLOW CONTROL VALVE

RELIEF VALVE

PUMP ROTOR

RESERVOIR

FIGURE 4–47

154. Which of the following is MOST LIKELY to cause steering wheel shimmy?
- **a.** A bent steering knuckle (spindle)
- **b.** A bent steering arm
- **c.** Too much positive caster
- **d.** Out-of-balance tires

155. A manual steering gear feels rough throughout its entire travel range.

Technician A says that this may be because of defective worm bearings.

Technician B says that this may be because of a gouge in the worm gear.

Who is right?
- **a.** A only
- **b.** B only
- **c.** Both A and B
- **d.** Neither A nor B

156. Which of the following statements is true regarding the front wheel bearing assembly on a RWD car?
- **a.** If a cone and roller assembly is defective, replace the cup also.
- **b.** Generally, they require no preloading.
- **c.** The grease seal should be replaced when packing or replacing wheel bearings.
- **d.** All of the above

157. Caster spread on the front wheels of most cars should not exceed:
- **a.** 1/2°. **b.** 1/4°. **c.** 1°. **d.** 3/4°.

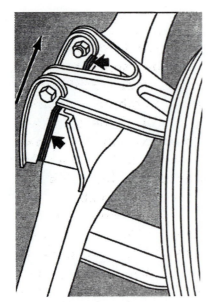

FIGURE 4–48

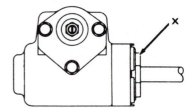

FIGURE 4–49

158. With reference to Figure 4–48, which statement is true?
  a. Removing an equal number of shims from the front and the rear will make camber more positive.
  b. Removing shims from the front shim pack only will make caster more positive.
  c. Both a and b
  d. Neither a nor b

159. A car owner says that the front end of her car vibrates while driving.
  Technician A says that this could be caused by excessive tire runout.
  Technician B says that this could be caused by out-of-balance tires.
  Who is right?
  a. A only
  b. B only
  c. Both A and B
  d. Neither A nor B

160. In a recirculating ball type steering gearbox, the teeth on the sector (pitman) shaft are meshed with:
  a. the ball nut teeth.
  b. the worm gear.
  c. the steering shaft gear.
  d. None of the above

161. What steering gearbox adjustment is made at point X in Figure 4–49?
  a. Worm preload
  b. Spool valve centering
  c. Lash
  d. Gear face contact

162. One procedure that is almost always recommended by the factory when adjusting a recirculating ball steering gearbox is to:
  a. raise front wheels off the shop floor.
  b. inflate front tires to correct pressure.
  c. disconnect the pitman arm from the sector shaft.
  d. make adjustments 45° from the right or left stop.

163. A vehicle is equipped with power steering. The owner complains of a buzzing noise when the engine is running at a fast idle speed. As soon as the wheels are turned, the noise disappears. What is the MOST LIKELY cause?
  a. Loose belt
  b. Restricted hose
  c. Sticking flow control valve
  d. Scored pump bearing shaft

164. The ride height at the right rear of a vehicle is off. This could be caused by:
  a. worn links on the left front.
  b. wear on the right rear shock.
  c. Both a and b
  d. Neither a nor b

165. All of the following methods are approved by car manufacturers to correct camber on MacPherson strut suspension systems EXCEPT:
  a. replacing strut.
  b. lengthening slots in upper plate.
  c. turning cam bolt.
  d. heating and bending strut.

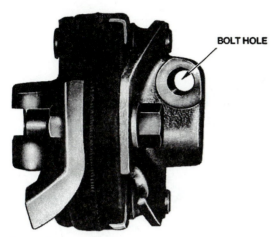

FIGURE 4–50

166. On most vehicles, what tool would be used to remove the bolt that fits into the hole in Figure 4–50?
a. An 8-point socket
b. A 12-point socket
c. An Allen wrench
d. A crowfoot wrench

167. Technician A says that tire conicity can cause a car to pull.
Technician B says that a tire conicity problem can be verified by switching the tires.
Who is right?
a. A only
b. B only
c. Both A and B
d. Neither A nor B

168. The rear thrust angle on a FWD car is incorrect. This can cause:
a. an offset steering wheel.
b. irregular tire wear.
c. dog tracking.
d. All of the above

169. Technician A says that loose rack and pinion mounting studs can cause tire feather edging.
Technician B says that worn strut cartridges can cause tire cupping.
Who is right?
a. A only
b. B only
c. Both A and B
d. Neither A nor B

170. A power steering system makes a faint "buzz" noise at the locks.
Technician A says that this could be caused by a slipping belt.
Technician B says that this could be considered normal.
Who is right?
a. A only
b. B only
c. Both A and B
d. Neither A nor B

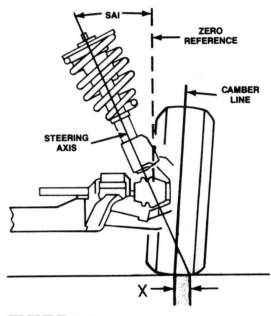

FIGURE 4–51

171. Dimension X in Figure 4–51 shows:
a. negative scrub radius.
b. positive scrub radius.
c. turning angle.
d. thrust angle.

172. Technician A says that if the top nut for a strut assembly is tightened down too much, memory steer can result.
Technician B says that if a rack and pinion steering gear is not securely mounted, bump steer can result.
Who is right?
a. A only
b. B only
c. Both A and B
d. Neither A nor B

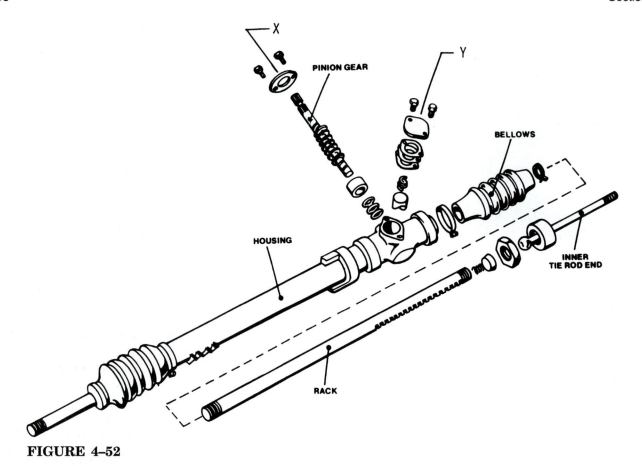

X

PINION GEAR

Y

BELLOWS

HOUSING

INNER
TIE ROD END

RACK

FIGURE 4–52

173. A rack and pinion steering system is shown in Figure 4–52.

Technician A says that rack lash is adjusted at point X.

Technician B says that pinion preload is adjusted at point Y.

Who is right?

a. A only
b. B only
c. Both A and B
d. Neither A nor B

174. A 4-wheel alignment needs to be done on a car.

Technician A says to set the rear wheels before the front ones.

Technician B says to set the rear toe before rear camber.

Who is right?

a. A only
b. B only
c. Both A and B
d. Neither A nor B

175. Cradle misalignment can cause a car to have:
a. a pulling condition.
b. a dramatic change in caster on one side.
c. stretched control cables.
d. All of the above

Desired Specs.	Actual Readings
Toe 1/8″ (3.18 mm)	1/8″
Camber 1/4 deg.	−1/4 deg. both sides
Caster 0 deg.	2° both sides

176. Refer to the chart above and compare the actual front wheel alignment readings on a vehicle against specs.

Technician A says that these readings may cause the car to pull.

Technician B says that these readings may cause the car to have hard steering.

Who is right?

a. A only
b. B only
c. Both A and B
d. Neither A nor B

177. While driving on a straight road, a car has a pronounced pull to the left. This could be caused by:
a. a bent frame.
b. a bent axle housing.
c. Both a and b
d. Neither a nor b

FRONT

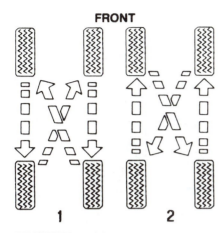

FIGURE 4–53

178. Refer to the tire rotation patterns in Figure 4–53.

Technician A says that pattern 1 can be used for front-wheel drive cars equipped with radial tires.

Technician B says that pattern 2 can be used for rear-wheel drive cars equipped with radial tires.

Who is right?
a. A only
b. B only
c. Both A and B
d. Neither A nor B

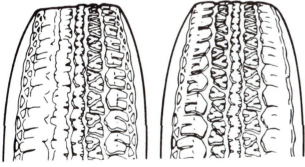

FIGURE 4–54

179. A car equipped with all-season radial tires shows outer tread wear on both non-drive axle tires (see Figure 4–54).

Technician A says that this could be caused by excessive camber.

Technician B says that this could be caused by excessive toe.

Who is right?
a. A only
b. B only
c. Both A and B
d. Neither A nor B

180. On a car equipped with electronic ride control, which of these statements could be considered true?
a. The shock absorber damping rods rotate.
b. Trouble codes can be stored and retrieved.
c. A computer sends current to actuators.
d. All of the above

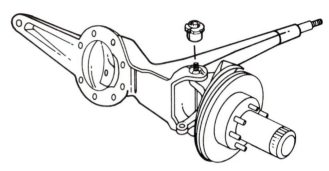

FIGURE 4–55

181. Technician A says that the bushing in Figure 4–55 is used to set camber.

Technician B says that the bushing is used to set caster.

Who is right?
a. A only   c. Both A and B
b. B only   d. Neither A nor B

182. A rack and pinion gear assembly has fluid in both boots and low fluid level in the reservoir.

Technician A says that this could be caused by a bad end seal.

Technician B says that this could be caused by a bad center seal.

Who is right?
a. A only   c. Both A and B
b. B only   d. Neither A nor B

183. The steering wheel on a power rack and pinion system surges when turning with the engine running (especially during parking).

Technician A says that this could be caused by insufficient pump pressure.

Technician B says that this could be caused by a sticky flow control valve.

Who is right?
a. A only   c. Both A and B
b. B only   d. Neither A nor B

184. Technician A says that toe is measured in inches or degrees.

Technician B says that S.A.I. helps assist the wheels back to the straight-ahead position after a turn is completed.

Who is right?
a. A only   c. Both A and B
b. B only   d. Neither A nor B

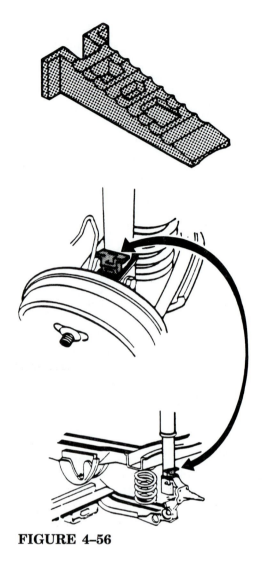

FIGURE 4–56

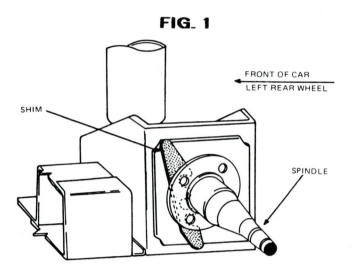

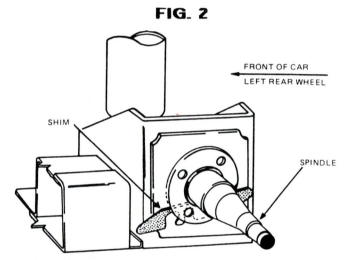

FIGURE 4–57

185. Technician A says that the wedge in Figure 4–56 is used to set camber.

Technician B says that the wedge is used to set caster.

Who is right?
a. A only
b. B only
c. Both A and B
d. Neither A nor B

186. A pick-up truck owner complains of a "clattering" noise when driving off-road.

Technician A says that this could be caused by worn shackle bushings.

Technician B says that this could be caused by worn spring eye bushings.

Who is right?
a. A only   c. Both A and B
b. B only   d. Neither A nor B

187. Refer to Figure 4–57.

Technician A says that Figure 1 shows installing a shim for more positive camber.

Technician B says that Figure 2 shows installing a shim for more toe-in.

Who is right?
a. A only
b. B only
c. Both A and B
d. Neither A nor B

188. New king pins have just been installed. The technician finds too much up-and-down movement. What needs to be done?
a. Replace the axle.
b. Replace the steering knuckle.
c. Replace the axle and steering knuckle.
d. Add shims.

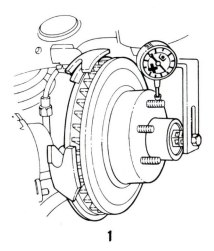

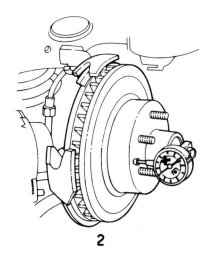

1   **2**

FIGURE 4–58

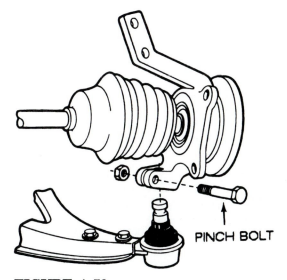

PINCH BOLT

FIGURE 4–59

189. Excessive wheel and tire runout occurs on a car. However, the runout does not occur during off-car testing.

Technician A says that measurement 1 shown in Figure 4–58 could be the problem.

Technician B says that measurement 2 could be the problem.

Who is right?

a. A only
b. B only
c. Both A and B
d. Neither A nor B

190. When replacing the ball joint in Figure 4–59:

a. widen the slit in the steering knuckle with a chisel
b. beat the pinch bolt into place with a hammer.
c. Both a and b
d. Neither a nor b

191. A vane type power steering pump is being tested as shown in Figure 4–60. What could cause the gauge reading to read low?

a. The pressure relief valve could be frozen.
b. The pump vanes could be sticking in their slots.
c. Either a or b
d. Neither a nor b

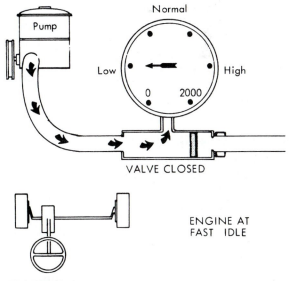

FIGURE 4–60

192. Technician A says that bump steer can be caused by a rack and pinion steering gear that is not mounted level.

Technician B says that torque steer can be caused by unequal drive axle angles.

Who is right?

a. A only
b. B only
c. Both A and B
d. Neither A nor B

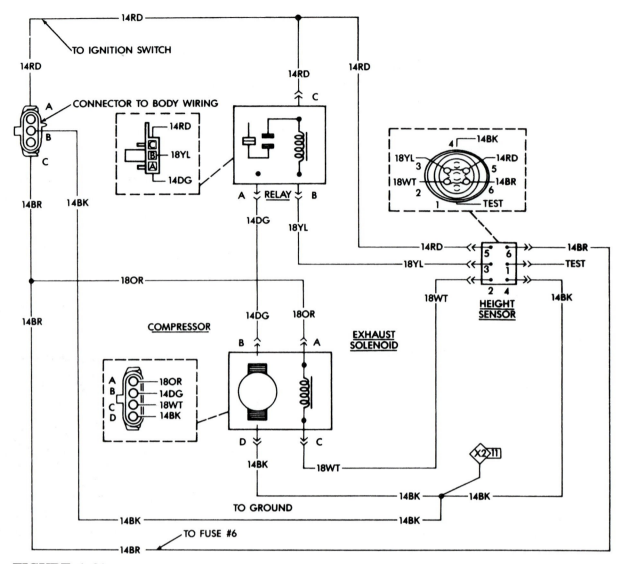

FIGURE 4–61

193. A car is equipped with an automatic air load leveling system. The compressor is inoperative and the car sits low. According to the wiring schematic in Figure 4–61, what could be the cause?
   a. Bad relay
   b. Open height sensor ground circuit
   c. Both a and b
   d. Neither a nor b

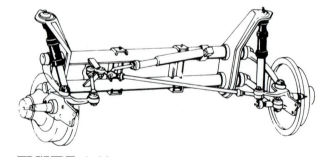

FIGURE 4–62

194. Which of the following would be the LEAST LIKELY cause of excessive front tire wear?
   a. Weak shock absorbers
   b. Underinflated tires
   c. An incorrect toe setting
   d. An incorrect caster setting

195. The front suspension system in Figure 4–62 is equipped with:
   a. torsion bars.
   b. a steering damper.
   c. Both a and b
   d. Neither a nor b

FIGURE 4-63

196. A fleet of FWD vehicles has developed irregular tread patterns on the rear tires (see Figure 4–63).

Technician A says that this could be caused by axle flex.

Technician B says that this could be caused by incorrect toe.

Who is right?

a. A only
b. B only
c. Both A and B
d. Neither A nor B

197. A wheel and tire assembly is going to be balanced on an off-car computerized balancer.

Technician A says to always place the proper size cone against the front surface of the wheel.

Technician B says that wheel width, wheel diameter, and a distance measurement setting are usually required.

Who is right?

a. A only
b. B only
c. Both A and B
d. Neither A nor B

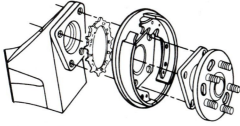

FIGURE 4-64

198. A rear wheel alignment shim is being installed (see Figure 4–64).

Technician A says to tighten all four bolts starting at the thin end of the shim.

Technician B says to install the shim with the letters facing to the right (passenger) side of the car.

Who is right?

a. A only
b. B only
c. Both A and B
d. Neither A nor B

199. Technician A says that match-mounting (vectoring) can be used to often reduce radial or lateral runout of a wheel and tire assembly.

Technician B says that radial force variation can often be corrected by grinding rubber from the tread area of the tire.

Who is right?

a. A only
b. B only
c. Both A and B
d. Neither A nor B

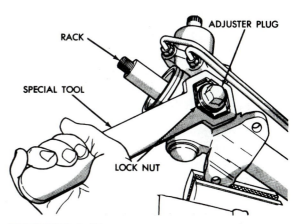

FIGURE 4-65

200. When making the adjustment in Figure 4–65:
a. turn adjuster plug until it bottoms, then back off.
b. tighten lock nut while holding adjuster plug.
c. Both a and b
d. Neither a nor b

201. A rack and pinion steering gear has fluid leaking from one tie-rod boot.

Technician A says that this could be caused by a damaged inner rack seal.

Technician B says that this could be caused by a damaged pinion seal.

Who is right?

a. A only
b. B only
c. Both A and B
d. Neither A nor B

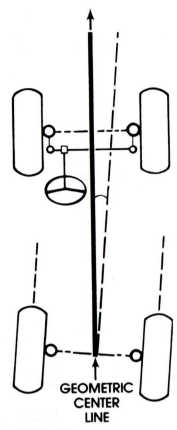

GEOMETRIC
CENTER
LINE

FIGURE 4–66

202. What alignment angle is illustrated in Figure 4–66?
   a. Cross camber
   b. Total toe
   c. Steering wheel
   d. Thrust

203. Technician A says that tire noise can be caused by cupped tires being driven on paved roads.

   Technician B says that tire noise can be caused by off-road tires being driven on paved roads.

   Who is right?
   a. A only
   b. B only
   c. Both A and B
   d. Neither A nor B

204. If a centrifugal force vibration occurs at 690 rpm, what is the frequency of vibration in hertz?
   a. 14.4 Hz
   b. 11.0 Hz
   c. 11.5 Hz
   d. 41.4 Hz

205. Match-mounting procedure can reduce the amount of runout on a good wheel by:
   a. aligning the high spot on the tire with the valve stem on the wheel.
   b. aligning the high spot on the tire opposite the valve stem on the wheel.
   c. Either A or B
   d. Alignment of the high spot will NOT affect runout.

206. A vehicle has had all four wheels and tires balanced using both a computer balancer and an on-car finish balancer. The wheels and tires are within runout specifications, yet a wheel tramp condition still exists.

   Technician A says that the problem could be caused by a tire with radial force variation.

   Technician B says that the problem could be caused by a dragging brake.

   Who is right?
   a. A only
   b. B only
   c. Both A and B
   d. Neither A nor B

207. As the steering wheel is moved lock-to-lock on a MacPherson strut suspension system, a "creaking" noise is heard and a strut spring twists.

   Technician A says this could be caused by a seized top plate bearing.

   Technician B says to replace the strut spring.

   Who is right?
   a. A only
   b. B only
   c. Both A and B
   d. Neither A nor B

208. A set of front tires looks good, except the tires show tire "chew" on the inner and outer edges.

   Technician A says that this can be caused by driving on curved roads with too much positive caster.

   Technician B says that this can be caused by overinflated tires.

   Who is right?
   a. A only
   b. B only
   c. Both A and B
   d. Neither A nor B

209. A vehicle is being aligned that is equipped with electronic leveling control (ELC).

Technician A says to activate the ELC system to help assure that overall ride height is correct.

Technician B says that air temperature can cause ELC air bags to contract or expand and change ride height.

Who is right?

a. A only
b. B only
c. Both A and B
d. Neither A nor B

210. Technician A says that if an extremely heavy person drives a vehicle equipped with I-beam suspension, LF camber will change in a negative direction.

Technician B says that if an extremely heavy person drives a vehicle equipped with strut suspension, LF camber will change in a positive direction.

Who is right?

a. A only
b. B only
c. Both A and B
d. Neither A nor B

211. Technician A says that some FWD vehicles have stabilizer bar frame bushing mounts that may be shifted rearward or forward to change caster.

Technician B says that some FWD vehicles have a cradle that is easily shifted left or right to change caster and/or camber.

Who is right?

a. A only
b. B only
c. Both A and B
d. Neither A nor B

212. Rack and pinion steering gear tie rods are going to be inspected.

Technician A says to inspect the inner tie rods for looseness by cutting a slit in the bellows boot.

Technician B says to inspect the outer tie rods for looseness by turning the adjustment sleeve.

Who is right?

a. A only
b. B only
c. Both A and B
d. Neither A nor B

213. The front wheels on a FWD car are aligned to the centerline, but the rear wheels are not parallel to the centerline. This will cause:

a. uneven front tire wear.
b. outside edge wear on the rear tires.
c. a more positive steering axis inclination.
d. the turning angle to be off for one front wheel.

214. Lead/pull may be caused by:

a. worn wheel bearings.
b. worn outside tie rod ends.
c. excessive lateral runout in the wheel.
d. a belt in a radial tire which is off center.

215. Which of the following can cause memory steer?

a. Worn centerlink
b. Worn tie rod ends
c. Worn control arm bushings
d. Windup in the top of the MacPherson strut

216. Variable effort steering (VES) systems:

a. vary driver steering effort proportional to vehicle speed.
b. vary driver steering effort proportional to engine speed.
c. provide different steering efforts for different drivers.
d. provide different steering efforts based on ambient temperature.

217. A vehicle with a supplemental inflatable restraint (SIR) system requires steering column service.

Technician A says to have the ignition key in the LOCK position when removing the steering wheel.

Technician B says to have the front wheels turned FULL RIGHT when installing the ribbon coil assembly.

Who is right?

a. A only
b. B only
c. Both A and B
d. Neither A nor B

Section 5

BRAKES

STUDY OUTLINE

I. Basic Fundamentals
   A. Hydraulic System
      1. Pressure requirements
      2. Dual and diagonally split systems
   B. Master and Wheel Cylinders
   C. Drum Brakes
   D. Disc Brakes (Single Piston Floating and Sliding Caliper Design)
      1. Advantages
      2. Adjustment
      3. Special tools
      4. Four wheel disc system
   E. Power Brakes
   F. Basic Troubleshooting
II. Hydraulic Control Devices
   A. Master Cylinder (Tandem)
      1. Operation
      2. Construction (position of parts)
      3. Nomenclature of parts
      4. Reconditioning procedures (include cleaning and inspection)
      5. Push rod adjustment (effects)
      6. Bench bleeding and installation
      7. Failure diagnosis
      8. Leakage (internal and external)
   B. Step Bore Master Cylinder
   C. Quick Take-up Master Cylinder
   D. Proportioning Valve
      1. Purpose
      2. Symptoms if defective
      3. Height sensing type
      4. Dual proportioning valves
      5. Servicing
   E. Metering Valve
      1. Purpose
      2. Must be open when pressure tank bleeding
      3. Symptoms if defective
      4. Hold open tools
   F. Pressure Differential Switch
      1. Operation
      2. Centering
      3. Testing the dash lamp
      4. Testing the warning light switch

   G. Residual Valve
      1. Purpose
      2. Drum brakes only
   H. Combination Valve
      1. Inspect and test
      2. By-pass
      3. Two-function type
      4. Three-function type
      5. Servicing
   I. Wheel Cylinders
      1. Nomenclature
      2. Inspection
      3. Reconditioning
      4. Purpose of expanders
   J. Brake Fluids
      1. Boiling points
      2. Water contamination
      3. Silicone type
      4. Changing fluid
      5. Handling and storage
   K. Hydraulic Tubing, Fittings, and Hoses (Copper Gaskets and Flare Nut Wrenches and Tools)
   L. Anti-lock Devices
   M. Pressure Test System by Applying Force to Pedal
      1. Hold for 15 seconds
      2. Inspect for leaks
III. System Service
   A. Bendix Type Brake
      1. Common
      2. Servo-action
      3. Nomenclature of parts (self-adjusting type)
      4. Construction (position of parts)
      5. Adjustment
      6. Anchor pin location
   B. Leading/Trailing Shoe Type Brake
      1. Nomenclature of parts
      2. Construction
      3. Adjustment
      4. Anchor pin location
   C. Drum Removal, Inspection, and Reconditioning
      1. Bell-mouthing
      2. Taper
      3. Out-of-round

4. Machining
  a. Chatter band
  b. Reasons for poor finish
5. Hard spots
6. Scoring
7. Oversize limits (machining and discard)
8. Drum micrometer
9. Removing drum front hub
  a. Swedged studs
10. Front wheel bearings (RWD and FWD)
  a. Service
  b. Diagnosis/repair
  c. Adjustment
  d. Seal installation

D. Rotor Inspection and Use of Tools
1. Runout (including the hub surface)
2. Parallelism
3. Thickness minimum (machining and discard)
4. RMS finish
5. Flatness
6. Machine on lathe (include swirl finish)
7. Importance of torquing lug nuts when installing
8. Rotor balance
9. Rotor ventilation
10. Scoring limits

E. Brake Shoes
1. Inspection
  a. Lining wear limits
  b. Shoe damage
2. Arcing
  a. Purpose
  b. Oversize lining
  c. Pre-arced lining
3. Primary and secondary shoes
4. Lubricate shoe support pads (ledges)
5. Replacement procedures (including use of brake shoe setting gauge)

F. Brake Bleeding Procedures
1. Pressure tank
  a. Diaphragm type
  b. Advantages
2. Manual bleeding
3. Pressure bleeding
4. Surge bleeding
5. Vacuum bleeding
6. Bleeder screw location
7. Bleeding sequences
8. Flushing

G. Wheel Cylinders and Calipers
1. Inspection
2. Reconditioning procedures and use of tools
3. Caliper design
  a. Fixed
  b. Floating
  c. Piston number difference
  d. Rear wheel types
  e. Low drag
  f. Phenolic pistons

4. Rubber parts and mounting hardware
5. Rebuilding (including use of assembly lubricant)

H. Disc Brake Pads
1. Inspection
2. Removal (including caliper dismount)
3. Replacement procedures/break-in
  a. Drain fluid
  b. Clean and lubricate component parts
  c. Torque caliper
4. Edge coding (including semimetallic material)

I. Parking Brake
1. Nomenclature
2. Adjustment/cable replacement
3. Test light circuit
4. Lubrication

J. Stop Light Switch
1. Operational check
2. Servicing

IV. Power Brakes
A. Vacuum Suspended
B. Atmospheric Suspended
C. Integral, Pedal Assist, and Multiplier Types
D. Testing/Diagnosis
1. Vacuum supply
2. Loss of fluid
3. Hard pedal
4. Rough idle with brake pedal depressed
5. Hidden brake fluid loss
6. Brake drag test
7. Air tightness test
8. Vacuum system test
E. Push Rod Adjustment
F. Purpose of Check Valve
G. Hydro-Boost System
1. Basic test
2. Accumulator test
3. Seal leaks
4. Troubleshooting
5. Bleeding procedure

V. Brake Problem/Diagnosis
A. Pulling to One Side
B. Grabbing
C. Chatter
D. Pedal Pulsation
E. Spongy Pedal
F. Squeals
G. Rising Pedal (Stop Light Stays On)
H. Low Pedal
I. Pedal Sinks Slowly to Floor with Pressure Applied
J. Loss of Pedal on Rough Roads
K. Wheel and Axle Seal Leakage
L. Wheel Bearing Noise
M. Poor Stopping
N. Dragging

O. Grinding Noise

P. Clicking Noise

Q. Vibration When Braking

R. No Stop Lights

S. Fluid Leaks

T. Failure to Self-Adjust

U. Fade

V. Hard Pedal

W. Wheel Lock-Up

X. Dive (Front End Dips Excessively)

Y. Sensitive Brakes

VI. Brake Service Philosophy

    A. Should Drums and Rotors on the Same Axle Be Turned the Same Size?

B. How Should Lining Be Broken In?

C. What Constitutes a Complete Brake Job?

D. Metallic vs. Nonmetallic Lining?

E. How Should Backing Plates and Brake Parts Be Cleaned?

VII. Anti-lock Braking Systems

    A. Theory of Operation/Nomenclature of Parts

    B. Precautions

    C. Operational Checks/Scan Tool Data

    D. Testing (Including Pulling Trouble Codes)

---

1. The outer bearing race (cup) is loose (spinning) in a front hub. The customer should be sold a:
   a. new cup and bearing.
   b. new cup only.
   c. new hub only.
   d. new cup, bearing, and hub.

2. When working on a Hydro-Boost brake system, which of these should you do first?
   a. Release master cylinder pressure.
   b. Disconnect hydraulic lines at the steering pump.
   c. Disconnect hydraulic lines at the booster.
   d. Release accumulator pressure.

3. Technician A says that weak retraction springs can cause rapid lining wear on drum-type brakes.

   Technician B says that weak hold-down springs can cause rapid lining wear on drum-type brakes.

   Who is right?
   a. A only
   b. B only
   c. Both A and B
   d. Neither A nor B

4. The brakes "grab" on a car that is equipped with the system in Figure 5–1.

   Technician A says that this could be caused by a broken spool return spring.

   Technician B says that this could be caused by binding pedal linkage.

   Who is right?
   a. A only   c. Both A and B
   b. B only   d. Neither A nor B

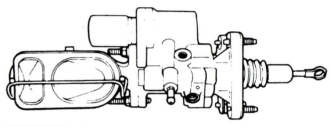

FIGURE 5–1

5. A car with a Hydro-Boost system has a vibrating brake pedal. This could be caused by:
   a. a loose power steering pump belt.
   b. low power steering fluid level.
   c. Both a and b
   d. Neither a nor b

6. All of the following could cause the brake lights on a car to not work EXCEPT a:
   a. bad ground at sockets.
   b. bad flasher.
   c. bad directional switch.
   d. bad wire.

7. A car with a disc/drum system pulls to the left when braking. This could be caused by:
   a. air bubbles in the left front caliper.
   b. a seized piston in the right caliper.
   c. Both a and b
   d. Neither a nor b

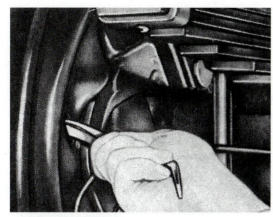

FIGURE 5–2

8. Technician A says that the parking brake is being adjusted in Figure 5–2.

    Technician B says that the star wheel is being turned.

    Who is right?
a. A only
b. B only
c. Both A and B
d. Neither A nor B

9. Before measuring front rotor runout on the spindle of a RWD vehicle, which of these should you do?
a. Check caliper mounts.
b. Check wheel bearing adjustment.
c. Check hub concentricity.
d. Check thickness of brake pads.

10. The primary and secondary shoes are switched at one wheel on the front of a car. This would MOST LIKELY result in a:
a. spongy pedal.
b. pulsating pedal.
c. brake pull.
d. clicking noise.

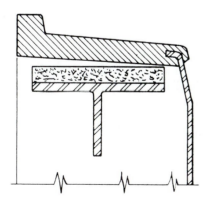

FIGURE 5–3

11. The fit between a drum and a shoe assembly is shown in Figure 5–3.

    Technician A says that this drum is bell-mouthed.

    Technician B says that this fit can cause brake fade.

    Who is right?
a. A only
b. B only
c. Both A and B
d. Neither A nor B

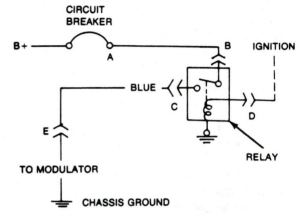

FIGURE 5–4

12. What would be the best way to determine if power is coming out of the anti-lock brake relay in Figure 5–4?
a. Turn on the ignition; disconnect the blue wire at E and touch to ground.
b. Turn on the ignition; hook up a voltmeter (+ to C and − to ground).
c. Hook up a voltmeter (+ to B and − to ground).
d. Hook up an ohmmeter (attach one lead to A and the other to ground).

13. Which of these should be used to clean the bores on wheel cylinders?
a. Cleaning solvent
b. Murphy's oil soap
c. Hot water
d. Isopropyl alcohol

14. A car with a vacuum booster requires too much pedal effort.

    Technician A says that this could be caused by a diaphragm leak.

    Technician B says that this could be caused by a restricted vacuum line.

    Who is right?
a. A only
b. B only
c. Both A and B
d. Neither A nor B

15. With the engine stopped, a technician holds the power brake pedal in the depressed position. When the engine is started (with the pedal still depressed), the pedal sinks slightly. What does this indicate?
   a. A defective control valve
   b. A leaking check valve
   c. A bad reaction disc
   d. A normal operating booster

16. After a new master cylinder is installed, the brakes drag. Which of these would be the MOST LIKELY cause?
   a. Bad master cylinder
   b. Brakes adjusted wrong
   c. Breather port clogged
   d. Pushrod adjusted wrong

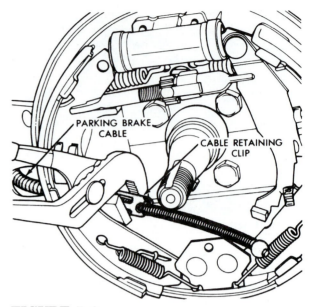

FIGURE 5–6

FIGURE 5–5

17. The special tool in Figure 5–5 is used to:
   a. reset the brake warning light.
   b. hold the metering valve open.
   c. test the proportioning valve.
   d. adjust the bypass valve.

18. The power brake hose on a vehicle collapses when the engine is idling. This could be caused by:
   a. a bad hose.
   b. a bad check valve.
   c. Both a and b
   d. Neither a nor b

19. The tool shown in Figure 5–6 is being used to:
   a. adjust parking brake tension.
   b. install the brake cable.
   c. free up the linkage.
   d. remove the brake cable.

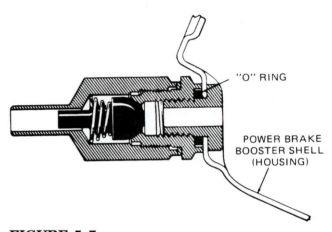

FIGURE 5–7

20. The valve in Figure 5–7:
   a. operates in one direction only.
   b. maintains vacuum in the booster.
   c. Both a and b
   d. Neither a nor b

21. When you apply the brakes hard, a car has a pull which is accompanied by a vibration. Which of the following could cause this condition?
   a. Collapsing strut rod bushings
   b. Incorrect tire pressure
   c. Leaky wheel cylinder
   d. All of the above

22. The brake pedal is spongy on a car with a disc/drum system. This could be caused by:
   a. a missing master cylinder diaphragm.
   b. air in the system.
   c. Both a and b
   d. Neither a nor b

23. A car with floating caliper disc brakes pulls to the right. This could be caused by:
   a. a frozen caliper.
   b. incorrect tire pressure.
   c. Both a and b
   d. Neither a nor b

24. A rotor has excessive thickness variation (parallelism). This would MOST LIKELY cause:
   a. a low pedal.
   b. a "nervous" (pulsating) pedal.
   c. wheel lockup.
   d. air to enter the hydraulic system.

FIGURE 5–8

25. Technician A says that the part in Figure 5–8 is mounted on the primary brake shoe.
   Technician B says that the part is mounted on the secondary brake shoe.
   Who is right?
   a. A only   c. Both A and B
   b. B only   d. Neither A nor B

26. When turning a drum, generally leave at least _____ under the discard size to allow for wear.
   a. .030″   b. .060″   c. .090″   d. .110″

27. Which of these is generally used to check rotor parallelism?
   a. Straightedge
   b. Micrometer
   c. Dial indicator
   d. Special service tool (SST)

28. Any of these could cause a parking brake not to hold EXCEPT:
   a. rear brakes out-of-adjustment.
   b. cables out-of-adjustment.
   c. worn linkage.
   d. fluid leak.

29. The rubber strap wrapped around the brake drum during machining is to:
   a. cool the drum.
   b. shield the operator from flying chips.
   c. prevent drum expansion.
   d. reduce chatter.

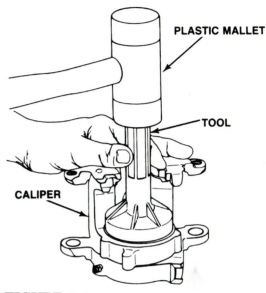

FIGURE 5–9

30. What operation is being performed in Figure 5–9?
   a. Installing square-cut seal
   b. Installing caliper piston
   c. Installing dust boot
   d. None of the above

31. On drum-type brakes, which of the following could cause a rising pedal on successive brake applications?
   a. Insufficient pedal free travel
   b. Master cylinder piston not returning to its stop
   c. Both a and b
   d. Neither a nor b

FIGURE 5–10

32. Identify the item in Figure 5–10.
   a. Disc brake stabilizer plate
   b. Caliper retaining clip
   c. Brake cable equalizer clip
   d. Brake hose lock

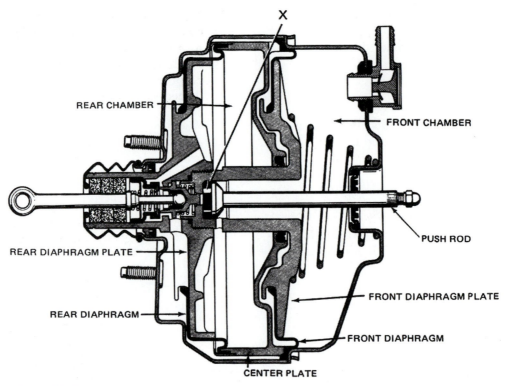

FIGURE 5–11

33. A technician is replacing a master cylinder. The pushrod (see Figure 5–11) is accidently pulled out, causing part X to fall into the bottom of the front chamber. This could cause:
   a. sensitive brakes.
   b. excessive pedal travel.
   c. Both a and b
   d. Neither a nor b

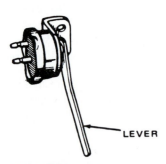

FIGURE 5–12

34. Technician A says that the switch in Figure 5–12 can be tested with a jumper wire.
   Technician B says that the switch above can be tested by grounding either terminal.
   Who is right?
   a. A only   c. Both A and B
   b. B only   d. Neither A nor B

35. A shop does a complete brake job on a car with drum brakes. One week later, the car returns with a low pedal.
   Technician A says that this could be caused by installing the star wheels on the wrong side.
   Technician B says that this could be caused by glazed lining.
   Who is right?
   a. A only
   b. B only
   c. Both A and B
   d. Neither A nor B

36. Which of these can cause the brake warning light to come on?
   a. Shorted light circuit
   b. Worn master cylinder
   c. Leak in brake line
   d. All of the above

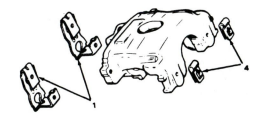

FIGURE 5–13

37. Refer to the disc brake exploded view illustration in Figure 5–13. Which arrow is pointing to the part(s) responsible for the self-adjusting action?
a. #1   **b.** #2   **c.** #3   **d.** #4

38. A car is losing fluid from the master cylinder. There is brake fluid on the bulkhead (firewall).

Technician A says that this could be caused by a defective secondary cup on the primary piston.

Technician B says that this could be caused by a defective primary cup on the secondary piston.

Who is right?
a. A only   **c.** Both A and B
b. B only   **d.** Neither A nor B

39. A car has just had a complete brake job.

Technician A says to make several fast hard stops to seat the linings.

Technician B says that the hotter the brakes, the better the linings will seat.

Who is right?
a. A only   **c.** Both A and B
b. B only   **d.** Neither A nor B

40. The front end of a car dips too much with light braking. Which of these would be the MOST LIKELY cause?
a. Bad master cylinder
b. Bad metering valve
c. Bad proportioning valve
d. Bad vacuum check valve

41. A car with a disc/drum system locks-up during moderate braking. This could be caused by:
a. a bad proportioning valve.
b. a bad pressure differential valve.
c. Both a and b
d. Neither a nor b

42. A car equipped with a disc/drum system has brake pedal pulsation. Lateral rotor runout is okay. This could be caused by:
a. incorrect tightening of the wheel lug nuts.
b. bulging flex-line hoses.
c. sticking m/c secondary piston.
d. installation of pads that are too hard.

FIGURE 5–14

43. The tool in Figure 5–14 is used to:
a. install shoe return springs.
b. remove shoe hold-down springs.
c. Both a and b
d. Neither a nor b

44. A car owner says that fluid drips on the carpet when the brake pedal is depressed. Which of the following is the MOST LIKELY cause?
a. Torn pushrod boot
b. Overfilled master cylinder
c. Leaking piston stop bolt
d. Defective cup

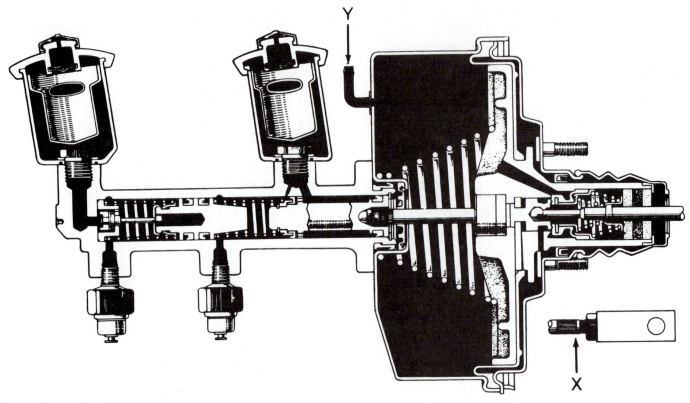

FIGURE 5–15

45. The master cylinder shown in Figure 5–15 must be removed and replaced.

Technician A says to bleed the fluid at point Y.

Technician B says to check the adjustment at point X.

Who is right?

a. A only   **c.** Both A and B
b. B only   **d.** Neither A nor B

46. A car owner says that fluid drips on the carpet when the brake pedal is depressed. Which of the following is the MOST LIKELY cause?

a. Torn booster diaphragm
b. Cracked reservoir
c. Leaking tube seats
d. Defective primary piston

47. The brakes on a vehicle equipped with a height sensing-type "P" valve must be bled.

Technician A says to raise the vehicle and allow the axle to hang down.

Technician B says to disconnect the rear shock absorbers.

Who is right?

a. A only   **c.** Both A and B
b. B only   **d.** Neither A nor B

48. A firm, steady pressure on the brake pedal results in the pedal sinking slowly to the floor. No external fluid leaks can be seen. This could be caused by:

a. a defective master cylinder residual check valve.
b. an internal master cylinder leak.
c. Both a and b
d. Neither a nor b

FIGURE 5–16

49. The brake pedal is low and spongy on a vehicle equipped with the master cylinder in Figure 5–16. This could be caused by:

a. improper bleeding procedure.
b. a faulty quick take-up valve.
c. Both a and b
d. Neither a nor b

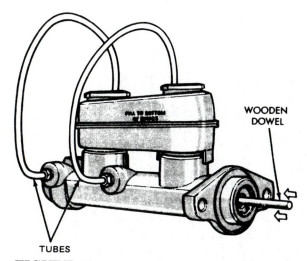

FIGURE 5–17

TUBES

WOODEN DOWEL

50. Refer to Figure 5–17.

Technician A says that both reservoirs must be filled.

Technician B says that depressing the wooden dowel will remove air.

Who is right?

a. A only

b. B only

c. Both A and B

d. Neither A nor B

51. A wheel has cracks running from stud hole to stud hole. This could have been caused by:

a. loose lug nuts.

b. loose studs.

c. Both a and b

d. Neither a nor b

52. Technician A says to use a broom to clean loose dirt from a backing plate.

Technician B says to use compressed air to clean loose dirt from a backing plate.

Who is right?

a. A only

b. B only

c. Both A and B

d. Neither A nor B

53. Technician A says that lug nuts should be final tightened with an impact wrench.

Technician B says that lug nuts should be final tightened in a star pattern.

Who is right?

a. A only

b. B only

c. Both A and B

d. Neither A nor B

54. Brake shoes are being replaced on a car.

Technician A says to lubricate the backing plate ledges (bosses).

Technician B says to groove the backing plate ledges (bosses) to match the shoe arc.

Who is right?

a. A only

b. B only

c. Both A and B

d. Neither A nor B

55. The edgebrand on a brake shoe lining is "R/M 4924-1 FE."

Technician A says that the "R/M" identifies the friction material.

Technician B says that the "FE" is the friction code.

Who is right?

a. A only

b. B only

c. Both A and B

d. Neither A nor B

56. Technician A says to replace the guide pins when rebuilding a caliper.

Technician B says to replace the piston seal when rebuilding a caliper.

Who is right?

a. A only

b. B only

c. Both A and B

d. Neither A nor B

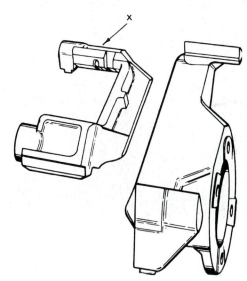

X

FIGURE 5–18

57. The area marked X on the brake part in Figure 5–18 is badly rusted. This could cause:

a. noise when braking.

b. tapered pad wear.

c. Both a and b

d. Neither a nor b

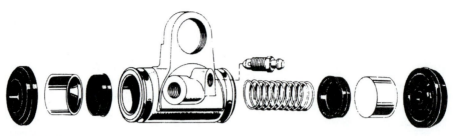

FIGURE 5–19

58. Figure 5–19 shows the layout of a wheel cylinder prior to reassembly. Which part is in the wrong position?
   a. Boot
   b. Expander
   c. Cup
   d. Piston

59. New front disc brake pads are going to be installed on a car.
   Technician A says that some brake fluid should be removed from the master cylinder.
   Technician B says that it may be necessary to bottom the caliper pistons.
   Who is right?
   a. A only
   b. B only
   c. Both A and B
   d. Neither A nor B

60. After new front pads have been installed and the calipers rebuilt, excessive pedal effort is needed to stop. This could be caused by:
   a. the wrong pad material.
   b. air in the system.
   c. Both a and b
   d. Neither a nor b

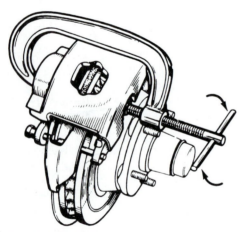

FIGURE 5–20

61. The set up in Figure 5–20 shows the:
   a. pads being seated.
   b. outboard pad being clinched to the caliper.
   c. caliper mounting pin being pressed out.
   d. caliper piston being pushed into its bore.

62. The parking brake cable on a car does not snap to the OFF position when the release is operated. This could be caused by:
   a. a cable bind inside the conduit.
   b. a lack of seepage from the wheel cylinders to lubricate the cable.
   c. Both a and b
   d. Neither a nor b

63. During the teardown phase of a brake job, you discover the front wheel bearings are badly damaged from too much end play. Which brake pedal complaint would this MOST LIKELY have caused?
   a. Spongy
   b. Hard
   c. Rising
   d. Pulsating

FIGURE 5–21

64. The adjustment in Figure 5–21, if incorrect, can cause:
   a. too much pedal travel.
   b. the brakes to drag.
   c. Both a and b
   d. Neither a nor b

65. A car has drum brakes. Which of these conditions is LEAST LIKELY to cause vibration (chatter) during braking?
   a. Incorrect toe and heel clearance
   b. Hard spots on drum
   c. Loose backing plate
   d. Torn wheel cylinder boot

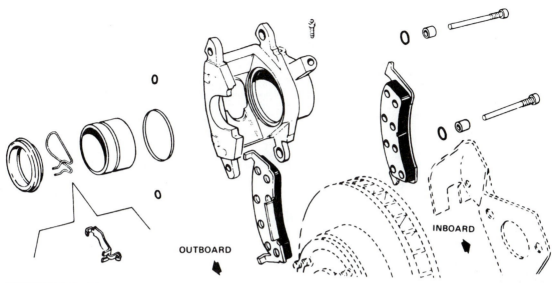

OUTBOARD

INBOARD

FIGURE 5–22

66. A car has the type of disc brake on the front wheels shown in Figure 5–22. The inboard pad is badly worn. The outboard pad shows barely any wear. This can be caused by:
   a. a hard piston seal.
   b. too much rotor runout.
   c. Both a and b
   d. Neither a nor b

67. The brake lights (stop lights) do not work on a car. This could be caused by:
   a. a bad turn signal switch.
   b. a bad ground.
   c. Both a and b
   d. Neither a nor b

68. The brake warning indicator light on a car stays lit while driving. This could be caused by:
   a. a stuck closed parking brake switch.
   b. a bent parking brake pedal mounting bracket.
   c. Both a and b
   d. Neither a nor b

69. Technician A says that an ohmmeter can be used to check continuity in an anti-lock braking system.
   Technician B says that an ohmmeter can be used to check resistance in an anti-lock braking system.
   Who is right?
   a. A only
   b. B only
   c. Both A and B
   d. Neither A nor B

70. A car has brake drag. This can be caused by:
   a. a binding parking brake cable.
   b. a weak parking brake retractor spring.
   c. Both a and b
   d. Neither a nor b

71. A power brake booster has a vacuum leak. All of the following conditions would exist EXCEPT:
   a. pedal pulsation.
   b. rough engine idle.
   c. hissing sound.
   d. hard pedal.

72. Technician A says to adjust brake shoes before adjusting the parking brake.
   Technician B says to hold the brake pedal down when adjusting the parking brake.
   Who is right?
   a. A only
   b. B only
   c. Both A and B
   d. Neither A nor B

73. A set of good brake linings becomes soaked with rear axle lubricant.
   Technician A says that it is okay to wash the lining in solvent and reuse.
   Technician B says that it is okay to dry the lining with an oxy-acetylene torch and reuse.
   Who is right?
   a. A only
   b. B only
   c. Both A and B
   d. Neither A nor B

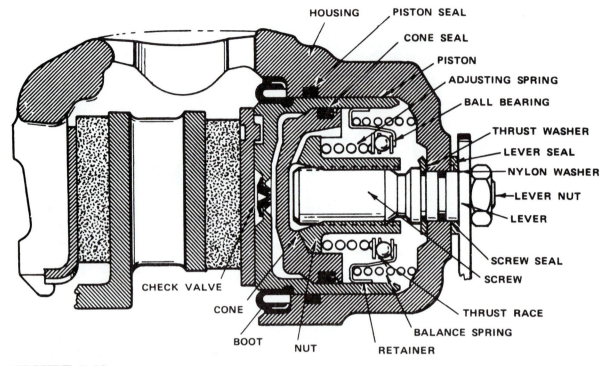

HOUSING   PISTON SEAL
CONE SEAL
PISTON
ADJUSTING SPRING
BALL BEARING
THRUST WASHER
LEVER SEAL
NYLON WASHER
LEVER NUT
LEVER
SCREW SEAL
SCREW
THRUST RACE
BALANCE SPRING
CHECK VALVE
CONE
BOOT   NUT   RETAINER

FIGURE 5-23

74. Refer to the rear disc brake caliper cross-section view shown in Figure 5–23.

Technician A says that the check valve prevents air from entering the piston assembly.

Technician B says that the housing contains an integral parking brake assembly.

Who is right?
a. A only
b. B only
c. Both A and B
d. Neither A nor B

75. A vehicle with the system in Figure 5–24 is losing brake fluid. There is no sign of external leakage. What should a technician do first?
a. Remove the check valve and measure manifold vacuum.
b. Remove the booster vacuum hose and check inside.
c. Check the brake pedal free travel.
d. Check for a dislodged disc inside the booster.

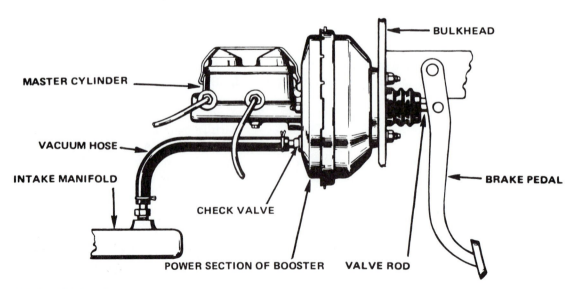

BULKHEAD
MASTER CYLINDER
VACUUM HOSE
INTAKE MANIFOLD
CHECK VALVE
POWER SECTION OF BOOSTER   VALVE ROD
BRAKE PEDAL

FIGURE 5-24

76. On drum brakes, which of the following is the MOST LIKELY cause of a spongy (springy) brake pedal?
   a. Loose wheel cylinder
   b. Air in system
   c. Weak return springs
   d. Self-adjuster not working

77. After both front calipers have been rebuilt, the brake warning light stays on. What must the technician do?
   a. Reset the pressure differential valve.
   b. Adjust pedal free play.
   c. Replace the warning light switch.
   d. Vacuum bleed the master cylinder.

78. Two technicians are discussing the replacement of a wheel bearing race (cup).
   Technician A says to drive in the race using a wooden dowel.
   Technician B says to drive in the race until it is flush with the top of the hub.
   Who is right?
   a. A only   **c.** Both A and B
   b. B only   **d.** Neither A nor B

79. A clean shop rag is used to wipe the old grease off an outer wheel bearing. A lot of shiny silver particles are observed on the rag afterward.
   Technician A says that the bearing needs to be replaced.
   Technician B says that the bearing cup needs to be replaced.
   Who is right?
   a. A only   **c.** Both A and B
   b. B only   **d.** Neither A nor B

80. You are replacing a right front inner wheel bearing that has failed (for the third time in several months). Which of these could be the cause?
   a. Use of the wrong grease
   b. A worn cup
   c. A bad spindle
   d. All of the above

81. The setup in Figure 5–25 is being used to:
   a. remove a frozen piston.
   b. install the boot retainer.
   c. press in a caliper sleeve.
   d. bottom the piston.

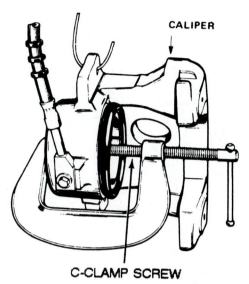

CALIPER

C-CLAMP SCREW

FIGURE 5–25

82. Technician A says that the mechanism in Figure 5–26 is adjusted by bending part X.
   Technician B says that the mechanism is positioned for a right side brake assembly.
   Who is right?
   a. A only   **c.** Both A and B
   b. B only   **d.** Neither A nor B

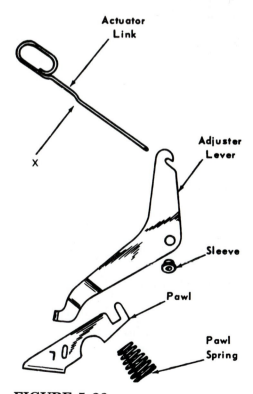

Actuator Link

Adjuster Lever

Sleeve

X

Pawl

Pawl Spring

FIGURE 5–26

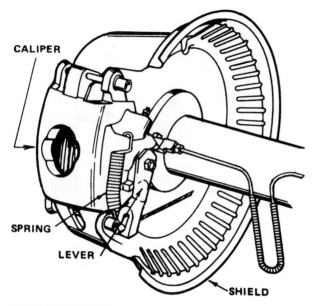

FIGURE 5–27

83. Technician A says that the lever in the assembly in Figure 5–27 applies the parking brake.
   Technician B says that the caliper in the assembly floats.
   Who is right?
   a. A only
   b. B only
   c. Both A and B
   d. Neither A nor B

84. A set of right front (RF) brake linings has become badly contaminated with grease.
   Technician A says to install new linings on the right front (RF) and on the left front (LF).
   Technician B says to inspect the wheel bearings.
   Who is right?
   a. A only
   b. B only
   c. Both A and B
   d. Neither A nor B

85. A cast iron wheel cylinder should generally not be honed more than _____ over the original diameter.
   a. .002″ **b.** .005″ **c.** .010″ **d.** .0005″

86. A car pulls to the right when the brakes are used. This could be caused by:
   a. a bad master cylinder.
   b. a bad proportioning valve.
   c. Both a and b
   d. Neither a nor b

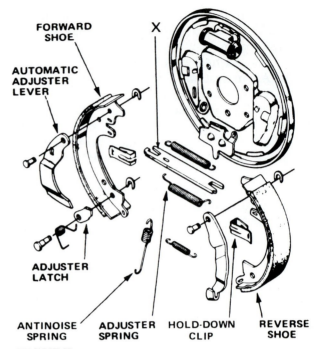

FIGURE 5–28

87. The purpose of part X in Figure 5–28 is to:
   a. center the shoes after each brake application.
   b. balance the force between the shoes during hard braking.
   c. Both a and b
   d. Neither a nor b

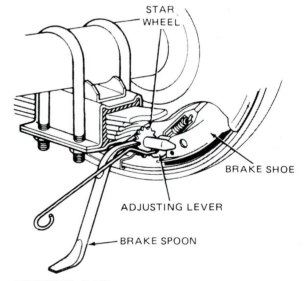

FIGURE 5–29

88. When making the adjustment in Figure 5–29:
   a. spin the tire.
   b. release the parking brake.
   c. Both a and b
   d. Neither a nor b

FIGURE 5-30

89. The part in Figure 5-30:
   a. eliminates the need for a residual pressure check valve.
   b. helps prevent water and dirt contamination.
   c. Both a and b
   d. Neither a nor b

90. The owner of a vehicle with front disc brakes says that the brake pedal pulsates during braking.
   Technician A says that this could be caused by a wheel bearing that is improperly adjusted.
   Technician B says that this could be caused by uneven rotor thickness.
   Who is right?
   a. A only
   b. B only
   c. Both A and B
   d. Neither A nor B

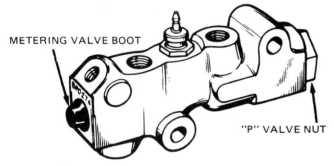

FIGURE 5-31

91. The valve assembly in Figure 5-31:
   a. delays pressure buildup to the front disc brakes.
   b. turns on the brake warning lamp.
   c. Both a and b
   d. Neither a nor b

92. A car pulls to one side when the brakes are applied.
   Technician A says that this could be caused by air in the brake lines.
   Technician B says that this could be caused by kinked brake lines.
   Who is right?
   a. A only
   b. B only
   c. Both A and B
   d. Neither A nor B

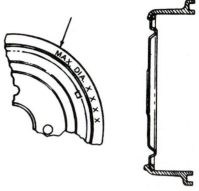

FIGURE 5-32

93. The marking in Figure 5-32 shows:
   a. the maximum outside drum diameter.
   b. the cutting dimension to use when installing new lining.
   c. Both a and b
   d. Neither a nor b

94. A driver complains of a clicking noise when applying the brakes. This could be caused by:
   a. grooved backing plate ledges.
   b. a loose anchor pin.
   c. Both a and b
   d. Neither a nor b

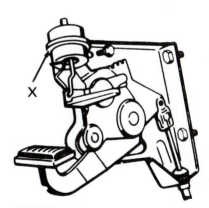

FIGURE 5-33

95. Technician A says that part X in Figure 5-33 applies the parking brake.
   Technician B says that part X releases the parking brake.
   Who is right?
   a. A only
   b. B only
   c. Both A and B
   d. Neither A nor B

96. Technician A says that silicone brake fluid is hygroscopic.

Technician B says that silicone brake fluid will attack and remove paint.

Who is right?

a. A only   **c.** Both A and B

b. B only   **d.** Neither A nor B

97. Which of the following can cause the brake warning light to come on?

a. Shorted light circuit

b. Worn master cylinder

c. Leak in brake line

d. All of the above

98. A master cylinder is being rebuilt.

Technician A says to use solvent to clean parts.

Technician B says to use brake fluid to clean parts. Who is right?

a. A only   **c.** Both A and B

b. B only   **d.** Neither A nor B

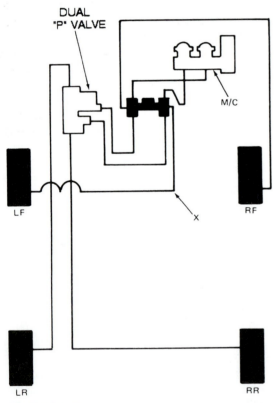

FIGURE 5–34

99. A car is equipped with the hydraulic brake system in Figure 5–34. There is a hole in the line at point X. This will cause a pressure loss at:

a. the RF brake.   **c.** Both a and b

b. the RR brake.   **d.** Neither a nor b

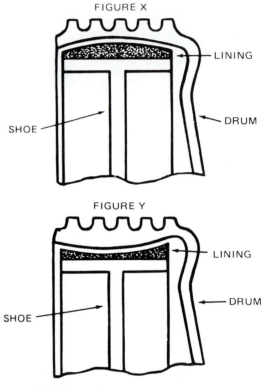

FIGURE 5–35

100. Which figure in Figure 5–35 shows a correct lining-to-drum fit?

a. X only   **c.** Both X and Y

b. Y only   **d.** Neither X nor Y

101. A power brake system needs to be bled.

Technician A says to reuse the old fluid.

Technician B says to maintain vacuum in the booster.

Who is right?

a. A only   **c.** Both A and B

b. B only   **d.** Neither A nor B

102. A car has a disc/drum system. The rear wheels lock up too quickly during hard brake application. Which of these is the MOST LIKELY cause?

a. Plugged compensating port

b. Bad booster unit

c. Trapped air

d. Bad proportioning valve

103. Technician A says that it is normal for a flexible brake hose to bulge a slight amount when the brakes are applied.

Technician B says that whenever a flexible brake hose is replaced, it is common practice to install the next longer size.

Who is right?

a. A only   **c.** Both A and B

b. B only   **d.** Neither A nor B

104. A wheel cylinder needs to be installed on a backing plate that has piston stops.

Technician A says to put on the piston boots after installing the cylinder.

Technician B says to remove the piston stops before installing the cylinder.

Who is right?
a. A only
b. B only
c. Both A and B
d. Neither A nor B

105. After a master cylinder cover is removed, it is observed that the primary reservoir is almost empty of fluid and the secondary reservoir contains too much fluid. This could be caused by:
a. a defective seal in the middle of the cylinder bore.
b. a defective seal on the primary piston.
c. Both a and b
d. Neither a nor b

106. The rear brakes grab (lock up) on a car. This could be caused by:
a. brake fluid on the linings.
b. out-of-round drums.
c. Both a and b
d. Neither a nor b

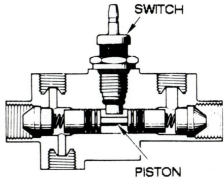

FIGURE 5–36

107. The piston in Figure 5–36:
a. may move during bleeding, but will recenter itself.
b. causes a ground circuit to be completed.
c. Both a and b
d. Neither a nor b

108. A new master cylinder (see Figure 5–37) has just been installed on a vehicle.

Technician A says to lubricate the piston assemblies with engine oil before filling the reservoirs with brake fluid.

Technician B says to watch for a spurt of brake fluid in the front reservoir when the brake pedal is depressed.

Who is right?
a. A only
b. B only
c. Both A and B
d. Neither A nor B

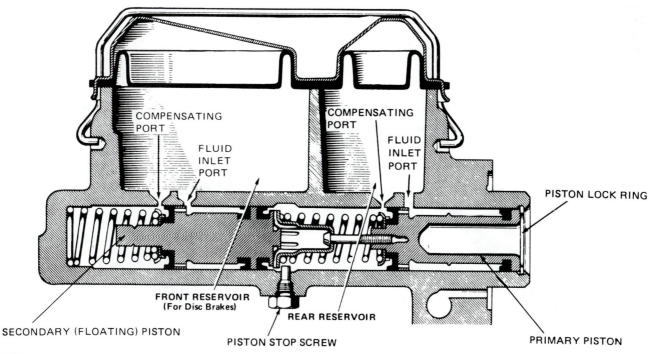

FIGURE 5–37

109. A heavy drag is felt while rotating a rear wheel that has drum brakes. This could be caused by:
   a. grooves in the backing plate.
   b. a broken shoe return spring.
   c. Both a and b
   d. Neither a nor b

110. On a vehicle with front disc brakes, violent cornering or rough roads may cause:
   a. excessive pedal travel.
   b. a drop in fluid pressure.
   c. Both a and b
   d. Neither a nor b

111. Which of these would be the Ra surface finish generally desired for a disc brake rotor?
   a. 80 to 100
   b. 15 to 80
   c. 0 to 15
   d. 100 to 240

112. A Bendix self-adjusting brake is being assembled.
   Technician A says to lubricate the retracting spring coils.
   Technician B says to lubricate the anchor pin.
   Who is right?
   a. A only
   b. B only
   c. Both A and B
   d. Neither A nor B

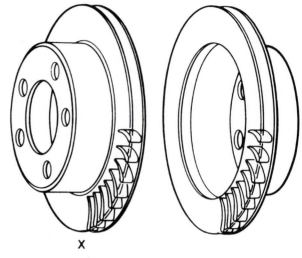

X

FIGURE 5–38

113. Technician A says that the type of rotors in Figure 5–38 SHOULD NOT be machined.
   Technician B says that rotor X is for a left wheel.
   Who is right?
   a. A only
   b. B only
   c. Both A and B
   d. Neither A nor B

114. The tool in Figure 5–39 checks:
   a. drum out-of-roundness.
   b. drum diameter.
   c. Both a and b
   d. Neither a nor b

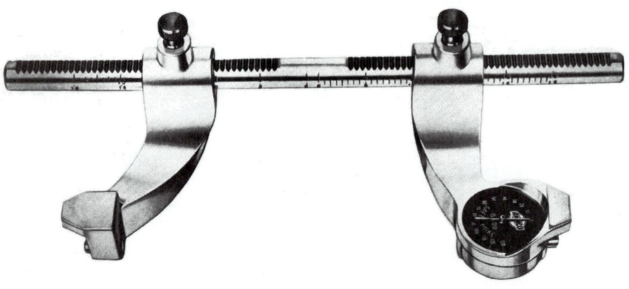

FIGURE 5–39

115. Which of the following front wheel bearing settings would you consider MOST NORMAL for a rear wheel drive car equipped with front disc brakes?
a. 12 inch lbs.—back off one flat
b. 90 foot lbs.—back off one flat
c. .000″–.004″ end play
d. .010″–.020″ end play

116. Technician A says that vibration should be dampened when machining a rotor.
Technician B says that a rotor should be swirl finished after machining.
Who is right?
a. A only   c. Both A and B
b. B only   d. Neither A nor B

117. When taking a caliper apart, a technician notices that the piston is pitted and the bore slightly rusted. What should be done?
a. Replace the piston and the caliper.
b. Crocus cloth the piston and replace the caliper.
c. Bore out the caliper and install a new oversize piston.
d. Crocus cloth the caliper bore and replace the piston.

118. Before installing new front disc pads, a technician removes some brake fluid from the master cylinder. This will:
a. permit gravity bleeding of the calipers.
b. allow front and rear fluid pressure to equalize.
c. prevent fluid overflow.
d. prevent the brake warning light from coming on.

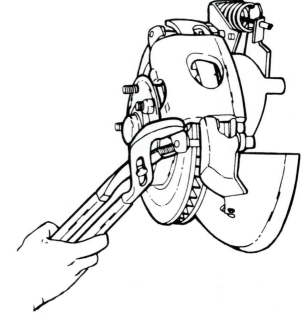

FIGURE 5–40

119. What is being done in Figure 5–40?
a. Locating the positioners
b. Crimping the outer shoe ears
c. Seating the guide pins
d. Removing the shoe clips

120. Adjustment of the parking brake mechanism in Figure 5–41 is made at point:
a. #1.   b. #2.   c. #3.   d. #4.

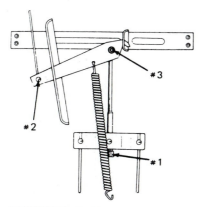

FIGURE 5–41

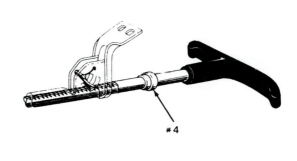

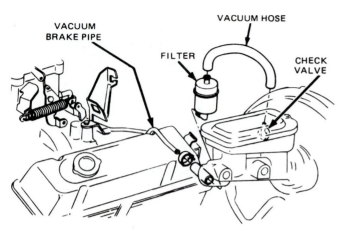

FIGURE 5–42

121. What is the purpose of the filter in Figure 5–42?
a. Increase vacuum level to the brake booster
b. Prevent fuel vapors from collecting in the brake booster
c. Both a and b
d. Neither a nor b

122. In a diagonal split brake system:
a. the left-front and right-rear brakes are connected.
b. two proportioners are used.
c. Both a and b
d. Neither a nor b

123. Technician A says that brake drum hard spots can be removed by machining the drum with a carbide tool bit.

Technician B says that brake drum hard spots can be removed by grinding the drum. However, they may reappear when heat is applied.

Who is right?
a. A only
b. B only
c. Both A and B
d. Neither A nor B

124. The brakes on a car heat up during driving and fail to release. This could be caused by:
a. the metering valve being incorrectly installed.
b. the stop light switch being improperly adjusted.
c. Both a and b
d. Neither a nor b

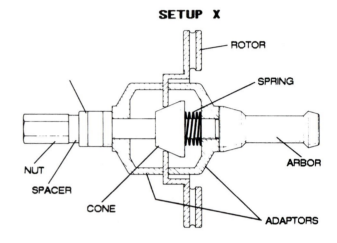

SETUP X

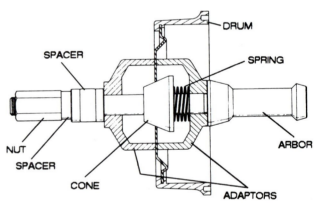

SETUP Y

FIGURE 5–43

125. Refer to the brake lathe mounting setups in Figure 5–43.

Technician A says that setup X is incorrect.
Technician B says that setup Y is incorrect.
Who is right?
a. A only
b. B only
c. Both A and B
d. Neither A nor B

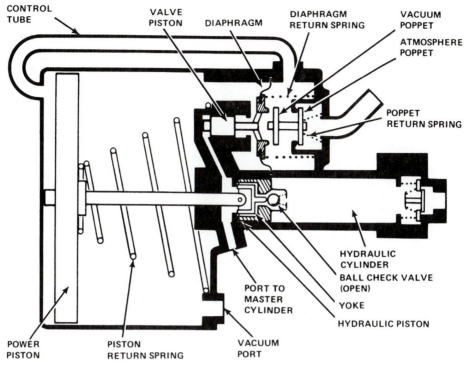

FIGURE 5–44

126. The power brake booster in Figure 5–44 is:
    a. "slaved" to the vehicle master cylinder.
    b. a pressure multiplier.
    c. Both a and b
    d. Neither a nor b

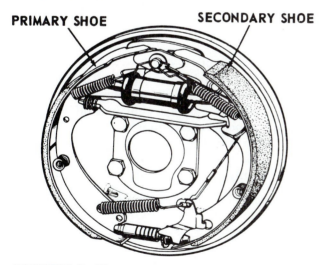

FIGURE 5–45

127. Refer to Figure 5–45.
    Technician A says that a front brake assembly is shown.
    Technician B says that a right side brake assembly is shown.
    Who is right?
    a. A only   **c.** Both A and B
    b. B only   **d.** Neither A nor B

128. When checking disc brake rotor runout:
    a. use a ruler.
    b. use a micrometer.
    c. remove the caliper from the steering knuckle.
    d. readjust wheel bearings when finished.

129. The vent on a master cylinder reservoir cover becomes plugged. This can cause:
    a. the brakes to drag.
    b. a spongy brake pedal.
    c. Both a and b
    d. Neither a nor b

130. Too much pedal effort is required to stop a vehicle with power disc brakes. This could be caused by:
    a. air in the hydraulic system.
    b. a master cylinder not working properly.
    c. Both a and b
    d. Neither a nor b

131. On a wet highway, what prevents the front disc brakes from locking up at light pedal pressure before the rear drum brakes develop enough stopping force?
    a. Proportioning valve
    b. Residual valve
    c. Quick take-up valve
    d. None of the above

132. The disc brake reservoir portion of a dual master cylinder is low on fluid. This could be caused by:
    a. worn front pads.
    b. a faulty power brake booster.
    c. Both a and b
    d. Neither a nor b

FIG. 1

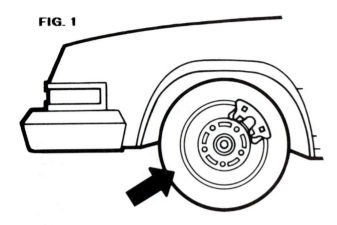

FIG. 2

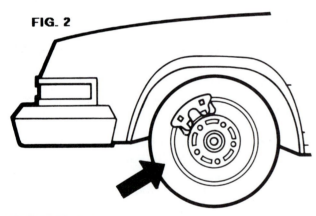

FIGURE 5–46

133. Technician A says that front calipers are mounted as shown in Figure 1 in Figure 5–46.
    Technician B says that front calipers are mounted as shown in Figure 2.
    Who is right?
    a. A only
    b. B only
    c. Both A and B
    d. Neither A nor B

134. Which of the following pressure ranges is generally used when bleeding the brakes with a pressure tank?
    a. 2 to 8 psi
    b. 15 to 30 psi
    c. 40 to 65 psi
    d. 60 to 80 psi

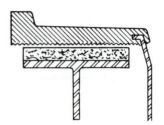

FIGURE 5–47

135. The brake drum in Figure 5–47 was turned at too fast a feed. This condition will MOST LIKELY cause:
    a. low-speed squeal.
    b. a snapping noise as brakes are released.
    c. vibration.
    d. fade.

136. Drum brake fade can be caused by:
    a. glazed lining.
    b. bell-mouthed drums.
    c. Both a and b
    d. Neither a nor b

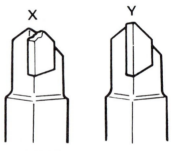

FIGURE 5–48

137. Refer to Figure 5–48.
    Technician A says that tool bit X is sharp and ground to the correct shape.
    Technician B says that tool bit Y will produce a poor surface finish.
    Who is right?
    a. A only
    b. B only
    c. Both A and B
    d. Neither A nor B

138. On-vehicle rotor turning equipment is often used to:
    a. compensate for stacked tolerances that can cause runout.
    b. help eliminate brake pulsation.
    c. Both a and b
    d. Neither a nor b

139. Swollen cups in a master cylinder could be caused by:
    a. solvent contamination.
    b. water contamination.
    c. Both a and b
    d. Neither a nor b

140. Problem: You have assembled a Bendix-type brake with a cable self-adjusting mechanism. You notice that the adjusting lever is below the centerline of the star wheel adjuster. Which of these could be the cause?
    a. The cable guide is not firmly seated against the primary shoe.
    b. The cable is stretched.
    c. Both a and b
    d. Neither a nor b

141. After a car with disc/drum brakes sits overnight, the pedal is low for the first stop in the morning. The rest of the day, the brakes are okay.
    Technician A says that this could be caused by low brake fluid level.
    Technician B says that this could be caused by a leaking residual valve.
    Who is right?
    a. A only   c. Both A and B
    b. B only   d. Neither A nor B

142. A hydraulic brake system pedal goes to the floor.
    Technician A says that this could be caused by out-of-adjustment shoes.
    Technician B says this could be caused by an out-of-adjustment master cylinder pushrod.
    Who is right?
    a. A only   c. Both A and B
    b. B only   d. Neither A nor B

143. The driver of a car with power brakes says that braking is fine during normal stops. However, the pedal becomes very hard during severe stops.
    Technician A says that this could be caused by a restricted vacuum hose.
    Technician B says that this could be caused by a dislodged reaction disc.
    Who is right?
    a. A only
    b. B only
    c. Both A and B
    d. Neither A nor B

144. When replacing a hydraulic brake line, which of these is correct?
    a. Use copper tubing with double-flared ends.
    b. Use seamless steel tubing with compression sleeves.
    c. Both a and b
    d. Neither a nor b

145. Some cars with front disc brakes use a metering valve. When bleeding this type of system:
    a. a pressure tank must be used.
    b. the metering valve plunger must be pushed to the closed position.
    c. Both a and b
    d. Neither a nor b

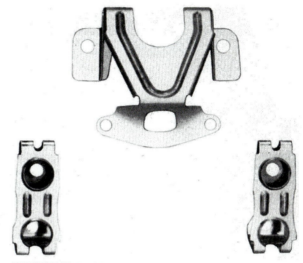

FIGURE 5–49

146. The parts in Figure 5–49 are defective. This can cause:
    a. brake pull.
    b. excessive up-and-down caliper movement on bumpy roads.
    c. Both a and b
    d. Neither a nor b

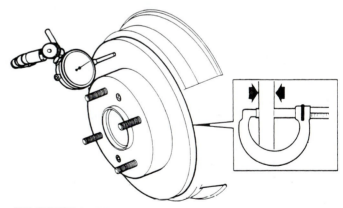

FIGURE 5–50

147. When making the checks in Figure 5–50, which of these readings would be considered as maximum allowable for most car applications?
    a. .010″   c. .030″
    b. .020″   d. None of these

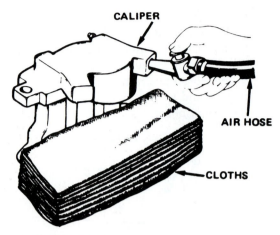

FIGURE 5–51

148. The procedure in Figure 5–51 shows the:
  a. caliper-to-piston bore clearance being checked.
  b. piston being removed.
  c. dust boot being checked for leakage.
  d. square-cut seal being checked for wear.

FIGURE 5–52

149. The hardware part in Figure 5–52 is designed to:
  a. keep the secondary shoe from vibrating.
  b. keep the primary shoe from vibrating.
  c. reduce parking brake strut rattle and vibration.
  d. reduce parking brake lever rattle and vibration.

150. The figure .0005″ is the dimension commonly used for maximum:
  a. rotor lateral runout.
  b. rotor parallelism.
  c. rotor radial runout.
  d. caliper bore wear.

151. On a disc/drum brake system, which of the following would MOST LIKELY cause a pulsating brake pedal?
  a. Leaking wheel cylinder
  b. Glazed linings
  c. Plugged master cylinder port
  d. Parking brake set while the drums are hot

152. Disc brakes generally use no residual pressure check valve. This is because:
  a. disc brakes use a metering valve.
  b. disc brakes use a proportioning valve.
  c. residual pressure would cause rotor drag.
  d. residual pressure would delay pad application.

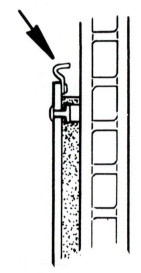

FIGURE 5–53

153. The arrow in Figure 5–53 is pointing to:
  a. an anti-rattle clip.
  b. a stabilizer.
  c. an anchor plate.
  d. a wear indicator.

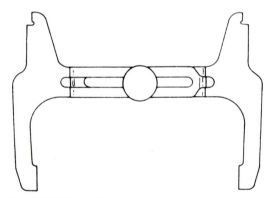

FIGURE 5–54

154. Technician A says that the tool in Figure 5–54 sets lining-to-drum clearance.
  Technician B says that the tool sets toe and heel clearance.
  Who is right?
  a. A only
  b. B only
  c. Both A and B
  d. Neither A nor B

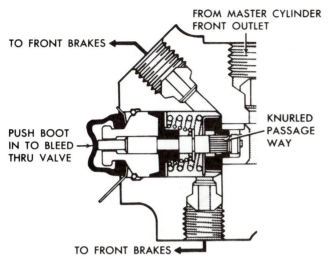

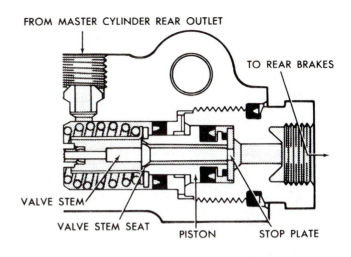

FIGURE 5–55

155. The illustrations in Figure 5–55 show:
  a. two types of "P" valves.
  b. two types of metering valves.
  c. a "P" valve and a metering valve.
  d. Neither a "P" valve nor a metering valve.

156. Which of these methods can be used to prove that the master cylinder compensating ports are open?
  a. Bleed wheel cylinder located closest to the master cylinder and observe fluid squirt.
  b. Remove master cylinder cover, jab the brake pedal, and observe fluid squirt.
  c. Both a and b
  d. Neither a nor b

157. Technician A says that a proportioning valve reduces pressure to the front brakes.
  Technician B says that a proportioning valve delays pressure application to the rear brakes.
  Who is right?
  a. A only   **c.** Both A and B
  b. B only   **d.** Neither A nor B

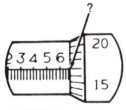

FIGURE 5–56

158. What is the micrometer reading shown in Figure 5–56?
  a. .647″   **c.** .698″
  b. .683″   **d.** None of the above

159. The valve in Figure 5–57 is part of the brake system on a light truck.
  Technician A says that this valve helps to reduce the chance of rear wheel lock-up.
  Technician B says that this valve must be disconnected from its linkage when adjusting the rear shoes.
  Who is right?
  a. A only
  b. B only
  c. Both A and B
  d. Neither A nor B

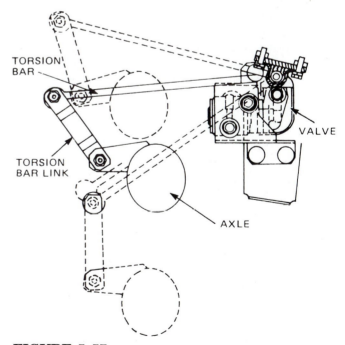

FIGURE 5–57

160. The brake warning light on a car does not work. This could be caused by all of the following EXCEPT:
  a. a bad bulb socket.
  b. open wiring.
  c. defective pressure differential valve.
  d. a defective metering valve.

161. A car is equipped with wheels that have built-in directional vanes.

Technician A says that the vanes are designed to pump air past the brakes.

Technician B says that switching such wheels from left to right can cause overheated brakes.

Who is right?
  a. A only
  b. B only
  c. Both A and B
  d. Neither A nor B

162. Technician A says that cars equipped with ABS generally have an amber brake light on the instrument panel.

Technician B says that cars equipped with ABS generally measure wheel speed using electronic sensors.

Who is right?
  a. A only
  b. B only
  c. Both A and B
  d. Neither A nor B

163. The brake warning indicator light in the circuit in Figure 5–58 stays on when the parking brake is fully released.

Technician A says that this could be caused by a poorly grounded brake pressure switch.

Technician B says that this could be caused by a bad 20 amp gauge fuse.

Who is right?
  a. A only
  b. B only
  c. Both A and B
  d. Neither A nor B

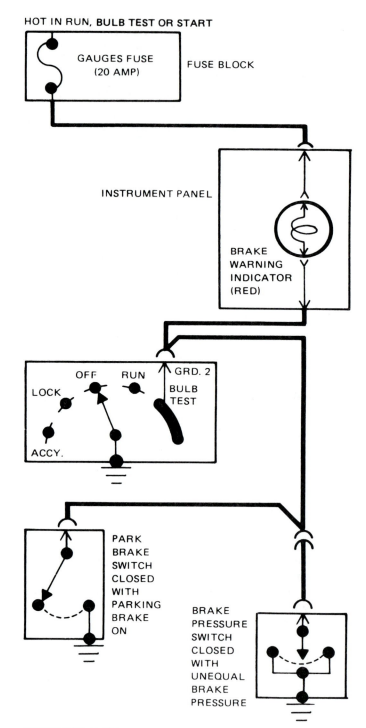

FIGURE 5–58

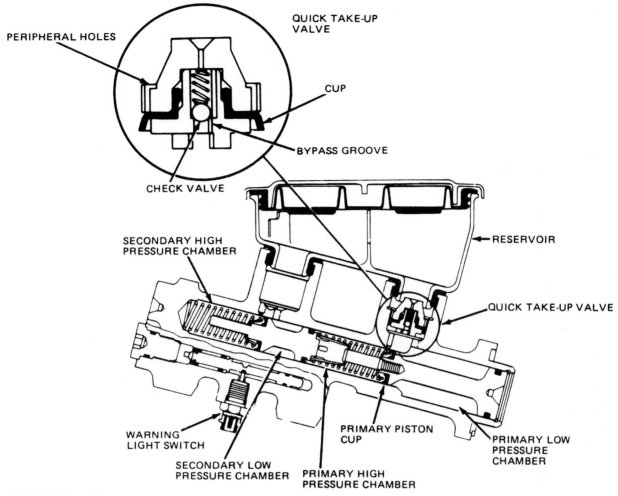

FIGURE 5–59

164. Refer to Figure 5–59.

Technician A says that this is a step bore master cylinder.

Technician B says that a higher pressure will be produced in the secondary section than in the primary section.

Who is right?

a. A only

b. B only

c. Both A and B

d. Neither A nor B

165. Two brake lines are pictured in Figure 5–60.

Technician A says that brake line X is ISO flared.

Technician B says that brake line Y is double flared.

Who is right?

a. A only   **c.** Both A and B

b. B only   **d.** Neither A nor B

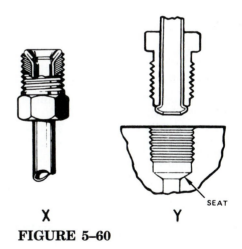

FIGURE 5–60

166. An anti-lock brake system controller determines wheel lock-up by:

a. pressure build-up in the brake lines.

b. signals from the wheel sensors.

c. input from the vacuum sensor on the engine.

d. All of the above

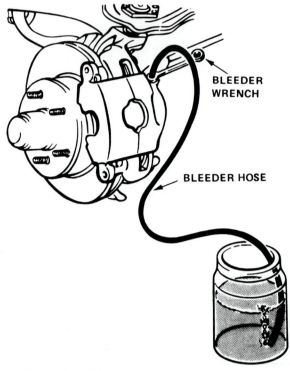

FIGURE 5–61

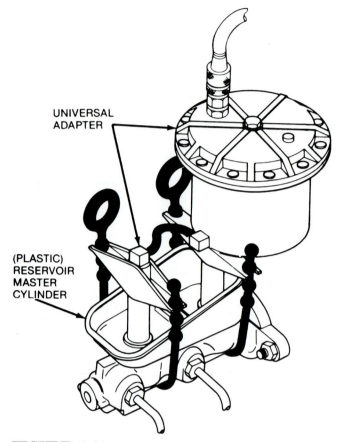

FIGURE 5–62

167. The procedure in Figure 5–61 is being performed on a car.

Technician A says to open the bleeder screw at least one full turn.

Technician B says to keep the hose end submerged in fluid.

Who is right?

a. A only
b. B only
c. Both A and B
d. Neither A nor B

168. An aluminum bore master cylinder is badly pitted. What should be done?

a. Install a new liner.
b. Wipe and install new rubber.
c. Hone and rebuild it.
d. Replace it.

169. The pedal pulsates during hard braking on a car equipped with an anti-lock system. This is MOST LIKELY an indication of:

a. an out-of-round drum.
b. a warped rotor.
c. a bad actuator.
d. normal system function.

170. When using the equipment in Figure 5–62:

a. make sure the pressure tank contains no fluid.
b. make sure the pressure in the tank is no less than 100 psi.
c. Both a and b
d. Neither a nor b

171. Technician A says that before performing system service on an anti-lock system, pump the pedal at least 20 times.

Technician B says that before performing system service on an anti-lock system, turn the ignition off.

Who is right?

a. A only   **c.** Both A and B
b. B only   **d.** Neither A nor B

172. Low brake fluid level in an anti-lock system can cause:

a. a warning light to come on.
b. the controller to shut down the anti-lock function.
c. Both a and b
d. Neither a nor b

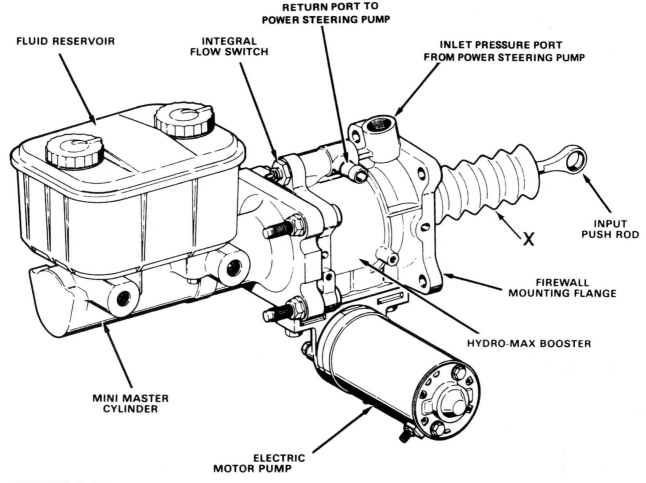

FLUID RESERVOIR

INTEGRAL FLOW SWITCH

RETURN PORT TO POWER STEERING PUMP

INLET PRESSURE PORT FROM POWER STEERING PUMP

INPUT PUSH ROD

X

FIREWALL MOUNTING FLANGE

HYDRO-MAX BOOSTER

MINI MASTER CYLINDER

ELECTRIC MOTOR PUMP

FIGURE 5–63

173. A Hydro-Max brake booster is shown in Figure 5–63.

Technician A says that part X provides the driver "pedal feel" during application of the brake pedal.

Technician B says that the electric motor provides power for reserve stops if the engine quits running.

Who is right?
a. A only   c. Both A and B
b. B only   d. Neither A nor B

174. A vehicle equipped with anti-lock brakes is being cranked.

Technician A says that the amber light should be off.

Technician B says that the red light should be on.

Who is right?
a. A only   c. Both A and B
b. B only   d. Neither A nor B

175. The amber anti-lock light comes on while driving.

Technician A says to replace the wheel sensors.

Technician B says to replace the electronic controller.

Who is right?
a. A only   c. Both A and B
b. B only   d. Neither A nor B

176. You've removed the first piston and boot from a 2-piston caliper. The second piston stayed in place. What is the best method for getting it out?
a. Slightly heat the caliper with a torch until the piston is loose.
b. Pry the piston out with a screwdriver.
c. Insert a slide hammer into the center of the piston and pull it out.
d. Reinsert the first piston with a suitable spacer, then apply compressed air.

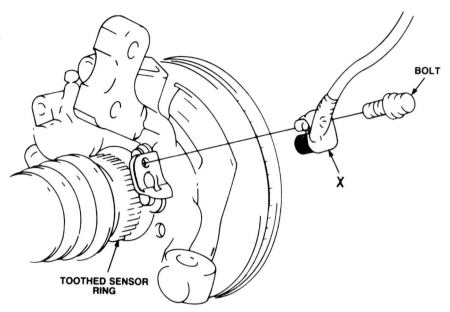

FIGURE 5–64

177. See component X pictured in Figure 5–64.

Technician A says that component X sends out an electrical signal.

Technician B says that component X may have an adjustable air gap.

Who is right?

a. A only   **c.** Both A and B
b. B only   **d.** Neither A nor B

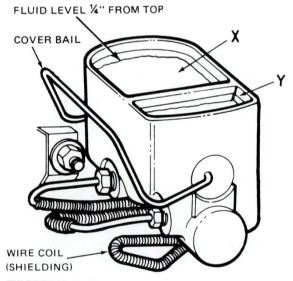

FIGURE 5–65

178. A master cylinder is shown in Figure 5–65.

Technician A says that arrow X points to the drum brake reservoir.

Technician B says that reservoir Y should be filled completely to the top.

Who is right?

a. A only   **c.** Both A and B
b. B only   **d.** Neither A nor B

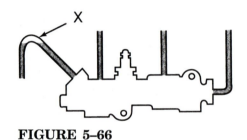

FIGURE 5–66

179. Brake line blockage is shown at point X in Figure 5–66.

Technician A says that the rear brakes will not work.

Technician B says that this will cause a hard pedal.

Who is right?

a. A only   **c.** Both A and B
b. B only   **d.** Neither A nor B

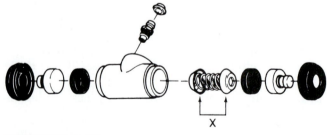

FIGURE 5–67

180. What is the purpose of part X in Figure 5–67?

a. To keep cup sealing lips in constant contact with the cylinder bore
b. To prevent air from entering past the cups
c. Both a and b
d. Neither a nor b

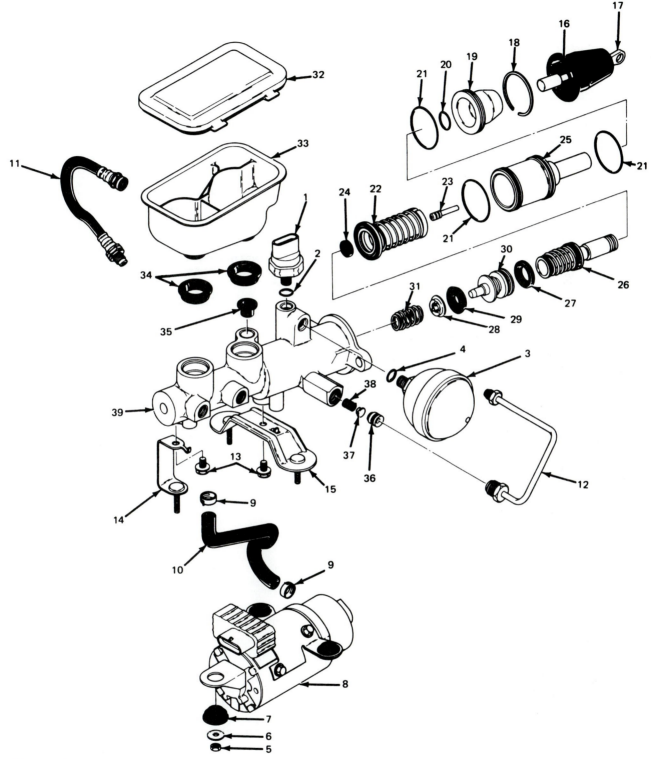

FIGURE 5–68

181. A power brake apply system is illustrated in Figure 5–68.

Technician A says that part 1 activates part 8.

Technician B says that pressure from part 3 acts on part 25.

Who is right?
a. A only
b. B only
c. Both A and B
d. Neither A nor B

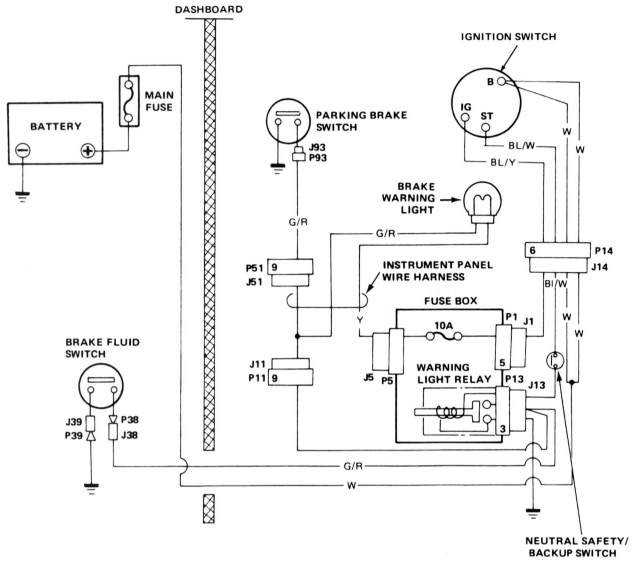

FIGURE 5–69

182. The brake warning lamp in the system in Figure 5–69 stays on while driving.

   Technician A says that this could be caused by a blown main fuse.

   Technician B says that this could be caused by the brake fluid level being too low.

   Who is right?

   a. A only
   b. B only
   c. Both A and B
   d. Neither A nor B

183. The red "brake" lamp and "anti-lock disabled" message is displayed on every brake application on a car equipped with ABS.

   Technician A says that this could be caused by cut accumulator seals.

   Technician B says that this could be caused by loss of accumulator pre-charge.

   Who is right?

   a. A only
   b. B only
   c. Both A and B
   d. Neither A nor B

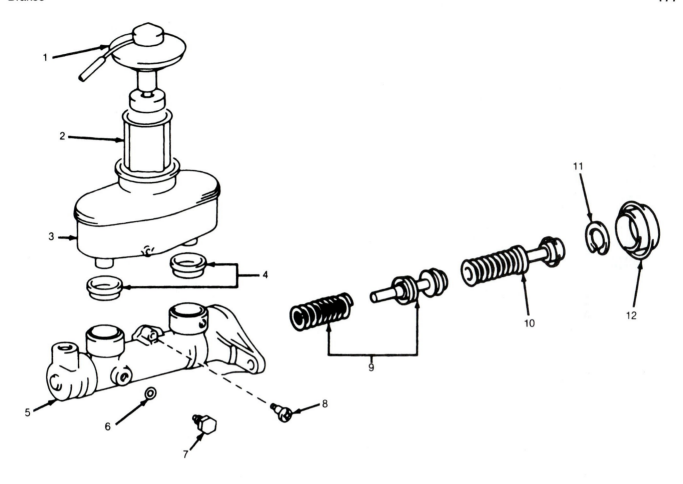

1. CAP
2. STRAINER
3. RESERVOIR
4. GROMMET

5. CYLINDER BODY
6. GASKET
7. STOPPER BOLT
8. SCREW

9. SECONDARY PISTON AND SPRING
10. PRIMARY PISTON AND SPRING
11. SNAP RING
12. BOOT

FIGURE 5–70

184. Refer to the exploded-view picture in Figure 5–70.

Technician A says that the cap assembly contains a reed switch.

Technician B says that the secondary piston is positioned backwards.

Who is right?

a. A only
b. B only
c. Both A and B
d. Neither A nor B

185. The setup in Figure 5–71 is used to:
a. produce a directional finish.
b. deglaze.
c. eliminate pedal pulsation.
d. correct parallelism.

FIGURE 5–71

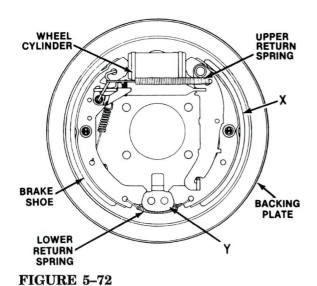

FIGURE 5–72

186. A leading/trailing shoe brake is shown in Figure 5–72.

Technician A says that brake shoe X faces towards the front of the car.

Technician B says that anchor Y is stationary.

Who is right?

a. A only
b. B only
c. Both A and B
d. Neither A nor B

187. A "ticking" noise can be heard when turning a brake drum.

Technician A says that the chatter band probably needs repositioning.

Technician B says that the drum probably has hard spots.

Who is right?

a. A only
b. B only
c. Both A and B
d. Neither A nor B

188. Technician A says that disconnecting ABS components with the ignition key on can cause damage.

Technician B says that arc welding on a vehicle equipped with ABS can cause damage.

Who is right?

a. A only
b. B only
c. Both A and B
d. Neither A nor B

189. Refer to the ABS layout in Figure 5–73.

Technician A says that part 5 cycles part 2.

Technician B says that part 4 sends an analog signal to part 5.

Who is right?

a. A only   c. Both A and B
b. B only   d. Neither A nor B

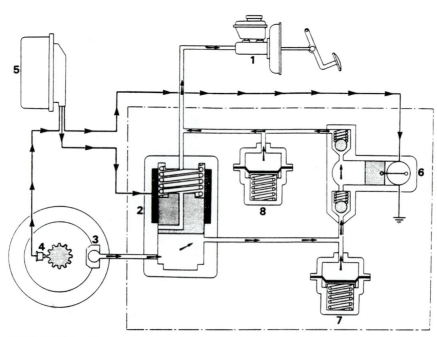

FIGURE 5–73

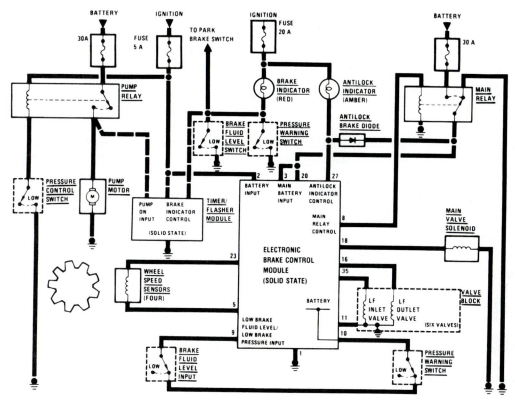

FIGURE 5–74

190. Study the anti-lock brake system (ABS) electrical schematic shown in Figure 5–74. The electric pump motor that supplies operating pressure to the system is controlled by the:
   a. main relay.
   b. pressure control switch.
   c. control module.
   d. park brake switch.

191. The amber ABS warning light comes on as a car is being driven.
   Technician A says that a faulty wheel bearing can cause this problem.
   Technician B says that mismatched tire size can cause this problem.
   Who is right?
   a. A only   c. Both A and B
   b. B only   d. Neither A nor B

192. Technician A says that sealed ball bearings are used for the front wheel bearings on FWD vehicles.
   Technician B says that sealed roller bearings are used.
   Who is right?
   a. A only   c. Both A and B
   b. B only   d. Neither A nor B

193. Technician A says to use a new hub nut when replacing a nonserviceable FWD front wheel bearing.
   Technician B says to use a new cotter pin when replacing a RWD front wheel bearing.
   Who is right?
   a. A only
   b. B only
   c. Both A and B
   d. Neither A nor B

194. A RWD vehicle equipped with a disc/drum brake system shows uneven pad wear on one side. The inboard pad is worn to 9/16″ thickness and the outboard pad is worn to 1/32″ thickness.
   Technician A says that this could be caused by a hard square-cut seal.
   Technician B says that this could be caused by rusty slides.
   Who is right?
   a. A only
   b. B only
   c. Both A and B
   d. Neither A nor B

195. What is the correct type of brake fluid to use in the majority of vehicles equipped with ABS?
a. DOT 3
b. DOT 4
c. Either DOT 3 or DOT 4
d. DOT 5

196. Technician A says that when fabricating brake pipes, cut pipe to length using a fine toothed saw.

Technician B says that when fabricating brake pipes, install fittings on the pipe before starting flare.

Who is right?
a. A only
b. B only
c. Both A and B
d. Neither A nor B

197. Semimetallic disc brake pads are being installed on a vehicle.

Technician A says to turn the rotors with a slow cross feed rate of .002″ per revolution.

Technician B says to break in the pads by making 20–25 hard stops.

Who is right?
a. A only
b. B only
c. Both A and B
d. Neither A nor B

198. Always refinish a rotor when:
a. replacing pads.
b. the customer complains of a hard pedal.
c. the customer complains of a brake "squeal."
d. None of the above

199. A diagonal split hydraulic brake system:
a. requires a combination valve.
b. is limited to truck applications.
c. is normally utilized on RWD vehicles.
d. is normally utilized on FWD vehicles.

200. In order to measure rotor thickness variation:
a. tighten wheel bearings to take out any free play.
b. measure at six or more points, equally spaced around the rotor.
c. mount a dial indicator to a fixed part of the suspension.
d. All of the above

Section 6

ELECTRICAL/ELECTRONIC SYSTEMS

STUDY OUTLINE

I. Types of Circuits (Understand Voltage, Amperage, and Resistance Relationships in Each)
   A. Series
   B. Parallel
   C. Series-parallel

II. Circuit Devices/Symbols
   A. Fuses
   B. Circuit Breakers
   C. Fusible Links
   D. Relays
   E. Switches
   F. Solenoids
   G. Diodes (Include Zener-Type and LEDs)
   H. Transistors (NPN and PNP)
   I. Motors
   J. Lamps
   K. Resistors
   L. Ground
   M. Battery
   N. Connections (Male and Female)

III. Circuit Test Equipment and Hook-Up (Know How to Read the Different Scales on Meters)
   A. Voltmeter
   B. Ammeter
   C. Ohmmeter
   D. 12-Volt Test Light and Logic Probe
   E. Self-Powered Test Light
   F. Short Detectors (Buzzers and Circuit Breakers)
   G. Jumper Wires
   H. High Impedance DVOM

IV. Circuit Testing (You Will Be Asked to Use Schematics in Locating Diagnosis Test Points)
   A. Shorted Circuit
   B. Open Circuit
   C. Grounded Circuit
   D. Intermittent Circuit Problems
   E. Voltage Drops
   F. Truth Table Interpretation

V. Lighting Systems (Understand the Typical Operation for Each Circuit)
   A. Headlight Circuit
      1. High beam lamps
      2. Low beam lamps
      3. Dimmer switch
      4. Switch rheostat
      5. Wiring
      6. Test, aim, and replace headlights
   B. Stop Lamp Circuit
      1. Adjust stop light switch
      2. Test stop light portion of turn signal switch
   C. Directional Signal Circuit
      1. Flasher types
      2. Switch replacement
      3. Flashing speed
   D. Hazard Warning Lights
   E. Tail Lamp Circuit
   F. Back-Up Lamp Circuit
   G. Instrument Panel Displays and Interior Lights
      1. Printed circuit boards/connectors/wires
   H. Problem/Diagnosis
      1. Intermittent, dim, or no headlight operation
      2. No dash light brightness control
      3. No flash on one or both sides
      4. No hazard flasher lights
      5. Brighter than normal lights
      6. No back-up lights
      7. No tail lamps
      8. No stop lamps

VI. Accessory Systems
   A. Basic Theory of Operation for Each Component/Circuit
   B. Basic Troubleshooting Procedures (Including Printed Circuits)
      1. Oil sending unit
      2. Fuel gauge and tank sending unit
      3. Temperature warning
      4. Horns
      5. Constant voltage regulator for dash instruments
      6. Buzzer/relays/timers
      7. Air bags
      8. Wiper/washer circuit

9. Power side window
10. Power tailgate
11. Power seat circuit
12. Electric door locks
13. Defogger switches, grid, and blower motors
14. Radio power circuit
15. Radio speaker and antenna (trim procedure)
16. Cruise control cables, regulator, servo, and hoses
17. Clock circuit
18. Cigar lighter circuit
19. Sunroof and convertible top circuits
20. Keyless lock/unlock circuits
21. Anti-theft circuits
22. Electric door lock circuits
23. Miles-to-empty fuel circuit

C. Problem/Diagnosis
1. Slow, intermittent, or no power window operation
2. Radio static
3. Weak, intermittent, or no radio reception
4. Unregulated, intermittent, or no cruise control
5. Constant, intermittent, or no horn operation
6. Wiper speed control and park problems (including pulsating type)
7. No windshield washer operation
8. High, low, or no gauge readings
9. Constant warning buzzer operation
10. Poor rear window defogger operation
11. No power seat operation
12. No power window operation
13. Poor or no electric door lock operation
14. No keyless lock/unlock device operation
15. No electric sunroof or convertible top operation
16. Poor heated mirror operation
17. No clock operation

VII. Battery
A. Safety Procedures
B. Open Flame and Explosion Hazard
C. Removal and Installation Procedure
D. Basic Construction and Chemical Action
E. Sizes and Ratings
F. Testing/Service
1. State of charge (built-in indicator)
2. Cell voltage (light load test)
3. Capacity test
4. Sulphation (3-minute charge test)
5. Battery charging procedure (slow and fast)
6. Clean/fill/replace
7. Jump starting
8. Replace cables and clamps
9. Constant battery drain (including computer draw)
G. Interpretation of Test Results
H. Problem/Diagnosis
1. Corroded connections
2. Leakage (dirt on battery top)

3. No start complaints
4. Slow cranking complaints
5. Excessive water use
6. Discharges overnight (heavy current drain)
7. Damaged plates
I. Storage
1. Dry charge
2. Wet charge
3. Putting into service procedure

VIII. Charging System
A. Basic System Components/Purpose/Operation
1. Diodes
2. Rotor
3. Stator
4. Slip rings
5. Load input to ECM (computer) circuitry
B. Circuit Operation
1. Various system schematics
2. Voltage regulation
3. Current control
4. Light relay
5. Field relay
6. Ammeter circuit (instead of charge indicator light)
C. Test Equipment
1. Voltmeter
2. Ammeter
3. Ohmmeter
4. Quarter Ω resistor/rheostat
5. Knife switch
6. Diode testers
7. Lab scope
D. Test Hook-Up/Interpretation of Results
1. Field circuit (current draw)
2. Rotor tests (shorts, grounds, continuity)
3. Stator tests (shorts, grounds, continuity)
4. Diode tests
5. Output test
6. Voltage regulator setting
7. Insulated and ground circuit tests (voltage drop)
E. Replace Component Parts
1. Brushes/holders
2. Bearings and end frames
3. Diodes (including soldering techniques)
4. Stator
5. Rotor
6. Capacitor
7. Warning light/driver information circuit
8. Rectifier bridge
9. Integral regulator
10. Electro-mechanical regulator
11. Diode trio
F. Problem/Diagnosis
1. Loose belts
2. Open rotor circuit
3. Grounded rotor circuit

4. Defective diode(s)
5. Noises
   a. Bearings
   b. Belts
   c. Mounting
   d. Diode
6. Undercharge conditions
7. No-charge conditions
8. Overcharge conditions
9. Defective regulator
   a. "Full-field" procedure (include precautions)
   b. Fusible links/in-line fuses
   c. Light relay
   d. Integral regulators
G. Alternator Rebuilding Procedures/Tools

IX. Starter (Cranking) System
A. Basic Function
B. Types and Basic Differences
   1. Moveable pole shoe
   2. Permanent magnet types
   3. Gear reduction types
C. Relays and Solenoids
D. Construction and Nomenclature of Parts
E. Starter Drives
   1. Bendix
   2. Overrunning clutch
   3. Inspect and replace
F. Testing/Service
   1. Current draw using BST
   2. Field coil tests (shorts, grounds, continuity)
   3. Armature tests (shorts, grounds, continuity)
      a. Growler and test light
      b. Free-running bench test
   4. Insulated circuit voltmeter readings (drop)
   5. Ground circuit voltmeter readings (drop)
   6. Remote cranking
   7. Rebuilding procedures
      a. Turning commutator
      b. Don't wash starter drive in solvent

c. Torque test
d. Replace components (include bushings and end frames)
8. Inspecting control circuit wiring
G. Problem/Diagnosis
   1. Dragging armature
   2. Defective starter drive
   3. Worn bushings
   4. Worn flywheel ring gear
   5. Starter alignment (shims)
   6. Noise when cranking
   7. High current draw
   8. Low current draw
   9. Thrown armature windings
   10. Will not crank
   11. Cranks slowly
   12. Burned commutator
   13. Worn brushes/holders
   14. Spins but will not engage
   15. Solenoid plunger vibrates back and forth

X. Starter Circuit Controls (Understand Basic Operation)
A. Relays
B. Solenoids
C. Neutral Safety Switches
D. Resistor By-pass
E. Ignition Switches (Including Removal and Replacement)
F. Circuit Testing
   1. Voltage drop acceptable readings
   2. Solenoid/relay tests
   3. Supply circuit and control circuit
G. Problem/Diagnosis
   1. "Chatter"
   2. Ignition switch contact corrosion
   3. Poor solenoid contact disc connection
   4. Starter motor won't stop turning after ignition switch is placed in run position
   5. Broken drive nose
   6. Overheat failure

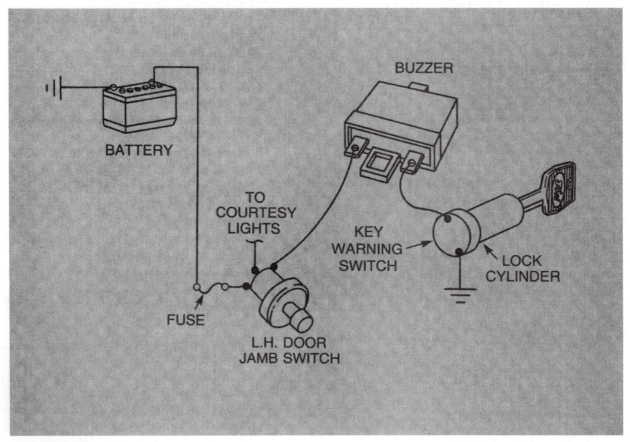

FIGURE 6–1

1. The buzzer in the warning system in Figure 6–1 does not sound.
    Technician A says that this could be caused by a blown fuse.
    Technician B says that this could be caused by a bad door jamb switch.
    Who is right?
    a. A only
    b. B only
    c. Both A and B
    d. Neither A nor B

2. On a multiple gauge instrument panel, one gauge reads incorrectly. Which of these would be the LEAST LIKELY cause?
    a. Bad printed circuit
    b. Bad gauge
    c. Bad sending unit
    d. Bad instrument voltage regulator

3. The battery is disconnected on a car that is equipped with a computer.
    Technician A says that the programmed settings of the digital clock and the AM/FM radio may be lost.
    Technician B says that it may take up to 200 miles of driving to reprogram certain computer functions.
    Who is right?
    a. A only   **c.** Both A and B
    b. B only   **d.** Neither A nor B

4. You are testing a cranking motor armature. If a self-powered lamp lights when one test prod is placed on the armature core and the other prod is placed on the commutator bars, the armature is:
    a. shorted.   **c.** open circuited.
    b. grounded.   **d.** testing normal.

5. The brushes in an alternator carry:
    a. field current.
    b. output current.
    c. voltage regulator current.
    d. Both a and b

FIGURE 6-2

6. The electrical component in Figure 6-2 is good. When measuring this part with an ohmmeter and then measuring again with the leads reversed, you should have:
   a. two low readings.
   b. two high (infinite) readings.
   c. one high (infinite) and one low reading.
   d. None of the above

7. An automobile is towed into the repair shop. The technician attempts to start it. The engine cranks very slowly and will not start. Also, the headlights dim considerably during cranking. Which of these could be the problem?
   a. Worn starter brushes
   b. Shorted field windings in the starter
   c. High resistance in the insulated or ground circuit
   d. None of the above

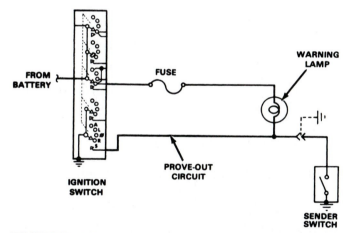

FIGURE 6-3

8. A warning light does not come on when it is supposed to, but glows when you ground the wire connected to the sender switch (see Figure 6-3).

   Technician A says that the prove-out circuit is bad.

   Technician B says that the sender switch or its ground is bad.

   Who is right?
   a. A only
   b. B only
   c. Both A and B
   d. Neither A nor B

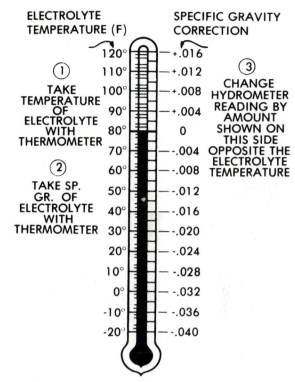

FIGURE 6-4

9. If a battery hydrometer reading is 1.280 and the electrolyte temperature reading is 50°F, the temperature corrected reading is (refer to the conversion scale in Figure 6-4).
   a. 1.160.   b. 1.292.   c. 1.400.   d. 1.268.

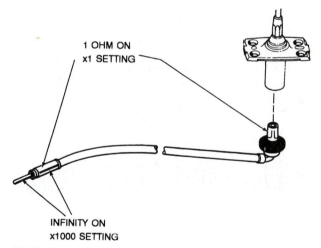

FIGURE 6-5

10. A radio antenna with a detachable cable and mast has been tested with an ohmmeter as shown in Figure 6-5. Which ohmmeter readings would you consider satisfactory?
    a. 1 only   c. Both 1 and 2
    b. 2 only   d. Neither 1 nor 2

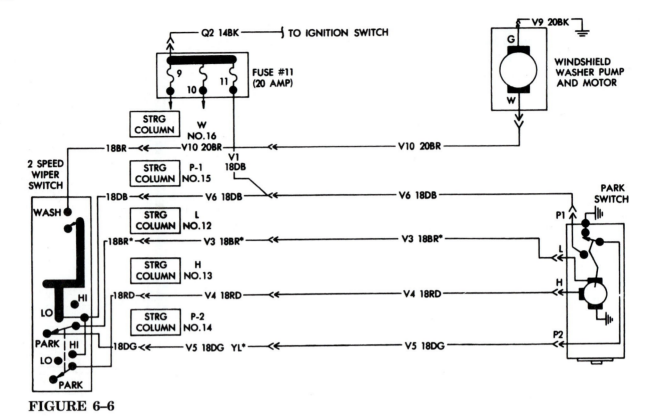

FIGURE 6–6

11. The 2-speed wiper motor shown in Figure 6–6 works okay, but will not park when the switch is turned OFF.

    Technician A says that this could be caused by a bad wiper motor ground.

    Technician B says that this could be caused by continuity at the wiring harness side between points L and P2.

    Who is right?
    a. A only
    b. B only
    c. Both A and B
    d. Neither A nor B

12. You are going to remove the battery from a negative ground system automobile and replace it with a new one. Which of the following procedures is correct?
    a. Disconnect the ground cable first, and reconnect the positive cable first.
    b. Disconnect the ground cable first, and reconnect the positive cable last.
    c. Disconnect the positive cable first, and reconnect the ground cable first.
    d. Disconnect the positive cable first, and reconnect the ground cable last.

13. Which of the following is true of the overrunning clutch type starter drive?
    a. Uses a shift lever
    b. Will slip if the cranking load becomes too great
    c. Both a and b
    d. Neither a nor b

14. An alternator regulator generally controls output voltage by:
    a. grounding the stator coils at the "Y" or "Delta" connection.
    b. grounding the diodes.
    c. grounding the field coil or inserting resistance in the circuit feeding battery current to the field coil.
    d. grounding the rectifier bridge.

15. A car radio has weak AM reception.
    Technician A says to check the antenna trimmer for proper adjustment.
    Technician B says to check for a short in the radio power feed wire.
    Who is right?
    a. A only
    b. B only
    c. Both A and B
    d. Neither A nor B

16. You are going to make a battery capacity test on a battery. The battery is marked only with the following information: Cold Cranking Current @ 0°F = 330; Reserve Capacity (minutes) = 100.

What load should be applied with the BST carbon pile?

a. 100 A   **b.** 115 A   **c.** 165 A   **d.** 50 A

17. A field current draw test can be made on alternators (left mounted on the vehicle) to check for:

a. a shorted rotor.
b. a grounded field coil.
c. poor brush contact.
d. All of the above

18. A customer complains that the turn signals flash too slowly. This could be caused by:

a. the wrong type of flasher.
b. incorrect bulb wattage.
c. Both a and b
d. Neither a nor b

19. You are going to make a high-rate discharge (capacity) test on a 12-V battery. With the proper load applied, the battery voltage should fall not lower than:

a. 11 V after 30 seconds.
b. 9.6 V after 15 seconds.
c. 10.5 V after 30 seconds.
d. 6 V after 15 seconds.

20. A car owner says that the radio makes a "fast popping noise" only when the engine is running.

Technician A says that this could be ignition circuit noise.

Technician B says that this could be caused by a loose capacitor at the positive ignition coil terminal.

Who is right?

a. A only
b. B only
c. Both A and B
d. Neither A nor B

21. Which of the following specific gravity readings would indicate a full state of charge (in a temperate climate)?

a. 1.140
b. 1.200
c. 1.215
d. None of these

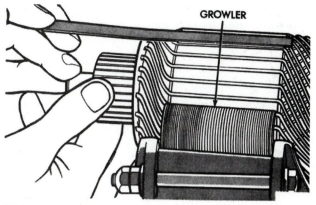

FIGURE 6–7

22. If the metal strip in Figure 6–7 vibrates, the armature is:

a. shorted.   **c.** open circuited.
b. grounded.   **d.** testing normal.

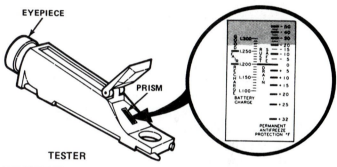

FIGURE 6–8

23. Checking a storage battery with the device in Figure 6–8 will indicate the:

a. capacity.   **c.** electrolyte mix.
b. voltage.   **d.** state-of-charge.

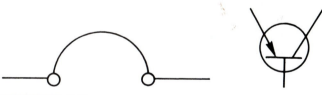

FIGURE 6–9

24. The electrical symbols drawn in Figure 6–9 represent which of the following?

a. Fuse and transistor
b. Circuit breaker and diode
c. Capacitor and transistor
d. None of the above

25. Convert 35 milliamperes to amperes. The answer would be:

a. 35 A.   **b.** 3.5 A.   **c.** .35 A.   **d.** .035 A.

26. Technician A says that worn bearings or a loose pulley can cause an alternator to be noisy.

Technician B says that a bad diode or a loose mounting bracket can cause an alternator to be noisy.

Who is right?

a. A only   **c.** Both A and B

b. B only   **d.** Neither A nor B

27. When soldering an electrical wiring connection use:

a. acid core flux.   **c.** Both a and b

b. rosin core flux.   **d.** Neither a nor b

FIGURE 6–10

28. You are testing an alternator with an oscilloscope. The waveform in Figure 6–10 appears. What would this indicate?

a. Normal condition

b. Open diode

c. Shorted diode

d. Open stator

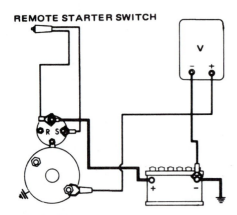

REMOTE STARTER SWITCH

FIGURE 6–11

29. A technician is performing a circuit resistance test according to the diagram in Figure 6–11. The voltmeter reads 0.2 V while the engine is being cranked. This indicates that the:

a. ground circuit is satisfactory.

b. ground circuit has excessive resistance.

c. insulated circuit has excessive resistance.

d. positive battery cable should be replaced.

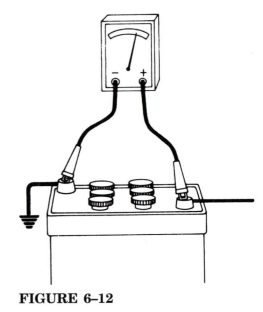

FIGURE 6–12

30. A voltmeter is connected across a 12-V battery according to the illustration in Figure 6–12. The ignition circuit is disabled to prevent the engine from starting. With the key turned on and the engine cranking, the voltmeter should not read less than:

a. 12.0 V.   **b.** 10.5 V.   **c.** 9.5 V.   **d.** 7.5 V.

31. When using an ammeter to perform a current draw test, a reading greater than specified would indicate:

a. an open circuit.

b. excessive circuit resistance.

c. a decrease in circuit resistance.

d. Either a or b above

32. Two lamps are wired in parallel. If another lamp is added in parallel:

a. the voltage will drop.

b. the total current will decrease.

c. the total resistance will increase.

d. the total resistance will decrease.

33. Technician A says that the quarter-ohm resistor setting on some older generator-alternator-regulator test machines is used to simulate a fully charged battery.

Technician B says that the quarter-ohm resistor is used during voltage regulator testing.

Who is right?

a. A only

b. B only

c. Both A and B

d. Neither A nor B

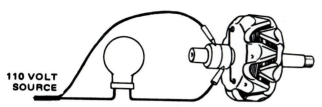

FIGURE 6–13

110 VOLT SOURCE

34. The test being performed in Figure 6–13 is a check for:
  a. shorts.   **c.** continuity.
  b. grounds.   **d.** high resistance.

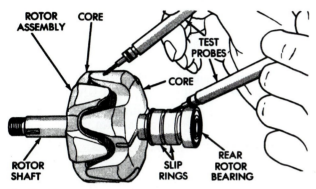

ROTOR ASSEMBLY   CORE   TEST PROBES   CORE   ROTOR SHAFT   SLIP RINGS   REAR ROTOR BEARING

FIGURE 6–14

35. The test being performed in Figure 6–14 is a check for:
  a. shorts.   **c.** continuity.
  b. grounds.   **d.** high resistance.

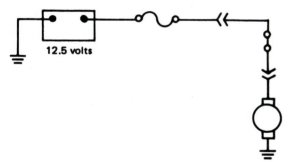

12.5 volts

FIGURE 6–15

36. The windshield wiper motor in Figure 6–15 has a 1.4-V drop in the power side of the circuit. There is a 0.1-V drop in the grounded side. How many volts are available to operate the motor?
  a. 11.0 **b.** 11.1 **c.** 12.4 **d.** 12.5

37. The no-load voltage across the terminals on a battery reads 12.2 V. However, the B+ terminal on the alternator reads zero volts. Which of these would be the MOST LIKELY cause?
  a. Open diode   **c.** Shorted regulator
  b. Poor ground   **d.** Open circuit

38. Battery electrolyte specific gravity should not vary more than _____ between cells.
  a. .10 **b.** .50 **c.** .050 **d.** .005

39. Technician A says that when using an analog ohmmeter, a low or zero reading indicates continuity.
  Technician B says that when using an analog ohmmeter, a full-scale reading (infinity) indicates no continuity.
  Who is right?
  a. A only   **c.** Both A and B
  b. B only   **d.** Neither A nor B

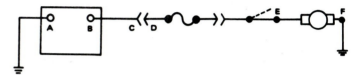

A   B   C   D   E   F

FIGURE 6–16

40. To measure current draw of the motor in Figure 6–16, how would you connect an ammeter?
  a. Red to E, black to F
  b. Red to B, black to F
  c. Red to C, black to D
  d. Black to A, red to F

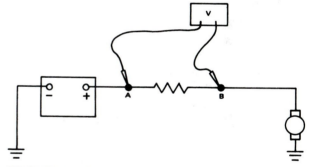

V   A   B

FIGURE 6–17

41. The voltmeter in the hook-up in Figure 6–17 reads 0 V. There is power to point A.
  Technician A says that the resistor could be shorted.
  Technician B says that the circuit beyond point B could be open.
  Who is right?
  a. A only   **c.** Both A and B
  b. B only   **d.** Neither A nor B

42. A battery is using excessive water. This can be caused by:
  a. a high voltage regulator setting.
  b. a shorted battery cell.
  c. a poor regulator ground.
  d. All of the above

43. The low beam headlamps on an automobile do not light.

Technician A says that this can be caused by a common ground.

Technician B says that this can be caused by a bad dimmer switch.

Who is right?
- **a.** A only
- **b.** B only
- **c.** Both A and B
- **d.** Neither A nor B

44. A 12-V battery that has just failed a capacity test is being charged at 40 A. After three minutes of charge, with the charger still operating, a voltmeter hooked across the battery reads 15.8 V. What does this indicate?
- **a.** The battery should be slow charged and put back into service.
- **b.** Everything is normal; continue fast charge for a half hour, and put back into service.
- **c.** The battery is sulphated and should be replaced.
- **d.** The battery electrolyte should be replaced.

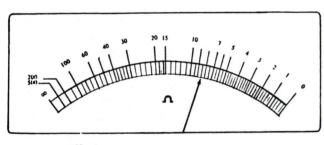

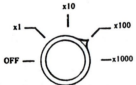

FIGURE 6–18

45. The analog meter reading in Figure 6–18 is:
- **a.** 8.5 Ω   **b.** 85 Ω   **c.** 850 Ω   **d.** 8,500 Ω

46. A customer complains that the left front directional light doesn't work. The left rear, right front, and right rear directional lights work. The MOST LIKELY cause would be a:
- **a.** faulty flasher.
- **b.** defective directional switch.
- **c.** burned out bulb.
- **d.** shorted out wire.

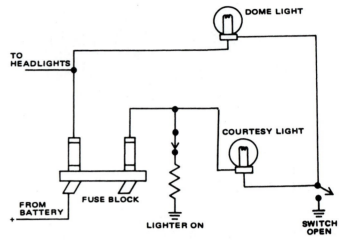

FIGURE 6–19

47. A customer complains that the cigarette lighter in his car doesn't pop out. Also, when the lighter is depressed, the dome light and courtesy light glow. According to the diagram in Figure 6–19, what could be wrong?
- **a.** A poor lighter ground
- **b.** A blown fuse
- **c.** Low circuit resistance
- **d.** A burned out lighter element

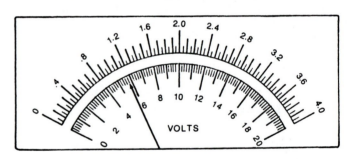

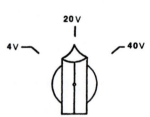

FIGURE 6–20

48. The analog meter reading in Figure 6–20 is:
- **a.** 4.9 V.   **b.** 5.08 V.   **c.** 5.4 V.   **d.** 5.8 V.

49. The built-in hydrometer on a sealed battery appears light yellow in color.

Technician A says to load test the battery.

Technician B says to charge the battery at 40A for 60 minutes.

Who is right?
- **a.** A only
- **b.** B only
- **c.** Both A and B
- **d.** Neither A nor B

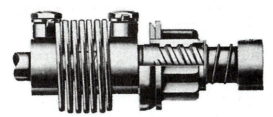

FIGURE 6–21

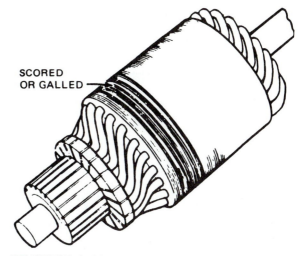

FIGURE 6–22

50. On the type of starter motor drive in Figure 6–21, how is the pinion gear engaged with the flywheel gear?
a. By the anti-drift spring
b. Through a shift lever
c. By release of pinion inertia
d. By the drive spring

51. A vehicle owner complains of a directional signal problem. You find that the left front light does not flash. Also, the left rear light flashes faster than normal. This could be caused by:
a. a bad left front bulb.
b. an open circuit between the switch and the left front bulb.
c. Both a and b
d. Neither a nor b

52. Every two days a battery goes "dead" for no apparent reason. A hidden current drain is suspected.
 Technician A says that this can be verified by hooking-up a voltmeter in series with the battery ground cable.
 Technician B says that this can be verified by hooking-up an ohmmeter in series with the battery ground cable.
 Who is right?
a. A only
b. B only
c. Both A and B
d. Neither A nor B

53. The starter solenoid "pumps" in and out when attempting to crank an engine.
 Technician A says that this could be caused by an undercharged battery.
 Technician B says that this could be caused by a bad solenoid.
 Who is right?
a. A only
b. B only
c. Both A and B
d. Neither A nor B

54. The condition in Figure 6–22 could be caused by:
a. worn bearings.
b. loose pole shoe.
c. bent armature shaft.
d. All of the above

55. In the schematic in Figure 6–23, connector C-512 is open. The result would be:
a. the courtesy lights and key reminder buzzer would be totally inoperative.
b. the dome and courtesy lamps would operate only from the left door jamb switch.
c. the dome and courtesy lamps would operate only from the headlamp switch.
d. the dome and courtesy lamps would operate only from the right door jamb switch or headlamp switch.

56. A radio speaker is going to be removed from a vehicle for testing.
 Technician A says to remove the radio fuse, as transistor damage can result if the radio is turned on with the speaker removed.
 Technician B says to test the speaker with an ohmmeter.
 Who is right?
a. A only   **c.** Both A and B
b. B only   **d.** Neither A nor B

57. A heater blower motor has a "squeak" that varies with motor speed. The MOST LIKELY cause would be:
a. excessive current flow.
b. loose pole shoes.
c. worn brushes.
d. dry or worn bearings.

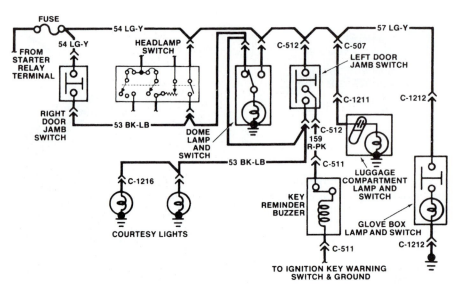

FIGURE 6–23

58. The dome lamp in Figure 6–23 will not come on when the driver's door is opened.

Technician A says that this could be caused by a stuck jamb switch.

Technician B says that this could be caused by no power to wire 54 at the fuse.

Who is right?

a. A only
b. B only
c. Both A and B
d. Neither A nor B

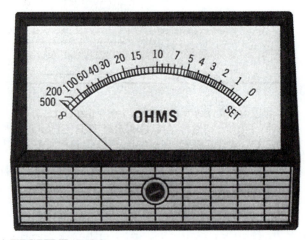

FIGURE 6–24

59. An electrical part needs to be accurately measured with the meter in Figure 6–24. You should begin with the range selector set at:

a. ×1000.   **c.** ×10.
b. ×100.   **d.** ×1.

60. A cranking motor has an unusually high amperage draw accompanied by slow cranking speed.

Technician A says that this could be caused by bad starter bushings.

Technician B says that this could be caused by the armature rubbing on the pole shoes.

Who is right?

a. A only
b. B only
c. Both A and B
d. Neither A nor B

61. A rectangular (4″ × 6.5″) high-low sealed beam headlight has a code designation of:
a. 1 A.   **b.** 2 A.   **c.** 2 B.   **d.** 2 C.

62. What would be the proper action to take with a battery that showed the following specific gravity readings (at 80° F)?

Cell 1	Cell 2	Cell 3	Cell 4	Cell 5	Cell 6
1.200	1.210	1.190	1.200	1.205	1.200

a. Load test the battery.
b. Replace the battery since the readings indicate that it is no longer fit for service.
c. Refill the battery with fresh electrolyte.
d. Recharge the battery.

63. A starter motor spins but does not crank the engine. This could be the result of:
a. a slipping drive.
b. worn crankshaft thrust.
c. Both a and b
d. Neither a nor b

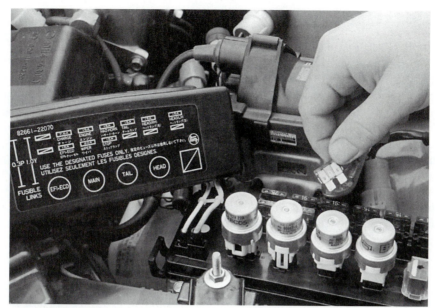

FIGURE 6–25

64. Technician A says that the rating of the item held in Figure 6–25 is indicated by a color code.

Technician B says that the rating of the item held above is indicated by a number marking.

Who is right?

a. A only
b. B only
c. Both A and B
d. Neither A nor B

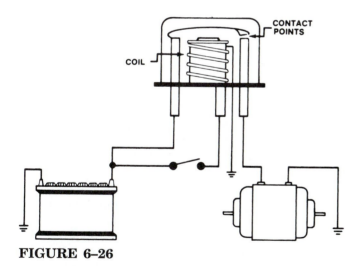

FIGURE 6–26

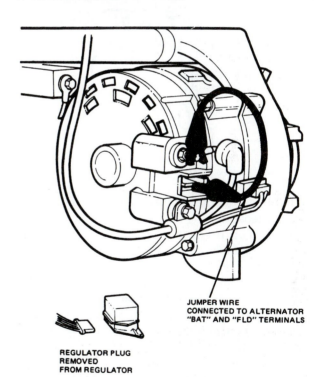

FIGURE 6–27

65. Technician A says that current is going through the coil when the motor is running in the circuit in Figure 6–26.

Technician B says that current is going through the contact points when the motor is running in the circuit.

Who is right?

a. A only
b. B only
c. Both A and B
d. Neither A nor B

66. A technician connects a jumper wire between the alternator B+ and F terminals during a field circuit and alternator test (see Figure 6–27).

Technician A says that if this corrects a low voltmeter reading, the wiring harness from the alternator to the regulator could be faulty.

Technician B says that this bypasses the voltage regulator.

Who is right?

a. A only
b. B only
c. Both A and B
d. Neither A nor B

67. Technician A says that a 10-gauge wire is smaller than a 14-gauge wire.

Technician B says that fusible links are generally one gauge size smaller than the wire in the circuit.

Who is right?

a. A only
b. B only
c. Both A and B
d. Neither A nor B

68. The instrument panel lamps, tail lamps, and headlamps do not operate on an automobile.

Technician A says that this could be caused by a bad headlamp switch.

Technician B says that this could be caused by a bad rheostat.

Who is right?

a. A only
b. B only
c. Both A and B
d. Neither A nor B

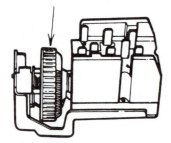

FIGURE 6–28

69. What is the arrow pointing to on the part in Figure 6–28?
a. Instrument lamp illumination control rheostat
b. Circuit breaker
c. ATO fuse
d. Resistor

70. A horn operates continuously without pressing the horn ring. Which of the following would be the MOST LIKELY cause?
a. An open wire to the relay
b. A shorted horn coil
c. An out-of-adjustment horn
d. A shorted relay

71. After charging a battery for 24 hours at 5 A, the cells read 1.220.

Technician A says that the battery needs to be charged more.

Technician B says that the battery is sulphated.

Who is right?

a. A only
b. B only
c. Both A and B
d. Neither A nor B

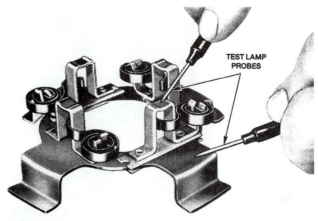

TEST LAMP PROBES

FIGURE 6–29

72. If a self-powered test lamp lights during the test in Figure 6–29, what is indicated?
a. The grounded brush holder is open.
b. The grounded brush holder is satisfactory.
c. The insulated brush holder is satisfactory.
d. The insulated brush holder is grounded.

73. A computer-controlled car is parked for 30 days and the battery goes "dead."

Technician A says that this could be caused by a bad diode.

Technician B says that this could be caused by the memory draw of the computer.

Who is right?

a. A only
b. B only
c. Both A and B
d. Neither A nor B

74. Technician A says that needle bearings are used to support the alternator rotor assembly.

Technician B says that ball bearings are used to support the alternator rotor assembly.

Who is right?

a. A only
b. B only
c. Both A and B
d. Neither A nor B

75. The cruise control on a vehicle does not always disengage when the brake pedal is depressed.

Technician A says that this could be caused by a bad servo.

Technician B says that this could be caused by a bad stop lamp and speed control switch.

Who is right?

a. A only
b. B only
c. Both A and B
d. Neither A nor B

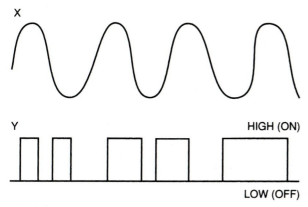

FIGURE 6–30

76. Technician A says that waveform X shown in Figure 6–30 represents a digital signal.

    Technician B says that waveform Y represents an analog signal.

    Who is right?
    a. A only
    b. B only
    c. Both A and B
    d. Neither A nor B

77. The cruise control on a vehicle does not engage when the set button is pressed and released.

    Technician A says that this could be caused by a misadjusted cruise control throttle cable.

    Technician B says that this could be caused by a vacuum leak.

    Who is right?
    a. A only
    b. B only
    c. Both A and B
    d. Neither A nor B

78. The word "shunt" describes a type of _____ circuit.
    a. open   b. series   c. parallel   d. ground

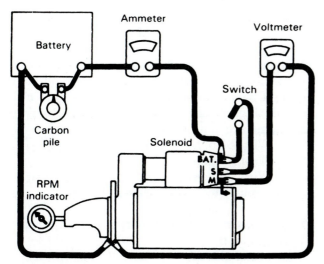

FIGURE 6–31

79. A starter free-running test is being made on the bench with a fully charged battery (see Figure 6–31). The current draw is higher than specs and the rpm level is lower.

    Technician A says that this could be caused by tight bushings.

    Technician B says that this could be caused by worn brushes.

    Who is right?
    a. A only
    b. B only
    c. Both A and B
    d. Neither A nor B

80. A vacuum fluorescent display (VFD) instrument cluster is being replaced.

    Technician A says that the odometer memory chip should be removed from the old cluster and installed in the new cluster.

    Technician B says that the odometer chip can be ruined by static electricity if not properly handled. Who is right?
    a. A only
    b. B only
    c. Both A and B
    d. Neither A nor B

81. What is the possible result from a too tight alternator drive belt?

    Technician A says that the belt can become glazed.

    Technician B says that alternator front bearing failure can result.

    Who is right?
    a. A only
    b. B only
    c. Both A and B
    d. Neither A nor B

82. An overrunning clutch-type starter is going to be disassembled.

    Technician A says to check the pinion gear teeth for wear.

    Technician B says to rotate the pinion gear; it should turn free in one direction and lock in the other direction.

    Who is right?
    a. A only
    b. B only
    c. Both A and B
    d. Neither A nor B

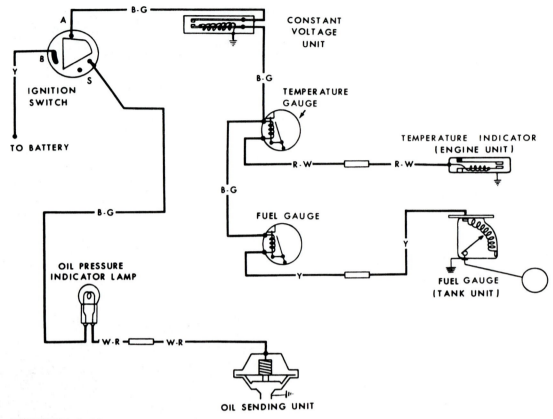

FIGURE 6–32

83. The temperature gauge in the circuit in Figure 6–32 functions correctly. However, the fuel gauge reads higher than the actual fuel level.

    Technician A says that this could be caused by stuck points inside the constant voltage unit.

    Technician B says that this could be caused by a defective rheostat inside the fuel tank.

    Who is right?
    a. A only
    b. B only
    c. Both A and B
    d. Neither A nor B

84. Electrical accessories on cars are protected against short circuit by:
    a. fusible links.
    b. circuit breakers.
    c. fuses.
    d. All of the above

85. A car owner says that the alternator warning lamp remains lighted at full brilliancy when the engine is running.

    Technician A says that this could be caused by a blown instrument cluster fuse.

    Technician B says that this could be caused by an open circuit.

    Who is right?
    a. A only   **c.** Both A and B
    b. B only   **d.** Neither A nor B

86. Refer to the circuit diagram in Figure 6–44 (p. 201). The left inboard and left outboard high beam filaments do not work. Both right side high beam filaments operate. Both low beams are okay. What could be wrong?
    a. Wire A open
    b. Wire B open
    c. Wire C open
    d. Ground wire G3 missing

87. The maximum current output of an alternator is limited by the:
    a. stator CEMF.   **c.** battery capacity.
    b. regulator.   **d.** diode size.

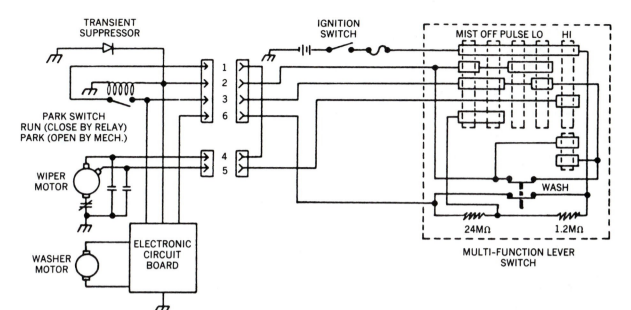

FIGURE 6–33

88. The circuit in Figure 6–33 incorporates a programmable windshield washer that does not work.

Technician A says that this could be caused by a bad ground connection.

Technician B says that this could be caused by a bad multifunction lever switch.

Who is right?
a. A only
b. B only
c. Both A and B
d. Neither A nor B

89. A starter motor is damaged beyond repair. The armature windings have been thrown outward, resulting in the destruction in Figure 6–34.

Technician A says that this could have been caused by the ignition switch not fully returning from START to ON position.

Technician B says that this could have been caused by a loose mounted starter.

Who is right?
a. A only
b. B only
c. Both A and B
d. Neither A nor B

90. If the feed wire in the power window circuit in Figure 6–35 becomes frayed and copper touches bare metal at point "X," what will be the result?
a. The fuse will blow.
b. The main relay coil will be damaged.
c. Both a and b
d. Neither a nor b

FIGURE 6–34

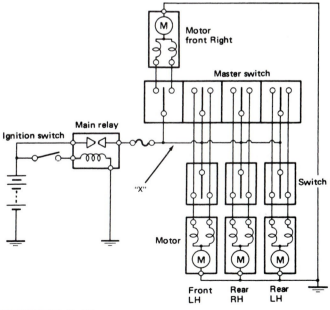

FIGURE 6–35

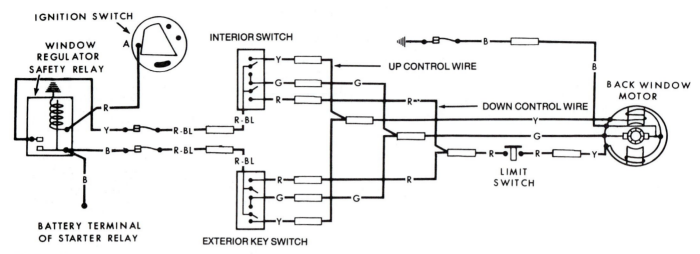

FIGURE 6–36

91. A station wagon is equipped with an electric tail gate window (see Figure 6–36). The window will operate in both directions through the exterior key switch. However, the window will not operate in either direction through the interior switch. What is wrong?

Technician A says that the limit switch could be defective.

Technician B says that the interior switch could be defective.

Who is right?

a. A only

b. B only

c. Both A and B

d. Neither A nor B

92. A vehicle has the headlamp cover system in Figure 6–37. The covers will not automatically open.

Technician A says that this can be caused by a defective light switch.

Technician B says that this can be caused by a kink in vacuum lines.

Who is right?

a. A only

b. B only

c. Both A and B

d. Neither A nor B

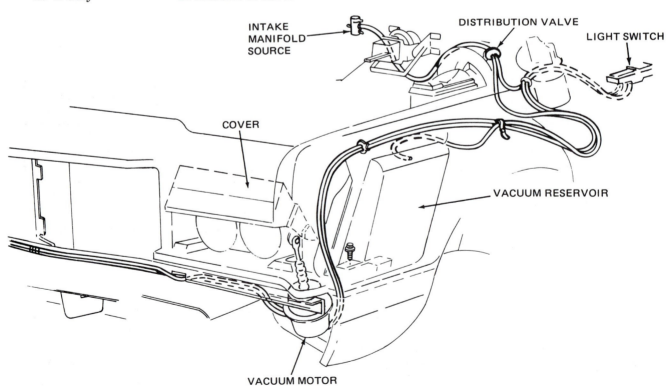

FIGURE 6–37

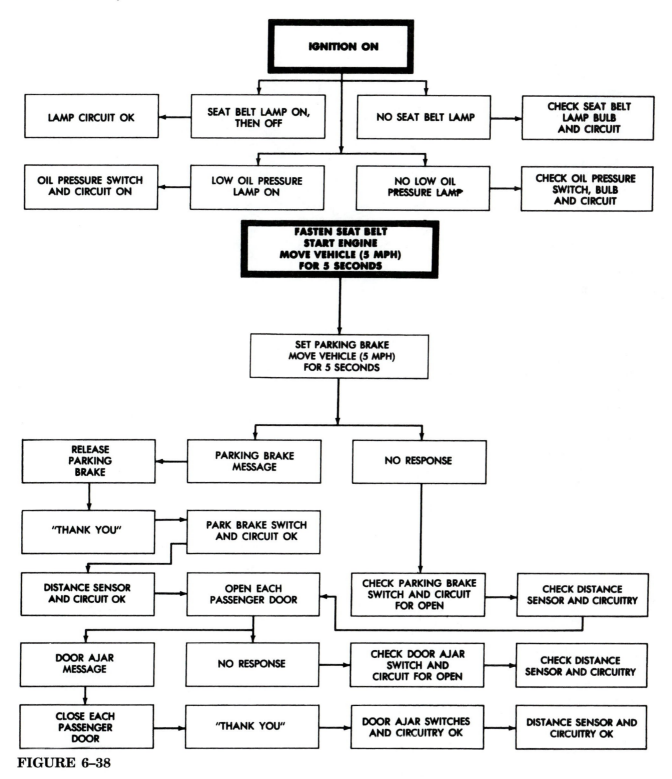

FIGURE 6–38

93. Refer to the electronic voice alert diagnosis chart shown in Figure 6–38.

Technician A says that no parking brake message response could be caused by a bad distance sensor.

Technician B says that no door ajar message response could be caused by an open circuit. Who is right?

a. A only   **c.** Both A and B

b. B only   **d.** Neither A nor B

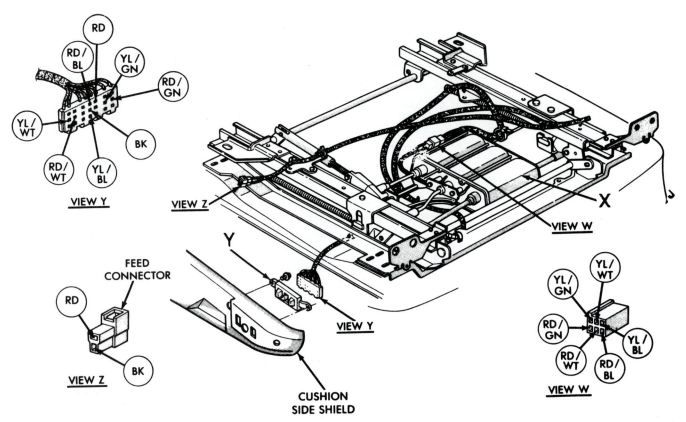

VIEW Y

VIEW Z

VIEW W

FEED CONNECTOR

CUSHION SIDE SHIELD

X

Y

FIGURE 6–39

94. The power seat in Figure 6–39 does not operate properly.

Technician A says that part X could be bad.
Technician B says that part Y could be bad.
Who is right?

a. A only
c. Both A and B
b. B only
d. Neither A nor B

95. The red charge indicator light fails to light with the ignition switch turned on to the RUN position with the engine stopped. What could be the problem?

a. This condition is normal on most cars.
b. The bulb is burned out.
c. The field relay is failing to close.
d. Both b and c above

96. You are using a jumper wire to bypass parts in the circuit in Figure 6–40. Which jumper is being used according to general recommended procedure?

a. A only
c. A and B only
b. B only
d. B, C, and D only

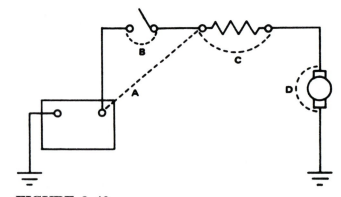

FIGURE 6–40

97. When soldering alternator diode connections, why are long nose pliers often used to hold the diode leads?

a. The pliers act as a heat sink.
b. To prevent overheating the stator windings
c. To prevent stator core damage
d. To prevent end frame damage

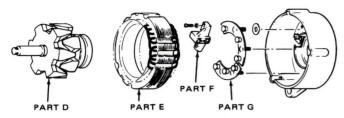

FIGURE 6-41

98. In the alternator assembly in Figure 6–41, where are the diodes located?
  a. Part D **b.** Part E **c.** Part F **d.** Part G

99. Both turn signals work, but will not cancel. What could be the cause?
  a. Wrong wattage flasher
  b. Steering wheel installed 180° out of correct position
  c. Bad turn signal switch
  d. Either b or c above

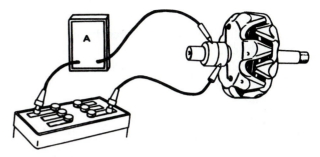

FIGURE 6-43

102. If the tail lights and rear side marker lights fail to operate in the circuit in Figure 6–44, but the license plate light does, the MOST LIKELY cause is:
  a. wire E is open.
  b. wire D is open.
  c. ground wire G2 is missing.
  d. ground wire G3 is missing.

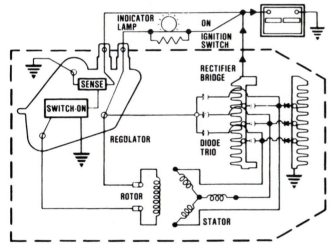

FIGURE 6-42

100. The indicator lamp in the Delco 10SI system in Figure 6–42 stays on when the engine is stopped (ignition switch OFF).

Technician A says that this could be caused by a faulty diode in the rectifier bridge.

Technician B says that this could be caused by an open circuit in the rotor.

Who is right?
  a. A only **c.** Both A and B
  b. B only **d.** Neither A nor B

101. The test in Figure 6–43 is generally made when testing for a(n):
  a. shorted circuit.
  b. grounded circuit.
  c. high resistance circuit.
  d. open circuit.

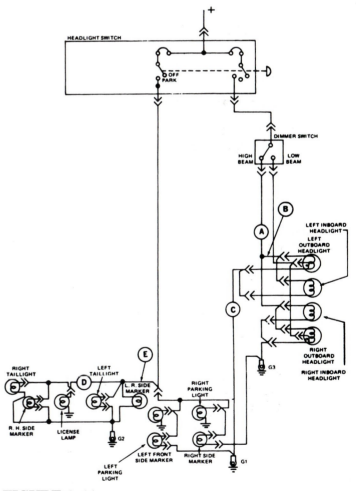

FIGURE 6-44

103. Technician A says that a chattering starter solenoid plunger can be caused by an open circuited hold-in winding.

Technician B says that the pull-in winding could be open circuited.

Who is right?

a. A only   **c.** Both A and B
b. B only   **d.** Neither A nor B

FIGURE 6–45

104. If the alternator component in Figure 6–45 is shorted, it can cause:

a. radio noise.
b. battery drain.
c. lower current output.
d. All of the above

105. Technician A says that a battery is likely to freeze during cold weather if it has a high specific gravity.

Technician B says that a battery is likely to freeze during cold weather if it has a low state of charge.

Who is right?

a. A only
b. B only
c. Both A and B
d. Neither A nor B

106. A rear window washer motor stays on when the engine is running (see Figure 6–46).

Technician A says that this could be caused by melted together switch contacts.

Technician B says that this could be caused by a shorted pump motor. Who is right?

a. A only
b. B only
c. Both A and B
d. Neither A nor B

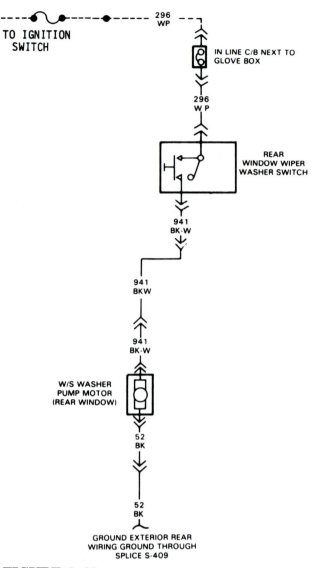

FIGURE 6–46

107. What occurs when two adjacent conductors make electrical contact and bypass a portion of a circuit?

a. A ground
b. An open
c. A short
d. The circuit resistance increases

108. The hazard warning lights will not flash. The turn signals function normally.

Technician A says that the hazard warning flasher could be inoperative.

Technician B says that the turn signal switch could be bad.

Who is right?

a. A only   **c.** Both A and B
b. B only   **d.** Neither A nor B

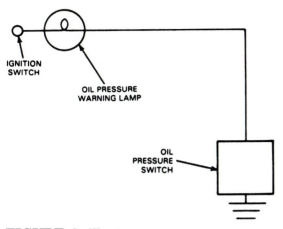

FIGURE 6–47

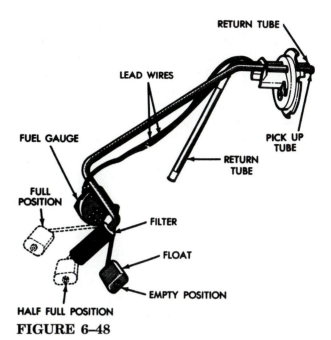

FIGURE 6–48

109. The red warning light in Figure 6–47 flickers ON and OFF when the car is driven down the road.

Technician A says that the wire could have come off at the pressure switch and is intermittently grounding.

Technician B says that the engine could be low on oil.

Who is right?
a. A only
b. B only
c. Both A and B
d. Neither A nor B

110. The basic purpose of an overrunning clutch in the starter drive is to:
a. disengage the armature when the engine starts.
b. pull the starter pinion gear out of mesh.
c. assist the solenoid during cranking.
d. keep the hold-in winding energized during cranking.

111. The item in Figure 6–48 has been removed from a vehicle. What would you use to check it accurately?
a. An ohmmeter
b. A self-powered test light
c. A shunt wound ammeter
d. A voltmeter

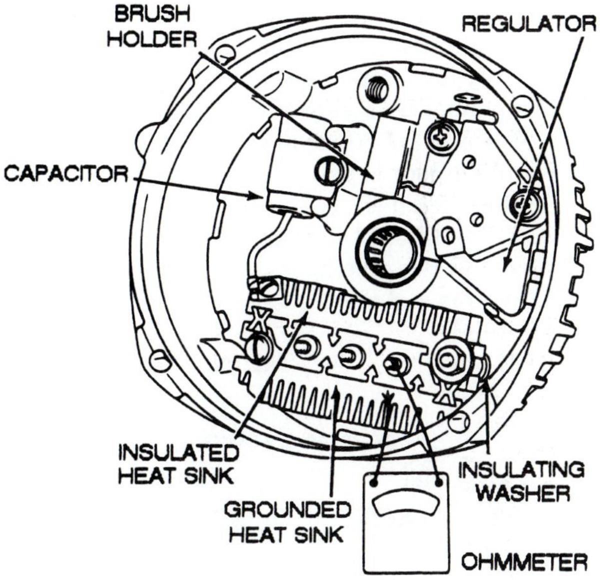

FIGURE 6–49

112. What alternator component is being tested in Figure 6–49?
a. Capacitor
b. Brush holder
c. Regulator
d. Rectifier bridge

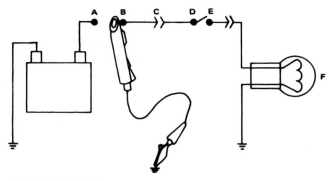

FIGURE 6–50

113. A self-powered test light has been connected to point B as shown in Figure 6–50. The light glows with bulb F disconnected and continues to glow as switch DE is opened. The light goes out when C is separated. What is indicated?
   a. Switch DE is shorted to ground.
   b. Wire CD is shorted to ground.
   c. The circuit is testing okay.
   d. Wire CD is open.

114. A starter draw test is being performed. An unusually low amperage reading is indicated (accompanied by a slow cranking speed).
   Technician A says that a possible cause could be poor brush or commutator condition.
   Technician B says that a possible cause could be lack of clearance between the armature and the pole shoes.
   Who is right?
   a. A only
   b. B only
   c. Both A and B
   d. Neither A nor B

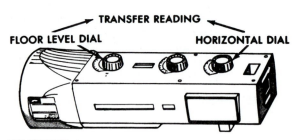

FIGURE 6–51

115. Technician A says that the headlamps have to be turned on when using the aimer in Figure 6–51.
   Technician B says that the car must be on a perfectly level surface when using the aimer.
   Who is right?
   a. A only
   b. B only
   c. Both A and B
   d. Neither A nor B

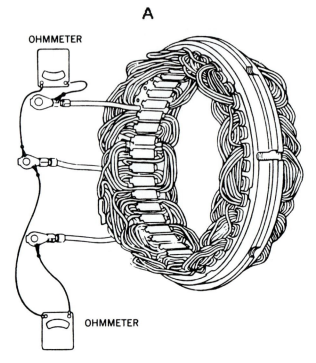

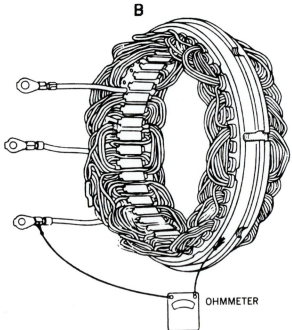

FIGURE 6–52

116. Technician A says that picture A in Figure 6–52 shows checking for grounds.
   Technician B says that picture B shows checking for an open.
   Who is right?
   a. A only
   b. B only
   c. Both A and B
   d. Neither A nor B

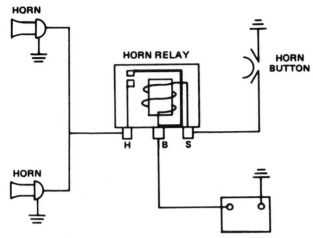

FIGURE 6–53

117. A customer complains that the horn does not honk. When wire B in Figure 6–53 is disconnected at the horn relay and touched to the H terminal connection, the horn honks.

Technician A says that the horn button mechanism could be defective.

Technician B says that the horn relay could be defective.

Who is right?
a. A only
b. B only
c. Both A and B
d. Neither A nor B

118. A vehicle is driven into the shop with an inoperative digital instrument cluster (DIC). This could be caused by:
a. a bad power supply.
b. bad ribbon board connectors.
c. bad grounds.
d. All of the above

119. Technician A says that an inoperative speedometer can be caused by a bad ground wire.

Technician B says that an inoperative speedometer can be caused by a bad speed sensor.

Who is right?
a. A only
b. B only
c. Both A and B
d. Neither A nor B

120. An engine has an intermittent start problem. When this happens, a click is heard.

Technician A says that this could be caused by a bent flywheel.

Technician B says that this could be caused by too many starter shims.

Who is right?
a. A only   c. Both A and B
b. B only   d. Neither A nor B

121. A fuel gauge does not read empty.

Technician A says that this can be caused by a deformed fuel tank.

Technician B says that this can be caused by a faulty printed circuit board.

Who is right?
a. A only
b. B only
c. Both A and B
d. Neither A nor B

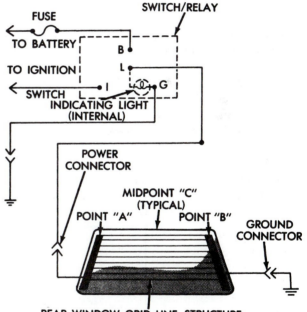

FIGURE 6–54

122. The electrically heated rear window pictured in Figure 6–54 will not warm the glass.

Technician A says that this could be caused by a break in one of the grid lines.

Technician B says that this could be caused by a loose power connector.

Who is right?
a. A only   c. Both A and B
b. B only   d. Neither A nor B

123. The windshield wipers on a car do not properly park. This could be caused by:
- **a.** loose linkage at the motor.
- **b.** wiper arms being set at an incorrect position.
- **c.** open park circuit wiring.
- **d.** All of the above

124. The halogen headlights on a vehicle are dim only when the engine is idling or shut off.

Technician A says that this could be caused by corroded battery terminals.

Technician B says that this could be caused by cracked sealed beam lenses.

Who is right?
- **a.** A only
- **b.** B only
- **c.** Both A and B
- **d.** Neither A nor B

125. The hard-shell connectors shown in Figure 6–55 require disengagement.

Technician A says to pry the connectors apart with a screwdriver.

Technician B says to release the locking tabs.
Who is right?
- **a.** A only
- **b.** B only
- **c.** Both A and B
- **d.** Neither A nor B

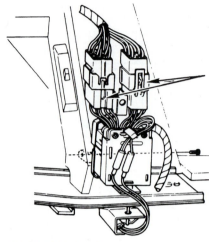

FIGURE 6–55

126. A car is equipped with the illuminated entry system shown in Figure 6–56. Everything works fine, except the interior courtesy lamps are inoperable when the right front door handle is lifted.

Technician A says that the light collector could be bad.

Technician B says that the door handle switch could be bad.

Who is right?
- **a.** A only
- **b.** B only
- **c.** Both A and B
- **d.** Neither A nor B

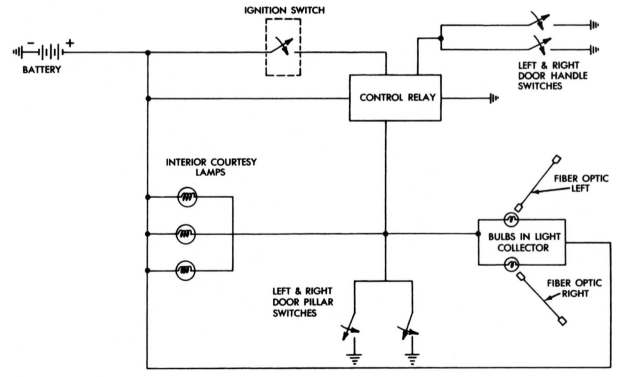

FIGURE 6–56

127. Technician A says that if the neutral safety switch is not installed correctly, the starter control circuit will not operate properly.

Technician B says that the back-up lights may not work properly.

Who is right?

a. A only

b. B only

c. Both A and B

d. Neither A nor B

128. The instrument voltage regulator (IVR) used in a gauge circuit needs to be tested.

Technician A says to connect a test light to the IVR output terminal; if the light flashes, the IVR is bad.

Technician B says to connect a test light to the coolant temperature sending unit; if the light flashes, the IVR is good.

Who is right?

a. A only

b. B only

c. Both A and B

d. Neither A nor B

129. Technician A says that solderless terminals should be installed with special crimping pliers.

Technician B says that a spade or ring terminal should be used when attaching a wire to a stud.

Who is right?

a. A only

b. B only

c. Both A and B

d. Neither A nor B

130. A car is equipped with a power door lock system (see component layout in Figure 6–57). All locks except the right front door work.

Technician A says that the harness could be bad.

Technician B says that the actuator could be bad.

Who is right?

a. A only

b. B only

c. Both A and B

d. Neither A nor B

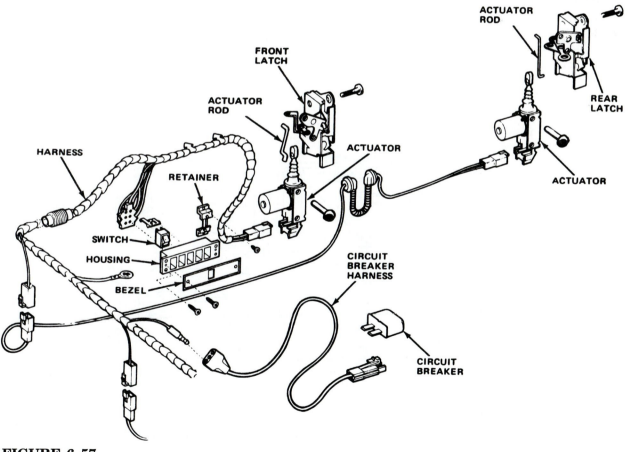

FIGURE 6–57

131. On a vehicle equipped with an automatic transmission, the starter will not crank and the solenoid does not "click."

Technician A says that this could be caused by a misadjusted neutral safety switch.

Technician B says that this could be caused by an open solenoid hold-in winding.

Who is right?
a. A only
b. B only
c. Both A and B
d. Neither A nor B

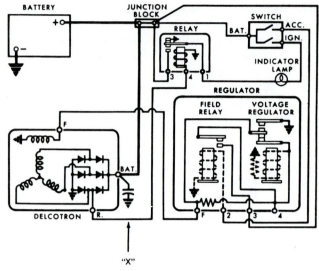

FIGURE 6–58

132. Where would the alternator heat sink be found?
a. Attached to the end frame
b. Mounted on the rotor shaft
c. Positioned between the stator coils
d. Connected to the slip rings

133. If alternator circuit wire R is broken at the "X" mark, what will happen? (Refer to the wiring diagram in Figure 6–58.)
a. The alternator will have no output.
b. The indicator lamp will stay on when the engine is running.
c. Both a and b
d. Neither a nor b

134. Refer to Figure 6–59.

Technician A says that this starter requires no field circuit testing.

Technician B says that this starter uses a gear assembly to help increase torque.

Who is right?
a. A only
b. B only
c. Both A and B
d. Neither A nor B

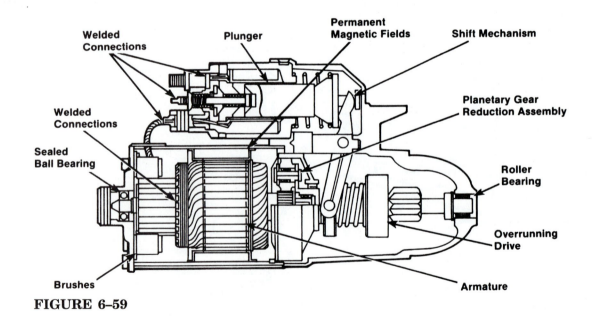

FIGURE 6–59

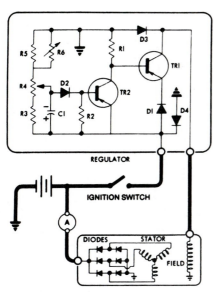

FIGURE 6–60

135. Technician A says that the regulator unit shown in Figure 6–60 has no moving parts when operating.

Technician B says that when the ignition switch is closed, current will flow through TR1.

Who is right?
a. A only
b. B only
c. Both A and B
d. Neither A nor B

136. Technician A says that some cars use a fusible link to protect the regulator contacts and the alternator field circuit.

Technician B says that some cars use a fusible link in the main wiring harness at the junction block in the engine compartment.

Who is right?
a. A only   c. Both A and B
b. B only   d. Neither A nor B

137. A carmaker's theft deterrent system might include:
a. a special resistor pellet in the ignition key.
b. door jamb switches.
c. a starter interlock.
d. Any of the above

138. If a carburetor electric choke is wired into an alternator circuit, where would the connection MOST LIKELY be?
a. At the alternator FLD terminal
b. At the alternator STA terminal
c. At the alternator BAT terminal
d. At the regulator A+ terminal

139. In the schematic in Figure 6–62, the indicator lamp will light when the ignition switch is turned on. Where does this lamp obtain its ground?
a. In the voltage coil
b. In the field coil
c. In the field relay
d. At the alternator BAT terminal

140. It is night and the headlamp doors in the system in Figure 6–61 will not open when the headlamp switch is turned on.

Technician A says to attempt opening the doors by jumping the 5-A circuit breaker.

Technician B says to attempt opening the doors by grounding the buss bar connection at the relay.

Who is right?
a. A only
b. B only
c. Both A and B
d. Neither A nor B

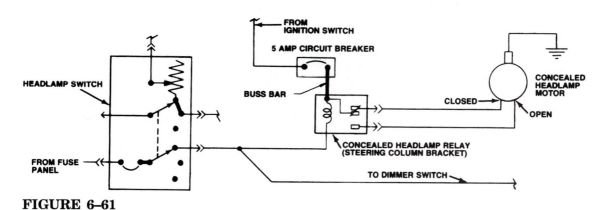

FIGURE 6–61

141. How is a DC voltmeter usually connected when making electrical checks?
   a. Across the circuit
   b. In parallel
   c. In series
   d. Both a and b above

142. Where would an ammeter MOST LIKELY be placed in an alternator circuit for an output check?
   a. In series with the alternator STA terminal
   b. In series with the alternator FLD terminal
   c. In parallel with the alternator BAT terminal
   d. In series with the alternator BAT terminal

143. Technician A says to "full-field" the alternator in Figure 6–62, you would take a jumper wire and ground the F terminal at the alternator.

   Technician B says to disconnect the multiple connector at the regulator and connect a jumper wire from F to 4 in the connector.

   Who is right?
   a. A only
   b. B only
   c. Both A and B
   d. Neither A nor B

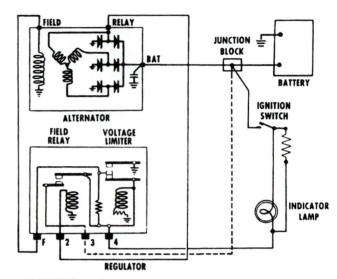

FIGURE 6–62

144. Two technicians are discussing the importance of the pigtail wire in Figure 6–63.

   Technician A says that a loose terminal connection at the fender panel can result in dim or flickering headlights.

   Technician B says that a loose terminal connection at the fender panel can cause failure of various bushings in the automatic transmission.

   Who is right?
   a. A only   c. Both A and B
   b. B only   d. Neither A nor B

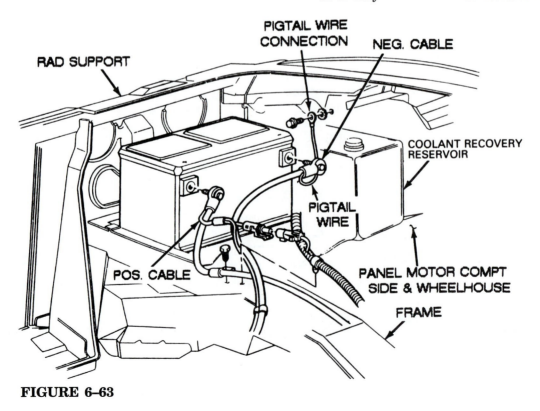

FIGURE 6–63

145. A 7.4-liter gasoline engine cranks slowly. The technician finds that the starter draw is 90 A and the battery voltage while cranking is 11 V. What should the technician do next?
a. Charge the battery.
b. Replace the starter; a short is indicated.
c. Make a voltage drop test.
d. Make a battery capacity test.

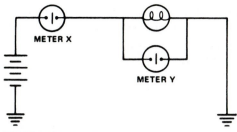

FIGURE 6–65

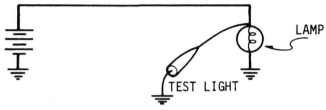

FIGURE 6–64

146. A lamp is not as bright as it should be. Yet a test light "burns" at normal brightness when placed in the circuit as shown in Figure 6–64.

Technician A says that the lamp could have a poor ground.

Technician B says that the wiring circuit from the battery to the lamp has to be good.

Who is right?
a. A only
b. B only
c. Both A and B
d. Neither A nor B

147. The setup in Figure 6–65 is being used by a technician for testing. Which of the following correctly identifies the meters?
a. Meter X is an ohmmeter and Y is a voltmeter.
b. Meter X is an ammeter and Y is a voltmeter.
c. Meter X is a voltmeter and Y is an ammeter.
d. Meter X is an ammeter and Y is an ohmmeter.

148. The cigar lighter in the ground distribution schematic in Figure 6–66 is not working. However, the clock is working.

Technician A says that the G200 connection could be bad.

Technician B says that the wire from S205 to G200 could be bad.

Who is right?
a. A only
b. B only
c. Both A and B
d. Neither A nor B

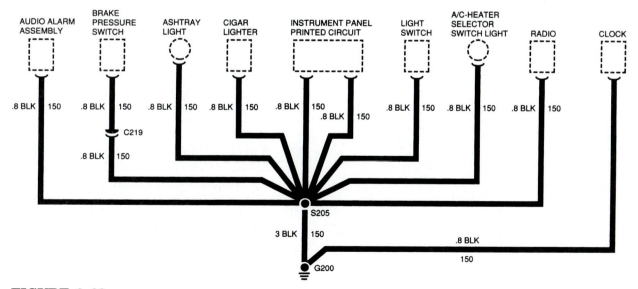

FIGURE 6–66

149. A gas gauge reads on "F" (full) position whenever the ignition switch is turned on.

Technician A says that this problem can be checked out by grounding the sending unit at the tank.

Technician B says that this problem can be checked out by feeding 12 V directly to the gauge.

Who is right?

a. A only
c. Both A and B
b. B only
d. Neither A nor B

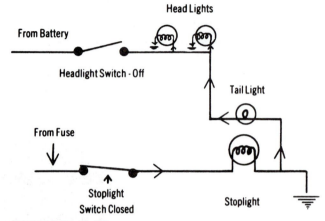

FIGURE 6–67

150. A car owner says that the headlights glow during the day whenever the brake pedal is depressed. According to the diagram in Figure 6–67, what could be wrong?

a. A burned out taillight
b. A bad stoplight ground
c. A bad headlight ground
d. A bad headlight switch

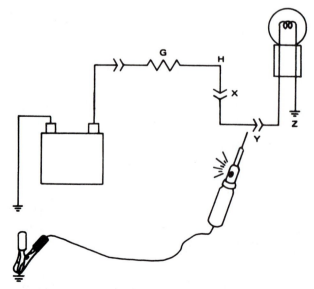

FIGURE 6–68

151. The test light in Figure 6–68 does not light when the point is placed at Y. It lights when placed at H or X. What is indicated?

a. Resistor G is open
b. Bad ground at Z
c. Wire XY is open
d. Bulb is burned out

152. Technician A says that a clock may lose time if there is low voltage at its B + connector.

Technician B says that a clock may not operate if its ground wire is rusted.

Who is right?

a. A only
c. Both A and B
b. B only
d. Neither A nor B

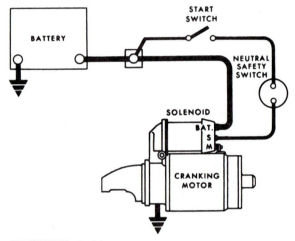

FIGURE 6–69

153. An engine with the starting system in Figure 6–69 will not crank when the start switch is closed. However, when a jumper cable is connected from the solenoid BAT terminal to the solenoid M terminal, the engine cranks.

Technician A says that the battery ground cable could have a loose connection.

Technician B says that the neutral safety switch could be incorrectly positioned.

Who is right?

a. A only
c. Both A and B
b. B only
d. Neither A nor B

154. A driver complains that her car has dim headlights. In checking, you find that the low beams are normal brightness and the high beams are quite dim on both headlamps. Which of the problems listed below would MOST LIKELY cause these symptoms?

a. A shorted headlamps switch
b. The headlamps have been installed upside down.
c. A poor headlamp ground
d. The high beam circuit has excessive resistance.

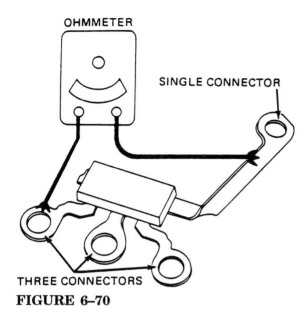

FIGURE 6–70

155. The alternator component in Figure 6–70 is being tested.

Technician A says to note the reading, then reverse the meter leads; both readings should be the same.

Technician B says that each pair of the three stator lead connectors must be checked.

Who is right?

a. A only   **c.** Both A and B

b. B only   **d.** Neither A nor B

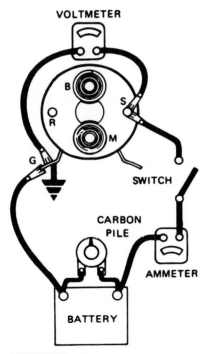

FIGURE 6–71

156. Refer to the starter solenoid in Figure 6–71. Which of the following is correct?

a. The hold-in winding is being adjusted.

b. The pull-in winding is being tested.

c. Terminal R supplies current directly to the ignition coil.

d. Terminal M supplies current to the ignition by-pass.

157. A 3-minute charge test is being performed on a battery in a vehicle.

Technician A says that the battery cables must be disconnected.

Technician B says that this test indicates if the battery plates are hardened (sulphated).

Who is right?

a. A only   **c.** Both A and B

b. B only   **d.** Neither A nor B

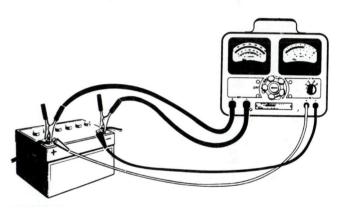

FIGURE 6–72

158. A battery is being tested as pictured in Figure 6–72.

Technician A says to maintain the load for 30 seconds.

Technician B says to apply a load equal to the cold cranking rating of the battery.

Who is right?

a. A only   **c.** Both A and B

b. B only   **d.** Neither A nor B

159. Technician A says that hazard and directional signal flashers can be interchanged, with no problems.

Technician B says that a 2-lamp directional signal flasher can be interchanged with a 3-lamp directional signal flasher, with no problems.

Who is right?

a. A only   **c.** Both A and B

b. B only   **d.** Neither A nor B

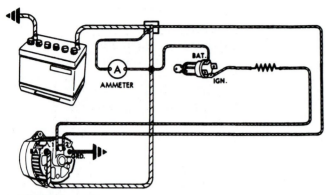

FIGURE 6–73

160. The meter hookup in the charging system in Figure 6–73 will show:
  a. IR drop.
  b. alternator draw.
  c. battery drain.
  d. None of the above

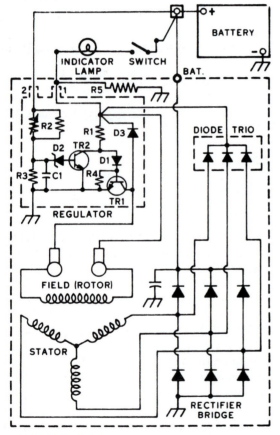

FIGURE 6–74

161. The charge indicator lamp in the charging circuit in Figure 6–74 stays lit at all engine speeds.

Technician A says that this could be caused by a bad diode trio.

Technician B says that this could be caused by system voltage being too high or too low.

Who is right?
  a. A only
  b. B only
  c. Both A and B
  d. Neither A nor B

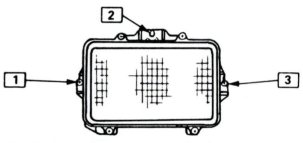

FIGURE 6–75

162. A front headlamp is shown in Figure 6–75. When making the vertical aim adjustment, which adjusting screw would you turn?
  a. 1　**b.** 2　**c.** 3　**d.** None of the above

163. One headlight on a car flickers (goes OFF and ON) while driving.

Technician A says that this could be caused by a loose connector.

Technician B says that this could be caused by a circuit breaker kicking in and out.

Who is right?
  a. A only
  b. B only
  c. Both A and B
  d. Neither A nor B

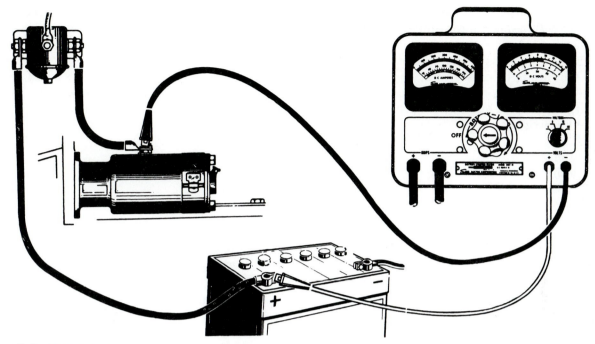

FIGURE 6-76

164. A circuit test is being made on a starting system (see Figure 6-76). While cranking, the voltmeter reads 0.4 V.

Technician A says to replace the starter switch; it is bad.

Technician B says that the ground cable is too small to carry the current.

Who is right?
a. A only
b. B only
c. Both A and B
d. Neither A nor B

165. The test in Figure 6-77 is being made on an alternator.

Technician A says that the field rheostat controls the voltage.

Technician B says that the carbon pile controls the current.

Who is right?
a. A only
b. B only
c. Both A and B
d. Neither A nor B

166. The fuel gauge, oil gauge, and water temperature gauge on a car all read high (they are "pegged").

Technician A says to make sure that the IVR mounting screw on the printed circuit board is tight.

Technician B says to check voltage at the IVR output terminal.

Who is right?
a. A only   **c.** Both A and B
b. B only   **d.** Neither A nor B

167. The sound quality is poor when a stereo tape is played. This could be caused by:
a. a dirty head.
b. a bad tape.
c. an incorrectly installed speaker.
d. Any of the above

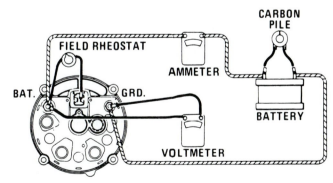

FIGURE 6-77

168. The fusible link in a charging circuit is replaced with a piece of conventional wire of the same size.

Technician A says that this can cause the charge rate to be excessive at high speeds.

Technician B says that this can cause the charge rate to be less at low speeds.

Who is right?
   a. A only
   b. B only
   c. Both A and B
   d. Neither A nor B

169. A car is equipped with 6-way power seats. One adjuster will not operate horizontally.

Technician A says that this could be caused by a disconnected or damaged horizontal drive cable.

Technician B says that this could be caused by a bad horizontal actuator.

Who is right?
   a. A only
   b. B only
   c. Both A and B
   d. Neither A nor B

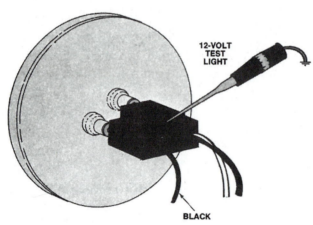

FIGURE 6–78

170. A headlamp is being tested with a 12-V test light as shown in Figure 6–78.

Technician A says that the headlamp filament is open if the test light does not light.

Technician B says to replace the dimmer switch if the test light does not light.

Who is right?
   a. A only
   b. B only
   c. Both A and B
   d. Neither A nor B

171. A power window circuit draws excessive current. The voltage drops in the circuit are okay.

Technician A says that this could be caused by a worn motor.

Technician B says that this could be caused by a bent regulator mechanism.

Who is right?
   a. A only
   b. B only
   c. Both A and B
   d. Neither A nor B

172. A voltage drop test on the insulated side of a charging circuit shows 2.5 V.

Technician A says that high resistance is indicated.

Technician B says to replace the alternator.

Who is right?
   a. A only
   b. B only
   c. Both A and B
   d. Neither A nor B

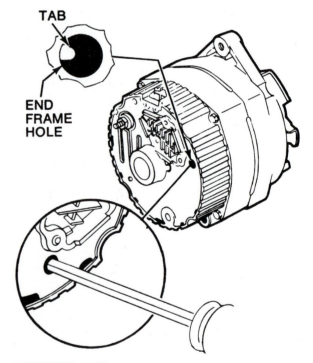

FIGURE 6–79

173. What procedure is being performed in Figure 6–79?
   a. Grounding the field winding
   b. Checking the field relay
   c. Adjusting voltage
   d. Holding the brushes during reassembly

174. The starting system circuitry in a car needs to be completely checked out.

Technician A says that a high-reading ammeter will be required.

Technician B says that a high-impedance DVOM will be required.

Who is right?
a. A only
b. B only
c. Both A and B
d. Neither A nor B

175. You are using a digital ohmmeter to measure a part that has approximately 500-Ω resistance. However, the meter display window keeps showing a 1.0 reading.

Technician A says that the meter could be overranged.

Technician B says to try using a 2K range scale.

Who is right?
a. A only
b. B only
c. Both A and B
d. Neither A nor B

176. A vehicle is being jump started according to the hookup in Figure 6–80.

Technician A says that this hookup is for negative ground systems.

Technician B says that the vehicles must touch when using this hookup.

Who is right?
a. A only
b. B only
c. Both A and B
d. Neither A nor B

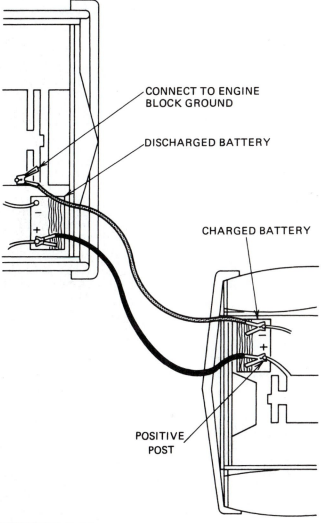

CONNECT TO ENGINE BLOCK GROUND

DISCHARGED BATTERY

CHARGED BATTERY

POSITIVE POST

FIGURE 6–80

177. Technician A says that an analog voltmeter can load down a computer circuit.

Technician B says that a digital voltmeter is preferred to an analog voltmeter when checking computer circuits.

Who is right?
a. A only
b. B only
c. Both A and B
d. Neither A nor B

ALTERNATOR FAULT CODE CHART

Code	Type	Power Loss Lamp	Circuit	When Monitored By The Logic Module	When Put Into Memory
16	Fault	Yes	Battery Voltage Sensing (Charging System)	All the time after one minute from when the engine starts.	If the battery sensing voltage drops below 4 or between 7½ and 8½ volts for more than 20 seconds.
41	Fault	No	Alternator Field Control (Charging System)	All the time when the ignition switch is on.	If the field control fails to switch properly.
44	Fault	No	Battery Temperature Sensor (Charging System)	All the time when the ignition switch is on.	If the battery temperature sensor signal is below .04 or above 4.9 volts.
46	Fault	Yes	Battery Voltage Sensing (Charging System)	All the time when the engine is running.	If the battery sense voltage is more than 1 volt above the desired control voltage for more than 20 seconds.
47	Fault	No	Battery Voltage Sensing (Charging System)	When the engine has been running for more than 6 minutes. engine temperature above 160°F and engine rpm above 1,500 rpm.	If the battery sense voltage is less than 1 volt below the desired control voltage for more than 20 seconds.

FIGURE 6–81

178. An alternator fault code chart is shown in Figure 6–81.

Technician A says that a code will be set if charging system voltage is higher than the specs for more than 20 seconds.

Technician B says that a code 47 indicates a low charging voltage.

Who is right?

a. A only
b. B only
c. Both A and B
d. Neither A nor B

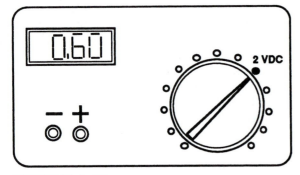

FIGURE 6–82

179. How much voltage is shown on the DVOM pictured in Figure 6–82?

a. 6/1000 V
b. 6/10 V
c. 6 V
d. None of the above

FIGURE 6–83

180. In the dual headlighting system shown in Figure 6–83:
   a. both outside lamps are double filament low and high beam.
   b. both outside lamps are double filament high beam only.
   c. Both inside lamps are double filament low and high beam.
   d. Both inside lamps are double filament high beam only.

181. The cruise control setting on a vehicle will not hold on bumpy roads.

Technician A says that the cause could be a misadjusted brake switch.

Technician B says that the cause could be a bad resume switch.

Who is right?

a. A only
b. B only
c. Both A and B
d. Neither A nor B

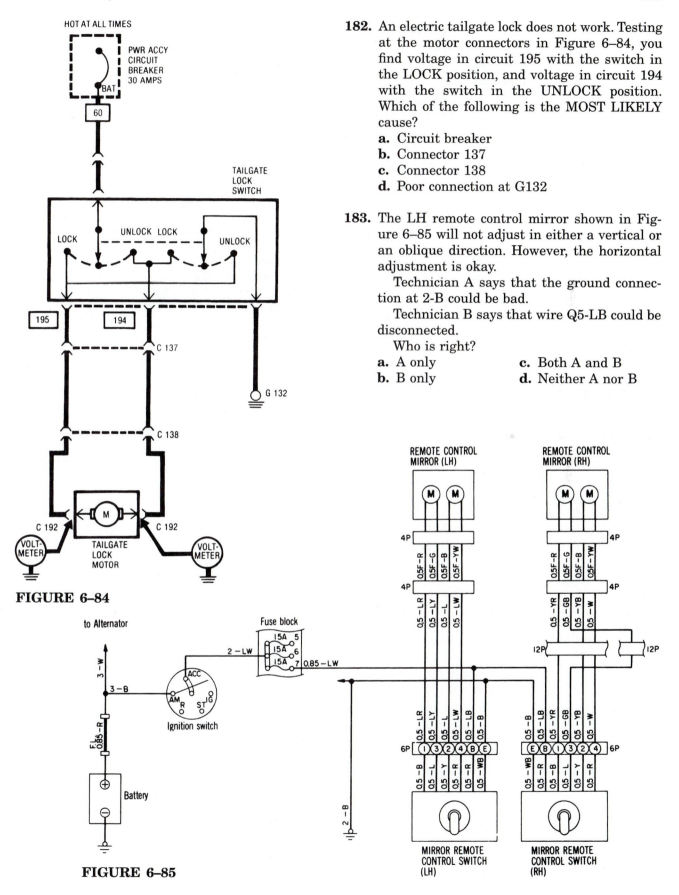

FIGURE 6–84

FIGURE 6–85

182. An electric tailgate lock does not work. Testing at the motor connectors in Figure 6–84, you find voltage in circuit 195 with the switch in the LOCK position, and voltage in circuit 194 with the switch in the UNLOCK position. Which of the following is the MOST LIKELY cause?

a. Circuit breaker

b. Connector 137

c. Connector 138

d. Poor connection at G132

183. The LH remote control mirror shown in Figure 6–85 will not adjust in either a vertical or an oblique direction. However, the horizontal adjustment is okay.

Technician A says that the ground connection at 2-B could be bad.

Technician B says that wire Q5-LB could be disconnected.

Who is right?

a. A only

b. B only

c. Both A and B

d. Neither A nor B

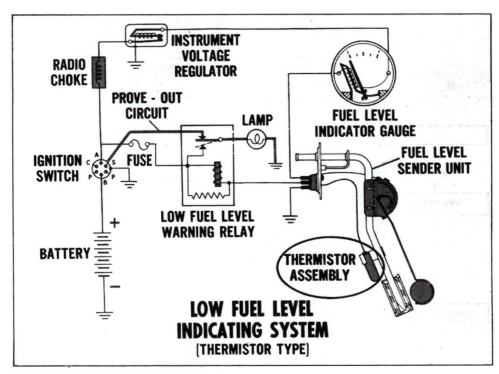

FIGURE 6–86

184. The low fuel warning light shown in Figure 6–86 will not go out when the fuel tank is full.

 Technician A says that the problem could be a short.

 Technician B says that the problem could be a bad relay.

 Who is right?
 a. A only
 b. B only
 c. Both A and B
 d. Neither A nor B

185. An air bag system needs to be temporarily disabled in order to perform steering column service. Which of these procedures would be correct?
 a. Disconnect the negative battery cable and wait 10 minutes.
 b. Remove the fasteners and connectors holding the air bag module to the steering wheel.
 c. Place the air bag module on a bench away from work areas.
 d. All of the above

186. During a starter voltage drop test, the reading across the negative battery cable was recorded at 0.1 V. What can be assumed?
 a. The cable is a gauge size too small.
 b. The cable is okay.
 c. The cable needs replacement.
 d. This is an inconclusive test.

187. During a voltage measurement, a DVOM displays "1", or the "OL", or the display starts to flash. What does this indicate?
 a. The circuit being tested exceeds the range being used.
 b. The polarity of the leads should be reversed.
 c. The battery in the DVOM should be replaced.
 d. The next lower scale should be selected.

188. Which panel display usually requires some sort of back lighting in order to see it operate?
 a. Vacuum tube fluorescent
 b. Liquid crystal
 c. Light emitting diode
 d. Gas vapor

189. The ignition in a vehicle is turned on in the "run" position. When a voltmeter is placed across the starter solenoid "BAT" and "MOTOR" terminals, it reads 12 V. What can be determined by this observation?
 a. The solenoid is bad.
 b. The starter is bad.
 c. The solenoid contacts need cleaning.
 d. This is normal.

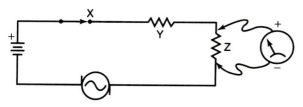

FIGURE 6–87

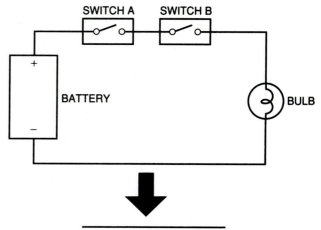

FIGURE 6–88

190. The voltmeter in the circuit in Figure 6–87 reads 0 V. There is power to point X in the circuit.

Technician A says that resistor Y could be too many watts.

Technician B says that resistor Z could be not enough ohms.

Who is right?

a. A only
b. B only
c. Both A and B
d. Neither A nor B

191. A simple mechanical circuit along with a corresponding AND-gate truth table is shown in Figure 6–88.

Technician A says that if either A or B are off (represented as zero), the output is zero and the bulb will not come on.

Technician B says that if both A and B are on (represented as 1), the output is 1 and the bulb will come on.

Who is right?

a. A only   c. Both A and B
b. B only   d. Neither A nor B

Section 7

HEATING AND
AIR CONDITIONING

STUDY OUTLINE

I. Air Conditioning System
  A. Basic Principles of Refrigeration
    1. Temperature/pressure relationship
    2. Latent heat of evaporation/condensation
  B. System Components, Purpose, Operation of Each, Inspection, and Service
    1. Evaporator
      a. Water drain
      b. Blower fan
    2. Compressor
      a. Various types
      b. Electromagnetic clutch
    3. Condenser
    4. Receiver-Drier
      a. Installation
      b. Fusible safety plug
      c. Desiccant
      d. Sight glass
    5. Expansion valve/orifice tube
      a. Sensing bulb (internally or externally equalized)
      b. Inlet screen
    6. Accumulator
  C. Refrigerant Flow
  D. Types of Systems (Temperature Controls) and Test Procedures
    1. Cycling
    2. STV and STV/BPO
    3. POA
    4. EPR
    5. VIR and EEVIR
    6. Fixed orifice tube
    7. Manual and vacuum controls (blend type)
    8. ETR
    9. "H" valve
    10. Combination valve
    11. Automatic systems
      a. Sensors
      b. Servos
      c. Amplifiers
      d. Aspirators
      e. Programmers
      f. Trouble codes

  E. High and Low Side
  F. "Touch" Test
  G. Condition of Refrigerant at Various Circuit Points
  H. Basic Controls for Compressor Operation
    1. Ambient temperature switch
    2. Thermostatic switch
    3. Cycling clutch switch
    4. Low pressure cut-out switch
    5. High pressure cut-out switch
    6. High pressure relief valve
    7. Thermal limiter and superheat switch
    8. Compressor control valve
    9. Pressure sensing switch

II. System Service
  A. Manifold Gauge Set
    1. Hose hook-up
      a. Purging test hoses
      b. Stabilizing system
      c. Attachment with third gauge (auxiliary gauge)
    2. Hand valve positions
    3. Normal gauge readings
  B. Service Valves
    1. Schrader connections
  C. Safety in Handling of Refrigerant
    1. Storage
    2. Discharging
    3. Recycling
    4. Can tap installation
    5. Phosgene gas
    6. Environmental concerns (use of R-134a)
  D. Evacuation Procedure
  E. Isolation of Compressor
  F. Check and Add Compressor Oil (Including Oil Injector Use)
  G. Charging Procedures
  H. Recovery and Recycling
    1. Adding refrigerant as a liquid
    2. Charging with vapor
    3. Adding refrigerant to accumulator type systems
    4. EPA regulations

 I. Leak Testing
  1. Halide
  2. Electronic
  3. Soap (bubble)
  4. Dytel
 J. Compressor Reed Valve Replacement
 K. Compressor Front Seal Replacement
 L. Replace Low Pressure Protection Devices
 M. Replace Clutch Components
 N. Replace Hoses, Lines, Fittings, and Seals
 O. Expansion Valve Screen Replacement
 P. VIR Overhaul
 Q. Receiver-Drier/Desiccant Replacement
 R. Accumulator Replacement
 S. Expansion Tube Replacement
 T. STV and EPR Valve Replacement
 U. Compressor Replacement/Flushing System
 V. Adding Alcohol with a Charging Station
III. Problem/Diagnosis
 A. Engine Overheating
 B. Noisy System Operation
  1. Mounts
  2. Bearings (pulley/clutch)
  3. Belts
  4. Excessive high or low charge
  5. Moisture in the refrigerant
 C. Insufficient Cooling
 D. Intermittent Cooling
 E. No Cooling at All
 F. Windshield Fogging
 G. Abnormal Low-Side Readings
 H. Abnormal High-Side Readings
 I. Frost on Evaporator
 J. Sight Glass
  1. Clear
  2. Foam (bubbles)
  3. Oily
  4. Cloudy
 K. Electrical Circuit Problems
  1. Blown fuse
  2. Defective wiring
  3. Bad connections
  4. Defective thermostat
  5. Magnetic clutch
 L. Effects of Moisture in System
 M. POA Systems/Pressures
 N. EPR Systems/Pressures
 O. Air Distribution
  1. Vacuum motors
  2. Manual cables

  3. Blower motor
   a. Relays
   b. Fuses
   c. Resistors
 P. Driveability/Compressor Control Check Areas
  1. Constant run relay
  2. Time delay relay
  3. Wide open throttle switch
  4. Low vacuum switch
  5. Power steering pressure switch
  6. Power brake time relay
  7. High coolant temperature switch
  8. Electronic control module delay timer
  9. Anti-dieseling relay
IV. Heating Systems
 A. Components
  1. Blend doors
  2. Blower motor
  3. Control valves
  4. Plenum chamber
  5. Vacuum reservoir and check valve
  6. Electrical controls
 B. Flow Control Valve Operation
  1. "Bowden" cable operated
  2. Restricted heater (touch)
  3. Small hose usually inlet
 C. Thermostat and By-pass (Function)
 D. Radiator, Pressure Cap, and Expansion Tank Operation
 E. Service
  1. Electrolysis damage
  2. "Bloc-Chek" test
  3. Testing radiator pressure cap
  4. Reverse flushing
  5. Fluid fan inspection
  6. Replace heater coolant control valve
  7. Replace heater core
  8. Replace hoses
  9. Replace drive belts
  10. Replace pulleys
  11. Replace fan shroud
  12. Replace electric fan
  13. Replace control panel
 F. Problem/Diagnosis
  1. No heat
  2. Too much heat (cannot control)
 G. Blower Motors
  1. Ducting—ac/heating
  2. Heater core position
  3. Evaporator position
  4. Inspect/test/replace resistors

1. A "thumping" noise can be heard after turning off an engine. It is overheated; yet the top tank of the radiator is cool.

   Technician A says that this could be caused by a stuck closed thermostat.

   Technician B says that this could be caused by a slipping water pump belt.

   Who is right?
   a. A only   c. Both A and B
   b. B only   d. Neither A nor B

2. Technician A says that radiators having plastic tanks must use special coolant.

   Technician B says that radiators having plastic tanks must not be pressure tested.

   Who is right?
   a. A only   c. Both A and B
   b. B only   d. Neither A nor B

3. If a can of R-12 refrigerant was released to the atmosphere (at sea level), it would start to "boil" rapidly at a temperature of:
   a. −80°F.   b. −22°F.   c. 0°F.   d. 212°F.

4. In an air conditioning system, the refrigerant is a _____ as it leaves the compressor.
   a. low pressure gas
   b. high pressure liquid
   c. high pressure gas
   d. low pressure liquid

5. The condenser:
   a. changes high pressure vapor into low pressure liquid.
   b. changes high pressure vapor into high pressure liquid.
   c. changes low pressure vapor into low pressure liquid.
   d. changes high pressure liquid into low pressure liquid.

6. The refrigerant line leading from the evaporator to the compressor contains:
   a. low pressure gas.
   b. low pressure liquid.
   c. high pressure gas.
   d. high pressure liquid.

7. In normal operation, the line mentioned in question 6 should feel:
   a. cold to the touch.
   b. hot to the touch.
   c. extremely hot to the touch.
   d. extremely cold to the touch.

8. What will the halide leak detector flame color be when a large refrigerant leak is present?
   a. Red
   b. Yellow-green
   c. Blue-green
   d. Pale blue

9. If R-12 comes into contact with a flame:
   a. it will explode.
   b. it will turn to a non-toxic gas.
   c. iodine crystals are formed.
   d. phosgene gas will form.

10. Any storage container or air conditioning system containing liquid R-12 (at rest and subject to an ambient temperature of 70°F) will have an internal pressure of approximately:
    a. 220 psi.   c. 70 psi.
    b. 125 psi.   d. 30 psi.

11. Technician A says never to steam clean near the components or lines of an air conditioning system because the heat can cause excessive pressure buildup.

    Technician B says never to discharge R-12 into a closed area, because it is heavier than air and can displace the air you breathe.

    Who is right?
    a. A only
    b. B only
    c. Both A and B
    d. Neither A nor B

12. Which air conditioning components separate the high pressure side from the low pressure side?
    a. Evaporator and condenser
    b. Condenser and expansion valve
    c. Compressor and expansion valve
    d. Evaporator and condenser

13. Of the following readings, which is closest to a normal low-side operating gauge pressure?
    a. 5–10 psi   c. 35–50 psi
    b. 15–30 psi   d. 180–205 psi

14. When evacuating an air conditioning system, the manifold gauge hand valves are in which position?
    a. Both sides closed
    b. Both sides open
    c. Low side open, high side closed
    d. Low side closed, high side open

EVAPORATOR PRESSURE GAUGE READING P.S.I.	EVAPORATOR TEMPERATURE °F	HIGH PRESSURE GAUGE READING P.S.I.	AMBIENT TEMPERATURE °F
0	-21	72	40
4.5	-10	105	60
11.2	4	113	64
13.4	8	122	68
15.8	12	129	71
18.3	16	134	73
21	20	140	75

FIGURE 7–1

15. According to the chart in Figure 7–1, if the temperature of the outside air reaching a normal working air conditioner is 71°F, the pressure in the discharge side of the system is:
    a. 129 psi.   c. 12 psi.
    b. 15.8 psi.   d. None of the above

16. Excessive moisture in an air conditioning system will MOST LIKELY cause freezing at the:
    a. receiver-drier.
    b. evaporator.
    c. thermostatic expansion valve.
    d. compressor.

17. A car owner says that his air conditioner is not properly cooling.
    Technician A says that an overcharge of R-12 could be the cause.
    Technician B says that the heater water valve could be the cause.
    Who is right?
    a. A only   c. Both A and B
    b. B only   d. Neither A nor B

18. The low pressure gauge reads 20″ Hg after 15 minutes of evacuation. This would indicate:
    a. that further evacuation is needed.
    b. that evacuation is completed.
    c. a large leak in the system.
    d. a normal condition.

19. A technician discovers that an air conditioning system has way too much "head pressure." The MOST LIKELY cause of this problem is:
    a. the condenser is clogged by bugs.
    b. a leaking thermal bulb.
    c. an open by-pass valve.
    d. a malfunctioning thermostatic switch.

20. Moisture contamination in the refrigeration system can cause:
    a. corrosion, rust, and sludge.
    b. hydrochloric and hydrofluoric acid.
    c. ice.
    d. All of the above

21. An air conditioning unit (switch de-icing type) freezes the coils regardless of temperature control setting.
    Technician A says that a seized clutch bearing could be the problem.
    Technician B says that moisture in the system could be the problem.
    Who is right?
    a. A only   c. Both A and B
    b. B only   d. Neither A nor B

22. Technician A says that when installing the receiver-drier, be sure the arrow points away from the evaporator.
    Technician B says that the receiver-drier should be installed as nearly vertical as possible.
    Who is right?
    a. A only   c. Both A and B
    b. B only   d. Neither A nor B

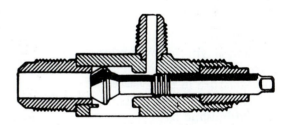

FRONT SEATED

FIGURE 7–2

23. What is the position of the service valve in Figure 7–2?
    a. Front seated
    b. Back seated
    c. Mid-position
    d. Normal operating position

24. Technician A says that if refrigerant will not enter the system due to low temperature, place the R-12 container in 125°F water.
    Technician B says to warm up the R-12 container with a propane torch.
    Who is right?
    a. A only   c. Both A and B
    b. B only   d. Neither A nor B

25. Technician A says that no bubbles in the sight glass could indicate too much refrigerant.
    Technician B says that no bubbles could indicate a complete loss of refrigerant.
    Who is right?
    a. A only
    b. B only
    c. Both A and B
    d. Neither A nor B

26. A heater core has just been boiled out. The car owner complains of insufficient heat.
    Technician A says that the trouble could be an improperly functioning blend door.
    Technician B says that a defective thermostat could be the trouble.
    Who is right?
    a. A only
    b. B only
    c. Both A and B
    d. Neither A nor B

27. When evacuating an air conditioning system, which manifold gauge hose is connected to the vacuum pump?
    a. High pressure hose
    b. Low pressure hose
    c. Center hose
    d. Either a or b above

28. Air conditioning system pressures vary with:
    a. humidity.
    b. altitude.
    c. temperature.
    d. All of the above

29. The compressor clutch will not engage with a system having a low pressure cut-off switch. What could be the cause?
    a. Moisture in the system
    b. A plugged receiver-drier
    c. Both a and b
    d. Neither a nor b

30. The control head is set to the "auto" position on a heating, ventilating, and air conditioning (HVAC) system. There is no response to temperature changes inside the vehicle, yet the blower and clutch work okay. What could be the cause?
    a. An undercharged system
    b. No air flow past the sensor
    c. Both a and b
    d. Neither a nor b

31. What could cause the evaporator to freeze on a cycling clutch air conditioning system?
    a. A bad thermostatic switch
    b. Too much refrigerant in system
    c. Both a and b
    d. Neither a nor b

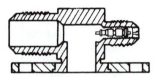

FIGURE 7–3

32. Technician A says that when servicing a system with the type of service valve in Figure 7–3, the compressor cannot be isolated.
    Technician B says that the valve permits a direct reading of the suction and discharge lines without having to front seat or back seat manually.
    Who is right?
    a. A only
    b. B only
    c. Both A and B
    d. Neither A nor B

33. The valve pictured in question 32 is known as a(n):
    a. POA valve.
    b. hot gas bypass valve.
    c. Schrader valve.
    d. EPR valve.

34. You are testing an air conditioning system with an EPR valve.
    Technician A says that the high-side gauge reading should be in the range of 90–110 psi.
    Technician B says that the auxiliary gauge should read 15 psi or more.
    Who is right?
    a. A only
    b. B only
    c. Both A and B
    d. Neither A nor B

35. Technician A says that windshield fogging can be caused by a plugged evaporator drain.
    Technician B says that a leaking heater core can be the cause.
    Who is right?
    a. A only
    b. B only
    c. Both A and B
    d. Neither A nor B

36. On a cycling clutch air conditioning system, the low pressure gauge reading is high. The high pressure gauge reads low.
    Technician A says that an expansion valve stuck open could be the cause.
    Technician B says that a restricted receiver-drier could be the cause.
    Who is right?
    a. A only
    b. B only
    c. Both A and B
    d. Neither A nor B

37. On a cycling clutch air conditioning system the low pressure gauge reading is low. The high pressure gauge reads low also.

    Technician A says that o-ring leakage is a possible cause.

    Technician B says that the expansion valve bulb might be located in the wrong place.

    Who is right?
    a. A only
    b. B only
    c. Both A and B
    d. Neither A nor B

38. Technician A says that the high-side gauge will read in the lower normal range with high ambient temperature.

    Technician B says that the high-side gauge will read in the upper normal range with low ambient temperature.

    Who is right?
    a. A only
    b. B only
    c. Both A and B
    d. Neither A nor B

39. On a cycling clutch air conditioning system, the low-side reading is normal. The high-side reading is too low.

    Technician A says that compressor internal leakage is indicated.

    Technician B says that an overcharge of refrigerant oil is indicated.

    Who is right?
    a. A only
    b. B only
    c. Both A and B
    d. Neither A nor B

40. "Purging" a system too fast will result in:
    a. forming phosgene gas.
    b. pulling oil from the compressor.
    c. reed valve damage.
    d. suction accumulator damage.

41. You are performing a system evacuation. The vacuum pump should be operated a minimum of _____ upon reaching 29″ Hg.
    a. 5 minutes
    b. 15 minutes
    c. 30 minutes
    d. 45 minutes

42. Temperature of stored R-12 must never exceed:
    a. 40°F. b. 72°F. c. 90°F. d. 120°F.

43. An air conditioning system is contaminated with metal particles.

    Technician A says to flush the system using distilled water.

    Technician B says to flush the system using special solvent.

    Who is right?
    a. A only
    b. B only
    c. Both A and B
    d. Neither A nor B

44. STV, POA, ETR, and EPR valves are designed to:
    a. control evaporator temperature.
    b. control condenser pressure.
    c. control compressor pressure.
    d. Both a and c

45. Technician A says that the suction throttling valve (STV) can be cable controlled.

    Technician B says that it is adjustable.

    Who is right?
    a. A only
    b. B only
    c. Both A and B
    d. Neither A nor B

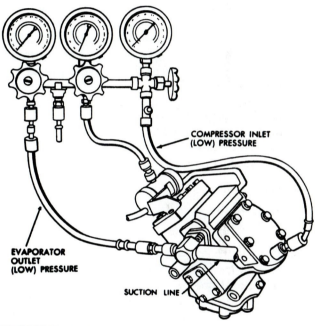

COMPRESSOR INLET (LOW) PRESSURE

EVAPORATOR OUTLET (LOW) PRESSURE

SUCTION LINE

FIGURE 7–4

46. A THIRD gauge is often used in combination with a conventional high and low pressure manifold gauge set (see Figure 7–4). This THIRD gauge permits the technician to:
    a. compare the THIRD gauge reading with the low-side gauge reading.
    b. compare the THIRD gauge reading with the high-side gauge reading.
    c. compare the THIRD gauge reading with figures listed in a pressure/temperature relationship chart.
    d. compare the THIRD gauge reading with discharge air temperature at the evaporator outlet register.

47. A car equipped with a transversally mounted engine is overheating. This could be caused by:
  a. an open coolant temperature switch.
  b. a bad thermostatic fan clutch.
  c. Both a and b
  d. Neither a nor b

48. Which of these could be responsible for drive belt problems?
  a. An overcharge of freon
  b. Misaligned pulleys
  c. Both a and b
  d. Neither a nor b

49. The low-side gauge reads 40 psi; the high-side gauge reads 150 psi; the auxillary gauge reads 5 psi. Ambient air temperature is 80°F. The system has an evaporator pressure control valve and cools poorly. The cause could be:
  a. a bad condenser.
  b. damaged compressor reed valves.
  c. Both a and b
  d. Neither a nor b

50. The low-side gauge reads 1 psi; the high-side gauge reads 200 psi; ambient air temperature is 100°F. The cause could be:
  a. poor air circulation over the condenser.
  b. receiver-drier plugged.
  c. Both a and b
  d. Neither a nor b

51. The low-side gauge reads 60 psi; the high-side gauge reads 110 psi; ambient air temperature is 85°F. Which of these would be the MOST LIKELY cause?
  a. Bad air circulation blower motor
  b. Bad valve plate
  c. Restricted expansion valve
  d. Restricted receiver-drier

52. Refer to the electrical circuit diagram in Figure 7–5. When the blower switch is in the MEDIUM-2 speed position, how many resistors are in the circuit to control blower motor speed?
  a. 3 **b.** 2 **c.** 1 **d.** 0

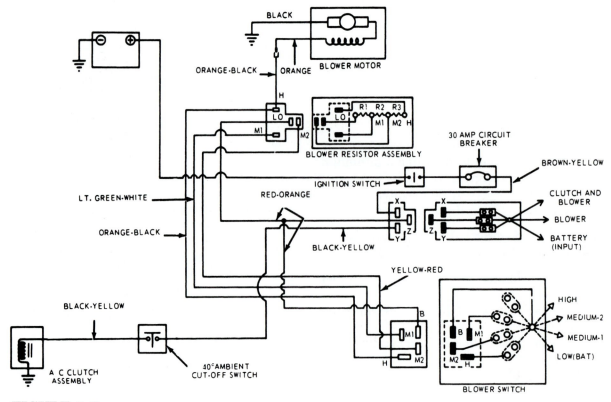

FIGURE 7–5

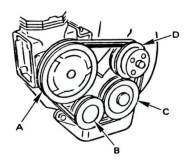

FIGURE 7–6

53. When replacing the compressor drive belt in Figure 7–6, at which pulley would the tension MOST LIKELY be adjusted?
a. Pulley A
c. Pulley C
b. Pulley B
d. Pulley D

54. Which of the following figures would best represent the size of the opening in the expansion valve that the R-12 has to pass through before entering the evaporator?
a. 1/4″　b. 1/8″　c. 0.008″　d. 0.0005″

55. Technician A says that the discharge side hose is smaller than the suction side hose.

Technician B says that the discharge side hose should be cool when given the "touch" test.

Who is right?
a. A only
b. B only
c. Both A and B
d. Neither A nor B

56. Refer to Figure 7–5. What would prevent the a/c clutch from engaging?

Technician A says that the 30-A circuit breaker could be defective.

Technician B says that the red-orange wire could be open.

Who is right?
a. A only
b. B only
c. Both A and B
d. Neither A nor B

57. With the air conditioning system operating, insert a thermometer into the evaporator with the tip touching the coil. The temperature should be around:
a. 35°F.
b. 55°F.
c. 72°F.
d. None of the above

58. A manifold gauge set has been hooked up to the suction and discharge sides of the compressor. The center hose has been blocked off.

Technician A says that system pressure is read when the gauge hand valves are open.

Technician B says that system pressure is read when the gauge hand valves are closed.

Who is right?
a. A only
b. B only
c. Both A and B
d. Neither A nor B

59. Clutch bearing failure noise on a York compressor would typically be:
a. much less when the compressor is engaged.
b. much worse when the compressor is engaged.
c. the same whether or not the compressor is engaged.
d. heard only when the compressor is engaged.

60. An air conditioning system is being charged with vapor. Which of the following is correct?
a. Close the high-side hand valve.
b. Open the low-side hand valve.
c. Hold the refrigerant drum upright.
d. All of the above

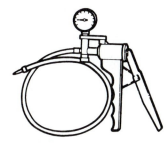

FIGURE 7–7

61. You are testing a blend door vacuum motor using the tool in Figure 7–7. You connect the tool into the line going to the motor, and obtain a zero vacuum reading. This would indicate:
a. the door is restricted.
b. the line to the motor is plugged or kinked.
c. the vacuum motor is defective.
d. Any of the above

62. Which of the following statements is true?
  a. Refrigerant gas is heavier than air and will rapidly drop to the floor as it flows from a point of leakage.
  b. The total refrigerant charge circulates through the entire system at least once each minute.
  c. Just one drop of water added to the refrigerant system can result in corrosion.
  d. All of the above

63. Which of the following leak detection methods indicates a leak by a red-colored stain?
  a. Halide   **c.** Flame
  b. Dytel   **d.** Electronic

64. A heater core is rust-corroded and needs flushing.
  Technician A says to clean the core by high pressure reverse flushing.
  Technician B says to clean the core by flushing with a gentle water stream.
  Who is right?
  a. A only
  b. B only
  c. Both A and B
  d. Neither A nor B

65. You are recharging an air conditioning system. The refrigerant is being added as a liquid. Which of the following is correct?
  a. Tip the refrigerant can upside-down.
  b. Open the low-side hand valve.
  c. Open the high-side hand valve and run the engine.
  d. None of the above

66. When "touching" the inlet and outlet of the receiver-drier, the temperature:
  a. should feel warm at the inlet and cold at the outlet.
  b. should feel cold at the inlet and warm at the outlet.
  c. should feel almost identical at the inlet and outlet.
  d. should feel warm at the inlet and hot at the outlet.

67. The arrow in Figure 7–8 is pointing to:
  a. an expansion valve.
  b. an EPR valve.
  c. a VIR valve.
  d. None of the above

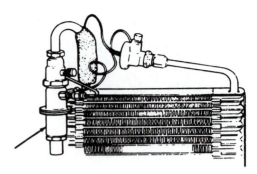

FIGURE 7–8

68. An air conditioning system is equipped with an EPR valve. When a THIRD gauge is connected into the compressor service port it will read:
  a. line pressure.
  b. compressor high-side pressure.
  c. discharge pressure.
  d. suction pressure.

69. Technician A says that a suction throttling valve not regulating properly could cause insufficient air flow from the instrument panel registers.
  Technician B says that a suction throttling valve not regulating properly could cause the evaporator to ice up.
  Who is right?
  a. A only
  b. B only
  c. Both A and B
  d. Neither A nor B

70. Technician A says that a defective POA valve can cause evaporator pressure to be either too high or too low.
  Technician B says that adjustment is possible on POA valves.
  Who is right?
  a. A only
  b. B only
  c. Both A and B
  d. Neither A nor B

71. You observe a slight seepage of compressor oil from the compressor shaft seal. This condition is:
  a. normal.
  b. a sign that the seal requires immediate replacement.
  c. an indication that the compressor shaft surface is damaged.
  d. Either b or c above

72. An air conditioning system is being evacuated (pumped down).

Technician A says that this is to remove refrigerant.

Technician B says that this is to remove dirt particles.

Who is right?

a. A only   **c.** Both A and B

b. B only   **d.** Neither A nor B

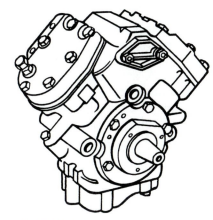

FIGURE 7–9

73. How would you check oil level in the compressor in Figure 7–9?

a. By draining the oil

b. With a special inducer tool

c. With a special dipstick

d. With a pressure gauge

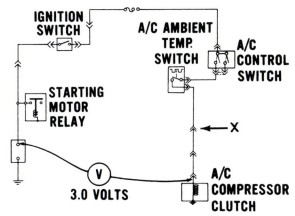

FIGURE 7–10

74. The meter in Figure 7–10 reads 3.0 V.

Technician A says that this is an unacceptable reading.

Technician B says that a bad connection at point X could be the cause of this reading.

Who is right?

a. A only   **c.** Both A and B

b. B only   **d.** Neither A nor B

75. Restricted air flow through the condenser will cause:

a. the low-side to read high.

b. the high-side to read low.

c. Both a and b

d. Neither a nor b

76. The refrigerant in the receiver-drier is a:

a. high pressure liquid.

b. high pressure vapor.

c. low pressure liquid.

d. low pressure vapor.

77. The high-side pressure in an air conditioning system is too high.

Technician A says that this could be caused by a slipping compressor drive belt.

Technician B says that this could be caused by a broken compressor reed valve.

Who is right?

a. A only   **c.** Both A and B

b. B only   **d.** Neither d.A nor B

78. A compressor has seized (because of a broken crankshaft) and is being replaced.

Technician A says that the drier must be replaced.

Technician B says that the complete system must be flushed.

Who is right?

a. A only   **c.** Both A and B

b. B only   **d.** Neither A nor B

79. The ETR (evaporator temperature regulator) valve:

a. is operated electrically.

b. is installed in the compressor inlet.

c. is designed to be normally open.

d. All of the above

FIGURE 7–11

80. Which view in Figure 7–11 would you see through the sight glass if everything within the air conditioning system was normal?

a. 1   **c.** Either 1 or 2

b. 2   **d.** Neither 1 nor 2

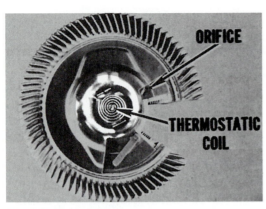

FIGURE 7–12

81. Many cooling systems use a thermal control fan drive coupling (see Figure 7–12).

Technician A says that the thermostatic coil controls the opening and closing of the orifice inside the coupling.

Technician B says that when the thermostatic coil is cold, the orifice is open.

Who is right?

a. A only
b. B only
c. Both A and B
d. Neither A nor B

FIGURE 7–13

82. Technician A says that when using the torch in Figure 7–13, check the legality of it in your area.

Technician B says that the copper element must be red hot.

Who is right?

a. A only
b. B only
c. Both A and B
d. Neither A nor B

83. A 6-cylinder compressor is being rebuilt. When installing the ceramic seal seat, what procedure is correct?

a. Coat the seal face with clean compressor oil.
b. Depress the seal seat retainer ring into position by tapping it with a hammer.
c. Avoid touching the seal seat face with your fingers.
d. Both a and c

84. A customer complains that the blower motor speed does not increase when the selector is moved from low to defrost position.

Technician A says that a blower resistor could be the problem.

Technician B says that a faulty blower motor ground could be the problem.

Who is right?

a. A only
b. B only
c. Both A and B
d. Neither A nor B

85. Outside temperature is 85° F. With the engine running, an air conditioning gauge set reads as follows:

Low side—5″ Hg (vacuum)
High side—190 psi

Technician A says that these readings could be caused by a blown compressor gasket.

Technician B says that these readings could be caused by low refrigerant charge.

Who is right?

a. A only
b. B only
c. Both A and B
d. Neither A nor B

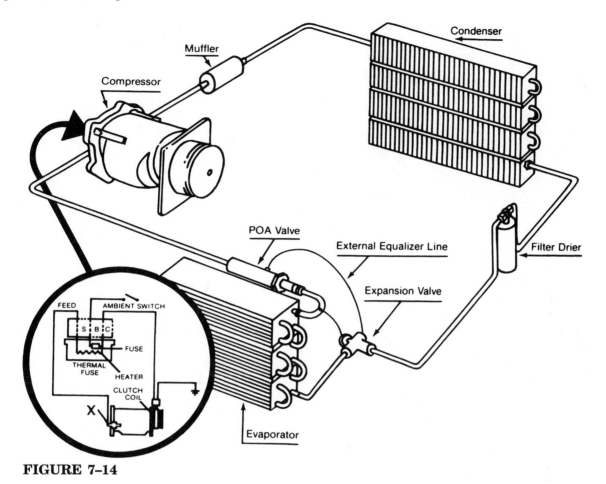

FIGURE 7–14

86. A vehicle is equipped with the air conditioning circuit in Figure 7–14. Arrow X is pointing to:
   a. the ambient switch.
   b. the superheat switch.
   c. the high pressure switch.
   d. None of the above

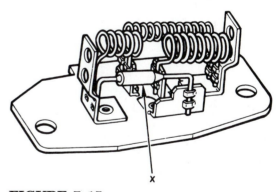

FIGURE 7–15

87. Technician A says that part X in Figure 7–15 is an overheating protective device.
   Technician B says that part X helps prevent damage to the evaporator case assembly.
   Who is right?
   a. A only
   b. B only
   c. Both A and B
   d. Neither A nor B

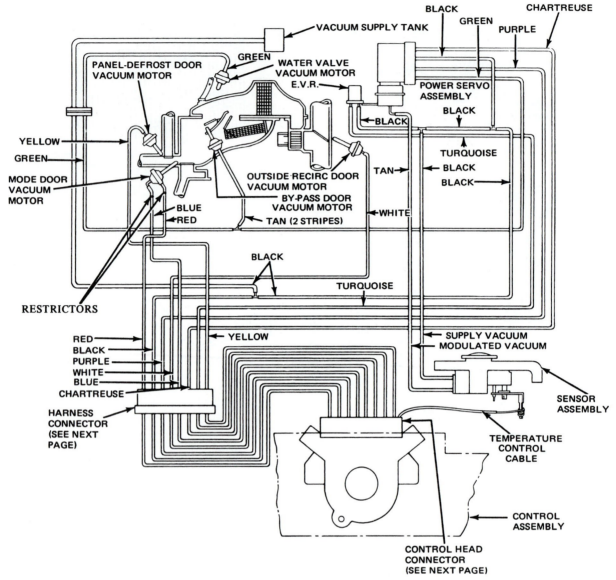

FIGURE 7–16

88. Refer to the automatic temperature control (ATC) vacuum system in Figure 7–16.

   A car owner says that the VENT and AC air come out the defroster opening instead of the panel registers. What could be the cause of this problem?
   a. Disconnected yellow vacuum hose
   b. Bad power servo
   c. Both a and b
   d. Neither a nor b

89. Technician A says that a "combo" valve assembly controls evaporator pressure.

   Technician B says that a "combo" valve assembly is similar in function and operation to a VIR assembly.
   Who is right?
   a. A only   c. Both A and B
   b. B only   d. Neither A nor B

90. Technician A says that a bad TPS can prevent compressor-clutch engagement.

   Technician B says that a bad coolant sensor can prevent compressor-clutch engagement.
   Who is right?
   a. A only   c. Both A and B
   b. B only   d. Neither A nor B

91. A technician is connecting a manifold gauge set that has color-coded hoses. The blue hose is connected to:
   a. a vacuum source.   **c.** the low side.
   b. the refrigerant.   **d.** the high side.

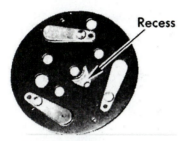

FIGURE 7–17

92. What is the name of the part in Figure 7–17?
   a. Front discharge valve plate assembly
   b. Suction reed plate
   c. Rear discharge valve plate assembly
   d. None of the above

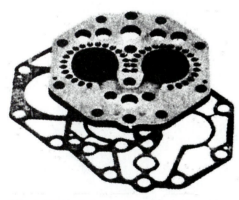

FIGURE 7–18

93. The 2-cylinder compressor part shown in Figure 7–18 is a:
   a. cylinder head.
   b. wobble plate.
   c. valve plate.
   d. suction cross-over cover.

94. A car owner complains of low heater output. All of these could be the cause EXCEPT:
   a. low coolant level in the engine.
   b. core sand lodged in the cooling system thermostat.
   c. a restricted heater water valve.
   d. using ethylene glycol type antifreeze.

FIGURE 7–19

95. The valve in Figure 7–19 has been installed backwards.
   Technician A says that this can cause the engine to overheat.
   Technician B says that this can cause cold air output from the heater.
   Who is right?
   a. A only   **c.** Both A and B
   b. B only   **d.** Neither A nor B

96. Two technicians are discussing heater water valves.
   Technician A says that some types are vacuum closed.
   Technician B says that some types are vacuum opened.
   Who is right?
   a. A only   **c.** Both A and B
   b. B only   **d.** Neither A nor B

97. When both manual service valves are in the back-seated position:
   a. the compressor is isolated.
   b. service procedures can be performed.
   c. the suction side and discharge side of the compressor are cut off.
   d. the compressor is in normal operating position.

98. The outlet heater hose that leads to the water pump has been removed. The engine is started, and the heater control switch is turned ON. The heater core outlet shows no water flow.
   Technician A says that the heater core could be plugged.
   Technician B says that the heater water valve could be defective.
   Who is right?
   a. A only   **c.** Both A and B
   b. B only   **d.** Neither A nor B

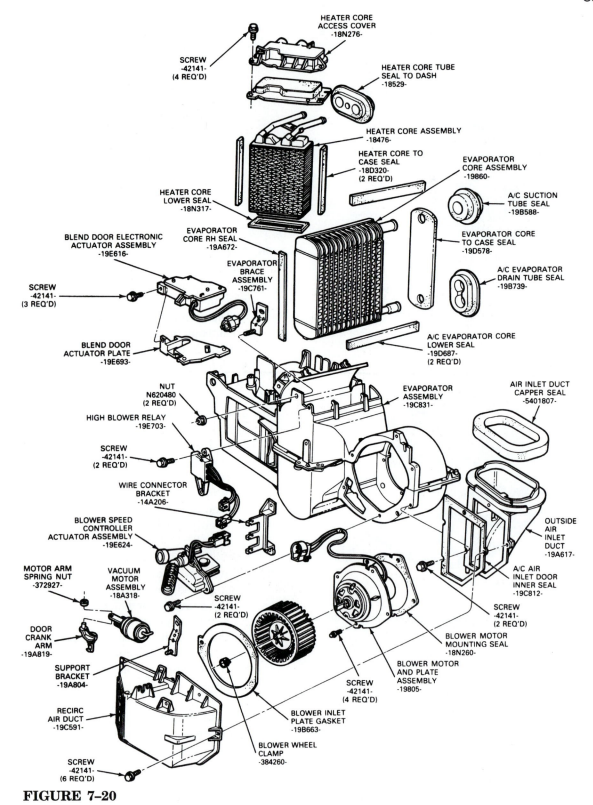

FIGURE 7–20

99. The evaporator needs to be removed from a vehicle (see Figure 7–20).

Technician A says to disconnect the battery ground cable.

Technician B says to discharge the refrigerant from the air conditioning system.

Who is right?

a. A only
b. B only
c. Both A and B
d. Neither A nor B

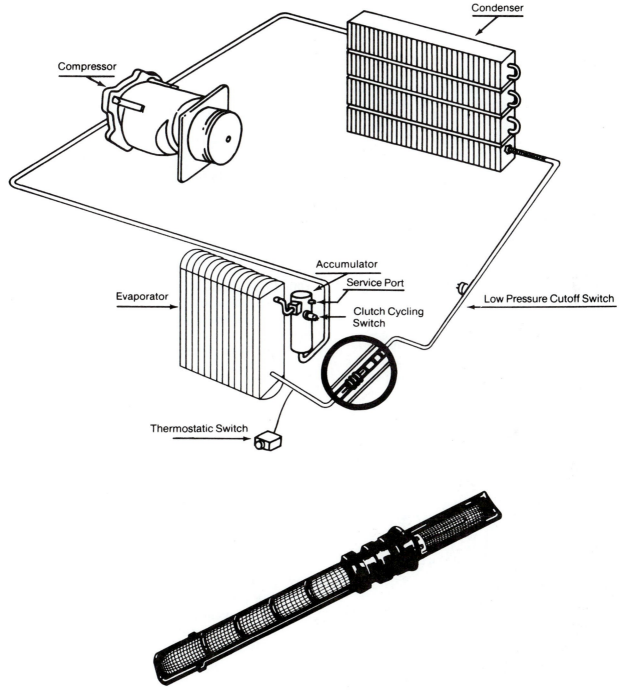

Condenser

Compressor

Accumulator

Service Port

Evaporator

Clutch Cycling Switch

Low Pressure Cutoff Switch

Thermostatic Switch

FIGURE 7–21

100. A vehicle is equipped with the cycling clutch orifice tube (CCOT) air conditioning system in Figure 7–21.

Technician A says that the drying agent is in the accumulator.

Technician B says that special aftermarket tools are available for removing the orifice tube.

Who is right?
a. A only
b. B only
c. Both A and B
d. Neither A nor B

101. A pressure tester is being used to check a cooling system. Gauge pressure rises when the engine is started.

   Technician A says that the radiator cap could be bad.

   Technician B says that the radiator core passages could be restricted.

   Who is right?

   a. A only   **c.** Both A and B

   b. B only   **d.** Neither A nor B

102. Refer to Figure 7–27 (p. 240). In either the high or low heat position, there is no heat to the floor. However, warm air flows from the defrosters. Which vacuum door is not working properly?

   a. 4   **c.** 6

   b. 5   **d.** None of the above

103. When performing cooling system service, air can become trapped in the heater core.

   Technician A says to bleed the trapped air by loosening the heater core outlet hose.

   Technician B says to bleed the trapped air by turning the heater on.

   Who is right?

   a. A only   **c.** Both A and B

   b. B only   **d.** Neither A nor B

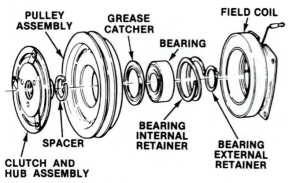

FIGURE 7–22

104. Refer to the exploded-view illustration in Figure 7–22.

   Technician A says that slight scoring of the drive plate is a normal condition.

   Technician B says that slight scoring of the driven plate is a normal condition.

   Who is right?

   a. A only

   b. B only

   c. Both A and B

   d. Neither A nor B

105. An extremely noisy compressor would MOST LIKELY be caused by:

   a. clutch wire shorted.

   b. high head pressures.

   c. slipping compressor clutch.

   d. defective ambient cut-off switch.

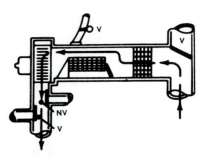

FIGURE 7–23

106. Refer to the heater-air conditioning system illustration in Figure 7–23. Which dash control setting would provide the air flow as shown?

   a. Recirculate air conditioning position

   b. Fresh air conditioning position

   c. Defrost position

   d. Maximum heat position

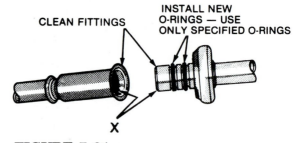

FIGURE 7–24

107. New o-rings are being installed on the spring lock coupling in Figure 7–24.

   Technician A says to lubricate surface X with refrigerant oil.

   Technician B says to assemble the coupling together by pushing with a slight twisting motion.

   Who is right?

   a. A only   **c.** Both A and B

   b. B only   **d.** Neither A nor B

108. When assembling a refrigerant tube and hose joint:

   a. lubricate the o-ring(s) with a thin film of wheel bearing grease.

   b. tighten the connection as tight as possible.

   c. Both a and b

   d. Neither a nor b

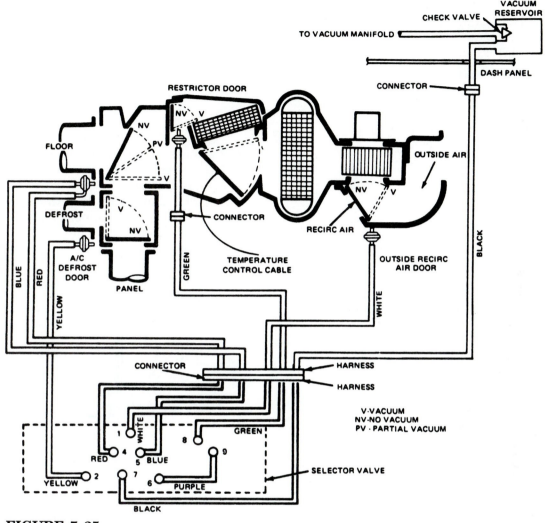

FIGURE 7–25

109. In the heater-air conditioning system in Figure 7–25, air comes out of the defroster outlet regardless of selector valve position.

Technician A says that this could be caused by a leaking vacuum reservoir tank.

Technician B says that this could be caused by a disconnected harness connector.

Who is right?

a. A only   **c.** Both A and B
b. B only   **d.** Neither A nor B

110. Technician A says that expansion valves are externally equalized.

Technician B says that expansion valves are internally equalized.

Who is right?

a. A only   **c.** Both A and B
b. B only   **d.** Neither A nor B

111. On a blend air type heating system, there is no heat.

Technician A says that this could be caused by an incorrect cable adjustment.

Technician B says that this could be caused by a faulty thermal bulb.

Who is right?

a. A only   **c.** Both A and B
b. B only   **d.** Neither A nor B

112. After a new heater core is installed, there is no air flow from the dash and floor registers.

Technician A says that the heater water valve could be disconnected.

Technician B says that the heater core could have an air lock.

Who is right?

a. A only   **c.** Both A and B
b. B only   **d.** Neither A nor B

FIGURE 7–26

113. The item in Figure 7–26 is used to:
   a. prevent compressor damage.
   b. break the clutch circuit.
   c. Both a and b
   d. Neither a nor b

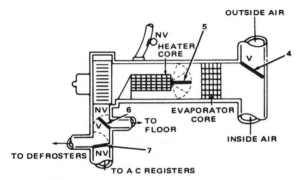

FIGURE 7–27

114. Refer to the heater-air conditioning system illustration in Figure 7–27. When the air conditioner is turned on, there is no cool air flowing from the air conditioning registers. However, cool air flows out of the defroster outlets. Which vacuum door is not operating?
   a. 4   **b.** 5   **c.** 6   **d.** 7

HIGH PRESSURE		LOW PRESSURE
•LIQUID LINE	•COMPRESSOR	
HIGH	HIGH	HIGH

FIGURE 7–28

115. The conditions in Figure 7–28 in a cycling-clutch air conditioning system could be caused by:
   a. insufficient closure of the heater water valve.
   b. poor contact at the expansion valve sensing bulb.
   c. Both a and b
   d. Neither a nor b

FIGURE 7–29

116. Technician A says that the rated cap in Figure 7–29 is commonly used on air conditioning equipped vehicles.
   Technician B says that that type of cap increases cooling system efficiency.
   Who is right?
   a. A only
   b. B only
   c. Both A and B
   d. Neither A nor B

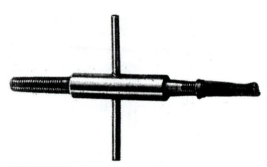

FIGURE 7–30

117. The special tool shown in Figure 7–30 is a(n):
   a. ceramic seal seat remover.
   b. expansion valve screen remover.
   c. CCOT remover.
   d. hub and shoe thread restorer.

FIGURE 7–31

118. The part in Figure 7–31:
   a. is an evaporator pressure regulator (EPR) valve.
   b. senses refrigerant pressure.
   c. Both a and b
   d. Neither a nor b

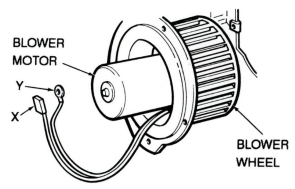

FIGURE 7–32

119. The blower motor in Figure 7–32 will not work when turned on by the dash switch. However, it works when battery voltage is fed into point X with a jumper wire and point Y is grounded with a jumper wire.

Technician A says that the motor armature could be bad.

Technician B says that the motor ground could be bad.

Who is right?

a. A only

b. B only

c. Both A and B

d. Neither A nor B

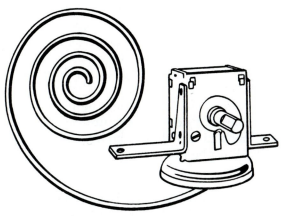

FIGURE 7–33

120. The switch in Figure 7–33 is used in a cycling-clutch air conditioning system.

Technician A says that this switch closes when the gas inside the coiled tube contracts.

Technician B says that this switch is placed in series with the compressor clutch circuit.

Who is right?

a. A only

b. B only

c. Both A and B

d. Neither A nor B

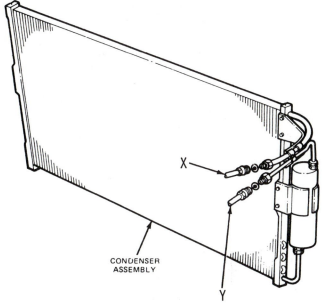

FIGURE 7–34

121. Refer to Figure 7–34. The discharge line from the compressor would be hooked to:

a. line X.   **c.** either X or Y.

b. line Y.   **d.** neither X nor Y.

FIGURE 7–35

122. When performing the test in Figure 7–35 on a safety-type radiator cap:

a. be sure the cap lever is in the down position.

b. the gauge hand should fall comparatively fast.

c. Both a and b

d. Neither a nor b

123. Which of the following would be considered the MOST NORMAL compressor clutch air gap clearance?
a. .0025″ **b.** .025″ **c.** 1/16″ **d.** .100″

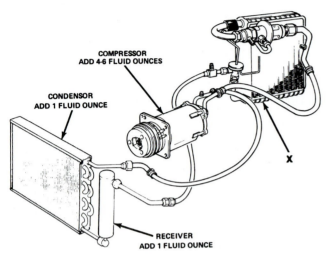

COMPRESSOR
ADD 4-6 FLUID OUNCES

CONDENSOR
ADD 1 FLUID OUNCE

X

RECEIVER
ADD 1 FLUID OUNCE

FIGURE 7–36

124. Part X shown in Figure 7–36 is going to be replaced.

Technician A says that it is not necessary to cap all open connections since all inlet and outlet connections are small in size.

Technician B says to pour several ounces of refrigerant oil into the new part X before installing.

Who is right?
a. A only
b. B only
c. Both A and B
d. Neither A nor B

125. Technician A says that on a factory installed air conditioning-heater system, air flow through the evaporator is controlled by the position of the blend door.

Technician B says that on a factory installed air conditioning-heater system, inlet air can come from the outside or from the inside of the vehicle.

Who is right?
a. A only
b. B only
c. Both A and B
d. Neither A nor B

126. A customer drives her car back into the shop for the third time with all the R-12 gone.

Technician A says that this could have been caused by failure to check for leakage at the evaporator drain.

Technician B says that this could have been caused by failure to check for leakage at the compressor service valves.

Who is right?
a. A only
b. B only
c. Both A and B
d. Neither A nor B

127. An air conditioning system on a late model vehicle incorporates a thermal limiter (fuse) and superheat switch.

Technician A says to use a jumper wire and by-pass when charging the system.

Technician B says to disconnect the superheat switch when charging the system.

Who is right?
a. A only
b. B only
c. Both A and B
d. Neither A nor B

128. Which of the following statements is true?
a. Do not use a superheat compressor on a high pressure system.
b. Do not use a high pressure compressor on a superheat system.
c. Either compressor may be used on a system that does not require the use of a superheat switch or a high pressure switch.
d. All of the above

129. Technician A says that gauge lines should be purged when gauges are connected to a charged air conditioning system.

Technician B says that purging should be done with the engine running.

Who is right?
a. A only
b. B only
c. Both A and B
d. Neither A nor B

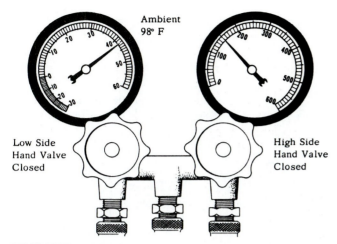

Ambient 98° F

Low Side Hand Valve Closed

High Side Hand Valve Closed

FIGURE 7-37

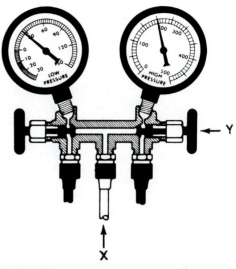

←— Y

↑
X

FIGURE 7-38

130. A customer complains that his car's interior does not cool down sufficiently for comfort. A gauge set is installed and the readings in Figure 7–37 are obtained.

Technician A says that the cause could be worn rings in the compressor.

Technician B says that the cause could be leaking reed valves.

Who is right?

a. A only
b. B only
c. Both A and B
d. Neither A nor B

131. An air conditioning clutch does not engage the compressor. However, there is B+ voltage at the clutch coil feed wire.

Technician A says that the clutch coil could be bad.

Technician B says that the clutch coil ground could be bad.

Who is right?

a. A only
b. B only
c. Both A and B
d. Neither A nor B

132. Refrigerant is being added to a non-accumulator air conditioning system.

Technician A says to connect a can of R-12 to hose X in Figure 7–38.

Technician B says to start the engine and open hand valve Y.

Who is right?

a. A only
b. B only
c. Both A and B
d. Neither A nor B

133. An air conditioning-heating system will not hold vacuum. A vacuum gauge "tee-ed" into the supply line shows a reading of 18″ that drops slowly to zero when the engine is shut-off.

Technician A says that the manifold check valve could be bad.

Technician B says that the vacuum supply tank could be "pin-holed."

Who is right?

a. A only
b. B only
c. Both A and B
d. Neither A nor B

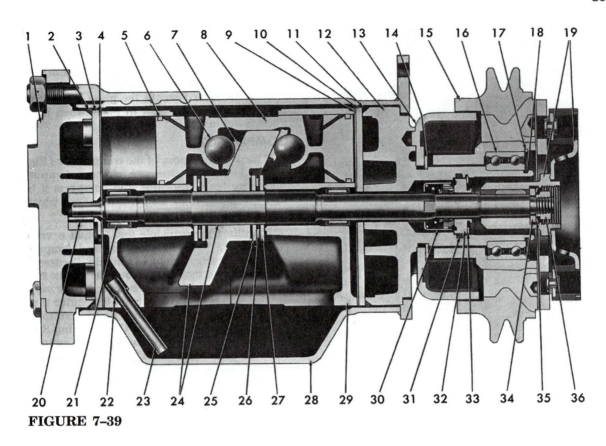

FIGURE 7–39

134. The sectional view of a 6-cylinder compressor is pictured in Figure 7–39.

Technician A says that part 24 changes rotating motion into reciprocating motion.

Technician B says that arrow 20 points to the oil pump gears.

Who is right?
a. A only
b. B only
c. Both A and B
d. Neither A nor B

135. Technician A says that the MAX A/C mode in some systems provide for up to 20% fresh air.

Technician B says that a fresh air supply of 100% is generally provided in the MAX HEAT mode.

Who is right?
a. A only
b. B only
c. Both A and B
d. Neither A nor B

136. The air conditioning compressor shaft on a vehicle does not rotate and the pulley freewheels. But, when a jumper wire is connected to the clutch, it engages.

Technician A says that an ambient switch could be bad.

Technician B says that a fuse could be bad.

Who is right?
a. A only
b. B only
c. Both A and B
d. Neither A nor B

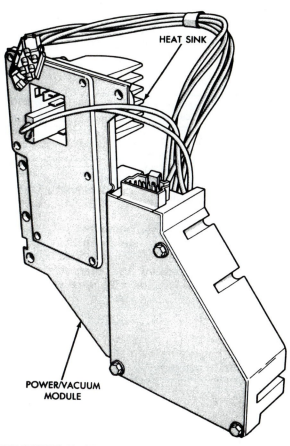

HEAT SINK

POWER/VACUUM
MODULE

FIGURE 7–40

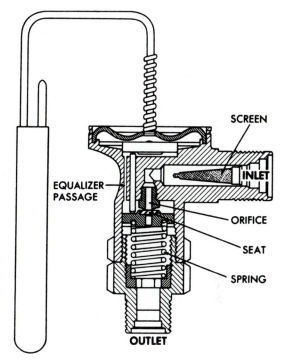

EQUALIZER
PASSAGE

SCREEN

INLET

ORIFICE

SEAT

SPRING

OUTLET

FIGURE 7–41

137. A power/vacuum module (PVM) from an automatic temperature control system is pictured in Figure 7–40.

Technician A says that an ohmmeter can be used to measure PVM input signals from the computer.

Technician B says that a voltmeter can be used to measure PVM output signals.

Who is right?

a. A only   c. Both A and B
b. B only   d. Neither A nor B

138. Technician A says that leak detecting dye can curdle and block the inlet screen of the expansion valve or orifice tube.

Technician B says that electronic leak detectors are generally best for locating small leaks.

Who is right?

a. A only
b. B only
c. Both A and B
d. Neither A nor B

139. The valve in Figure 7–41 is being checked on-the-car.

Technician A says that low-side pressure should rise when the bulb is warmed in your hand.

Technician B says that the valve should open wide when the bulb is warmed in your hand.

Who is right?

a. A only
b. B only
c. Both A and B
d. Neither A nor B

140. Technician A says that the compressor low-side to high-side ratio on cycling clutch systems is approximately 1:10.

Technician B says that on non-cycling clutch systems with evaporator pressure regulators, the ratio is approximately 1:5.

Who is right?

a. A only
b. B only
c. Both A and B
d. Neither A nor B

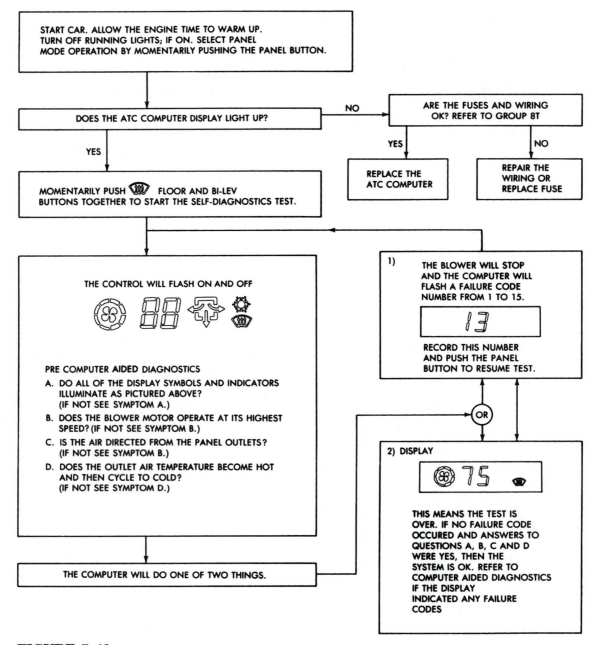

FIGURE 7–42

141. An automatic temperature control (ATC) diagnostic flowchart is shown in Figure 7–42.

Technician A says to momentarily push the FLOOR and BI-LEV buttons together to begin self-diagnostics.

Technician B says that this particular system has 20 failure (fault) codes.

Who is right?

a. A only
b. B only
c. Both A and B
d. Neither A nor B

142. Technician A says that the changing of refrigerant oil is considered to be part of seasonal service.

Technician B says that refrigerant oil is very pure and light (about 525 viscosity).

Who is right?

a. A only
b. B only
c. Both A and B
d. Neither A nor B

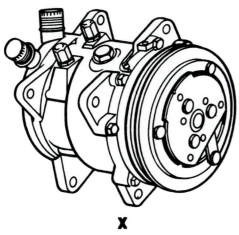
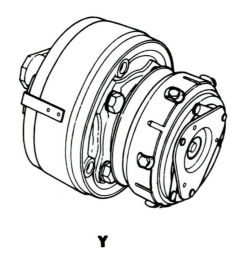

X   **Y**

FIGURE 7–43

143. Technician A says that compressor X shown in Figure 7–43 has 4 cylinders and uses no connecting rods.

Technician B says that compressor Y shown above has five pistons and uses a "swash" plate.

Who is right?
- **a.** A only
- **b.** B only
- **c.** Both A and B
- **d.** Neither A nor B

144. An air conditioning system cools satisfactorily during the early morning or late evening. But, it does not cool during the hot part of the day. NOTE: While testing, the low-side gauge may read normal and then drop into a vacuum.

Technician A says that ice could be forming on the expansion valve tip.

Technician B says that the drier could be saturated with moisture.

Who is right?
- **a.** A only
- **b.** B only
- **c.** Both A and B
- **d.** Neither A nor B

145. An air conditioning system does not cool the car. The low-side gauge reads 45 psi; the high-side gauge reads 250 psi; ambient air is 95°F; there is a heavy sweat on the suction hose and from the evaporator. What could be the problem?
- **a.** The thermal bulb has lost its charge.
- **b.** A clogged expansion valve screen
- **c.** Both a and b
- **d.** Neither a nor b

146. An operational check needs to be made on an automatic temperature control system.

Technician A says to turn on the system, set the temperature degree dial to 75° F, and blow hot air from a hair dryer around the in-car temperature sensor and aspirator. The system should go into the heating mode.

Technician B says to spray R-12 around the in-car temperature sensor and aspirator. The system should go into the heating mode.

Who is right?
- **a.** A only
- **b.** B only
- **c.** Both A and B
- **d.** Neither A nor B

147. Technician A says that liquid-charging into the high side with the engine off is accepted procedure when using a charging station.

Technician B says that you can measure exactly how much refrigerant has been delivered into the system when using a charging station.

Who is right?
- **a.** A only
- **b.** B only
- **c.** Both A and B
- **d.** Neither A nor B

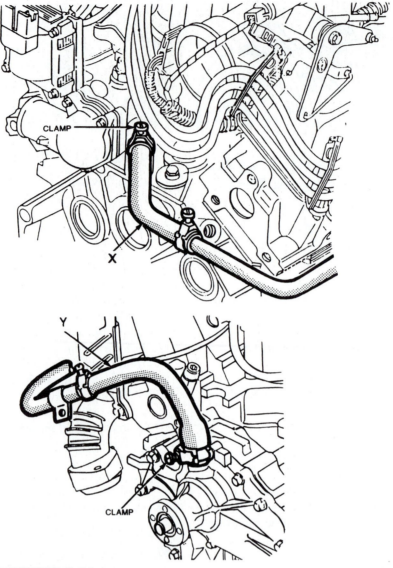

FIGURE 7–44

148. Technician A says that heater hose X and hose Y pictured in Figure 7–44 are improperly connected to the engine; they need to be reversed.

Technician B says that reversed heater hoses can result in unsatisfactory heater operation.

Who is right?

a. A only   **c.** Both A and B
b. B only   **d.** Neither A nor B

149. Technician A says that the Montreal Protocol Agreement was established to protect the earth's ozone layer.

Technician B says that R-12, R-22, R-500, and R-502 refrigerants can be recovered and recycled.

Who is right?

a. A only   **c.** Both A and B
b. B only   **d.** Neither A nor B

150. An ATC power module has failed several times in a row.

Technician A says that this could be caused by a shorted clutch diode.

Technician B says that this could be caused by a poor module ground.

Who is right?

a. A only   **c.** Both A and B
b. B only   **d.** Neither A nor B

151. An engine stalls at idle when the air conditioning is turned on. This could be caused by:

a. a bad fan controller.

b. a bad throttle kicker.

c. Both a and b

d. Neither a nor b

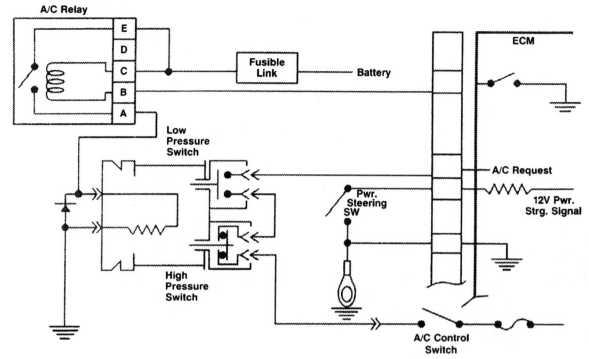

FIGURE 7–45

152. Refer to the a/c control circuit in Figure 7–45.
Technician A says that the high pressure switch can be checked with an ohmmeter.

Technician B says that the low pressure switch will show very low resistance if okay (with normal system pressure).

Who is right?
a. A only
b. B only
c. Both A and B
d. Neither A nor B

153. What is the function of the transistor in the mode door circuit in Figure 7–46?
a. Turn on the LED
b. Provide a ground for the solenoid
c. Both a and b
d. Neither a nor b

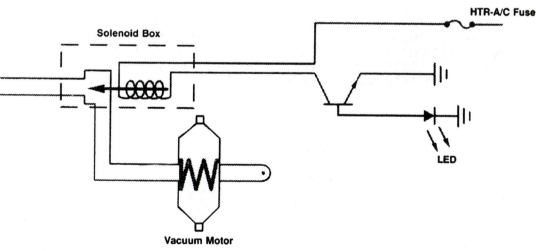

FIGURE 7–46

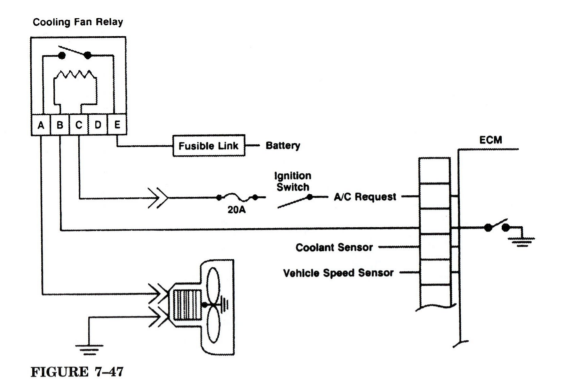

FIGURE 7–47

154. With the engine running and the air conditioning turned on, the cooling fan shown in Figure 7–47 does not operate.

   Technician A says that the ECM could be bad.

   Technician B says that the fan relay could be bad.

   Who is right?

   a. A only
   b. B only
   c. Both A and B
   d. Neither A nor B

155. Technician A says that a self-balancing bridge temperature control/connector diagram is shown in Figure 7–48.

   Technician B says that the voltmeter below should read 0 V regardless of the temperature control position.

   Who is right?

   a. A only
   b. B only
   c. Both A and B
   d. Neither A nor B

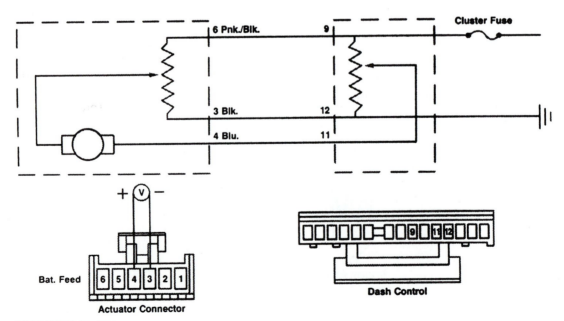

FIGURE 7–48

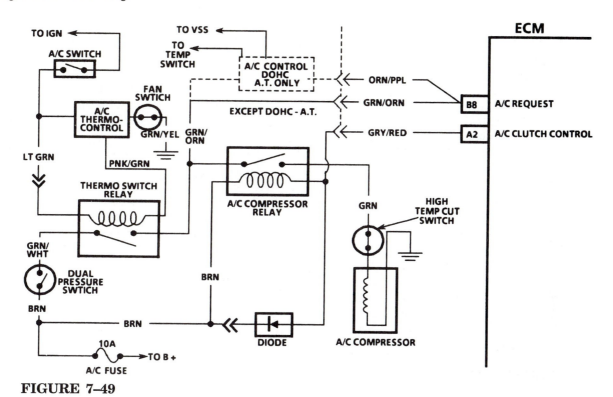

FIGURE 7–49

156. A technician finds that the air conditioning compressor is inoperative in the circuit in Figure 7–49. What could cause this condition?
   a. An open to ECM terminal B8
   b. Stuck closed triple switch contacts
   c. Both a and b
   d. Neither a nor b

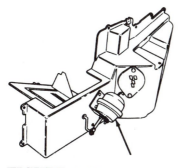

FIGURE 7–50

157. The arrow in the illustration in Figure 7–50 is pointing to a:
   a. vacuum door motor.
   b. water valve.
   c. vacuum supply tank.
   d. plenum chamber.

158. An old orifice (expansion) tube breaks apart inside the evaporator inlet tube when removal is attempted with a pair of needle-nose pliers.
   Technician A says that you can cut off the evaporator inlet tube and splice in a repair kit.
   Technician B says that a heat gun can be used to assist the removal of old orifice tubes.
   Who is right?
   a. A only   **c.** Both A and B
   b. B only   **d.** Neither A nor B

159. A factory installed air conditioning system has an R-12 capacity of 60 ounces.
   Technician A says that this equals 5 hand cans.
   Technician B says that this equals 3.75 lbs.
   Who is right?
   a. A only   **c.** Both A and B
   b. B only   **d.** Neither A nor B

160. Technician A says that it's okay to adapt R-12 manifold gauges for use on R-134a systems because the gauges are calibrated the same.
   Technician B says that service ports on R-134a systems are different from those on R-12 systems.
   Who is right?
   a. A only   **c.** Both A and B
   b. B only   **d.** Neither A nor B

161. Refrigerant has just been recovered from a system. How long should you wait after turning off the recovery/recycling unit to see if the system still has pressure?
  a. At least 2 hours
  b. At least 1 hour
  c. At least 10 minutes
  d. At least 5 minutes

162. Compared to a filter-drier designed for use with R-12, an R-134a filter-drier:
  a. is about the same size.
  b. is less efficient.
  c. has greater moisture capacity.
  d. does not use desiccant material.

163. Technician A says that if additional refrigerant is needed to detect a leak, only enough refrigerant should be added to produce a positive pressure.
  Technician B says that only a visual inspection is needed before charging a leaking system.
  Who is right?
  a. A only
  b. B only
  c. Both A and B
  d. Neither A nor B

164. To prevent overfilling a container with recycled refrigerant, never fill the container to more than what percent of its gross weight rating?
  a. 85% **b.** 60% **c.** 50% **d.** 35%

165. Technician A says that a shop must have two separate recovery/recycling stations in order to avoid mixing of refrigerant from R-12 and R-134a systems.
  Technician B says that a shop must have two separate vacuum pump motors in order to avoid mixing of refrigerant from R-12 and R-134a systems.
  Who is right?
  a. A only
  b. B only
  c. Both A and B
  d. Neither A nor B

166. Recovery/recycling equipment should have shut-off valves located within 12 inches (30 cm) of the hose's service end.
  Technician A says that this allows the filter to be changed without disconnecting the hoses.
  Technician B says that this allows oil to be added to the refrigerant.
  Who is right?
  a. A only   **c.** Both A and B
  b. B only   **d.** Neither A nor B

167. Any container of recycled refrigerant should not be used until it has been checked for what?
  a. Noncondensable gases
  b. CFCs
  c. Halon
  d. Chlorine

168. Technician A says that PAG oil used in R-134a systems is compatible with R-12 systems.
  Technician B says that refrigerant hoses used in R-134a systems can be used on R-12 systems.
  Who is right?
  a. A only   **c.** Both A and B
  b. B only   **d.** Neither A nor B

169. A recovery/recycling operation is being performed on an R-12 system.
  Technician A says that the refrigerant recovered must be weighed.
  Technician B says that special fittings to stop the refrigerant from discharging when disconnecting manifold hoses are available.
  Who is right?
  a. A only   **c.** Both A and B
  b. B only   **d.** Neither A nor B

170. Technician A says that a corona discharge leak detector CANNOT be used on R-12 systems.
  Technician B says that a corona discharge leak detector CANNOT be used on R-134a systems.
  Who is right?
  a. A only   **c.** Both A and B
  b. B only   **d.** Neither A nor B

Section 8

ENGINE PERFORMANCE

STUDY OUTLINE

I. Fuel and Induction System
  A. Intake Manifolds
    1. Runner configuration (fuel distribution)
    2. Exhaust crossover/heat riser/heaters
    3. Vacuum leak areas
    4. Bolt torque tightening pattern
    5. Poor gasket seating (oil consumption)
    6. Electronic fuel injection (EFI) plenum/throttle body injection (TBI)
  B. Fuel Supply System
    1. Fuel tank and safety cap
    2. Filters
    3. Lines and hoses
    4. Fuel pumps/controls
    5. Cold enrichment systems (EFI vehicles)
    6. Acceleration enrichment systems (EFI vehicles)
    7. EFI fuel circulation loop
    8. Cleaning
    9. Inertia switch
    10. Roll-over valve
  C. Carburetor Circuit (Understand Principles of Operation)
    1. Float
    2. Idle and low-speed
    3. Main metering
    4. Pump
    5. Power
    6. Automatic choke
    7. Identify components from circuits above
      a. Float, needle, and seat
      b. Accelerator pump
      c. Bowl vents (mechanical and electrical)
      d. Compensator valves
      e. Anti-dieseling solenoids
      f. Cold enrichment parts
      g. Closed-loop system parts
      h. Idle speed electrical/electronic parts
      i. Decel system (fuel cut-off) parts
      j. Dashpot
  D. Crankcase Ventilation System
    1. PCV valve
    2. Testing/servicing
    3. Problem/diagnosis
      a. Stuck open
      b. Stuck closed
      c. Incorrect valve
    4. Replace filter, tubes, breathers, and hoses
  E. Air Cleaners
    1. Types
    2. Servicing
II. Fuel and Induction System Problem/Diagnosis
  A. Fuel Pumps
    1. Typical specifications
    2. Pressure testing
    3. Vacuum testing
    4. Volume test
    5. Porous diaphragm (oil consumption)
    6. Noise
    7. Blown fuse (electric fuel pump)
    8. Rest pressure test
    9. Maximum output test (electric fuel pump on EFI vehicles)
  B. Carburetor
    1. Flooding
    2. Hard cold starting
    3. Hard hot starting
    4. Hesitation (off-idle)
    5. Surging
    6. Poor mileage
    7. Rough idle
    8. Loss of power
    9. Flat-spot when accelerating
    10. Vacuum leaks (internal and external)
    11. Plugged air bleeds
    12. Misaligned throttle plates
    13. Defective choke pull-off diaphragm
    14. Defective anti-percolator valve
    15. Dieseling
    16. Black smoke from exhaust pipe during idle
    17. Engine will not idle below 1500 rpm
    18. Burned-through choke stove
  C. Carburetor Adjustments/Effects if Incorrect
    1. Float level and float drop
    2. Unloader
    3. Fast idle setting
    4. Curb idle setting
    5. Choke plate pull-off
    6. Idle mixture (sealed plugs)

7. Pump stroke
8. Secondary lock-out
9. Idle solenoid settings
10. Choke plate tension
11. Propane enrichment mixture setting method
12. Lean best idle mixture setting method
13. CO meter idle mixture setting method
14. Rich/lean stops

D. Know the Typical Procedure for Making Each of the Just Listed Adjustments

E. Carburetor Cleaning Procedures

F. Replace Components

III. Fuel Injection Systems

A. Theory of Operation

B. Manifold Pressure Controlled

C. Air Flow Controlled

D. Continuous Injection with Lambda Control

E. Throttle Body and Port Comparison

F. Component Parts

G. Problem/Diagnosis
1. No starting
2. Hard starting
3. Surging
4. Misfire
5. Power loss
6. Gas consumption too high
7. Rough idle
8. Flooding
9. Hesitation
10. Stalling

IV. Exhaust System

A. Manifold Heat Control Valve Operation

B. Heated Air Intake System Ducting

C. Choking
1. Exhaust gas heated air
2. Hot water
3. Electric (stator current)

V. Exhaust System Problem/Diagnosis

A. Leaks

B. Collapsed Pipe (Restricted on the Inside) or Plugged "Cat"
1. Testing with a vacuum gauge
2. Testing with a pressure gauge

C. Manifold Heat Control Valve
1. Stuck open
2. Stuck closed
3. Lubrication
4. Replacement procedure
5. Vacuum/thermal controls

VI. Ignition Systems (Including Theory of Operation)

A. Primary (Low Voltage)
1. Battery
2. Ignition switch
3. Ballast resistor or resistance wire
4. Coil primary winding

5. Pickup coil
6. Module
7. Harness wiring
8. System grounds

B. Secondary (High Voltage)
1. Coil secondary winding
2. Distributor cap
3. Rotor
4. Spark plug wiring
5. Plugs
6. System grounds

C. Distributor Spark Timing Mechanisms (Including Test Procedures)
1. Vacuum diaphragms
2. Centrifugal weight assembly
3. Adjusting timing
4. Initial (base) timing
5. Total advance
6. Electrical/electronic components
7. Thermal, mechanical, or vacuum components and hoses

D. Electronic Ignition (Includes Hall Effect)
1. Components/diagnosis

E. Distributorless Ignition (DIS)
1. Components/diagnosis

VII. Ignition System Problems/Diagnosis

A. Engine Missing
1. At idle
2. Under load
3. Spark plug condition
4. Incorrect timing
5. Bad control unit (module)
6. Bad pickup coil or triggering device
7. Bad wiring harness or connectors
8. Bad coil(s)
9. Bad cap or rotor

B. Engine Cranks but Will Not Start

C. Engine Backfires
1. Spark plug wire routing
2. Carbon tracking

D. Engine Lacks Power/Poor Driveability

E. Engine Starts During Crank but Quits When Key Is Released to Run Position

F. Spark Timing Problems
1. Breaker plate wear
2. Worn bushings
3. Bent distributor shaft
4. Sticking weights
5. Incorrect vacuum diaphragm hose hook-up
6. Low octane fuel
7. "Ping" (wrong PROM)

G. Engine Difficult to Start When Cold

H. Engine Difficult to Start When Hot

I. Excessive Voltage Drop in the Primary Circuit

J. Electronic Ignition System Continuity and Available Voltage Tests

VIII. Use of Test Equipment (Adjustments or Repair to Bring Vehicle to Specification)
  A. Voltmeter
  B. Ammeter
  C. Ohmmeter
    1. Electronic ignition system distributor pickup and ignition coil checks
    2. Electronic ignition system control unit (module) checks
  D. Compression Gauge
  E. Cylinder Leakage Test
  F. Cylinder Balance
  G. Distributor Synchograph
  H. Oscilloscope/Engine Analyzer
    1. Basic patterns (know the sections)
      a. Primary
      b. Secondary
      c. Superimposed
      d. Parade
      e. Raster
    2. Diagnostic tests/pattern interpretation
      a. Reversed polarity
      b. Coil output
      c. Ignition reserve
      d. Rotor gap KV requirement
      e. Shorted coil
      f. Secondary insulation
      g. Worn distributor shaft bushings
      h. Open plug wire
      i. Fouled plug
      j. Lean mixture
      k. Coil tower corrosion
      l. Spark line slopes upward
      m. Spark line slopes downward
  I. Tach/Dwell Meter
    1. Set rpm
    2. Check duty cycle solenoids
  J. Infrared Analyzer
    1. Meter interpretation
      a. High HC
      b. High CO
      c. Low CO
      d. Fluctuating HC reading
      e. Engine mechanical, ignition, or fuel problems
      f. Low O_2
      g. High O_2
      h. CO_2 less than 13%
    2. 2500 rpm test
  K. Interpretation of Vacuum Gauge Readings
  L. Determine Needed Repairs on Electronic/Computer-Controlled Systems
    1. Scan tool and lab scope diagnostics
    2. Digital and analog meter usage
    3. Replace sensor and actuator components

IX. Basic Emission Control Systems (The Test Does Not Emphasize Makes or Models; Be Concerned with Principles of Operation)
  A. Crankcase Ventilation Devices
    1. See Section I-D
  B. Combustion Controls
    1. Air injection reactor (AIR)
    2. Improved combustion (IMPCO)
    3. Clean air systems (CAS)
    4. Pulse-type systems
    5. Testing/servicing
      a. Air pump (includes pulleys and belts)
      b. Relief valve
      c. Check valve
      d. Diverter or gulp valve and sensing hose
      e. Air manifold/nozzles
      f. Vacuum advance control valves and hoses
      g. Filters
      h. Pulleys and belts
      i. Catalytic converter
    6. Replace components
  C. Vapor Control Systems
    1. Crankcase storage
    2. Carbon canister storage
      a. Filter
      b. Purge valve
    3. Vapor separator
    4. Check valves, hoses, and lines
    5. Tank caps
    6. Air cleaner connections
    7. Testing/service
    8. Problem/diagnosis
      a. Liquid gas in carbon canister
      b. Collapsed tank
      c. No purge
      d. Surging
    9. Replace components (thermal, vacuum, and electrical controls)
  D. Temperature Controlled Air Cleaner/Purpose
    1. Vacuum motor
    2. Air door
    3. Temperature sensor or thermostat bulb
    4. Testing/service
    5. Problem/diagnosis
      a. Effects of vacuum loss
      b. Vacuum motor defects
      c. Temperature sensor defects
      d. Stuck air door
      e. Heat stove shroud missing
  E. Exhaust Gas Recirculating System (EGR)/Purpose
    1. Vacuum/pressure control
    2. EGR valve diaphragm/position sensor
    3. Passages
    4. Testing/service
    5. Problem/diagnosis
      a. Rough idle
      b. No EGR valve stem movement
    6. Replace components and hoses

7. Inspect, test, repair, and replace electrical/electronic controls and wiring

F. Distributor Advance Control Systems
   1. See section VI-C
   2. For NO$_x$ control
   3. Vacuum retard (dual diaphragm distributors)
   4. Electric retard solenoid
   5. Transmission controlled spark (TCS)
   6. Thermal controls, vacuum amplifiers, delay diaphragms, and hoses
   7. Computer control
   8. Testing/service
   9. Problem/diagnosis
      a. Engine overheating
      b. Lack of power

G. Catalytic Converter System/Purpose
   1. Components (including air management devices)
   2. Converter construction (two-way and three-way)
   3. Testing/service
   4. Problem/diagnosis
      a. Converter overheating
      b. Don't remove spark plug wires when engine is running
      c. "Rotten egg" exhaust gas smell

   d. Infrared service tap
   e. Plugged converter

H. Mixture/Idle Speed Control Systems
   1. Solenoids, vacuum valves, switches, and hoses
   2. Feedback carburetor/closed-loop fuel injection
      a. Electronic sensors and actuators
      b. Confirming closed-loop operation

X. Engine Related Service
   A. Adjustments
      1. Valve lash (mechanical or hydraulic lifters)
      2. Belts (timing, serpentine, and v-type)
   B. Checks
      1. Cooling system pressure tests
      2. Fan clutch/fan shroud/fan control devices
      3. Battery hydrometer and capacity test
      4. Self-diagnostic computer system tests
   C. General Diagnosis
      1. Road test procedures
      2. Unusual exhaust color, odor, and sound
      3. Fuel, oil, coolant, and other leaks
      4. Engine vacuum (manifold absolute pressure) tests
      5. Turbocharger system tests
      6. Basic engine electrical system tests (battery, starting, and charging)

---

1. An engine has excessive oil consumption. Both wet and dry compression tests are acceptable.
   Technician A says that the engine could have bad valve stem seals.
   Technician B says that there could be a problem in the PCV system.
   Who is right?
   a. A only
   b. B only
   c. Both A and B
   d. Neither A nor B

2. A vehicle equipped with electronic ignition will not start.
   Technician A says that the cause could be a bad module.
   Technician B says that the pick-up coil connections could be corroded.
   Who is right?
   a. A only
   b. B only
   c. Both A and B
   d. Neither A nor B

3. A car has driveaway hesitation during cold weather warm-up. Which of these would be the LEAST LIKELY cause of this?
   a. A plugged intake manifold crossover
   b. A stuck heat riser
   c. A bad hot air intake system
   d. An unpurged cannister

4. Technician A says that overfilling the battery can cause corrosion of the cables and clamps.
   Technician B says that overfilling the battery can cause sulfation of the plates.
   Who is right?
   a. A only
   b. B only
   c. Both A and B
   d. Neither A nor B

5. Typical charging system voltage on a 12-V system would be:
   a. 14.5–16.0 V.
   b. 13.0–14.5 V.
   c. 7.5–9.0 V.
   d. 11.9–13.3 V.

6. A computer-controlled engine will not go into closed loop.
   Technician A says that the oxygen sensor could be coated with carbon.
   Technician B says that the wrong thermostat could have been installed.
   Who is right?
   a. A only
   b. B only
   c. Both A and B
   d. Neither A nor B

7. A computer-controlled vehicle runs poorly when cold.

Technician A says that a bad coolant temperature sensor could be the cause.

Technician B says that improper hose routing to a TVS could be the cause.

Who is right?
a. A only
b. B only
c. Both A and B
d. Neither A nor B

8. A heated air intake system has a leak in the vacuum diaphragm.

Technician A says that this can cause poor cold weather performance.

Technician B says that this will cause poor hot engine driveability.

Who is right?
a. A only
b. B only
c. Both A and B
d. Neither A nor B

9. A cold wet rag is placed on the temperature bulb of a thermostatically controlled air cleaner that is on a warm, idling engine. The air door should:
a. move to closed position.
b. move to open position.
c. not change its position.
d. flutter.

10. You are checking ignition coil available voltage with an oscilloscope. What is the procedure on a non-DIS ignition system?
a. Disconnect any plug wire at its plug and ground it.
b. Disconnect any plug wire at its plug and hold it away from ground.
c. Disconnect the high tension lead at the coil and ground it.
d. Disconnect the primary pigtail at the coil and ground it.

11. An engine equipped with a distributorless ignition system (DIS), as shown in Figure 8–1, won't start.

Technician A says that this could be caused by a faulty crank sensor.

Technician B says that this could be caused by a wiring problem.

Who is right?
a. A only
b. B only
c. Both A and B
d. Neither A nor B

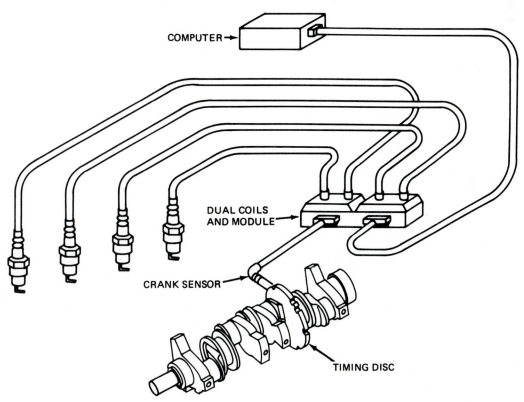

FIGURE 8–1

12. Technician A says that ignition timing is generally adjusted while running the engine with the computer power feed disconnected.

Technician B says that ignition timing is generally adjusted while running the engine at 2,500 rpm.

Who is right?
a. A only
b. B only
c. Both A and B
d. Neither A nor B

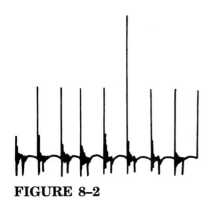

FIGURE 8–2

13. The oscilloscope pattern shown in Figure 8–2 indicates what problem?
a. Bad coil
b. Bad transistor
c. Shorted module
d. Open spark plug wire

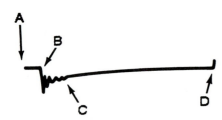

FIGURE 8–3

14. Refer to the electronic ignition scope pattern in Figure 8–3. Which letter indicates where the ignition module transistor turns off the primary current?
a. A **b.** B **c.** C **d.** D

15. Which device below incorporates a "Hall" switch?
a. MAP sensor
b. Coolant temperature sensor
c. MAF sensor
d. None of these

16. Technician A says that distributor vacuum diaphragms are used to retard spark timing.

Technician B says that distributor vacuum diaphragms are used to advance spark timing.

Who is right?
a. A only
b. B only
c. Both A and B
d. Neither A nor B

17. An engine starts with the key switch in the crank position. When the switch is released to the run position, the engine dies. What is the MOST LIKELY cause of this problem?
a. Bad ignition resistor
b. Bad coil
c. Bad starter solenoid
d. Bad neutral switch

18. An on-board computer PROM:
a. can only be written to by the computer.
b. stores data pertinent to a certain application.
c. is Permanently Retained On-board Memory.
d. can be written to but not read by the computer.

19. An engine generally requires the richest air–fuel mixture during:
a. starting, idling, and full-throttle operation.
b. starting, acceleration, and full-throttle operation.
c. starting, part-throttle, and full-throttle operation.
d. hot weather, high altitude, and high-speed operation.

20. An engine performs poorly on a cranking vacuum test.

Technician A says that this could be caused by bad rings.

Technician B says that this could be caused by improper cam timing.

Who is right?
a. A only
b. B only
c. Both A and B
d. Neither A nor B

21. During a cylinder leakage test on a 4-cylinder engine, air is heard escaping from the #3 spark plug hole as the #4 cylinder is checked.

Technician A says that this could be due to a blown head gasket.

Technician B says that this could be due to a cracked block.

Who is right?
a. A only
b. B only
c. Both A and B
d. Neither A nor B

22. The choke thermostatic coil spring tends to _____ the choke plate, and the choke vacuum diaphragm tends to _____ the choke plate.
a. open, close
b. close, open
c. close, close
d. open, open

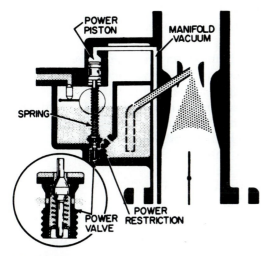

FIGURE 8–4

23. An engine is equipped with the carburetor in Figure 8–4. When engine load is increased, the power piston is moved _____ by _____ to _____ the power valve.
a. down, spring tension, open
b. up, vacuum, open
c. down, vacuum, open
d. up, spring tension, close

24. Technician A says that some carburetors are designed to have hot water (radiator coolant) going into the choke coil housing.

Technician B says that some carburetors are designed to have exhaust gas going into the choke coil housing.

Who is right?
a. A only
b. B only
c. Both A and B
d. Neither A nor B

25. Setting carburetor float level lower than factory specification can cause:
a. too lean a mixture.
b. surge at cruising speeds.
c. Both a and b
d. Neither a nor b

26. A carburetor has a malfunctioning automatic choke. The choke housing is corroded inside and there are heavy carbon accumulations on the choke piston.

Technician A says to replace the carburetor.

Technician B says to check the manifold heat pipe for cracks.

Who is right?
a. A only
b. B only
c. Both A and B
d. Neither A nor B

FIGURE 8–5

27. To set the air gap on the electronic ignition system shown in Figure 8–5, a technician would use:
a. a special meter.
b. a brass feeler gauge.
c. a self-powered test lamp.
d. an ohmmeter.

28. A carburetor has a power valve that is leaking. How would this MOST LIKELY be indicated on an infrared analyzer?
a. High HC
b. High HC and low CO
c. High CO
d. The HC meter needle will fluctuate.

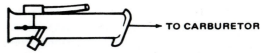

FIGURE 8–6

29. What is true about the thermostatically controlled air cleaner shown in Figure 8–6?
a. It is providing cool air to the carburetor.
b. The hot air passage is open.
c. Both a and b
d. Neither a nor b

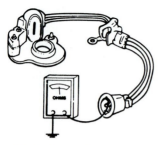

FIGURE 8–7

30. What electronic ignition system component is being tested in the picture in Figure 8–7?
a. Reluctor
b. Trigger wheel
c. Pickup coil
d. Compensating resistor

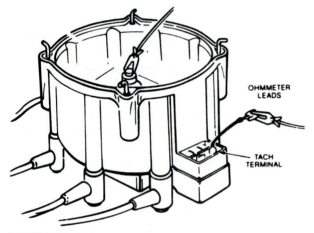

FIGURE 8–8

31. A high energy ignition (HEI) system is being checked. What test is being performed in Figure 8–8?
a. Ballast resistance
b. Ignition coil primary
c. Ignition coil secondary
d. None of the above

32. An engine with a closed crankcase system is idling rough. When a technician pulls the PCV valve out of the valve cover and places his thumb over the end, the idle smooths out.
   Technician A says that the hose from the air cleaner to the crankcase could be plugged.
   Technician B says that the PCV valve could be plugged.
   Who is right?
a. A only
b. B only
c. Both A and B
d. Neither A nor B

33. Valve lash on an overhead cam engine is being adjusted.
   Technician A says that not enough lash can cause valves to burn.
   Technician B says that too much lash can cause noise and poor engine performance.
   Who is right?
a. A only
b. B only
c. Both A and B
d. Neither A nor B

34. An air injection system car has a rough idle.
   Technician A says that this could be caused by a bad anti-backfire valve.
   Technician B says that this could be caused by an intake manifold gasket leak.
   Who is right?
a. A only
b. B only
c. Both A and B
d. Neither A nor B

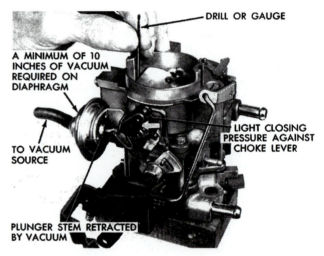

FIGURE 8–9

35. What is being checked in Figure 8–9?
   a. Choke plate lock-out
   b. Dashpot
   c. Unloader
   d. Vacuum break (pull-off)

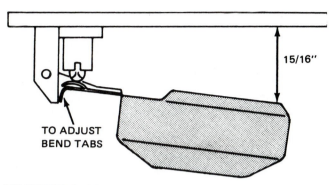

FIGURE 8–10

36. Figure 8–10 shows which carburetor adjustment?
   a. Float level   c. Float alignment
   b. Float drop   d. None of these

FIGURE 8–11

37. The part in Figure 8–11 is stuck open.
   Technician A says that this could cause poor gas mileage.
   Technician B says that this could cause less manifold vacuum, resulting in overheating.
   Who is right?
   a. A only   c. Both A and B
   b. B only   d. Neither A nor B

38. To turn on a transistor, the _____ circuit must be properly forward biased.
   a. collector   c. emitter
   b. trigger   d. base

39. A car starts, "coughs," and dies.
   Technician A says that this could be due to a PCV valve that is stuck in the open position.
   Technician B says that this could be due to a PCV vacuum hose that is disconnected from the carburetor base.
   Who is right?
   a. A only   c. Both A and B
   b. B only   d. Neither A nor B

40. The valve shown in Figure 8–12 would MOST LIKELY control what ignition timing mode?
   a. Retard during high temperature idle
   b. Advance during high temperature idle
   c. Retard during high speed driving
   d. Advance during deceleration

FIGURE 8–12

41. An AIR equipped vehicle has a badly burned (charred) hose above the check valve. This could be due to:
   a. advanced ignition timing.
   b. a bad smog pump.
   c. a bad gulp valve.
   d. a bad check valve.

42. Metering rods (used on some carburetors) are designed to vary the size of the:
   a. idle jets.   c. main jets.
   b. acceleration jets. d. floor jets.

43. A technician is adjusting hydraulic lifter lash. He turns to a specified setting past zero-lash. What is the reason for doing this?
   a. To position the plunger properly in the lifter body.
   b. To set proper valve lift.
   c. Both a and b
   d. Neither a nor b

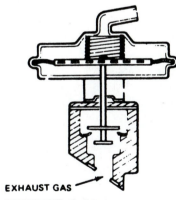

EXHAUST GAS

FIGURE 8–13

44. Technician A says that the valve in Figure 8–13 should reduce NO_x emissions if it is operating properly.
   Technician B says that the valve should not be open at engine idle.
   Who is right?
   a. A only   c. Both A and B
   b. B only   d. Neither A nor B

45. If a spark plug wire falls off a "non-cat" equipped car, the HC emissions will:
a. increase.
b. decrease.
c. remain low until about 2,500 rpm, and then increase.
d. not change.

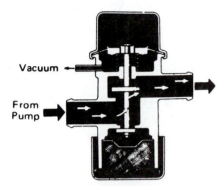

FIGURE 8–14

46. The valve pictured in Figure 8–14 is used on an automobile AIR system.

Technician A says that the purpose of the valve is to enrich the air-fuel mixture on deceleration.

Technician B says that the purpose of the valve is to prevent backfire.

Who is right?
a. A only   **c.** Both A and B
b. B only   **d.** Neither A nor B

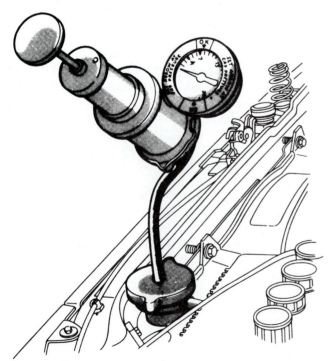

FIGURE 8–15

47. Technician A says that the tool in Figure 8–15 may be used to test the radiator cap to see if it holds pressure.

Technician B says that the tool may be used to test the vacuum valve in the radiator cap.

Who is right?
a. A only   **c.** Both A and B
b. B only   **d.** Neither A nor B

48. Refer to the part illustrated in Figure 8–13. How much vacuum should be applied during idle?

Technician A says that there should be zero inches when the engine is cold.

Technician B says that there should be 10 inches when the engine is warmed-up.

What is right?
a. A only   **c.** Both A and B
b. B only   **d.** Neither A nor B

49. A V-6 supercharged engine lacks power.

Technician A says that this could be caused by a tight drive belt.

Technician B says that this could be caused by a fixed oxygen sensor voltage.

Who is right?
a. A only   **c.** Both A and B
b. B only   **d.** Neither A nor B

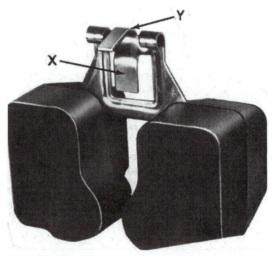

FIGURE 8–16

50. Refer to Figure 8–16.

Technician A says that float drop is adjusted at point X.

Technician B says that float level is adjusted at point Y.

Who is right?
a. A only   **c.** Both A and B
b. B only   **d.** Neither A nor B

51. Where is the fuel discharge hole for the carburetor idle circuit located?
   a. Slightly above the closed position of the throttle plate
   b. Slightly below the closed position of the throttle plate
   c. At the main discharge nozzle opening
   d. In the venturi cluster

52. Oxygen sensor voltage on a vehicle stays at the low end of its range. This could be caused by a:
   a. high float level.
   b. rich fuel mixture.
   c. misadjusted choke pull-off.
   d. rusted out air injection manifold.

53. Which of these would be the MOST LIKELY cause of catalytic converter overheating?
   a. High octane gas
   b. Stuck open EGR valve
   c. Choke valve stuck partly closed
   d. Disconnected air pump

54. What does the black colored cap that is attached to the automatic choke housing adjust?
   a. Fast-idle speed
   b. Choke plate opening time
   c. Curb-idle speed
   d. Choke pull-off setting

55. A car with a feedback carburetor has bad gas mileage.
   Technician A says that this could be caused by a bad O_2 sensor.
   Technician B says that this could be caused by a leaking accelerator pump intake.
   Who is right?
   a. A only
   b. B only
   c. Both A and B
   d. Neither A nor B

56. An automatic choke does not open and the engine is hot. This could be caused by:
   a. no spring tension in the choke system.
   b. no heat in the choke system.
   c. Both a and b
   d. Neither a nor b

57. An engine has a rough idle.
   Technician A says that this could be caused by a stuck open EGR valve.
   Technician B says that this could be caused by a partly blocked thermo-vacuum valve.
   Who is right?
   a. A only
   b. B only
   c. Both A and B
   d. Neither A nor B

58. Technician A says that a typical TCS system would deny distributor vacuum advance until about 35 mph.
   Technician B says that an exhaust gas recirculation valve is part of most TCS systems.
   Who is right?
   a. A only
   b. B only
   c. Both A and B
   d. Neither A nor B

59. What is true about a car equipped with TVRS plug wires?
   a. They should be checked with an ohmmeter.
   b. They should not be used with resistor spark plugs.
   c. Both a and b
   d. Neither a nor b

60. In a Hall Effect distributor, what does the ECM use as the reference?
   a. Top of the wave form
   b. Falling edge of the wave form
   c. Rising edge of the wave form
   d. Bottom edge of the wave form

61. What is true about a correctly operating EFE system?
   a. It should improve engine performance when the engine is warming up.
   b. It should improve engine performance when the engine is under heavy load.
   c. Both a and b
   d. Neither a nor b

62. An engine has weak spark at all the cylinder spark plug wires. Which of these would be the MOST LIKELY cause?
   a. Bad spark advance mechanism
   b. Bad secondary wire insulation
   c. Low resistance in the secondary circuit
   d. High resistance in the primary circuit

63. Technician A says that a spark plug that does not use a gasket should be tightened less than one that uses a gasket.
   Technician B says that a normal spark plug's firing end will generally turn gray or tan in use.
   Who is right?
   a. A only
   b. B only
   c. Both A and B
   d. Neither A nor B

64. A technician is performing a compression test on an engine. Which statement below is true?

   a. All cylinders reading higher than normal could be caused by excessive carbon accumulation.

   b. All cylinders reading even, but considerably lower than normal, could be caused by a slipped timing chain.

   c. Low identical readings on two adjacent cylinders could be caused by a blown head gasket.

   d. All of the above

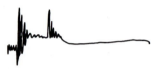

FIGURE 8–17

65. A customer has a hard start complaint. You observe the secondary superimposed pattern in Figure 8–17. What is wrong?

   a. The coil is shorted.

   b. The coil has series resistance.

   c. The coil is hooked up backwards.

   d. The rotor air gap is excessive.

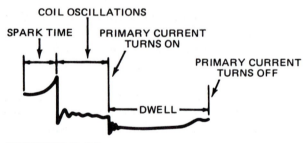

FIGURE 8–18

66. The scope display shown in Figure 8–18 is a:

   a. raster pattern.

   b. primary pattern.

   c. secondary parade pattern.

   d. solid-state ignition system secondary pattern.

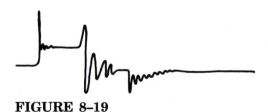

FIGURE 8–19

67. What are the oscillations directly to the right of the spark plug firing line (see Figure 8–19)?

   a. Coil buildup (saturation) time

   b. Dwell time

   c. Plug wire resistance peaks

   d. Coil and condenser discharge action

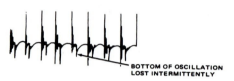

FIGURE 8–20

68. The bottom of a scope parade pattern oscillation is lost intermittently (see Figure 8–20). Why?

   Technician A says that spark plug wires could be routed incorrectly.

   Technician B says that the distributor cap could be cracked.

   Who is right?

   a. A only   **c.** Both A and B

   b. B only   **d.** Neither A nor B

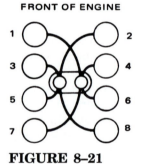

FIGURE 8–21

69. Refer to the intake manifold layout in Figure 8–21. When doing a minor tune-up, the technician observes that spark plugs 5, 6, 7, and 8 are blistered. The rest of the plugs are okay. What could be the problem?

   a. A lean mixture at the right-hand carburetor barrel

   b. A clogged or restricted cooling system

   c. Both a and b

   d. Neither a nor b

FIGURE 8–22

FIGURE 8–23

70. In the device shown in Figure 8–22, the plunger is stuck in the maximum flow position.
    Technician A says that this can cause rough engine idle.
    Technician B says that this can cause excessive oil consumption.
    Who is right?
    a. A only
    b. B only
    c. Both A and B
    d. Neither A nor B

71. A cylinder leakage test is being performed. When air is introduced into the cylinder, bubbles are seen in the radiator at the filler opening. What does this possibly indicate?
    a. A cracked cylinder block
    b. A blown head gasket
    c. Either a or b
    d. Neither a nor b

72. Technician A says that a dripping cold start injector can cause high CO when idling.
    Technician B says that zero vacuum to the pressure regulator can cause high CO when idling.
    Who is right?
    a. A only
    b. B only
    c. Both A and B
    d. Neither A nor B

73. You are testing a distributor on a testing machine. Eight stroboscope images appear. You compare the positions of the stroboscope images as they index the degree scale. The images vary ±4° from the normal 45° spacing interval. What does this indicate?
    a. A worn upper distributor shaft bushing
    b. A dirty advance weight mechanism
    c. Both a and b
    d. Neither a nor b

74. Figure 8–23 illustrates what combustion chamber situation?
    a. Detonation
    b. Over-advanced timing
    c. Pre-ignition
    d. Normal burning

75. You suspect that an exhaust pipe has collapsed on the inside. A vacuum gauge is hooked up to the intake manifold. What might the gauge read if a restriction is present?
    a. At idle there is a regular needle drop of about 3".
    b. At idle there is a regular needle drop of about 8".
    c. At 1,000 engine rpm the needle shows a continuous gradual drop.
    d. At idle the needle oscillates slowly between 16–21".

76. A cranking vacuum test reading is lower than specification. This could result in:
    a. hard starting.   c. Both a and b
    b. rough idle.   d. Neither a nor b

77. A 12-V battery removed from a vehicle has been sitting on a shelf for four months. How should this battery be put back into service?
    a. Dump the old electrolyte, fill with new electrolyte, and recharge.
    b. Put on half the normal charging rate for 50 to 100 hours.
    c. Both a and b
    d. Neither a nor b

78. Technician A says that an intake manifold gasket leak can cause spark plug fouling.
    Technician B says that an intake manifold gasket leak can cause oil consumption.
    Who is right?
    a. A only   c. Both A and B
    b. B only   d. Neither A nor B

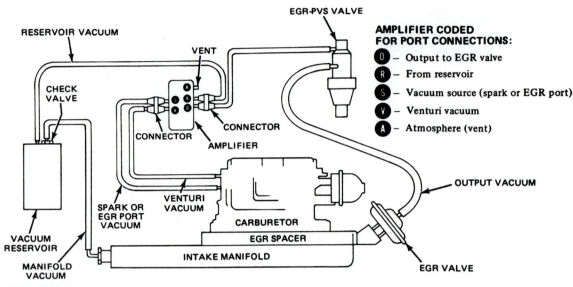

FIGURE 8–24

79. An engine is running at idle and warmed to operating temperature. When hand vacuum is applied to the EGR valve (see Figure 8–24), the engine dies.

    Technician A says to replace the EGR valve.

    Technician B says to replace the vacuum reservoir.

    Who is right?
    a. A only
    b. B only
    c. Both A and B
    d. Neither A nor B

80. A customer complains that the engine keeps running after the key is turned off.

    Technician A says that carbon deposits in the combustion chambers could be the cause.

    Technician B says that the idle speed could be set too high or the solenoid throttle stop plunger is stuck.

    Who is right?
    a. A only
    b. B only
    c. Both A and B
    d. Neither A nor B

81. High voltage is produced in the ignition coil secondary winding when:
    a. the condenser shorts out.
    b. the primary circuit closes.
    c. the primary circuit opens.
    d. the rotor makes contact.

82. A hot spark plug:
    a. has a long heat travel path.
    b. has a short heat travel path.
    c. is advisable for continuous high speed driving.
    d. produces less radio interference.

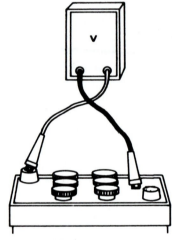

FIGURE 8–25

83. What is being checked in Figure 8–25?
    a. Post resistance
    b. Cell voltage
    c. Battery leakage
    d. Terminal voltage

84. Technician A says that the centrifugal spark advance mechanism adjusts ignition timing to suit changes in engine load.

    Technician B says that it adjusts ignition timing to suit changes in engine speed.

    Who is right?
    a. A only
    b. B only
    c. Both A and B
    d. Neither A nor B

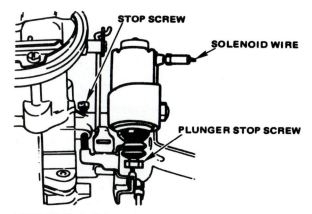

FIGURE 8–26

85. Many carburetors have been equipped with an idle stop solenoid (see Figure 8–26).

Technician A says that hot engine idle speed is adjusted by turning the plunger stop screw with the solenoid wire connected.

Technician B says that low speed idle is adjusted by turning the stop screw with the solenoid wire disconnected.

Who is right?

a. A only
c. Both A and B
b. B only
d. Neither A nor B

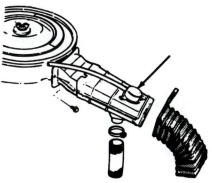

FIGURE 8–27

86. What is the name of the part that the arrow is pointing to in Figure 8–27?

a. Air bleed valve
b. Thermostat
c. Vacuum motor
d. Temperature sensor

87. Technician A says that intake manifold vacuum and engine load are not related.

Technician B says that the higher the engine speed, the higher the intake manifold vacuum.

Who is right?

a. A only
c. Both A and B
b. B only
d. Neither A nor B

FIGURE 8–28

88. The carburetor part shown in Figure 8–28 is designed to allow for:

a. easier cold starting.
b. easier hot starting.
c. the prevention of dieseling.
d. a richer mixture during hot weather.

89. You are rebuilding a carburetor. Which of the following can be ruined by soaking in carburetor cleaner?

a. Choke pull-off (vacuum break)
b. Hot idle compensating valve
c. Throttle positioner diaphragm
d. All of the above

90. Some carburetors are designed with a choke lock-out.

Technician A says that the purpose of the lock-out is to prevent the choke from closing once the engine is warm.

Technician B says that the lock-out prevents the secondary throttle plate(s) from opening when the choke is closed.

Who is right?

a. A only
c. Both A and B
b. B only
d. Neither A nor B

91. When abnormal parasitic load is suspected, verify with:

a. an ammeter.
c. an ohmmeter.
b. a voltmeter.
d. a dwell meter.

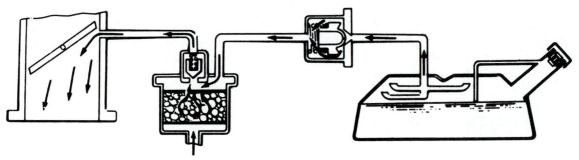

FIGURE 8–29

92. Refer to the evaporative control system illustrated in Figure 8–29. What is passing into the intake manifold?
    a. Liquid gas
    b. Evaporated gas
    c. Fresh air
    d. Both b and c

93. Under what condition would carburetor icing MOST LIKELY occur?
    a. Low humidity
    b. High humidity
    c. When water is in the gasoline.
    d. At any temperature below freezing.

94. Many cars use a device to prevent engine stalling due to automatic transmission drag during a sudden stop. What is the name of this item?
    a. A dashpot
    b. A kickdown lever
    c. An elastomer valve
    d. An over-travel spring

95. Which of the following statements is true?
    a. Using leaded fuel additive can poison and neutralize the effectiveness of a catalytic converter.
    b. An open spark plug wire can increase the temperature in the catalytic converter.
    c. A rich air–fuel mixture can cause a catalytic converter to plug.
    d. All of the above

96. Technician A says that carbon monoxide (CO) and carbon dioxide (CO_2) can be measured with an infrared analyzer.
    Technician B says that oxygen (O_2) and hydrocarbons (HC) can be measured with an infrared analyzer.
    Who is right?
    a. A only
    b. B only
    c. Both A and B
    d. Neither A nor B

97. An engine has a firing order of 1-8-5-4-6-3-7-2. The #1 piston is at TDC on compression. What position is #6 piston in?
    a. Half the distance up on compression
    b. Half the distance down on power
    c. TDC
    d. BDC

98. An engine is running in the shop at fast idle. With a normally operating carburetor, when the air horn is partly covered with a piece of cardboard, the engine should:
    a. slow down.
    b. speed up.
    c. surge.
    d. quit running.

99. A cylinder has a very low compression reading. When 30-wt. oil is squirted into the spark plug hole, the compression increases to a normal reading. What engine defect is MOST LIKELY indicated?
    a. A bad valve
    b. Defective piston rings
    c. A casting crack in the cylinder head
    d. A broken head gasket divider

100. In a closed crankcase system, the blow-by gases are routed through the:
    a. intake manifold.
    b. air cleaner.
    c. Both a and b
    d. Neither a nor b

101. A turbocharged engine has excessive oil consumption and emits blue exhaust smoke. This could be caused by:
    a. a "coked" oil drain line.
    b. a sludged center housing.
    c. Both a and b
    d. Neither a nor b

102. What could cause a high spark plug firing voltage?
a. Excessive resistance in the plug wires
b. Wide plug gap
c. Both a and b
d. Neither a nor b

103. A vacuum advance unit that uses "ported spark" receives its vacuum from the carburetor:
a. venturi.
b. air horn.
c. just below the throttle plates.
d. just above the throttle plates.

104. One voltmeter prod is grounded on the radiator. The other prod is inserted into the coolant. A reading of 4 V is obtained. What does this indicate?
a. Drain, flush, and refill the cooling system.
b. Corrosion is taking place.
c. Both a and b
d. Neither a nor b

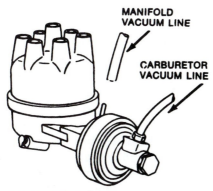

FIGURE 8–30

105. An engine is operating at idle speed. The carburetor vacuum line is connected to the outer diaphragm (see Figure 8–30). When the manifold vacuum line is connected to the inner diaphragm, what should happen to spark timing?
a. It should advance.
b. It should retard.
c. It will change and speed up the engine.
d. Nothing will happen at this speed.

106. A cylinder balance test shows two adjacent cylinders with higher HC readings than any of the other cylinders. Which of the following is the MOST LIKELY cause?
a. Blown head gasket
b. Bad control unit (module)
c. Worn timing gears
d. Bad ignition coil

107. Technician A says that a high HC reading at idle could be caused by an ignition, vacuum, or valve malfunction.
Technician B says that a high CO reading at idle could be caused by a leaky or stuck power valve.
Who is right?
a. A only
b. B only
c. Both A and B
d. Neither A nor B

FIGURE 8–31

108. What is the air injection system component pictured in Figure 8–31?
a. Air pump relief valve
b. Check valve
c. Diverter valve
d. Dump valve

109. A turbocharged engine lacks power.
Technician A says that this could be caused by a restricted air intake.
Technician B says that this could be caused by a restricted exhaust system.
Who is right?
a. A only
b. B only
c. Both A and B
d. Neither A nor B

110. An engine with electronic spark timing (EST) detonates badly under load.
Technician A says that this could be caused by low octane gas.
Technician B says that this could be caused by incorrect initial (base) timing.
Who is right?
a. A only
b. B only
c. Both A and B
d. Neither A nor B

111. If the EFE heat duct is missing, what is LEAST LIKELY to happen?
a. Throttle plate icing
b. Stumble on acceleration
c. Delayed opening of the choke
d. Stalling

112. An engine has a knocking noise on medium to hard acceleration. Which of these would be the MOST LIKELY cause?
a. Too rich fuel mixture
b. Restricted EGR passage
c. Leaking vacuum advance mechanism
d. Bad ignition pickup (trigger) coil

113. A piston has the top melted through the center. The cause could be:
a. detonation.   **c.** Both a and b
b. retarded timing.   **d.** Neither a nor b

114. A car owner complains of poor fuel economy.
Technician A says that this could be due to an improper accelerator pump travel adjustment.
Technician B says that this could be due to a stuck open power valve.
Who is right?
a. A only   **c.** Both A and B
b. B only   **d.** Neither A nor B

115. An engine idles okay, but will not run at a speed higher than idle.
Technician A says that this could be due to a pinched fuel line.
Technician B says that this could be due to a plugged fuel filter.
Who is right?
a. A only   **c.** Both A and B
b. B only   **d.** Neither A nor B

116. When setting basic ignition timing on an engine equipped with vacuum and centrifugal advance, which of the following statements is true?
a. The distributor vacuum lines are generally disconnected and plugged.
b. To advance the timing, rotate the distributor.
c. Both a and b
d. Neither a nor b

117. A car owner complains of erratic performance. A technician checks the timing. He notices the timing does not return to the same spot when the rpm is raised, then dropped. What could be causing this problem?
a. The weight and cam assembly needs lubrication.
b. A worn breaker plate
c. Both a and b
d. Neither a nor b

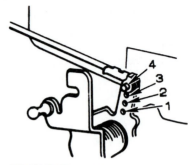

FIGURE 8–32

118. On the carburetor shown in Figure 8–32, what could happen if the rod was moved to hole #1?
a. The accelerator pump stroke will be changed.
b. The curb idle speed will change.
c. The fast idle cam position will change.
d. The idle CO will change.

119. A car is originally equipped with a vented gas tank cap. What can happen if someone puts a non-vented cap on the tank?
Technician A says that the gas tank may collapse.
Technician B says that the car may be starved for fuel, especially at high speeds.
Who is right?
a. A only   **c.** Both A and B
b. B only   **d.** Neither A nor B

120. A manifold heat control valve (heat riser) should be serviced when performing a tune-up using which of the following procedures?
a. Lubricate the valve with 30 wt. engine oil.
b. Disassemble the valve, clean, and reassemble.
c. Apply recommended lubricant to shaft ends; tap the valve lightly if necessary for free action.
d. Install a new valve.

121. What will happen when the infrared analyzer probe is placed near a fuel line leak?
Technician A says that a CO reading will be obtained.
Technician B says that an HC reading will be obtained.
Who is right?
a. A only   **c.** Both A and B
b. B only   **d.** Neither A nor B

122. Technician A says that an engine vacuum leak on a non-cat car will cause a CO reading to be higher than normal.

Technician B says that an engine misfire on a non-cat car will have little or no effect on a CO reading.

Who is right?
- **a.** A only
- **b.** B only
- **c.** Both A and B
- **d.** Neither A nor B

123. The alternator charge indicator lamp stays on when the engine is stopped (ignition switch OFF).

Technician A says that this could be caused by a faulty diode.

Technician B says that this could be caused by a bad rotor.

Who is right?
- **a.** A only
- **b.** B only
- **c.** Both A and B
- **d.** Neither A nor B

124. The primary ignition circuit on a vehicle is good. However, there is no spark coming out of the coil high tension wire. This could be caused by:
- **a.** a defective coil.
- **b.** an overheated transistor.
- **c.** a grounded rotor.
- **d.** Both a and b

125. A good spark is coming out of the coil high tension wire, but the engine will not start. Which of the following could be the cause?
- **a.** An open module
- **b.** A carbon tracked distributor cap
- **c.** A grounded rotor
- **d.** All of the above

126. A knock sensor equipped vehicle lacks power.

Technician A says that this could be caused by using low octane fuel.

Technician B says that this could be caused by carbon deposits.

Who is right?
- **a.** A only
- **b.** B only
- **c.** Both A and B
- **d.** Neither A nor B

127. In what carburetor circuit might a discharge weight be found?
- **a.** Float circuit
- **b.** High speed circuit
- **c.** Pump circuit
- **d.** Power circuit

128. What would be correct procedure when replacing a relief valve on an air pump?
- **a.** Remove the valve by twisting back and forth with a pipe wrench.
- **b.** Have the pump disassembled, and install the valve by using a large hammer and a piece of pipe for a driver.
- **c.** Both a and b
- **d.** Neither a nor b

129. An engine runs smooth at speeds above 2,500 rpm but idles rough.

Technician A says that this could be caused by a cracked intake manifold.

Technician B says that this could be caused by a poorly seated valve.

Who is right?
- **a.** A only
- **b.** B only
- **c.** Both A and B
- **d.** Neither A nor B

130. If you are checking a clamping diode with an analog ohmmeter on the X10 scale, and the diode is okay, what would you expect to see?
- **a.** Two high readings
- **b.** Two low readings
- **c.** Two mid-scale readings
- **d.** One high reading and one low reading

131. All of the spark plugs removed from an engine have a glazed yellowish-brown coating on the insulator nose. This could be caused by:
- **a.** excessive valve guide clearance.
- **b.** a plugged oil drain in the head.
- **c.** Both a and b
- **d.** Neither a nor b

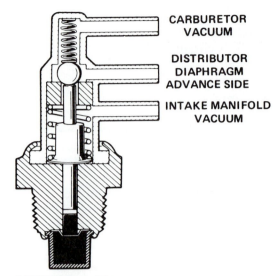

CARBURETOR VACUUM

DISTRIBUTOR DIAPHRAGM ADVANCE SIDE

INTAKE MANIFOLD VACUUM

FIGURE 8–33

132. Refer to the valve in Figure 8–33.

Technician A says that this valve controls ignition advance during high temperature idle.

Technician B says that this valve controls ignition advance during deceleration.

Who is right?
a. A only
b. B only
c. Both A and B
d. Neither A nor B

133. Technician A says that the EGR valve allows exhaust gases to enter the intake manifold.

Technician B says that the EGR system reduces combustion chamber temperature.

Who is right?
a. A only
b. B only
c. Both A and B
d. Neither A nor B

134. Which of these can cause a car to hesitate (stumble) when the gas pedal is opened quickly?
a. Low carburetor float level
b. Retarded ignition timing
c. Leaking accelerator pump ball check
d. All of the above

135. A cylinder leakage test shows all cylinders to be okay. Yet the engine just failed a compression test. What could be the reason for this?
a. Slow cranking rpm
b. An out-of-time camshaft
c. Both a and b
d. Neither a nor b

136. At times, an engine has a surge or cut-out. This is usually noticed when the accelerator is held in a steady position.

Technician A says that this could be caused by a plugged gas tank vent.

Technician B says that this could be caused by a leak in the fuel line.

Who is right?
a. A only
b. B only
c. Both A and B
d. Neither A nor B

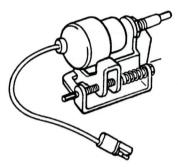

FIGURE 8–34

137. Technician A says that the device in Figure 8–34 controls engine fast idle during warm-up.

Technician B says that the device above opens the carburetor throttle plates when the ignition is ON.

Who is right?
a. A only
b. B only
c. Both A and B
d. Neither A nor B

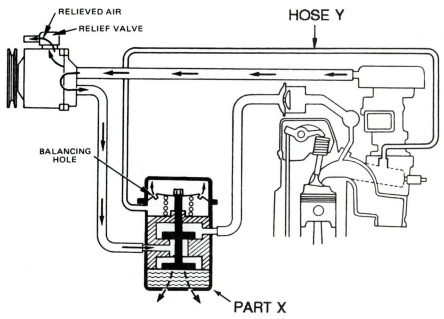

FIGURE 8–35

138. A car equipped with the air pump system in Figure 8–35 backfires when decelerating. This could be caused by:
a. part X being bad.
b. hose Y being broken.
c. Both a and b
d. Neither a nor b

140. A car owner complains of static noise in the radio. This could be caused by:
a. steel core ignition cables.
b. resistor spark plugs.
c. Both a and b
d. Neither a nor b

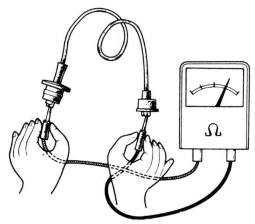

FIGURE 8–36

139. Technician A says that the test in Figure 8–36 SHOULD NOT indicate continuity.
   Technician B says that the test above checks resistance.
   Who is right?
a. A only
b. B only
c. Both A and B
d. Neither A nor B

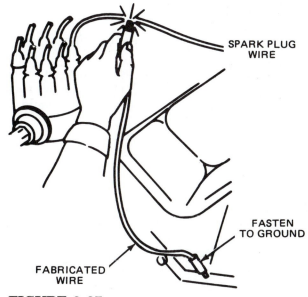

FIGURE 8–37

141. What is being checked in Figure 8–37?
a. Cylinder balance
b. Coil output
c. Plug wire insulation
d. None of these

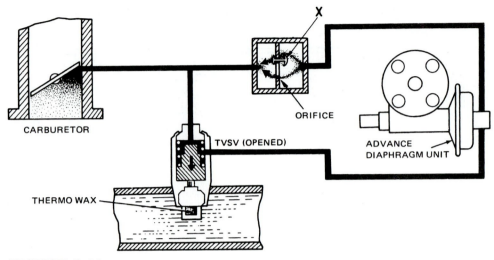

FIGURE 8–38

142. Refer to part X in Figure 8–38.

Technician A says that this part delays spark advance.

Technician B says that this part is often color coded.

Who is right?
a. A only
b. B only
c. Both A and B
d. Neither A nor B

143. Intake manifold vacuum is highest:
a. at idle speed.
b. during midrange cruise.
c. under load.
d. during deceleration and coasting.

144. A compression test has been made on an in-line 6-cylinder engine. All of the cylinder readings are higher than normal. This could be caused by:
a. a stretched timing chain.
b. excessive head milling.
c. Both a and b
d. Neither a nor b

145. Technician A says that the device in Figure 8–39 lessens carbon monoxide (CO) pollutants in the exhaust gas.

Technician B says that improper air-fuel ratio arriving to the device above can result in a "rotten egg" smell.

Who is right?
a. A only
b. B only
c. Both A and B
d. Neither A nor B

FIGURE 8–39

146. The meters in Figure 8–40 read as shown when hooked up to a new model engine running at 2,500 rpm.

Technician A says that the CO reading is rich.

Technician B says that the HC reading is high.

Who is right?
a. A only
b. B only
c. Both A and B
d. Neither A nor B

 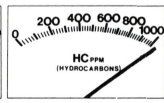

FIGURE 8–40

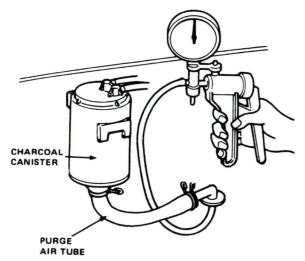

CHARCOAL CANISTER

PURGE AIR TUBE

FIGURE 8–41

147. A vacuum pump/gauge is connected as shown in Figure 8–41. When the engine is started and the speed raised to 2,500 rpm, a vacuum reading appears on the gauge. What does this indicate?
a. A plugged canister
b. A dirty purge air tube
c. Both a and b
d. Neither a nor b

148. A driver says that his automobile has reduced top speed.

Technician A says that this could be caused by a stuck power valve.

Technician B says that an improperly adjusted dashpot could be the cause.

Who is right?
a. A only
b. B only
c. Both A and B
d. Neither A nor B

149. A PCV pocket tester on the oil filter opening reads "good."

Technician A says that this indicates a buildup of pressure in the crankcase.

Technician B says that fresh air is flowing into the crankcase and there is a slight vacuum.

Who is right?
a. A only
b. B only
c. Both A and B
d. Neither A nor B

150. One plug in a set has badly burned (melted) electrodes. What is the MOST LIKELY cause?
a. Cross-fire
b. An open spark plug wire
c. A burned valve
d. A worn camshaft

151. A mechanical fuel pump is being tested using a standard vacuum/pressure gauge at the pump inlet.

Technician A says that this tests the condition of the diaphragm.

Technician B says that this tests the check valves in the pump.

Who is right?
a. A only
b. B only
c. Both A and B
d. Neither A nor B

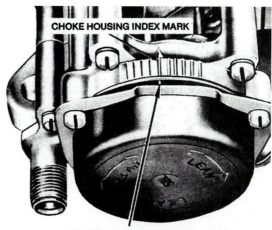

CHOKE HOUSING INDEX MARK

CHOKE COVER INDEX MARK

FIGURE 8–42

152. The index marks in Figure 8–42 are used to adjust the:
a. thermostatic spring tension.
b. choke plate tension.
c. Both a and b
d. Neither a nor b

153. A car equipped with an AIR system backfires when decelerating. Which of these should a technician check?
a. The air manifold(s) for restrictions
b. The operation of the diverter or gulp valve
c. The output pressure of the air pump
d. The operation of the exhaust manifold check

154. A TCS equipped car has no vacuum advance in third or fourth gear at all engine temperatures.

Technician A says that this could be due to a bad TCS switch on the transmission.

Technician B says that this could be due to a bad advance diaphragm on the distributor.

Who is right?
a. A only
b. B only
c. Both A and B
d. Neither A nor B

FIGURE 8–43

155. A spark plug has chunks of aluminum imbedded between the electrode and insulator (see Figure 8–43).

Technician A says that this can be caused by pre-ignition.

Technician B says that this can be caused by using low grade gasoline.

Who is right?

a. A only   **c.** Both A and B
b. B only   **d.** Neither A nor B

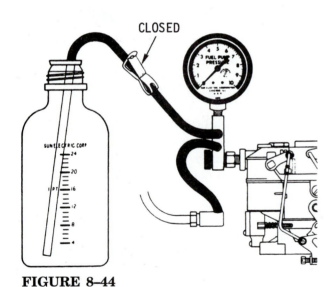

FIGURE 8–44

156. The setup in Figure 8–44 is checking for fuel pump:

a. volume.   **c.** Both a and b
b. pressure.   **d.** Neither a nor b

157. When a spark plug is shorted out on an engine equipped with EGR, the idle speed increases.

Technician A says that this is normal on certain model engines.

Technician B says that this can be caused by late ignition timing.

Who is right?

a. A only   **c.** Both A and B
b. B only   **d.** Neither A nor B

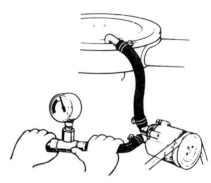

FIGURE 8–45

158. A low reading is obtained when making the test in Figure 8–45. This could be caused by:

a. worn carbon shoes.
b. a stuck open relief valve.
c. Either a or b
d. Neither a nor b

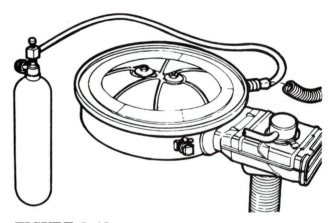

FIGURE 8–46

159. Technician A says that propane is used when making the check in Figure 8–46.

Technician B says that the rpm gain is noted when making this check.

Who is right?

a. A only   **c.** Both A and B
b. B only   **d.** Neither A nor B

160. Technician A says that combustion chamber temperatures will be lower when vacuum advance is denied.

Technician B says that exhaust gas temperatures increase when vacuum advance is denied.

Who is right?

a. A only
b. B only
c. Both A and B
d. Neither A nor B

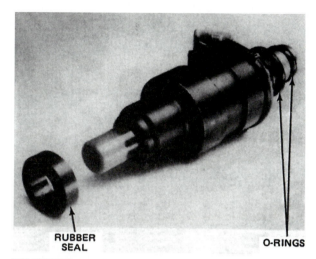

RUBBER SEAL   O-RINGS

FIGURE 8–47

161. Technician A says that if the rubber seal shown in Figure 8–47 is cracked, rough idle can result.

Technician B says that if the o-rings shown above are cut, gasoline fumes can result.

Who is right?

a. A only
b. B only
c. Both A and B
d. Neither A nor B

162. Technician A says that the lean drop method is used to adjust idle mixture.

Technician B says that the CO specification method is used to adjust idle mixture.

Who is right?

a. A only
b. B only
c. Both A and B
d. Neither A nor B

163. Technician A says that a MAP sensor measures engine load.

Technician B says that a typical MAP sensor produces a low voltage signal when manifold vacuum is high.

Who is right?

a. A only
b. B only
c. Both A and B
d. Neither A nor B

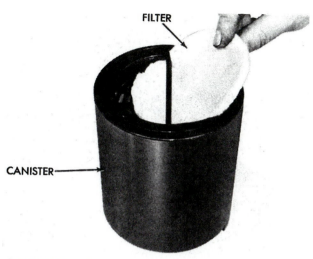

FILTER

CANISTER

FIGURE 8–48

164. The filter in Figure 8–48 is going to be replaced.

Technician A says to saturate the new one with oil.

Technician B says to rinse out the canister with cleaning solvent.

Who is right?

a. A only
b. B only
c. Both A and B
d. Neither A nor B

165. Technician A says that a typical TPS provides a voltage of less than 1 V at idle to near 5 V at wide open throttle.

Technician B says that a TPS can often be adjusted.

Who is right?

a. A only
b. B only
c. Both A and B
d. Neither A nor B

166. Which of the following statements regarding an oxygen sensor on most vehicles is true?

a. It monitors exhaust oxygen content.
b. It produces a signal of under 0.5 V with a lean mixture.
c. It will switch its signal from rich to lean (high to low) several times per second during closed loop operation.
d. All of the above

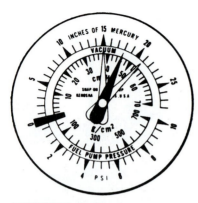

FIGURE 8–49

167. The gauge in Figure 8–49 shows a slow float-ing motion between 15 and 21 at idling speed.

Technician A says that this could be caused by a loose exhaust manifold.

Technician B says that this could be caused by a "stepped" idle mixture screw.

Who is right?

a. A only　　　　　**c.** Both A and B
b. B only　　　　　**d.** Neither A nor B

168. Technician A says that a pulse air system does not use an air pump.

Technician B says that a pulse air system reduces hydrocarbon and carbon monoxide emissions.

Who is right?

a. A only　　　　　**c.** Both A and B
b. B only　　　　　**d.** Neither A nor B

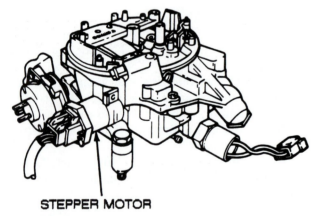

STEPPER MOTOR
FIGURE 8–50

169. Technician A says that the motor in Figure 8–50 is a device that increases throttle open-ing when the air conditioning turns on.

Technician B says that the motor is a device that varies carburetor air-fuel mixture.

Who is right?

a. A only　　　　　**c.** Both A and B
b. B only　　　　　**d.** Neither A nor B

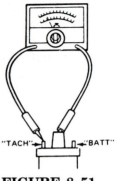

FIGURE 8–51

170. A technician is making the check in Figure 8–51 with a VOM. The MOST NORMAL read-ing would be:

a. infinity.　　　　　**c.** 100 ohms.
b. no resistance.　　**d.** 8,500 ohms.

171. Injectors are checked for all of the following, EXCEPT:

a. resistance.　　　　**c.** flow.
b. dripping.　　　　**d.** capacitance.

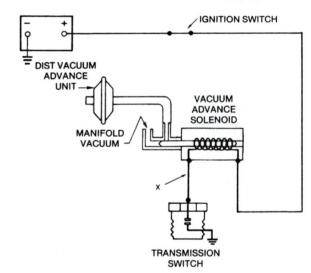

FIGURE 8–52

172. Wire X in Figure 8–52 is pinched and acci-dently grounded when a new transmission is installed. This will result in:

a. no vacuum advance in any transmission gear.
b. a battery drain when the ignition is turned off.
c. Both a and b
d. Neither a nor b

173. Technician A says that TVRS ignition wire prevents spark plug fouling.

Technician B says that TVRS ignition wire isn't easily damaged when pulled off the spark plugs.

Who is right?
a. A only
b. B only
c. Both A and B
d. Neither A nor B

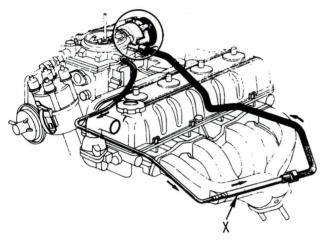

FIGURE 8-53

174. Tube X in Figure 8-53 is cracked.

Technician A says that this can result in hard starting.

Technician B says that this can cause the engine to overheat.

Who is right?
a. A only
b. B only
c. Both A and B
d. Neither A nor B

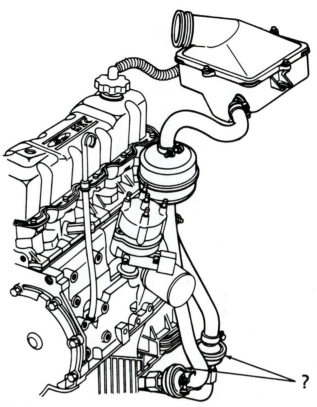

FIGURE 8-54

175. What are the air injection system components pictured in Figure 8-54?
a. Relief valves   c. Diverter valves
b. Check valves   d. Gulp valves

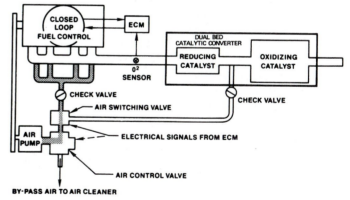

FIGURE 8-55

176. An air management system in the cold operation mode is shown in Figure 8-55.

Technician A says that air is being directed between the beds of the catalytic converter.

Technician B says that the air switching valve is energized by the ECM.

Who is right?
a. A only   c. Both A and B
b. B only   d. Neither A nor B

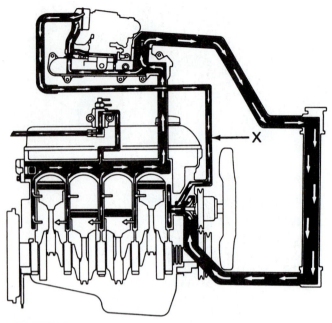

FIGURE 8–56

177. What is the purpose of hose X in the cooling system circuit in Figure 8–56?
   a. It allows trapped air to escape.
   b. It prevents cavitation.
   c. Both a and b
   d. Neither a nor b

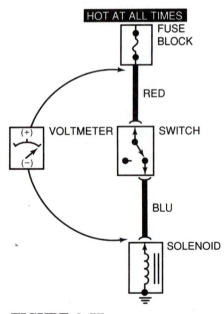

FIGURE 8–57

178. Technician A says that the meter in Figure 8–57 is testing for voltage drop.
   Technician B says that the above meter is testing for high resistances.
   Who is right?
   a. A only   c. Both A and B
   b. B only   d. Neither A nor B

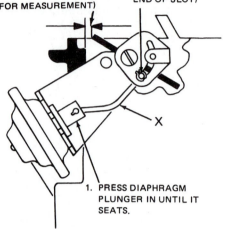

FIGURE 8–58

179. Study Figure 8–58.
   Technician A says that the diaphragm plunger helps to open the choke valve.
   Technician B says that the vacuum break clearance can be adjusted by bending the linkage rod at point X.
   Who is right?
   a. A only   c. Both A and B
   b. B only   d. Neither A nor B

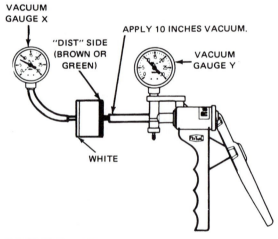

FIGURE 8–59

180. The valve in Figure 8–59 is being tested.
   Technician A says that gauge X should respond more slowly than gauge Y.
   Technician B says that gauge X and gauge Y should both read the same after a short delay.
   Who is right?
   a. A only   c. Both A and B
   b. B only   d. Neither A nor B

| ENGINE CONDITION | FUEL CONTROL SYSTEM OPERATION | | |
	INPUTS TO ECM	M/C SOLENOID OPERATION	DWELLMETER READING
STARTING (CRANKING)	• TACHOMETER LESS THAN 200 RPM	M/C SOLENOID OFF (RICH MIXTURE)	0°
WARM-UP	• TACH ABOVE 200 RPM (ENGINE RUNNING) • O_2 SENSOR LESS THAN 315°C (600°F) • COOLANT LESS THAN 19°C (66°F) • LESS THAN 10 SECONDS ELAPSED SINCE STARTING	FIXED COMMAND FROM ECM TO M/C SOLENOID	FIXED READING BETWEEN 10° AND 50°
WARM OPERATION IDLE AND CRUISING ("CONSTANT" ENGINE SPEED)	• O_2 SENSOR ABOVE 315°C (600°F) • COOLANT ABOVE 19°C (66°F) • MAP SENSOR	M/C SOLENOID SIGNAL DETERMINED BY OXYGEN SENSOR INFORMATION TO ECM	VARING ANYWHERE BETWEEN 10° AND 50° (NOMINAL 35°) (FASTER WITH HIGHER RPM)
ACCELERATION AND DECELERATION ("CHANGING" ENGINE SPEEDS)	• THROTTLE POSITION SENSOR (TPS) • MAP SENSOR • O_2 SENSOR	MOMENTARY PROGRAMMED SIGNAL FROM ECM DURING PERIOD AFTER THROTTLE CHANGE UNTIL OXYGEN SENSOR RESUMES CONTROL OF M/C SOLENOID	MOMENTARY CHANGE, CAN'T BE READ ON DWELLMETER. WILL BE VARYING, BUT HIGH OR LOW ON SCALE DEPENDING UPON OPERATING CONDITION(S)
WIDE-OPEN THROTTLE	• TPS FULLY OPEN • MAP SENSOR	VERY RICH COMMAND TO M/C SOLENOID	6°

FIGURE 8–60

181. A vehicle having the fuel control system in Figure 8–60 has just been started after being parked overnight.

  Technician A says that the mixture control (m/c) solenoid dwell should be fixed.

  Technician B says that the mixture control (m/c) solenoid signal is being determined by oxygen sensor information to the ECM.

  Who is right?

  a. A only **c.** Both A and B
  b. B only **d.** Neither A nor B

182. A heavy carburetor float can cause:
  a. hard starting. **c.** rough idle.
  b. poor gas mileage. **d.** All of the above

183. The engine cooling fans on a vehicle are operating at a 95% duty cycle. This means the fans are:
  a. almost turned off.
  b. varying as necessary.
  c. running at almost full speed.
  d. not synchronized.

184. A gasoline fuel injection system offers what advantage(s) over a carburetor system?
  a. No need for manifold heat
  b. Improved fuel economy
  c. Higher torque at lower speeds
  d. All of the above

185. A continuous injection system:
  a. eliminates electronic injector timing.
  b. uses an air flow sensor mechanically connected to a hydraulic valve.
  c. Both a and b
  d. Neither a nor b

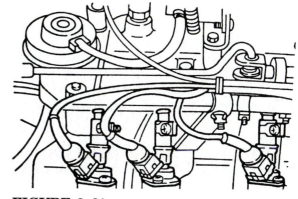

FIGURE 8–61

186. Technician A says that the injectors shown in Figure 8–61 have fuel pressure behind them after the engine is shut off.

  Technician B says that these injectors may be designed to operate on less than 12 V.

  Who is right?

  a. A only **c.** Both A and B
  b. B only **d.** Neither A nor B

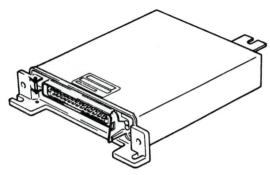

FIGURE 8–62

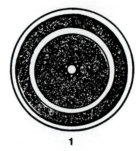

FIGURE 8–63

187. An automobile is equipped with an electronic ported fuel injection system.

Technician A says that the part in Figure 8–62 controls the injector pulse-width.

Technician B says that this part grounds the injectors.

Who is right?

a. A only   **c.** Both A and B

b. B only   **d.** Neither A nor B

188. A vehicle has an electronic ported fuel injection system with oxygen feedback.

Technician A says never arc weld on the vehicle unless the control unit is disconnected.

Technician B says never disconnect the control unit or any of its sensors unless the ignition is switched off.

Who is right?

a. A only   **c.** Both A and B

b. B only   **d.** Neither A nor B

189. An engine with electronic ported fuel injection surges at idle speed.

Technician A says that this could be caused by an air leak in the induction system.

Technician B says that this could be caused by a poor ground connection at the fuel pump relay.

Who is right?

a. A only   **c.** Both A and B

b. B only   **d.** Neither A nor B

190. A fuel injection system uses the air flow sensor plate in Figure 8–63: Which illustration above shows the correct alignment?

a. 1   **b.** 2   **c.** Both 1 and 2   **d.** Neither 1 or 2

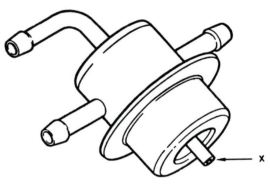

FIGURE 8–64

191. An EFI system uses the pressure regulator in Figure 8–64.

Technician A says that this regulator may be adjustable.

Technician B says that tube X connects to the intake manifold.

Who is right?

a. A only

b. B only

c. Both A and B

d. Neither A nor B

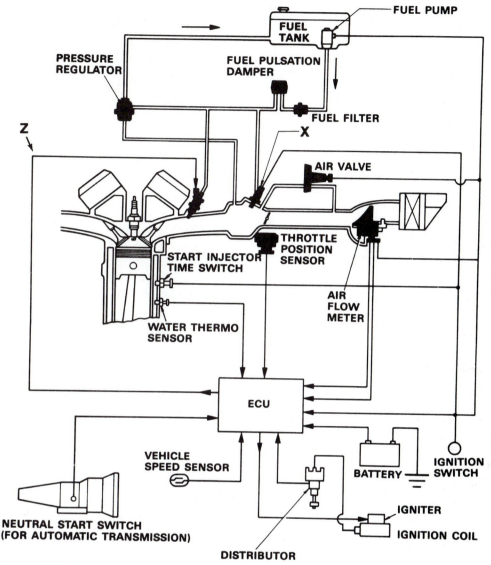

FIGURE 8–65

192. Technician A says that part X in Figure 8–65 gets current only when the starter is cranking.

Technician B says that the air valve works only when the engine is hot.

Who is right?
a. A only
b. B only
c. Both A and B
d. Neither A nor B

193. Refer to the schematic for question 192.

Technician A says that the fuel pressure regulator is vacuum sensitive.

Technician B says that engine speed should drop when wire Z is disconnected.

Who is right?
a. A only
b. B only
c. Both A and B
d. Neither A nor B

194. Refer to the schematic for question 192. How does the ECU (electronic control unit) know how much gasoline should be injected?
a. By the air flow meter
b. By the throttle position sensor
c. By the ignition coil
d. All of the above

195. Which of these could be the cause of high fuel consumption on a vehicle with EFI?
a. Fuel pressure set too high
b. Cracked pressure regulator vacuum hose
c. Restricted muffler
d. All of the above

196. Refer to the diagram in Figure 8–67.

Technician A says that fuel flow is governed by intake manifold pressure.

Technician B says that part X is designed to drip a small amount of fuel after the engine is warm and running.

Who is right?

a. A only   **c.** Both A and B
b. B only   **d.** Neither A nor B

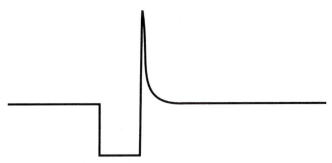

FIGURE 8–66

197. Figure 8–66 shows the injector pattern of a series resistor type injector. What does the pattern indicate?

a. A mechanically stuck injector
b. An open internal circuit
c. A partial short circuit
d. A normal condition

198. A car equipped with air flow controlled fuel injection will not start.

Technician A says that this could be caused by a blown fuse.

Technician B says that this could be caused by an air box leak.

Who is right?

a. A only   **c.** Both A and B
b. B only   **d.** Neither A nor B

199. Technician A says that the oxidation bed of a three-way catalytic converter is used to control carbon monoxide and carbon dioxide.

Technician B says that the reduction bed of a three-way catalytic converter is used to control oxides of nitrogen.

Who is right?

a. A only   **c.** Both A and B
b. B only   **d.** Neither A nor B

200. An engine equipped with manifold pressure controlled fuel injection quits whenever operating temperature rises above normal. Otherwise, the engine runs okay.

Technician A says that this could be caused by a faulty brain.

Technician B says that this could be caused by a defective temperature sensor.

Who is right?

a. A only
b. B only
c. Both A and B
d. Neither A nor B

201. Technician A says that the frequency of an analog signal is determined by current flow in the circuit.

Technician B says that it is determined by the amplitude of the signal being generated in the circuit.

Who is right?

a. A only
b. B only
c. Both A and B
d. Neither A nor B

202. An engine with a continuous injection system stalls sporadically.

Technician A says that this could be caused by a sticking fuel head (distributor).

Technician B says that this could be caused by misadjusted CO.

Who is right?

a. A only
b. B only
c. Both A and B
d. Neither A nor B

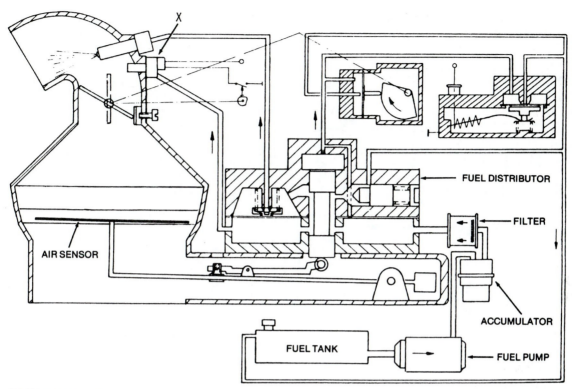

X

FUEL DISTRIBUTOR

FILTER

AIR SENSOR

ACCUMULATOR

FUEL TANK

FUEL PUMP

FIGURE 8–67

203. Technician A says that the accumulator in Figure 8–67 helps during hot starting.

Technician B says that the accumulator above holds the fuel pressure constant for an extended length of time after the engine has been turned off.

Who is right?
a. A only   c. Both A and B
b. B only   d. Neither A nor B

204. Excessive fuel consumption on a car with continuous fuel injection could be caused by:
a. "warm" control pressure being too low.
b. bad Lambda control system.
c. Either a or b
d. Neither a nor b

205. Which of these could be responsible for affecting a change in CO level?
a. Binding air flow sensor door
b. Change in O_2 sensor voltage
c. Both a and b
d. Neither a nor b

206. An EFI engine has poor acceleration when the throttle is suddenly opened wide. Idle and cruise performance are okay.

Technician A says that this could be caused by a shorted air flow sensor.

Technician B says that this could be caused by corroded throttle position switch contacts.

Who is right?
a. A only   c. Both A and B
b. B only   d. Neither A nor B

207. A car has electronic ported fuel injection. The engine has to crank longer than normal before it starts. Which of these would be the MOST LIKELY cause?
a. Grounded control unit
b. Faulty residual check valve
c. Improperly adjusted TPS
d. Bad pulsation damper

208. An engine will not start when cold. Which one of these would be the MOST LIKELY cause?
a. Bad fuel accumulator
b. Leaking injector seal
c. Binding auxiliary air regulator
d. Bad thermo-time switch

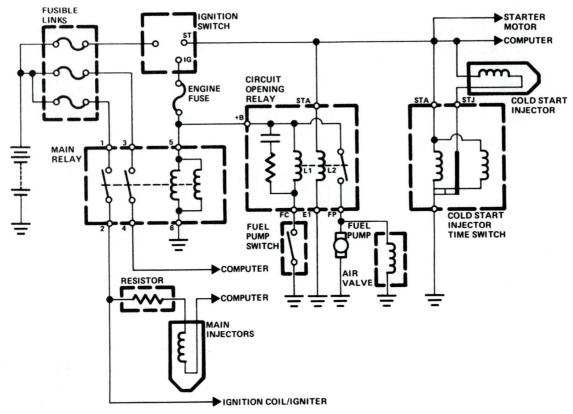

FIGURE 8–68

209. Refer to the EFI circuit schematic in Figure 8–68.

Technician A says that a bad main relay could cause a no-start condition.

Technician B says that the cold start injector should operate only during engine cranking.

Who is right?

a. A only
b. B only
c. Both A and B
d. Neither A nor B

210. An automobile equipped with continuous fuel injection and Lambda control is being driven with a disconnected frequency valve.

Technician A says that this will decrease the pressure in the lower chamber of the fuel distributor.

Technician B says that this will decrease the amount of fuel to the injectors.

Who is right?

a. A only
b. B only
c. Both A and B
d. Neither A nor B

211. When a pair of pliers is used to pinch off the hose to the auxiliary air regulator on a cold running engine, the rpm drops. This would indicate a:

a. bad air regulator.
b. normal condition.
c. manifold vacuum leak.
d. bad injector.

212. An engine with EFI surges at idle only when at operating temperature. The MOST LIKELY cause would be:

a. a wrong base idle speed setting.
b. a bad vehicle speed sensor.
c. a clogged injector.
d. a bad coolant temp. sensor.

213. A car equipped with EFI loses power slowly and dies. It restarts okay, then loses power and dies again. What could be the cause?

a. A dirty fuel tank sock
b. A collapsed hose between the fuel pump and the fuel tank
c. Both a and b
d. Neither a nor b

214. An engine hesitates during acceleration. Which of these should you check first?
   a. Air temperature sensor
   b. Cold start injector
   c. Rail pressure
   d. Air flow sensor flap

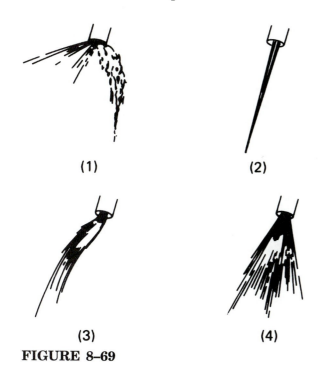

(1)   (2)

(3)   (4)

FIGURE 8–69

215. An injector is being checked. Which illustration in Figure 8–69 shows the correct spray pattern?
   a. #1 **b.** #2 **c.** #3 **d.** #4

216. A fuel injected engine has one cylinder misfiring at idle. This could be caused by:
   a. a leaking fuel injector.
   b. a leaking throttle shaft.
   c. Both a and b
   d. Neither a nor b

217. A fuel injected engine equipped with a "cat" is being checked with a 4-gas infrared analyzer.
   Technician A says that if the HC and CO are above specification, the CO_2 is low and the O_2 is 1% to 2%, the "cat" could be inoperative.
   Technician B says that if the O_2 rises above 2%, the engine may go into a lean misfire. If so, the HC will rise.
   Who is right?
   a. A only   **c.** Both A and B
   b. B only   **d.** Neither A nor B

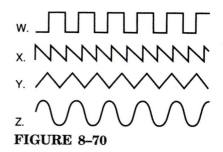

FIGURE 8–70

218. Refer to the waveforms in Figure 8–70.
   Technician A says that both Y and Z show normal output for a PM generator.
   Technician B says that both W and X show normal toggle for a buffer amplifier.
   Who is right?
   a. A only   **c.** Both A and B
   b. B only   **d.** Neither A nor B

219. Technician A says to measure pump pressure at point X in the fuel circulation loop in Figure 8–71.
   Technician B says to measure rest pressure at point Y in the loop.
   Who is right?
   a. A only   **c.** Both A and B
   b. B only   **d.** Neither A nor B

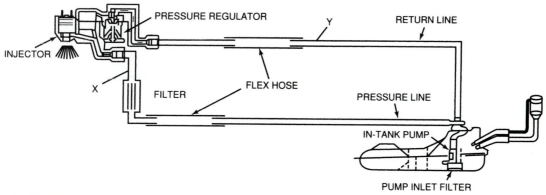

FIGURE 8–71

220. Deposit-fouled injectors can result in:
  a. stalling.
  b. an uneven spray pattern.
  c. hard starting.
  d. All of the above

221. Underhead valve deposits in a fuel injected engine can cause:
  a. cylinder flow characteristics to be upset.
  b. a lean operating condition during warm-up.
  c. Both a and b
  d. Neither a nor b

222. Refer to the fuel circulation loop shown in Figure 8–71.
  Technician A says that a pinched return line will cause a decrease in fuel pressure.
  Technician B says that the injector spray pattern can be checked with a timing light.
  Who is right?
  a. A only   **c.** Both A and B
  b. B only   **d.** Neither A nor B

223. A vacuum-operated EFE valve is pictured in Figure 8–72. There is a hole in hose X.
  Technician A says that this could cause sluggish cold engine throttle response.
  Technician B says that this could cause blistered spark plugs.
  Who is right?
  a. A only   **c.** Both A and B
  b. B only   **d.** Neither A nor B

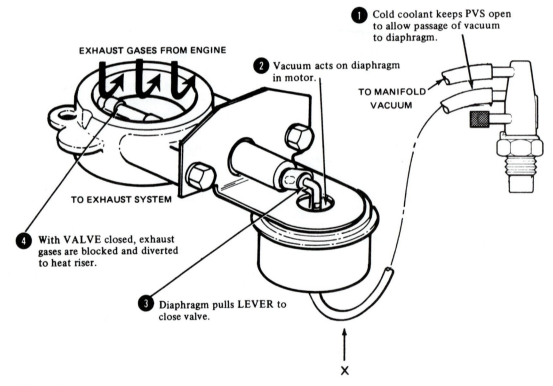

① Cold coolant keeps PVS open to allow passage of vacuum to diaphragm.

EXHAUST GASES FROM ENGINE

② Vacuum acts on diaphragm in motor.

TO MANIFOLD VACUUM

TO EXHAUST SYSTEM

④ With VALVE closed, exhaust gases are blocked and diverted to heat riser.

③ Diaphragm pulls LEVER to close valve.

X

FIGURE 8–72

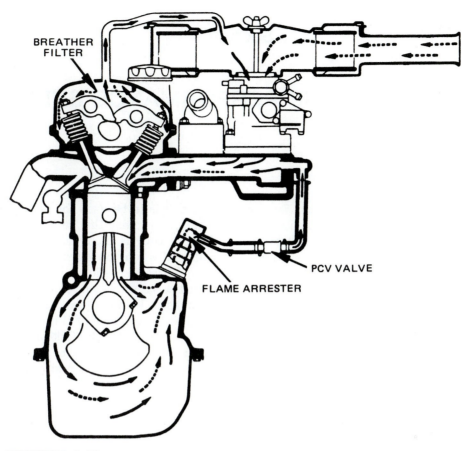

BREATHER
FILTER

PCV VALVE

FLAME ARRESTER

FIGURE 8–73

224. The air cleaner element in the engine in Figure 8–73 becomes oil soaked in a very short period of driving time.

Technician A says that a missing breather filter could be the cause.

Technician B says that the wrong weight engine oil could be the cause.

Who is right?

a. A only   **c.** Both A and B

b. B only   **d.** Neither A nor B

Note: Refer to the Engine Repair Test and the Electrical/Electronic Systems Test in this book. Some of these questions are applicable for use on the Engine Performance Test.

Section 9

ADVANCED ENGINE PERFORMANCE SPECIALIST

The Advanced Engine Performance Specialist (or L1) test is designed to measure a technician's ability to diagnose emission failures and drivability problems on computer-controlled engine systems. *NOTE: To register to take the ASE L1 test you must be currently certified in the Automobile Engine Performance area, and meet the two-year experience requirement.*

At present, this test consists of 45 multiple choice questions which require the use of a *Composite Vehicle Reference* booklet. This reference booklet will be sent to you prior to taking the actual test and is to be used for preparation. You will not be allowed to use this same booklet at the test site. A fresh copy is included with the test and will be collected when you finish.

Chart 9–1 shows how scan tool data (often called serial data) will be displayed for a number of Composite Vehicle questions. Different values will be shown with each of these questions.

Additionally, the following charts and their related information may be needed in order to help interpret certain Composite Vehicle questions. See *Charts 9–2* through *9–7*.

Chart 9–1
Serial Data

Engine Coolant Temperature Sensor (ECT) ⬇	Intake Air Temperature Sensor (IAT) ⬇	Manifold Absolute Pressure Sensor (MAP) ⬇	Throttle Position Sensor (TPS) ⬇
Engine Speed Sensor (RPM) ⬇	Heated Oxygen Sensor (HO2S) ⬇	Vehicle Speed Sensor (VSS) ⬇	Battery Voltage (B+) ⬇
Idle Air Control Valve (IAC) ⬇	Evaporative Emission Canister Solenoid (EVAP) ⬇	Torque Converter Clutch Solenoid (TCC) ⬇	EGR Valve Control Solenoid (EGR) ⬇
Malfunction Indicator Lamp (MIL) ⬇	Diagnostic Trouble Codes ⬇	Open/Closed Loop ⬇	Fuel Pump Relay (FP) ⬇
Measured Ignition Timing (°BTDC) ▶ Base: Actual:			

Chart 9–2
Diagnostic Trouble Code (DTC) Chart

P0105	Manifold Absolute Pressure (MAP) Sensor Circuit Malfunction
P0110	Intake Air Temperature (IAT) Sensor Circuit Malfunction
P0115	Engine Coolant Temperature (ECT) Sensor Circuit Malfunction
P0120	Throttle Position (TP) Sensor Circuit Malfunction
P0130	Oxygen Sensor (O2S) Circuit Malfunction
P0171	System Too Lean (O2S signal is continuously lean)
P0172	System Too Rich (O2S signal is continuously rich)
P0200	Fuel Injector Circuit Malfunction
P0230	Fuel Pump Relay Circuit Malfunction
P0300	Ignition Misfire Detected
P0320	Engine Speed (RPM) Sensor Circuit Malfunction
P0400	Exhaust Gas Recirculation (EGR) System Malfunction
P0440	Evaporative Emission (EVAP) Control System Malfunction
P0500	Vehicle Speed (VS) Sensor Circuit Malfunction
P0505	Idle Speed Control System Malfunction
P0560	System Voltage Malfunction
P0740	Torque Converter Clutch (TCC) System Malfunction

Chart 9–3
"Typical" Scan Tool Data Parameters/Values

Engine Speed	0—9999 rpm
Desired Idle	1—3187 rpm
Coolant Temperature	–40°C (–40°F)—151°C (304°F)
Startup Coolant Temperature	–40°C (–40°F)—151°C (304°F)
Coolant Temperature	–40°C (–40°F)—151°C (304°F)
Intake Air Temperature	–38°C (–36°F)—199°C (390°F)
MAP	11—105 kPa/0—5.1 Volts
BARO	11—105 kPa/0—5.1 Volts
Throttle Position	0—5.1 Volts
Throttle Angle	0—100%
Oxygen Sensor	0—1132 mV
Injector Pulse Width	0—998.4 mSEC
Fuel Integrator	0—255
Block Learn	0—255
Block Learn Cell	0—16
Block Learn Enable	No/Yes
Air/Fuel Ratio	0—25.5
Spark Advance	–90—90 Degrees
Knock Retard	0—45 Degrees
Knock Signal	No/Yes
"Open/Closed" Loop	"Open Loop"/"Closed Loop"
Converter High Temp.	No/Yes
Desired EGR Position	0—100%
Actual EGR Position	0—100%
EGR Pintle Position	0—5.1 Volts
EGR Duty Cycle	0—100%
EGR Auto-Zero	Not Complete/Complete
EGR Pintle Position	0—5.1 Volts
Idle Air Control	0—255
Park/Neutral	P-N—/R-DL
MPH KPH	0—255 0—255
TCC/Shift Light	Off/On
Fourth Gear Switch	Off/On
A/C Request	No/Yes
Battery/Ignition Volts	0—25.5 Volts
Fuel Pump Volts	0—25.5 Volts
IMTV Solenoid	Off/On
PROM ID	0—9999
Time from Start	0:00:00—18:12:15

Chart 9–4 a
MAP Sensor / Vacuum / Voltage Relationships

Vacuum at sea level [in. Hg]	Manifold Absolute Pressure [kPa]	Sensor Voltage	Fuel Mixture
0	101.3	4.0	Rich
3	91.2	3.5	
6	81.0	3.0	
9	70.8	2.5	
12	60.7	2.0	
15	50.5	1.5	
18	40.4	1.0	
21	30.2	0.5	
24	20.0	0.0	Lean

Chart 9–4b
ECT and IAT Sensors Temperature / Voltage Relationships

Temperature °F	Temperature °C	Sensor Voltage	Ohms Ω
248	120	0.25	—
212	100	0.46	177
176	80	0.84	332
150	66	1.34	—
140	60	1.55	667
104	40	2.27	1,459
86	30	2.60	2,238
68	20	2.93	3,520
32	0	3.59	9,420
−4	−20	4.24	28,680
−40	−40	4.90	100,700

Chart 9–5
Composite Vehicle Type 1 Electrical Schematic

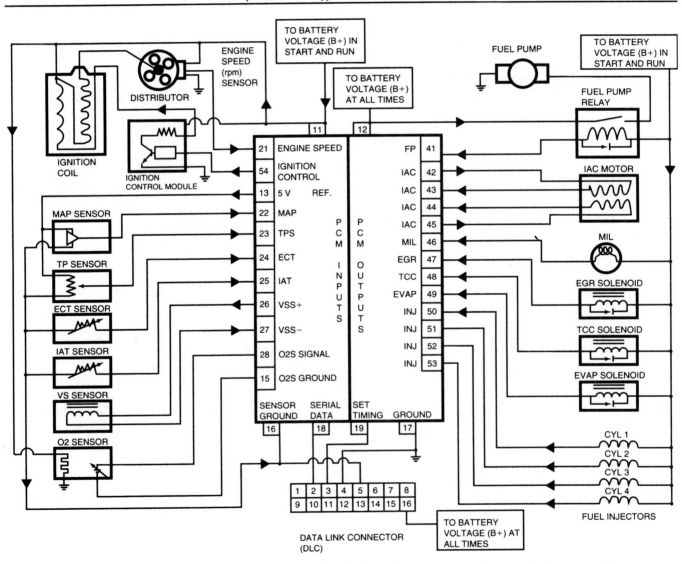

STUDY OUTLINE

I. Composite Vehicle **Type 1** Information
   A. General Description
      1. Generic
      2. Four cycle, four cylinder
      3. Speed-density, closed-loop system
   B. Powertrain Control Module (PCM)
      1. Receives sensor input
      2. Calculates ignition and fuel requirements
      3. Controls engine and transmission actuators
      4. Receives power from battery and ignition switch
      5. Provides regulated 5-volt supply for engine sensors
   C. Fuel System
      1. Sequential multiport fuel injection (SFI)
      2. Fuel pressure mechanically regulated with manifold vacuum
         a. Between 34 and 38 psi (234 and 262 kPa)
   D. Ignition System
      1. Distributor ignition (DI) with a single coil
      2. Engine speed input
      3. Spark timing
         a. Adjustable
         b. Specification is 10° BTDC
         c. Measure base with advance disabled
         d. Measure actual with advance enabled
         e. Jump pin 3 to pin 4 in the data link connector to disable advance
   E. Idle Speed
      1. Nonadjustable
      2. Normal no-load range is 850–900 rpm with an idle air control (IAC) value of 15–25%
   F. Sensors
      1. Engine speed (rpm) sensor
         a. Generates a signal for each cylinder as it reaches 30° BTDC
         b. Generates a sync pulse (camshaft position signal) on cylinder #1 for injector sequencing
      2. Manifold absolute pressure (MAP) sensor
         a. Senses intake manifold absolute pressure
         b. Voltage reading varies
         c. 4.0 volts at 101 kPa (key-on, engine-off, at sea level) to 0 volts at 20 kPa
         d. 1.0 volt (at sea level, no-load idle) with 18 inches of vacuum (40 kPa)
      3. Throttle position (TP) sensor
         a. Three-wire nonadjustable potentiometer
         b. Senses throttle position
         c. Voltage reading varies
         d. 0.5 volt at closed throttle
         e. 4.5 volts at maximum throttle
         f. Throttle opening of 80% or greater is "seen" as wide open throttle (WOT) by the PCM
         g. 3.7 volts at 80% opening
      4. Engine coolant temperature (ECT) sensor
         a. Negative temperature coefficient (NTC) thermistor
         b. Senses engine coolant temperature
         c. Values range from −40°C to 120°C
         d. 0.46 volt at 212°F (100°C)
      5. Intake air temperature (IAT) sensor
         a. NTC thermistor
         b. Senses air temperature in the air cleaner housing
         c. Values range from −40° to 248°F (−40°C to 120°C)
         d. 2.6 volts at 86°F (30°C)
      6. Oxygen sensor (O2S)
         a. Measures oxygen content in the exhaust manifold
         b. Output varies from 0.0 to 1.0 volt
         c. Less than 0.45 volt, oxygen content around sensor is high (lean mixture)
         d. More than 0.45 volt, oxygen content around sensor is low (rich mixture)
      7. Vehicle speed (VS) sensor
         a. Generates a signal
         b. Increases in frequency as vehicle speed increases
         c. Used by PCM to control torque converter clutch (TCC) and high-speed fuel cut-off
         d. Signal read in mph
   G. Actuators (All Solenoids and Relays Receive a Constant Battery Positive Voltage Feed from the Ignition Switch and Are Controlled by the PCM, Providing a Path to Ground)
      1. Fuel Injectors
         a. Electromechanical
         b. Individually energized once per camshaft revolution
         c. Timed to its cylinder's intake stroke
      2. Idle air control (IAC) valve
         a. Stepper motor
         b. Regulates air allowed to bypass throttle plate
         c. Controls engine idle speed during closed throttle operation
         d. Value of 0% indicates PCM command to fully close idle air bypass
         e. Value of 100% indicates PCM command to fully open idle air bypass
      3. Torque converter clutch (TCC) solenoid value
         a. Applied by redirecting hydraulic pressure in transaxle
         b. Solenoid energized when engine coolant temperature reaches 150°F (66°C) and vehicle is above 40 mph at cruise

4. Exhaust gas recirculation (EGR) valve control solenoid
   a. Duty cycle controlled solenoid
   b. When energized, supplies manifold vacuum to open EGR valve
   c. When not energized, blocks vacuum and EGR valve diaphragm is vented to close valve
   d. Value of 0% indicates PCM command to fully close EGR valve
   e. Value of 100% indicates a PCM command to fully open EGR valve
   f. Solenoid is energized when engine coolant temperature reaches 150°F (66°C) and the throttle is not closed or wide open
5. Fuel pump (FP) relay
   a. When energized, supplies battery voltage (B+) to the fuel pump
6. Ignition control module
   a. Closes and opens ignition primary circuit
   b. Ignition timing is controlled by the PCM based on engine speed and various sensor inputs
7. Malfunction indicator lamp (MIL)
   a. Indicates problems have been detected by the PCM
   b. With key-on, engine-off, the lamp turns on for bulb check
   c. Lamp stays on with engine running when diagnostic trouble code is set by PCM
8. Evaporative emission (EVAP) canister purge solenoid
   a. When energized, vapors stored in canister flow to intake manifold
   b. Solenoid is energized when engine coolant temperature reaches 150°F (66°C) and the throttle is not closed

H. SFI Operation and Component Functions
1. Starting mode
   a. With key-on, PCM energizes fuel pump relay for two seconds to pressurize fuel system
   b. Fuel pump relay is de-energized unless engine is cranked within this 2-second period
   c. Fuel pump relay is energized as long as engine speed (rpm) signal to PCM is 100 rpm or more
2. Clear-flood mode
   a. With throttle opening of 80% or greater and engine speed below 400 rpm, PCM turns off fuel injectors
3. Open-loop mode
   a. PCM does not use oxygen sensor signal
   b. Fuel injector pulse width is calculated from engine speed and various sensors
   c. System stays in open-loop until the heated oxygen sensor (HO2S) reaches operating temperature (600°F/315°C) and is sending a varying signal to the PCM
   d. System stays in open-loop until engine coolant temperature is above 150°F (66°C)

e. System stays in open-loop until 2 minutes have elapsed since start-up
   f. System stays in open-loop until the above three conditions (c, d, and e) are satisfied
4. Closed-loop mode
   a. PCM adjusts injector pulse width based on varying voltage signal from oxygen sensor
   b. Oxygen sensor signal below 0.45 volt causes PCM to increase injector pulse width
   c. Oxygen sensor signal above 0.45 volt causes PCM to decrease injector pulse width
   d. System goes into closed-loop when conditions stated in 3c, 3d, and 3e are met and throttle opening is less than 80%
5. Acceleration-enrichment mode
   a. Increase in manifold absolute pressure and change in throttle position is used by PCM to calculate increased injector pulse width
   b. During wide open throttle (WOT) operation, control system goes into open-loop mode
6. Deceleration-enleanment mode
   a. Decrease in manifold absolute pressure and change in throttle position is used by PCM to calculate decreased injector pulse width
7. Fuel cut-off mode
   a. For safety reasons, the PCM will turn off the fuel injectors when vehicle speed reaches 110 mph, or if engine speed exceeds 6000 rpm

II. Various Vehicle Applications
A. Sensors
1. Map (digital and analog signals)
2. Oxygen (zirconia and titania)
3. Throttle position (potentiometer and switched)
4. Crankshaft/camshaft position (magnetic, Hall Effect, and optical types)
5. Air flow (analog, digital, and potentiometer types)
6. Knock (piezo crystal)
   a. Retarding test
7. Vehicle speed (buffer amplifier)

B. Actuators
1. Injectors
   a. Pulse width modulated
   b. Peak and hold (current controlled)
   c. Throttle body
   d. Conventional (saturated switch)
2. Idle air control/idle speed control
   a. Duty cycle and voltage

C. Distributorless Ignition System (DIS)
1. Waste spark method
2. Dwell (10 to 15 milliseconds)
3. Magnetic triggering
4. Hall Effect triggering
5. Optical triggering

D. Testing/Evaluation
1. DVOM
2. Lab scope/ignition scope/burn time
3. Serial data
4. Root causes of failures

5. Five gas analysis
6. IM 240
7. Evaporative emission system pressure and purge tests

III. Composite Vehicle **Type 2** Information
  A. General Description
    1. Generic
    2. Four cycle, V6, single chain-driven camshaft
    3. Distributorless ignition, 12 valves
    4. Mass airflow-type closed-loop system
    5. Single exhaust with a three-way catalytic converter without secondary air injection
  B. Powertrain Control Module (PCM)
    1. Receives sensor input
    2. Calculates ignition and fuel requirements
    3. Controls engine and transmission actuators
    4. Has on-board diagnostic (OBD II) sensors and diagnostic capabilities
    5. Receives power from battery and ignition switch
    6. Provides regulated 5-volt supply for engine sensors
    7. Controls shifting for a four-speed automatic overdrive transaxle
    8. Controls vehicle's charging system
  C. Fuel System
    1. Sequential multiport fuel injection (SFI)
    2. Returnless fuel supply with electric fuel pump mounted inside the fuel tank
    3. Fuel pressure regulated by a mechanical regulator inside the fuel tank
      a. Constant 50 psi (345 kPa)
      b. Minimum 45 psi (310 kPa)
      c. Rest pressure minimum of 45 psi (310 kPa) for 2 minutes after engine is shut off
  D. Ignition System
    1. Distributorless ignition (DI) with three ignition coils
    2. Firing order: 1–2–3–4–5–6
      a. Cylinders 1, 3, and 5 are on bank 1
      b. Cylinders 2, 4, and 6 are on bank 2
    3. Spark timing
      a. Nonadjustable
      b. Determined by PCM using crankshaft position (CKP) sensor signal
  E. Idle Speed
    1. Nonadjustable closed throttle stop (minimum air rate)
    2. Normal no-load range is 850–900 rpm with an idle air control (IAC) value of 15–25%
  F. Sensors
    1. Crankshaft position (CKP) sensor
      a. Magnetic-type pulse generator
      b. Mounted on crankshaft just behind balancer pulley
      c. 36-toothed iron wheel with one narrow tooth
      d. Generates 36 pulses for each crankshaft revolution, including one synchronizing pulse at 60° BTDC for cylinder 1

      e. PCM uses the 60° BTDC signal to select which ignition coil to fire
    2. Mass airflow (MAF) sensor
      a. Senses airflow into the throttle body
      b. Voltage reading varies
      c. 0.2 volt (0 gm/sec) with key on, engine off
      d. 4.8 volts (175 gm/sec) at maximum airflow
      e. 0.7 volt (2.0 gm/sec) at sea level, no-load idle (850 rpm)
    3. Manifold absolute pressure (MAP) sensor
      a. Senses intake manifold absolute pressure
      b. Voltage reading varies
      c. Sensor signal only used by PCM for OBD II diagnostics
      d. 4.0 volts at 101 kPa (key on, engine off, at sea level) to 0.0 volt at 20 kPa
      e. 1.0 volt (at sea level, no-load idle) with 18 inches of vacuum (40 kPa)
    4. Throttle position (TP) sensor
      a. Three-wire nonadjustable potentiometer located on the throttle body
      b. Senses throttle position
      c. Voltage reading varies
      d. 0.5 volt at closed throttle
      e. 4.5 volts at maximum throttle
      f. Throttle opening of 80% or greater is "seen" as wide open throttle (WOT) by the PCM
      g. 3.7 volts at 80% opening
    5. Engine coolant temperature (ECT) sensor
      a. Negative temperature coefficient (NTC) thermistor
      b. Senses engine coolant temperature
      c. Values range from −40°C to 120°C (−40°F to 248°F)
      d. 0.46 volts at 212°F (100°C)
    6. Intake air temperature (IAT) sensor
      a. NTC thermistor
      b. Senses air temperature in the air cleaner housing
      c. Values range from −40° to 248°F (−40°C to 120°C)
      d. 2.6 volts at 86°F (30°C)
    7. Heated oxygen sensors (HO2S 1/1, HO2S 2/1, and HO2S 1/2)
      a. Electrically heated zirconia sensors
      b. Sensor 1/1 is located on bank 1 exhaust manifold
      c. Sensor 2/1 is located on bank 2 exhaust manifold
      d. Sensors 1/1 and 2/1 used for closed loop fuel control and OBD II monitoring (upstream)
      e. Sensor 1/2 mounted in exhaust pipe after catalytic converter (downstream)
      f. Sensor 1/2 used for OBD II monitoring of catalytic converter operation
      g. Output varies from 0.0 to 1.0 volt
      h. Less than 0.45 volt, oxygen content around sensor is high (lean mixture)
      i. More than 0.45 volt, oxygen content around sensor is low (rich mixture)

j. Key on, engine off, sensor readings are zero volts

8. Camshaft position (CMP) sensor
   a. Hall Effect sensor
   b. Generates single pulse 30 camshaft degrees BTDC compression for cylinder 1
   c. Generates three pulses 30 camshaft degrees BTDC compression for cylinder 3
   d. Generates two pulses 30 camshaft degrees BTDC compression for cylinder 5
   e. Signals allow PCM to determine injector sequencing
   f. Located on timing cover, with specially notched interruptor mounted on cam timing gear

9. Power steering pressure (PSP) switch
   a. Located in power steering high pressure hose
   b. Switch closes when high pressure is detected in power steering system
   c. Switch signal used by PCM to increase idle speed to compensate for added load from power steering pump

10. Brake pedal position (BPP) switch
    a. Located on brake pedal arm
    b. Switch closes when brake pedal is depressed (brakes applied)
    c. Switch signal used by PCM to release torque converter clutch (TCC)

11. A/C request switch
    a. Located on climate control panel
    b. Switch closes when vehicle operator requests a/c compressor operation

12. A/C pressure sensor
    a. Located on a/c high side liquid line
    b. Readings vary from 0.25 volt @ 25 psi to 4.50 volts @ 450 psi
    c. Signal used by PCM to control a/c compressor clutch, radiator fan, and to increase idle speed to compensate for added load from a/c compressor
    d. If pressure is below 40 psi or above 420 psi, PCM will disable compressor

13. Fuel tank pressure (FTP) sensor
    a. Located on top of fuel tank
    b. Readings vary from 0.5 volt @ 5" of water pressure to 4.5 volts @ 15" of water vacuum
    c. Output is 1.5 volts with no pressure or vacuum in fuel tank (gas cap removed)
    d. Signal used by PCM to monitor and test evaporative system

14. Transmission fluid temperature (TFT) sensor
    a. Located in transmission oil pan
    b. Negative temperature coefficient (NTC) thermistor
    c. Values range from −40°F to 248°F (−40°C to 120°C)
    d. Output is 0.46 volt @ 212°F (100°C)
    e. Signal used by PCM to modify shift points and control TCC operation

15. Vehicle speed sensor (VSS)
    a. Located on transaxle
    b. Magnetically generates a signal that increases in frequency as vehicle speed increases
    c. Signal used by PCM to control upshifts, downshifts, TCC, and high-speed fuel cutoff

16. Transmission turbine shaft speed (TSS) sensor
    a. Located on transaxle
    b. Magnetically generates a signal that increases in frequency as transmission input speed increases
    c. Signal used by PCM to control TCC operation and sense transmission slippage

17. Transmission range (TR) switch
    a. Located on transaxle housing
    b. Six-position switch that indicates position of manual select lever (park/neutral, reverse, manual low 1, second 2, drive 3, or overdrive)
    c. Signal used by PCM to control transmission line pressure, upshifting, and downshifting

G. Actuators (All Coils, Solenoids and Relays Receive a Constant Battery Positive Voltage Feed from the Ignition Switch and Are Controlled by the PCM, Providing a Path to Ground)

1. Idle air control (IAC) valve
   a. Stepper motor
   b. Regulates air allowed to bypass throttle plate
   c. Controls engine idle speed during closed throttle operation
   d. Value of 0% indicates PCM command to fully close idle air bypass
   e. Value of 100% indicates PCM command to fully open idle air bypass

2. Fuel pump (FP) relay
   a. When energized, supplys battery voltage (B+) to fuel pump

3. Exhaust gas recirculation (EGR) valve control solenoid
   a. Duty cycle controlled solenoid
   b. When energized, supplies manifold vacuum to open EGR valve
   c. When not energized, blocks vacuum and EGR valve diaphragm is vented to close valve
   d. Value of 0% indicates PCM command to fully close EGR valve
   e. Value of 100% indicates a PCM command to fully open EGR valve
   f. Solenoid is energized when engine coolant temperature reaches 150°F (66°C) and the throttle is not closed or wide open

4. Malfunction indicator lamp (MIL)
   a. With key on, engine off, lamp turns on for a bulb check
   b. With engine running, MIL will light only when fault occurs in a monitored circuit that could result in increased emissions
   c. Diagnostic trouble codes (DTCs) and freeze frame data are stored in PCM memory

d. MIL will flash if fault is engine misfire that could damage catalytic converter

e. MIL will turn off only if DTC is cleared with a scan tool, or if three consecutive "trips" are completed with the OBD II diagnostic monitor run and no faults occur

5. Torque converter clutch (TCC) solenoid valve
   a. Applied by redirecting hydraulic pressure in transaxle
   b. Solenoid energized when engine coolant temperature reaches 150°F (66°C) and vehicle is above 40 mph at cruise
   c. With a duty cycle of 0%, TCC is released
   d. With a duty cycle of 100%, TCC is fully applied
   e. Duty cycle cut to 0% if brake pedal position switch closes

6. Evaporative emission (EVAP) canister purge solenoid
   a. Duty cycle controlled
   b. Regulates flow of vapors stored in canister to intake manifold
   c. Enabled when engine coolant temperature reaches 150°F (66°C) and throttle not closed
   d. With a duty cycle of 0%, vapor flow is blocked
   e. With a duty cycle of 100%, vapor flow is maximum
   f. Duty cycle determined by PCM, based on engine speed and load
   g. Used for OBD II testing of evaporative emission system

7. Fuel injectors
   a. Electro-mechanical
   b. Individually energized once per camshaft revolution timed to its cylinder's intake stroke

8. Ignition coils
   a. Produce high voltage to create spark at two cylinders simultaneously
   b. Coil 1 provides spark for cylinders 1 and 4
   c. Coil 2 provides spark for cylinders 2 and 5
   d. Coil 3 provides spark for cylinders 3 and 6

9. Generator field
   a. Duty cycle controlled
   b. Determines field voltage of generator
   c. Increased duty cycle results in greater generator output

10. Fan control (FC) relay
    a. When energized, provides battery voltage (B+) to radiator/condenser cooling fan motor

11. A/C clutch relay
    a. When energized, provides battery voltage (B+) to a/c compressor clutch coil

12. Evaporative emission (EVAP) canister vent solenoid
    a. When energized, fresh air supply hose to canister is blocked
    b. Only energized for OBD II testing of evaporative emission system

13. Transmission pressure control (PC) solenoid
    a. Pulse width modulated (PWM)
    b. PCM controls line pressure by varying duty cycle of solenoid
    c. When duty cycle is minimum (10%), line pressure is maximized
    d. When duty cycle is maximum (90%), line pressure is minimized
    e. Helps control shift feel and slippage

14. Transmission shift solenoids (SS1 and SS2)
    a. Control fluid routed to the 1–2, 2–3, and 3–4 shift valves
    b. PCM makes gear changes as indicated by energizing or de-energizing the solenoids

Gear	SS 1	SS 2
P, N, or R	On	Off
1	On	Off
2	Off	Off
3	Off	On
4	On	On

H. SFI Operation and Component Functions
   1. Starting mode
      a. With key on, PCM energizes fuel pump relay for 2 seconds to pressurize fuel system
      b. Fuel pump relay is de-energized unless engine is cranked within this 2-second period
      c. Fuel pump relay is energized as long as engine speed (CKP) signal to PCM is 100 rpm or more
      d. Prior to cranking (key on), PCM is looking at engine coolant temperature, intake air temperature, and throttle position to determine initial injector pulse width

   2. Clear-flood mode
      a. With throttle opening of 80% or greater and engine speed below 400 rpm, PCM turns off fuel injectors

   3. Run mode (open-loop)
      a. Occurs when engine is first started and running above 400 rpm
      b. PCM does not use oxygen sensor signal
      c. Injector pulse width calculated from throttle position, coolant and intake air temperatures, MAF sensor, and CKP sensor

   4. Run mode (closed-loop criteria)
      a. Both upstream oxygen sensors (HO2S 1/1 and HO2S 2/1) sending a varying signal to PCM
      b. Engine coolant temperature is above 150°F (66°C)
      c. One minute elapsed time since start up
      d. Throttle opening less than 80%

   5. Injector pulse width (closed-loop mode)
      a. PCM adjusts injector pulse widths for bank 1 and bank 2 based on the varying voltage signals from the upstream oxygen sensors
      b. Oxygen sensor signal below 0.45 volt causes PCM to increase injector pulse width
      c. Oxygen sensor signal above 0.45 volt causes PCM to decrease injector pulse width

6. Acceleration enrichment mode
   a. PCM uses increase in intake airflow and change in throttle position to calculate increased injector pulse width
   b. During wide-open throttle (WOT) operation, control system goes into open-loop mode
7. Deceleration enleanment mode
   a. PCM uses decrease in intake airflow, vehicle speed, and change in throttle position to calculate decreased injector pulse width
8. Fuel cut-off mode
   a. For safety reasons, the PCM will turn off the fuel injectors when vehicle speed reaches 110 mph, or if engine speed exceeds 6000 rpm

I. OBD System Operation
1. Comprehensive component monitor
   a. Continuously monitors engine and transmission sensors and actuators for shorts, opens, and out-of-range values
   b. Any detected failure will set a DTC
   c. Any failure resulting in increased emissions will turn on the MIL, and freeze frame data will be captured
   d. MIL remains on until DTC is cleared, or until three consecutive trips are completed with the OBD II diagnostic monitor run and no faults found
   e. DTC remains stored in memory until cleared using a scan tool
2. Main monitor
   a. Actively tests some systems for proper operation while driving
   b. Fuel control and engine misfires are checked continuously
   c. CAT efficiency, EGR operation, EVAP integrity, oxygen sensor responses, and oxygen sensor heaters are tested once during each "trip"
   d. Fuel control monitor will store a DTC and turn on the MIL if long-term fuel trim is plus or minus 30% at any time during trip after warm up
   e. Engine misfire monitor uses CKP sensor signal to continuously detect engine misfires
   f. Catalytic converter moniter compares signals from heated oxygen sensors to determine CAT efficiency
   g. EGR monitor uses MAP sensor signal to detect changes in intake manifold pressure during EGR operation
   h. EVAP system monitor uses fuel tank pressure sensor signal to determine if the EVAP system has any leaks
   i. Oxygen sensors monitor checks maximum and minimum output voltage for all oxygen sensors, and switching times
   j. Oxygen sensor heaters monitor checks time from cold start until oxygen sensors begin to operate

3. Monitor readiness status . . .
   The monitor readiness status indicates whether or not a particular OBD II diagnostic monitor has been run since the last time that DTCs were cleared from PCM memory. If the monitor has not yet run, the status will display on the scan tool as "NO." If the monitor has been run, the status will display on the scan tool as "YES." This does not mean that no faults were found, only that the diagnostic monitor has been run. Whenever DTCs are cleared from memory, all monitor readiness status indicators are reset to "NO." The following monitor readiness statuses can be read on the scan tool:

Comprehensive component	YES/NO
Fuel control	YES/NO
Engine misfire	YES/NO
Catalytic converter	YES/NO
EGR system	YES/NO
EVAP system	YES/NO
Oxygen sensors	YES/NO
Oxygen sensor heaters	YES/NO

4. OBD II trip cycle . . .
   To run all OBD II diagnostic monitors, the vehicle must be driven under a variety of conditions. The following example drive cycle, or "trip," will allow all monitors to run on this vehicle.
   a. Start and warmup until ECT is at least 160°F (71°C)—one minute minimum.
   b. Accelerate to 40–55 mph at ¼ throttle and maintain speed for five minutes.
   c. Decelerate without using the brake to 20 mph or less, then stop the vehicle, allow the engine to idle for 10 seconds, turn the key off, and wait one minute.
   d. Restart and accelerate to 40–55 mph at ¼ throttle and maintain speed for two minutes.
   e. Decelerate without using the brake to 20 mph or less, then stop the vehicle, allow the engine to idle for 10 seconds, turn the key off, and wait one minute.
   f. Repeat steps d and e.
5. Freeze frame data . . .
   When a DTC is stored, the following "freeze frame" data is also captured. If a DTC for fuel control or engine misfire is stored at a later time, the newest data are stored and the earlier information is lost.

   Calculated load value
   Short-term fuel trim
   Vehicle speed
   Manifold absolute pressure
   DTC stored with the freeze frame
   Engine rpm
   Long-term fuel trim
   Engine coolant temperature
   Closed/open loop status
   Cylinder ID if misfire detected

Chart 9–6a
Scan Tool Data (The Following Information Can Be Displayed on the OBD II Scan Tool)

ECT:	−40 to 248°F/−40 to 120°C
IAT:	−40 to 248°F/−40 to 120°C
MAP:	30 to 101 kPa
MAF	0.2 to 4.8 v/0 to 175 gm/sec
TP:	0 to 100%
Tach:	0 to 6000 rpm
VSS:	0 to 110 mph
Calculated Load Value:	0 to 100%
HO2S1/1:	0 to 1000 mv
HO2S2/1:	0 to 1000 mv
HO2S1/2:	0 to 1000 mv
Loop:	Open/Closed
Bank 1 Injector Pulse Width:	0 to 15 ms
Bank 2 Injector Pulse Width:	0 to 15 ms
Long Term Fuel Trim:	−30% to +30%
Short Term Fuel Trim:	−30% to +30%
Timing Advance:	0 to 60°
IAC:	0 to 100%
Battery:	0 to 18 v.
Generator Field	0 to 100%
EGR:	0 to 100%
Evap Purge:	0 to 100%
Evap Vent:	On/Off
Fuel Tank Pressure:	+5 to −15 in. H$_2$O
P/S Switch:	On/Off
Brake Switch:	On/Off
A/C Request:	On/Off
A/C Pressure:	25 to 450 psi
A/C Clutch:	On/Off
Fan Control:	On/Off
Fuel Pump:	On/Off
TR:	P/N, R, 1, 2, 3, OD
TFT:	−40 to 248°F/−40 to 120°C
TSS:	0 to 6000 rpm
SS1:	On/Off
SS2:	On/Off
TCC:	0 to 100%
PC:	0 to 100%
MIL:	On/Off
DTCs:	
Misfire Cyl #:	

Chart 9–6b

Mass Airflow (gm/sec)	Sensor Voltage
0	0.2
2	0.7
4	1.0
8	1.5
15	2.0
30	2.5
50	3.0
80	3.5
110	4.0
150	4.5
175	4.8

Chart 9–7
Composite Vehicle Type 2 Electrical Schematic

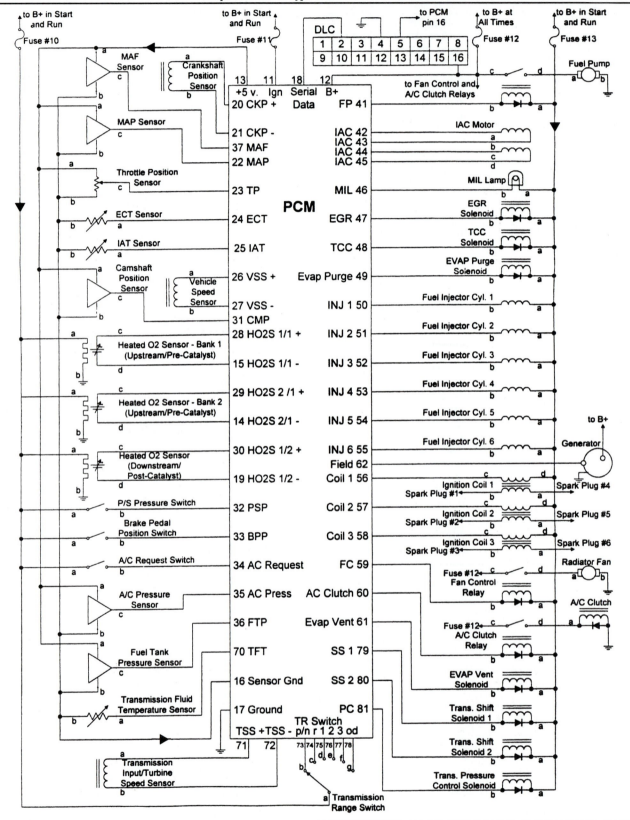

1. A vehicle has a rough idle and stalls intermittently when coming to a stop. It is able to restart but runs with a rough idle. Which of the following conditions could be the cause?
   a. Plugged EGR vent valve
   b. Stuck closed EGR control solenoid
   c. Both a and b
   d. Neither a nor b

2. A car runs rough and stalls repeatedly during the first two minutes after a cold start up. Ambient temperature is 70°F. The following scan tool data was obtained immediately after the cold start up:

Scan Tool Readings	
ECT	2.8 volts
IAT	2.8 volts
MAP	1–1.3 volts
Heated oxygen sensor (HO2S)	.7–.8 volt
IAC	45%

   Which of the following would be the MOST LIKELY cause?
   a. Bad ECT
   b. Bad HO2S
   c. Worn distributor bushings
   d. Intake valve deposits

3. A technician is checking EGR operation. He brings the engine up to 2000 rpm and disconnects and plugs the EGR vacuum supply hose. The engine speed climbs to 2200 rpm. Which of the following conditions could be the cause?
   a. Bad EGR control solenoid
   b. Plugged EGR passage
   c. Both a and b
   d. Neither a nor b

4. Technician A says that if base timing is incorrect, the PCM will not be able to correctly control spark advance.
   Technician B says that because of the ability of the PCM to control timing, the advance must be disabled in order to set base timing.
   Who is right?
   a. A only
   b. B only
   c. Both A and B
   d. Neither A nor B

5. An empty ("gutted") catalytic converter can cause which of the following items to function improperly?
   a. EVAP system   c. IAC motor
   b. EGR valve   d. PCV system

6. Technician A says that leaded fuel can "poison" a catalytic converter.
   Technician B says that there is no normal life expectancy of a catalytic converter.
   Who is right?
   a. A only   c. Both A and B
   b. B only   d. Neither A nor B

7. During a hot weather day, a vehicle fails an IM 240 test with high CO at idle. Which of these is the MOST LIKELY cause?
   a. Constant high oxygen sensor voltage
   b. EGR valve not seating
   c. Bad ignition module
   d. Stuck open EVAP purge solenoid

8. An engine is equipped with a speed density EFI system and runs rich. It is rough at idle and MAP voltage varies rapidly.
   Technician A says that this could be caused by a "jumped" timing belt.
   Technician B says that this can be caused by an intake manifold vacuum leak.
   Who is right?
   a. A only   c. Both A and B
   b. B only   d. Neither A nor B

9. During an IM 240 test, the vehicle fails because of high HC.
   Technician A says that a bad EFI spray pattern could be the cause.
   Technician B says that a restricted EGR passage could be the cause.
   Who is right?
   a. A only   c. Both A and B
   b. B only   d. Neither A nor B

10. Readings from a scanner on the Type 1 Composite Vehicle are normal except for a zero volts reading at the ECM v-ref. output pin.
    Technician A says that this could be caused by a short-to-ground in the ECT or the IAC.
    Technician B says that this could be caused by a short-to-ground in the MAP or the TPS.
    Who is right?
    a. A only   c. Both A and B
    b. B only   d. Neither A nor B

11. An engine has warmed up and the fuel injector pulse width is shorter than normal. HEGO voltage is 0.8 and fixed. Which of these could be the cause?
    a. Bad fuel pressure regulator
    b. Bad MAP
    c. Both a and b
    d. Neither a nor b

12. A car runs very rough at idle. Scan tool data is shown below:

Scan Tool Readings	
Loop status	closed
MAP	2.5 volts
Oxygen Sensor	0.1–0.9 volt
RPM	800
IAC	55%

Which of these is the MOST LIKELY cause?
    a. Dead oxygen sensor
    b. Stuck open EGR valve
    c. Stuck closed IAC valve
    d. Bad engine rpm signal

13. A car has poor mileage and sluggish performance. With ambient temperature near 100°F, it fails IM-240 with high HC and CO. Oxides of nitrogen are very low. Pressure and purge tests pass, but with high CO at idle. Which of these is the MOST LIKELY cause?
    a. Bad HEGO sensor
    b. Bad EVAP solenoid
    c. Short-to-ground at PCM pin 44 (see schematic on page 292 of this test section)
    d. Short-to-power at PCM pin 49 (see schematic on page 292 of this test section)

14. A vehicle runs okay, but the following four gas analyzer readings are indicated:

HC	25 ppm
CO	0.3%
O_2	7.5%
CO_2	8.0%

What is the MOST LIKELY cause for these readings?
    a. Bad PCV system
    b. Leaking EGR valve diaphragm
    c. Connected air pump
    d. Rich mixture

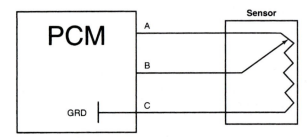

FIGURE 9–1

15. Use the circuit in Figure 9–1 to answer questions 15–18.
    Signal voltage returns to the PCM through which pin?
    a. A   b. B   c. C   d. None of the above

16. Voltage at pin A is called?
    a. Input
    b. Output
    c. Limiter
    d. Reference

17. Pin C voltage to ground should read less than?
    a. 0.10 volt
    b. 1.0 volt
    c. 4.5 volts
    d. 5.0 volts

18. To test signal return voltage, connect a voltmeter across which pins?
    a. A to B
    b. A to C
    c. A to battery negative
    d. B to C

19. Many temperature sensors are negative temperature coefficient (NTC) thermistors. Which of the following statements best describes the operation of this type of sensor?
   a. Their resistance goes down as the temperature goes up.
   b. Their resistance goes down as the temperature goes down.
   c. They produce a voltage that indicates temperature.
   d. They always return a negative polarity voltage to the computer.

20. When you disconnect the P/B booster hose, the oxygen sensor's voltage should:
   a. quickly drop between 0–0.4 volt.
   b. stay at 0.45 volt if the PCM is functioning properly.
   c. quickly rise between 0.5–1.0 volt.
   d. vary between 0.2–0.8 volt.

21. Technician A says a "hard" code indicates that a problem exits during the PCM's self-test.
   Technician B says a "hard" code indicates that a faulty circuit could exist, not necessarily a bad component.
   Who is right?
   a. A only   c. Both A and B
   b. B only   d. Neither A nor B

22. What method can be used to determine if the engine's fuel control system is in closed-loop?
   Technician A says to check for codes and as long as there are no "hard" codes, the engine is in closed-loop.
   Technician B says to check for a varying oxygen sensor signal that crosses the midpoint consistently.
   Who is right?
   a. A only
   b. B only
   c. Both A and B
   d. Neither A nor B

23. A lean EGO2 sensor will cause the PCM to:
   a. send a lean command.
   b. lower the idle speed.
   c. send a rich command.
   d. retard the spark.

24. Digital pressure sensors can be tested by using a multimeter and reading:
   a. AC hertz.   c. DC hertz.
   b. AC volts.   d. DC volts.

25. A computer-controlled car with air injection and a 3-way catalytic converter is started. Assuming that the engine is cold, which of the following conditions is true?
   a. EGR is on, closed-loop operation, air is being pumped into the air cleaner.
   b. EGR is off, open-loop operation, air is being pumped into the CAT.
   c. EGR is on, closed-loop operation, air is being pumped into the CAT.
   d. EGR is off, air is being pumped into the exhaust manifold.

26. A computer-controlled engine is operating under the parameters of high vacuum, low throttle position sensor voltage, and a high coolant sensor (NTC) voltage. What mode of engine operation is MOST LIKELY indicated?
   a. Warm engine at curb idle
   b. Cold engine at curb idle
   c. Cold engine at maximum throttle
   d. Warm engine at maximum throttle

27. Technician A says that the TPS measures throttle angle and sends a variable DC voltage signal to the computer.
   Technician B says that a MAF sensor measures air density and volume.
   Who is right?
   a. A only   c. Both A and B
   b. B only   d. Neither A nor B

28. Technician A says that the four gas readings below indicate a rich fuel mixture.
   Technician B says that the four gas readings below indicate a bad CAT.
   Who is right?
   a. A only   c. Both A and B
   b. B only   d. Neither A nor B

HC	50 ppm
CO	0.1%
O_2	2.0%
CO_2	15.0%

29. Technician A says that the electrical value "meg" is equal to 0.000001.
   Technician B says that the electrical value "milli" is equal to 1,000.
   Who is right?
   a. A only   c. Both A and B
   b. B only   d. Neither A nor B

30. The current flowing through a 2200 ohm resistor is 5 milliamps. What is the voltage being applied across the resistor?
  a. 11 volts
  c. 44 millivolts
  b. 44 volts
  d. None of the above

31. Technician A says that a measurement of infinity on an ohmmeter means the circuit has no resistance.

Technician B says that a measurement of zero on an ohmmeter means the circuit is open.

Who is right?
  a. A only
  c. Both A and B
  b. B only
  d. Neither A nor B

32. A PCM is faulty and requires replacement on a vehicle.

Technician A says that before replacing the PCM, check all its outputs for excessive current draw.

Technician B says that when installing the PCM wear a grounding device to prevent electrostatic discharge.

Who is right?
  a. A only
  c. Both A and B
  b. B only
  d. Neither A nor B

33. With the key ON and the engine OFF, the meter in Figure 9–2 reads 0.232 volt. What does this indicate?
  a. Faulty PCM
  b. Poor PCM power ground
  c. Normal condition
  d. Low reference signal

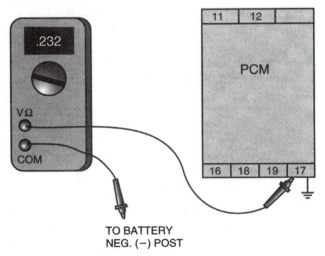

TO BATTERY
NEG. (−) POST

FIGURE 9–2

34. A vehicle has high CO during an IM 240 test. The oxygen sensor is brand new, but its voltage is always low. Which of these is the MOST LIKELY cause?
  a. A dripping injector
  b. High fuel rail pressure
  c. Air pump air staying upstream
  d. Restricted air intake

35. Technician A says that an open injector driver on a sequential fuel injected engine could cause a rich mixture.

Technician B says that spring breakage inside an electronic fuel injector could cause a rich mixture.

Who is right?
  a. A only
  c. Both A and B
  b. B only
  d. Neither A nor B

36. A multiport V-6 engine is running rough and the fuel mixture appears to be lean. Injecting propane improves idle quality, yet there are no vacuum leaks. According to a balance test, cylinders no. 1 and no. 5 are weak.

Technician A says that this problem could be caused by a bad quad driver.

Technician B says that this problem could be caused by the no. 3 injector having low resistance.

Who is right?
  a. A only
  c. Both A and B
  b. B only
  d. Neither A nor B

37. A vehicle equipped with a single overhead cam engine and TBI has a severe loss of power. During acceleration, the engine "shoots ducks" (backfires) through the throttle body. Which of the following is the MOST LIKELY cause?
  a. Timing belt advanced one cog
  b. Flat intake cam lobe
  c. Disengaged or broken exhaust valve rocker arm
  d. Advanced spark timing

38. A 5.7 L feedback carbureted vehicle stalls repeatedly and has little power. The MC solenoid dwell is fixed at 10 degrees. Additionally, the oxygen sensor voltage is fixed and low.

Technician A says that the PCM could be bad.

Technician B says that the float level could be too high.

Who is right?
  a. A only
  c. Both A and B
  b. B only
  d. Neither A nor B

39. A carbureted engine has gasoline dripping from the bottom of the carbon canister.

Technician A says that this could be caused by repeated overfilling of the fuel tank.

Technician B says that this could be caused by an inoperative purge solenoid.

Who is right?
a. A only
b. B only
c. Both A and B
d. Neither A nor B

40. Technician A says that, on many vehicles, the percentage that the EGR valve opens will vary according to the pulse width modulated signal from the PCM.

Technician B says that a value of 100% indicates a PCM command to fully close the EGR valve.

Who is right?
a. A only
b. B only
c. Both A and B
d. Neither A nor B

41. The insulator tips on all the spark plugs from an engine are chalk white with small gray-brown spots. Also, the electrodes are severely burned.

Technician A says that this condition could be caused by the plugs being loose.

Technician B says that this condition could be caused by too lean a fuel mixture.

Who is right?
a. A only
b. B only
c. Both A and B
d. Neither A nor B

42. When shifting the gear selector from P or N into either D or R, the engine in a vehicle stalls.

Technician A says that this could be caused by a stuck shift valve in the transmission valve body.

Technician B says that this could be caused by a stuck governor valve on the transmission output shaft.

Who is right?
a. A only   **c.** Both A and B
b. B only   **d.** Neither A nor B

43. A car has a high CO reading at idle. Scan tool information is listed below:

Scan Tool Readings	
MAP	1.1 volts
Heated oxygen sensor	0.7–0.9 volt
Engine speed	850 rpm

Technician A says that this could be caused by a plugged fuel pressure regulator hose.

Technician B says that this could be caused by injector o-ring leakage.

Who is right?
a. A only   **c.** Both A and B
b. B only   **d.** Neither A nor B

44. What is the ideal A/F ratio for a computer-controlled vehicle?
a. 15.9:1   **b.** 14.7:1   **c.** 13.5:1   **d.** 12.5:1

45. Refer to the wiring diagram in Figure 9–3. There are 12 volts measured at point X. However, when measuring voltage between point X and point Y with the control solenoid energized, there are only 9 volts. What is the source of the high resistance?
a. Poor B+ connection
b. EGR control solenoid
c. Bad PCM
d. Poor PCM ground

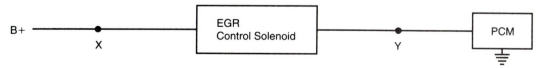

FIGURE 9–3

46. A/F ratios leaner than stoichiometric will create higher amounts of:
a. Carbon monoxide.
b. Carbon dioxide.
c. Sulfur oxide.
d. Oxides of nitrogen.

47. Technician A says that the enhanced emissions test measures CO and HC.

Technician B says that the enhanced emissions test measures CO_2 and O_2.

Who is right?
a. A only
b. B only
c. Both A and B
d. Neither A nor B

48. Technician A says that the PCM should energize the EVAP solenoid when the exhaust has low oxygen content.

Technician B says that the PCM should increase fuel delivery when the exhaust has low oxygen content.

Who is right?
a. A only
b. B only
c. Both A and B
d. Neither A nor B

49. A vehicle equipped with dual throttle body injection is running very rough. Each injector has a different spray pattern when strobed with a timing light. Injecting propane causes the engine to smooth out and to gain rpm. A lab scope shows each injector waveform to be identical except that one injector's voltage spike is considerably shorter than the other. Which of the following could be causing the problem?
a. Bad PCM
b. Corroded injector connector
c. Shorted injector winding
d. Low charging system voltage

50. All of the following mechanical problems can set a lean exhaust code, EXCEPT:
a. water-contaminated fuel.
b. low fuel pressure.
c. restricted fuel filter.
d. saturated evaporative canister.

51. Technician A says that diagnostic trouble codes (DTCs) are retrieved by using scan tools.

Technician B says that diagnostic trouble codes (DTCs) are retrieved by using the needle "sweeps" of an analog meter.

Who is right?
a. A only
b. B only
c. Both A and B
d. Neither A nor B

52. Technician A says that serial data displayed on a scan tool reflects what the PCM thinks is occurring.

Technician B says that serial data can be accessed by connecting a scan tool to the assembly line data link (ALDL) connector.

Who is right?
a. A only
b. B only
c. Both A and B
d. Neither A nor B

53. A vehicle has failed an IM 240 pressure test on the EVAP system. This could be caused by:
a. not holding pressure above 8 inches of water column.
b. a loose fuel filler cap or damaged filler neck.
c. Both a and b
d. Neither a nor b

54. An engine has unacceptable high levels of NO_X emissions during an IM 240 test.

Technician A says that this could be caused by a malfunctioning early fuel evaporation (EFE) system.

Technician B says that this could be caused by a malfunctioning EGR valve.

Who is right?
a. A only
b. B only
c. Both A and B
d. Neither A nor B

55. A vacuum assisted fuel pressure regulator has a punctured (leaking) diaphragm. This can cause:
a. a rich condition.
b. system pressure to increase.
c. Both a and b
d. Neither a nor b

56. ECT sensor input has been manipulated by disconnecting its connector leads and soldering a 100 kΩ resistor across them.

Technician A says that this can cause the electric cooling fan to run continuously.

Technician B says that this can cause excessive injector pulse width.

Who is right?
a. A only
b. B only
c. Both A and B
d. Neither A nor B

57. An engine is being "preconditioned" before emission testing. This ensures that:
a. evaporative canister purging is completed.
b. oxygen sensor feedback voltage is fixed.
c. Both a and b
d. Neither a nor b

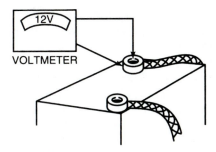

FIGURE 9–4

58. Given the situation pictured in Figure 9–4, what is the recommended service action?
a. Replace the battery
b. No action required; situation is normal
c. Check the charging system
d. Clean the battery cable connector

59. A transistor's typical forward bias voltage (base to emitter) is:
a. 600 millivolts.
b. 1.2 volts.
c. 120 millivolts.
d. 2.1 volts.

60. Data that is transmitted on a single line is considered:
a. serial data.
b. micro data.
c. parallel data.
d. All of the above

61. A clamping diode protects the circuit from:
a. voltage drops.
b. voltage surges.
c. static electricity.
d. high resistance.

62. Another term for a "pulsed-modulated" signal is:
a. analog.
b. digital.
c. logarithmic.
d. None of the above

63. Refer to the diagram in Figure 9–5.
   Technician A says that diode X is forward biased with the switch ON.
   Technician B says that diode Y is used to eliminate voltage spike when the switch is turned OFF
   Who is right?
a. A only   c. Both A and B
b. B only   d. Neither A nor B

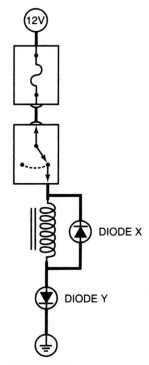

FIGURE 9–5

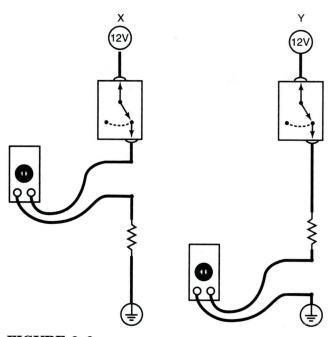

FIGURE 9–6

64. Technician A says that illustration X in Figure 9–6 demonstrates how to measure current.
   Technician B says that illustration Y above demonstrates how to measure voltage drop.
   Who is right?
a. A only   c. Both A and B
b. B only   d. Neither A nor B

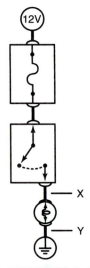

FIGURE 9–7

65. Technician A says that in the circuit in Figure 9–7, a short-to-ground at point X will cause the light to always be ON with the switch OFF.

Technician B says that in the above circuit, a short-to-ground at point Y will cause the fuse to blow when the switch is turned ON.

Who is right?

a. A only   **c.** Both A and B
b. B only   **d.** Neither A nor B

66. Technician A says that the drive cycle for the IM 240 test covers about ten miles at many different speeds.

Technician B says that exhaust emissions for the IM 240 test are measured in units of concentration.

Who is right?

a. A only   **c.** Both A and B
b. B only   **d.** Neither A nor B

67. A scan tool is hooked-up to an OBD II data-link connector. The display shows a "Code P0110—Intake air temperature circuit malfunction."

Technician A says that this circuit is functional, but not within its normal operating range.

Technician B says that this circuit could have a fixed value.

Who is right?

a. A only
b. B only
c. Both A and B
d. Neither A nor B

68. Technician A says that the upstream oxygen sensor provides the signal that causes the cylinder-misfire monitor to turn on the check engine light and store a trouble code.

Technician B says that the upstream and downstream oxygen sensors provide the signal that causes the catalyst-efficiency monitor to recognize improper operation of the catalytic converter.

Who is right?

a. A only   **c.** Both A and B
b. B only   **d.** Neither A nor B

69. Technician A says that an air leak after the MAF sensor can cause rough idle and a constantly low 02S voltage reading.

Technician B says that a stuck open downstream AIR valve can cause rough idle and a constantly low O2S voltage reading.

Who is right?

a. A only   **c.** Both A and B
b. B only   **d.** Neither A nor B

70. A battery runs down over a two-day period to 9 volts when the vehicle is not driven. This is MOST LIKELY caused by:

a. excessive current in a memory circuit.
b. a poor connection at the battery ground cable.
c. low voltage in a memory circuit.
d. high resistance in a memory B+ feed circuit.

71. A DVOM is being used to sweep test a TPS.

Technician A says that a DVOM may not be able to catch "glitches" that may be present.

Technician B says that a lab scope is more accurate to use when conducting a sweep test.

Who is right?

a. A only   **c.** Both A and B
b. B only   **d.** Neither A nor B

72. Technician A says that the failure of a MAP sensor will cause an engine no-start condition.

Technician B says that the absence of an RPM or crankshaft signal will cause an engine no-start condition.

Who is right?

a. A only
b. B only
c. Both A and B
d. Neither A nor B

73. Technician A says that a lab scope can be used to measure pulse width.

Technician B says that a lab scope can be used to measure frequency.

Who is right?

a. A only
c. Both A and B
b. B only
d. Neither A nor B

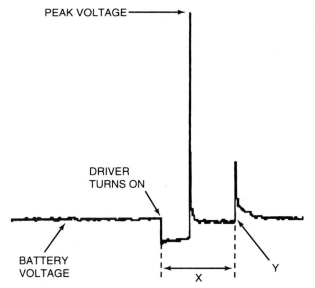

PEAK VOLTAGE

DRIVER TURNS ON

BATTERY VOLTAGE

X

Y

FIGURE 9–8

74. Refer to the peak and hold (current controlled) injector waveform in Figure 9–8.

Technician A says that section X represents the injector on-time.

Technician B says that point Y is where fuel flow ends.

Who is right?

a. A only
b. B only
c. Both A and B
d. Neither A nor B

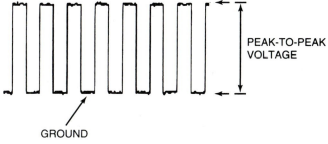

PEAK-TO-PEAK VOLTAGE

GROUND

FIGURE 9–9

75. A MAP sensor digital signal is shown in Figure 9–9.

Technician A says that the frequency of the signal will decrease as the throttle is opened.

Technician B says that the lower horizontal lines should almost reach ground.

Who is right?

a. A only
b. B only
c. Both A and B
d. Neither A nor B

76. Refer to the picture for question 75.

Technician A says that voltage drop to ground should NOT be greater than 400 mV.

Technician B says that peak-to-peak voltage should NOT be greater than one-half the reference voltage.

Who is right?

a. A only
b. B only
c. Both A and B
d. Neither A nor B

77. An engine is equipped with a Hall Effect crankshaft position sensor.

Technician A says that output voltage amplitude changes as rpm changes.

Technician B says that frequency changes as rpm changes.

Who is right?

a. A only
b. B only
c. Both A and B
d. Neither A nor B

78. An engine is equipped with a magnetic (variable reluctance) camshaft position sensor.

Technician A says that output voltage varies as vehicle speed changes.

Technician B says that frequency varies as vehicle speed changes.

Who is right?

a. A only
b. B only
c. Both A and B
d. Neither A nor B

79. One Hz equals one cycle per _____.

a. second
b. minute
c. revolution
d. millisecond

80. Which waveform in Figure 9–10 is a 95% pulse width modulated signal?

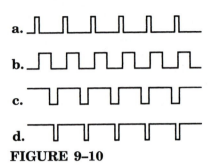

a.

b.

c.

d.

FIGURE 9–10

81. Which waveform in Figure 9–11 is serial data?

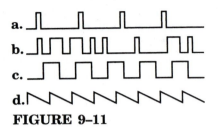

a.

b.

c.

d.

FIGURE 9–11

82. Refer to the multimeter shown in Figure 9–12.

Technician A says that button 8 is pushed when you want to record input changes of 100 milliseconds or longer.

Technician B says that button 13 is pushed when you want to measure duty cycle.

Who is right?

a. A only

b. B only

c. Both A and B

d. Neither A nor B

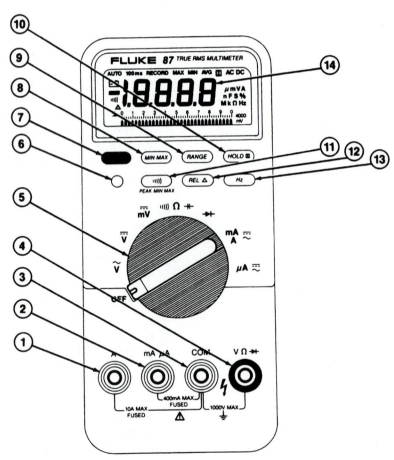

FIGURE 9–12

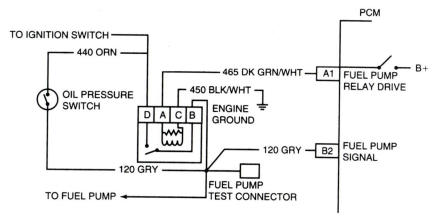

FIGURE 9–13

83. A vehicle equipped with the fuel pump relay circuit in Figure 9–13 will not start unless a jumper wire is hooked from B2 to D.

Technician A says that the PCM could be bad.

Technician B says that the relay could be bad.

Who is right?
a. A only
b. B only
c. Both A and B
d. Neither A nor B

84. An engine will not crank.

Technician A says that this could be caused by a bad clutch switch.

Technician B says that this could be caused by a bad PCM.

Who is right?
a. A only
b. B only
c. Both A and B
d. Neither A nor B

85. Technician A says that a coked IAC conical valve can cause engine stalling on deceleration.

Technician B says that IAC conical valve information may show up in a data stream as counts (0 to 255).

Who is right?
a. A only
b. B only
c. Both A and B
d. Neither A nor B

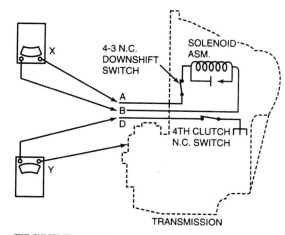

FIGURE 9–14

86. Technician A says that meter X as shown in Figure 9–14 cannot check the solenoid diode unless it's an analog type.

Technician B says that meter Y should be reading near zero.

Who is right?
a. A only
b. B only
c. Both A and B
d. Neither A nor B

87. A fuel pressure test is being performed on a vehicle. The fuel gauge reads lower than specs. This could be caused by all of the following, EXCEPT:
a. a bad pressure regulator.
b. a restricted fuel inlet sock.
c. a restricted fuel filter.
d. a restricted fuel return line.

88. Technician A says that a CO_2 reading of 14–16% in the exhaust gas is considered ideal.

Technician B says that a CO_2 reading lower than normal can be caused by a leaky exhaust system.

Who is right?

a. A only
b. B only
c. Both A and B
d. Neither A nor B

89. Technician A says that higher than normal O_2 and lower than normal CO readings can be caused by the air pump connected during diagnostic testing.

Technician B says that lower than normal O_2 and higher than normal CO readings can be caused by a fuel contaminated crankcase.

Who is right?

a. A only
b. B only
c. Both A and B
d. Neither A nor B

90. Type 1 Composite Vehicle has a rough idle. A stacked scope pattern shows a dwell variance of 6 distributor degrees.

Technician A says that this could be caused by an elongated distributor gear rollpin hole.

Technician B says that this could be caused by a worn camshaft sprocket.

Who is right?

a. A only   c. Both A and B
b. B only   d. Neither A nor B

91. When observing the height of the firing lines during a snap throttle test, voltage is high on one cylinder.

Technician A says that this could be caused by a bad plug wire.

Technician B says that this could be caused by a fouled plug.

Who is right?

a. A only   c. Both A and B
b. B only   d. Neither A nor B

92. A scan tool is connected to the Composite Vehicle that cranks but will not start when cold. The serial data in Figure 9–15 was obtained with the key ON, engine OFF. Which of these is the MOST LIKELY cause of the problem?

a. Bad MAP   c. Bad TPS
b. Bad ECT   d. Bad IAC

Chart 9–93
Serial Data

Engine Coolant Temperature Sensor (ECT)	Intake Air Temperature Sensor (IAT)	Manifold Absolute Pressure Sensor (MAP)	Throttle Position Sensor (TPS)
0.46 Volts	3.59 Volts	4 Volts	0.5 Volts
Engine Speed Sensor (RPM)	Heated Oxygen Sensor (HO2S)	Vehicle Speed Sensor (VSS)	Battery Voltage (B+)
0 RPM	0 Volts	0 MPH	12.5
Idle Air Control Valve (IAC)	Evaporative Emission Canister Solenoid (EVAP)	Torque Converter Clutch Solenoid (TCC)	EGR Valve Control Solenoid (EGR)
45 Percent	Off	Off	0 Percent
Malfunction Indicator Lamp (MIL)	Diagnostic Trouble Codes	Open/Closed Loop	Fuel Pump Relay (FP)
Off	None	Open	Off

Measured Ignition Timing (°BTDC)   Base: Actual:

FIGURE 9–15

Chart 9–94
Serial Data

Engine Coolant Temperature Sensor (ECT)	Intake Air Temperature Sensor (IAT)	Manifold Absolute Pressure Sensor (MAP)	Throttle Position Sensor (TPS)
0.45 Volts	2.5 Volts	0 Volts	0 Volts
Engine Speed Sensor (RPM)	Heated Oxygen Sensor (HO2S)	Vehicle Speed Sensor (VSS)	Battery Voltage (B+)
840 RPM	700 mV	0 MPH	13.3 Volts
Idle Air Control Valve (IAC)	Evaporative Emission Canister Solenoid (EVAP)	Torque Converter Clutch Solenoid (TCC)	EGR Valve Control Solenoid (EGR)
25 Percent	Off	Off	0 Percent
Malfunction Indicator Lamp (MIL)	Diagnostic Trouble Codes	Open/Closed Loop	Fuel Pump Relay (FP)
On	PO105, PO120	Open	On
Measured Ignition Timing (°BTDC)		Base: 10	Actual: 12

FIGURE 9–16

93. On a road test, the Composite Vehicle's engine runs rough, stumbles, and hesitates. According to the serial data in Figure 9–16 obtained at idle and the electrical schematic on page 292, the problem could be caused by:
   a. an open connection at PCM pin 23.
   b. an open connection at PCM pin 13.
   c. Both a and b
   d. Neither a nor b

94. As soon as the transmission on a vehicle is shifted into drive or reverse with the service brake pedal applied, the engine dies.
   Technician A says that this can be caused by a shorted TCC circuit.
   Technician B says that this can be caused by an open IAC circuit.
   Who is right?
   a. A only
   b. B only
   c. Both A and B
   d. Neither A nor B

95. The Composite Vehicle fails an IM 240 test because of a rich condition. All scan tool data is normal except for a fixed HO2S reading of 0.05 volt. The injectors have a wider than normal pulse width and a trouble code PO171 (system too lean) has been set.
   Technician A says that this could be caused by a bad HO2S.
   Technician B says that this could be caused by dirty injectors.
   Who is right?
   a. A only   c. Both A and B
   b. B only   d. Neither A nor B

96. The resistance of an EVAP solenoid is being checked. It measures 3 ohms. Specs are 30–40 ohms.
   Technician A says that the solenoid draw is more than its normal current.
   Technician B says that the PCM may need to be replaced.
   Who is right?
   a. A only   c. Both A and B
   b. B only   d. Neither A nor B

Chart 9–95
Serial Data

Engine Coolant Temperature Sensor (ECT)	Intake Air Temperature Sensor (IAT)	Manifold Absolute Pressure Sensor (MAP)	Throttle Position Sensor (TPS)
▼	▼	▼	▼
3.7 Volts	2.6 Volts	2.0 Volts	0.5 Volts
Engine Speed Sensor (RPM)	Heated Oxygen Sensor (HO2S)	Vehicle Speed Sensor (VSS)	Battery Voltage (B+)
▼	▼	▼	▼
1100 RPM	950 mV Fixed	0 MPH	13.5 Volts
Idle Air Control Valve (IAC)	Evaporative Emission Canister Solenoid (EVAP)	Torque Converter Clutch Solenoid (TCC)	EGR Valve Control Solenoid (EGR)
▼	▼	▼	▼
35 Percent	Off	Off	0 Percent
Malfunction Indicator Lamp (MIL)	Diagnostic Trouble Codes	Open/Closed Loop	Fuel Pump Relay (FP)
▼	▼	▼	▼
On	P0172, P0105	Open	On
Measured Ignition Timing (°BTDC) ▶		Base: 10	Actual: 10

FIGURE 9–17

97. The Composite Vehicle has just failed an IM 240 test. The owner says that for several months the vehicle has had very poor performance, gets lousy gas mileage, has a "stinky" exhaust smell, and the MIL lamp stays on. Using the serial data in Figure 9–17 (captured with the engine running at operating temperature) and the electrical schematic on page 292, the MOST LIKELY root of the problem is a:
a. bad ECT sensor.
b. bad TPS circuit.
c. bad MAP sensor.
d. plugged CAT.

98. A MAP sensor voltage signal "glitches" to a value lower than minimum specs. This can cause:
a. high CO reading at idle.
b. rich mixture at cruise.
c. Both a and b
d. Neither a nor b

99. Technician A says that improper TPS adjustment may cause an automatic transmission to shift erratically.
Technician B says that improper TPS voltage may prevent engine starting.
Who is right?
a. A only   c. Both A and B
b. B only   d. Neither A nor B

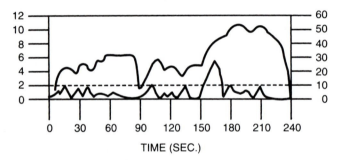

FIGURE 9–18

100. Refer to the NO$_X$ emissions trace in Figure 9–18 that was created during an enhanced emissions test. The cutpoint for this vehicle is 2.0 grams per mile.
Technician A says that the trace spikes show the vehicle failed.
Technician B says that the trace rightside numbers show the miles per hour.
Who is right?
a. A only
b. B only
c. Both A and B
d. Neither A nor B

101. Four injectors are wired in parallel. Each has a spec of 12 ohms. An ohmmeter is hooked across the circuit to measure total circuit resistance, and it reads 4 ohms. What is wrong?
    a. One injector is shorted
    b. One injector is open
    c. Three injectors are bad
    d. Nothing

102. At the conclusion of an IAC snap test, a technician notices that his final IAC counts are 7, but his initial counts at idle were 15. What does this indicate?
    a. IAC motor is functioning properly
    b. PROM calibration is incorrect
    c. ECM should be replaced
    d. IAC motor should be replaced

103. In the wiring diagram shown in Figure 9–20, where would you put your ohmmeter to check the heater part of the oxygen sensor?
    a. From B to D6
    b. From A to B with the key on
    c. From battery (B+) side of the 20A fuse to ground
    d. None of the above

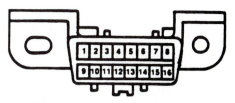

FIGURE 9–19

104. Technician A says that an OBD II data-link connector is shown in Figure 9–19.
    Technician B says that pin assignment number 5 is the signal ground.
    Who is right?
    a. A only   c. Both A and B
    b. B only   d. Neither A nor B

105. Refer to the wiring diagram in Figure 9–20.
    Technician A says that you can measure oxygen sensor voltage between the purple wire and ground.
    Technician B says that the red voltmeter lead should go on the purple wire and the black lead to a good ground.
    Who is right?
    a. A only
    b. B only
    c. Both A and B
    d. Neither A nor B

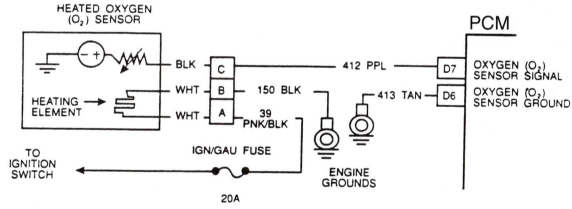

FIGURE 9–20

106. Injector rail pressure is below specs. When the return hose to the fuel tank is pinched, rail pressure increases. Which of these is the MOST LIKELY cause?
a. Bad pump
b. Bad regulator
c. Plugged filter
d. Vacuum loss to regulator

107. A computer-controlled engine has high CO and poor mileage. This could be caused by all of the following, EXCEPT:
a. stuck open thermostat.
b. high resistance in ECT circuit.
c. bad O_2S circuit.
d. low resistance in IAT circuit.

108. An OBD II vehicle won't accelerate at times when driving on rutted roads. Additionally, intermittent idling problems have developed.
Technician A says that this could be caused by a break in the PCM's internal soldering.
Technician B says that this could be caused by the PCM's round voltage being zero.
Who is right?
a. A only
b. B only
c. Both A and B
d. Neither A nor B

109. Two technicians are discussing the catalyst monitor on an OBD II vehicle.
Technician A says that when the catalytic converter is normal, downstream side oxygen sensor inversions are far fewer than those of the upstream side oxygen sensor.
Technician B says when the catalytic converter deteriorates, downstream side oxygen sensor inversions increase and become closer to those of the upstream side oxygen sensor.
Who is right?
a. A only
b. B only
c. Both A and B
d. Neither A nor B

110. Which of the following statements regarding a misfire on an OBD II vehicle is true?
a. It may "flash" the MIL.
b. It is detected by the CKP sensor.
c. It is stored as "freeze" frame data.
d. All of the above

111. A Type 2 Composite Vehicle cranks but won't start. Which of the following is the LEAST LIKELY cause?
a. Broken CKP sensor
b. Bad MAF sensor
c. Open CMP sensor circuit
d. Low TFT sensor voltage

112. A car owner has had four rebuilt PCMs installed in his Type 2 Composite Vehicle. Each PCM lasts about three months. What would you do first to fix this car?
a. Install a different rebuilt brand PCM.
b. Install an original equipment PCM.
c. Determine if the timing chain is "loose."
d. Ohm out the actuators and check against specifications.

Section 10

LIGHT VEHICLE COMPRESSED NATURAL GAS

STUDY OUTLINE

I. Vehicle Compatibility Analysis
  A. Customer Requirements
  B. Analyze Vehicle for Fitness of Conversion
    1. Weight
    2. Mileage
    3. Applicable emissions
    4. Safety standards
  C. Compressed Natural Gas Cylinders
    1. Determine appropriate size
    2. Determine location and mounting
    3. Determine location of venting system
    4. Space requirements and best location for related underhood components
  D. National Fire Protection Agency (NFPA 52) Standards

II. Parts Fabrication
  A. Cylinder Stabilization Brackets and Braces
  B. Brackets for Underhood Components
  C. Heat Shields
    1. Installation
  D. Protective Shields
    1. Installation
  E. Wiring Harnesses
    1. Installation
  F. Kit Installation
    1. Modification

III. Equipment Installation
  A. Fuel Storage System
    1. Recommended fasteners
    2. Cylinder venting
  B. Regulator Assemblies
    1. Replacing diaphragms
  C. Underhood Fuel Delivery System
    1. Lines, clamps, and vibration loops
  D. System Wiring
    1. Electrical and electronic component wiring
    2. Instrument panel components
  E. Valving
    1. PRD (pressure relief devices)
    2. Fittings
    3. Recommended fasteners

F. Required Documentation
    1. Safety labels
    2. Information labels
    3. Emergency shut-down procedures given to operator

IV. Leak Testing/Repairs
  A. Gasoline
  B. CNG (Compressed Natural Gas)
    1. Low pressure
    2. High pressure
    3. Filling cylinders
  C. Coolant
  D. Vapor Seal

V. Initial Adjustments
  A. Base Ignition Timing
  B. Regulator Pressure(s)
  C. Power Enrichment
  D. Idle Mixture
  E. Fuel Gauge Operation
    1. Adjust as needed
  F. Electronic Components Operation

VI. Engine Performance Diagnosis
  A. Emission Testing for CNG and Gasoline
  B. Road Testing
    1. Acceptable driveability
    2. Starting and restarting abilities
    3. Fuel changeover operation (bi-fuel vehicles)
    4. Handling and stability
    5. Check for abnormal noises
  C. On-Board Diagnostic Checks
    1. Determine needed repairs

VII. System Diagnosis/Repair
  A. Visual Inspection of Components
  B. Vacuum, Electrical, and Electronic Components
    1. Diagnose driveability problems
    2. Repair/replace
  C. Underhood Fuel Delivery System and Components
    1. Diagnose driveability problems
    2. Repair/replace
  D. Fuel Lines, Valves, Fittings, and PRD's
    1. Remove, repair, replace

E. Cylinders
  1. Remove and replace
  2. Venting
  3. Improper fueling procedures

F. GFI, IMPCO, GEM, MOGAS, and BAYTECH Conversions (Have a Fundamental Understanding of Each)

G. CNG Properties

---

1. A CNG cylinder has been mounted enclosed in a vehicle.

   Technician A says that the PRD vent line on the cylinder must be routed so that it will discharge past the rear bumper.

   Technician B says that the PRD vent line must be secured to the vehicle at 24″ intervals
   Who is right?
   a. A only
   b. B only
   c. Both A and B
   d. Neither A nor B

2. A CNG cylinder-mounting bracket must be capable of withstanding a force, applied in any direction, of _____ times the weight of a fully pressurized cylinder.
   a. 2 **b.** 4 **c.** 6 **d.** 8

3. Technician A says that NGV2 cylinders have a 15-year life, after which they must be removed from service.

   Technician B says that aluminum cylinders rated at 3600 psi must be submitted for testing every three years.
   Who is right?
   a. A only
   b. B only
   c. Both A and B
   d. Neither A nor B

4. Refer to the fuel delivery control schematic shown in Figure 10–1.

   Technician A says that when the filler door is opened, a ground circuit is closed.

   Technician B says that when the filler door is opened, the fuel tank solenoids close.
   Who is right?
   a. A only
   b. B only
   c. Both A and B
   d. Neither A nor B

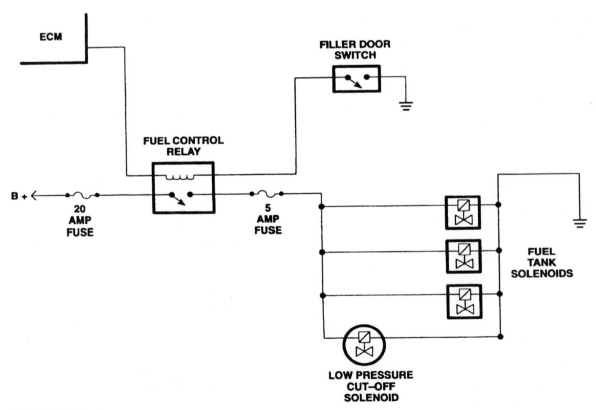

FIGURE 10–1

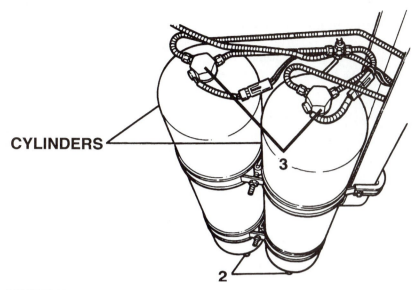

CYLINDERS ◄

3

2

FIGURE 10–2

5. A CNG cylinder is being mounted in the luggage compartment (trunk) of a car.

Technician A says to route the vent line into the wheel well.

Technician B says to route the vent line into the engine compartment.

Who is right?
a. A only   c. Both A and B
b. B only   d. Neither A nor B

6. Technician A says that "fast" filling of cylinders can result in heating of the gas and a reduction in driving range.

Technician B says that "slow" filling will minimize the heating of the gas.

Who is right?
a. A only   c. Both A and B
b. B only   d. Neither A nor B

7. Technician A says to always shut off the fuel pressure at the manual shut-off valve first when working on a low-pressure component.

Technician B says to always check for leaks with a match after any service is performed.

Who is right?
a. A only   c. Both A and B
b. B only   d. Neither A nor B

8. Technician A says that natural gas has a lower BTU content than gasoline.

Technician B says that natural gas fuel tanks (cylinders) hold 2000 psi when full.

Who is right?
a. A only   c. Both A and B
b. B only   d. Neither A nor B

9. Technician A says that number 2 in Figure 10–2 shows over/temperature over/pressure relief valves.

Technician B says that number 3 shows solenoid valves.

Who is right?
a. A only   c. Both A and B
b. B only   d. Neither A nor B

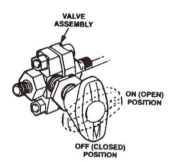

VALVE ASSEMBLY

ON (OPEN) POSITION

OFF (CLOSED) POSITION

FIGURE 10–3

10. Technician A says that the valve in Figure 10–3 is located between the CNG cylinder(s) and the pressure regulator.

Technician B says that the valve is a quarter-turn manual valve.

Who is right?
a. A only   c. Both A and B
b. B only   d. Neither A nor B

11. Before venting cylinders, always ground at the:
a. solenoid valve.
b. vehicle frame rail.
c. refueling connector.
d. over temperature/over pressure relief valve.

12. Technician A says that it is acceptable to mount a cylinder-mounting bracket to a vertical panel only.

Technician B says that it is acceptable to mount a cylinder-mounting bracket to a horizontal panel only.

Who is right?
a. A only
b. B only
c. Both A and B
d. Neither A nor B

13. Natural gas is:
a. heavier than air.
b. lighter than air.
c. 80–95% methane.
d. Both b and c

14. Technician A says that all CNG fuel lines between the cylinder(s) and the high pressure side of the regulator are made from high pressure annealed seamless stainless steel.

Technician B says that this line must be able to withstand in excess of 12,000 psi pressure.

Who is right?
a. A only
b. B only
c. Both A and B
d. Neither A nor B

15. Technician A says that if a CNG cylinder is mounted less than 8 inches from the exhaust system, a heat shield must be installed.

Technician B says that it is allowable to MIG weld a heat shield to an aluminum cylinder.

Who is right?
a. A only
b. B only
c. Both A and B
d. Neither A nor B

16. A cylinder PRD needs to be insolated in order to be serviced.

Technician A says to turn the quarter-turn valve off.

Technician B says to turn the ignition switch off.

Who is right?
a. A only
b. B only
c. Both A and B
d. Neither A nor B

17. A CNG vehicle drives into a repair shop. The driver says that the engine runs for a short time, then shuts off, and will not start again until it has sat for about 15 minutes. Which of the following is the MOST LIKELY cause?
a. Dirt holding regulator open
b. Low fuel pressure
c. Fuel system over-fueling (flooding) engine
d. Frozen regulator

18. Technician A says that PRDs have to be vented and bagged to the outside of the vehicle whenever they are mounted in a closed compartment.

Technician B says that PRDs do not need venting when in a closed compartment because natural gas molecules are smaller than oxygen molecules and natural gas is lighter than air.

Who is right?
a. A only
b. B only
c. Both A and B
d. Neither A nor B

19. Technician A says that a CNG conversion must comply with NFPA 52 standards and state and local standards.

Technician B says that a CNG conversion must be inspected by the local fire department.

Who is right?
a. A only
b. B only
c. Both A and B
d. Neither A nor B

20. When checking for a stuck open natural gas injector:
a. turn ignition ON and listen for "hiss" sound.
b. pump throttle and check for a "mist."
c. turn ignition to START and listen for "hiss" sound.
d. turn ignition OFF and listen for "hiss" sound.

21. Which of the following situations would represent the highest pressure on a CNG vehicle?
a. WOT (wide-open throttle)
b. Idle
c. Cruise
d. Refueling

22. Initial setup is being done on a bi-fuel CNG conversion.

Technician A says that a dual-timing curve may be needed because natural gas has a slower flame speed than gasoline.

Technician B says that the base timing should be advanced on gasoline to improve the driveability on natural gas.

Who is right?
a. A only
b. B only
c. Both A and B
d. Neither A nor B

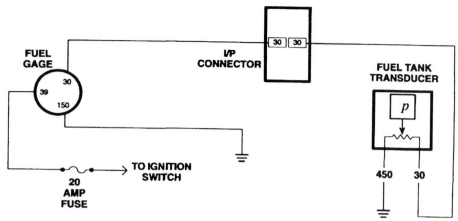

FIGURE 10–4

23. A fuel gauge electrical circuit is pictured in Figure 10–4.

    Technician A says that as fuel is used, pressure in the high side of the system drops, causing a reduced resistance to ground at the transducer.

    Technician B says that this fuel gauge electrical circuit is the same as a gasoline system, with the transducer substituting for a float.

    Who is right?
    a. A only
    b. B only
    c. Both A and B
    d. Neither A nor B

24. Regulator pressures are being checked during initial setup of a bi-fuel CNG conversion.

    Technician A says that a manometer can be used to set the secondary regulator pressure.

    Technician B says that the primary regulator typically reduces service pressure to somewhere between 75 and 200 psi.

    Who is right?
    a. A only
    b. B only
    c. Both A and B
    d. Neither A nor B

25. Which of the following is the correct procedure for repairing a bent fuel system line caused by an accident?
    a. Perform a leak check; if there are no leaks, line is okay.
    b. Remove line, straighten, and reinstall and leak check
    c. Both a and b
    d. Neither a nor b

26. A CNG cylinder is being installed in the bed of a pick-up truck.

    Technician A says that load spreaders should be used.

    Technician B says that rubber gaskets should be installed between the cylinder and brackets.

    Who is right?
    a. A only
    b. B only
    c. Both A and B
    d. Neither A nor B

27. Emission readings on a bi-fuel CNG conversion should be set to:
    a. AGA standards.
    b. local emission standards.
    c. NFPA 52 standards.
    d. kit manufacturer's specifications.

28. A service facility is equipped with overhead open flame-type heaters.

    Technician A says to always turn off heaters before servicing vehicles.

    Technician B says to always close the quarter-turn manual valve before servicing vehicles.

    Who is right?
    a. A only
    b. B only
    c. Both A and B
    d. Neither A nor B

29. Line-to-line and line-to-fitting connections on a natural gas fuel system require:
    a. o-ring sealant with Teflon.
    b. swagelok sealant.
    c. petroleum jelly.
    d. none of the above

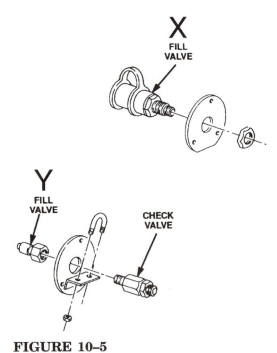

FIGURE 10–5

30. Refer to the filler valves shown in Figure 10–5.
    Technician A says that picture X shows a Sherex valve design.
    Technician B says that picture Y shows a Hansen valve design.
    Who is right?
    a. A only
    b. B only
    c. Both A and B
    d. Neither A nor B

31. A "dedicated" CNG vehicle has a rich mixture, stinky exhaust, rough idle, and stalls intermittently. The following diagnostic data below has been obtained:

Block learn	110
IAC	50–65
MAP	34–38
Fuel pressure	175 psi

   Which of these would be the MOST LIKELY cause?
   a. Stuck open injector
   b. Bad MAP sensor
   c. Bad fuel regulator
   d. Vacuum leak

32. Technician A says that CNG mixers are sealed units and the diaphragm(s) cannot be replaced.
    Technician B says that if a CNG mixer adaptor gasket is leaking, a rich condition will result.
    Who is right?
    a. A only
    b. B only
    c. Both A and B
    d. Neither A nor B

33. Item X in Figure 10–6 is a:
    a. fuel pressure test port.
    b. low pressure cut-off solenoid.
    c. coolant check valve.
    d. transducer.

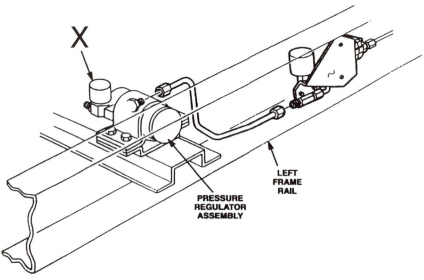

FIGURE 10–6

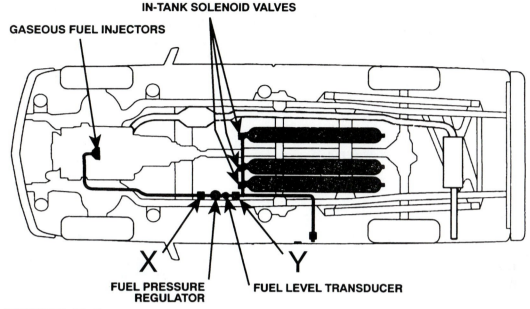

IN-TANK SOLENOID VALVES

GASEOUS FUEL INJECTORS

X Y

FUEL PRESSURE REGULATOR **FUEL LEVEL TRANSDUCER**

FIGURE 10–7

34. A "dedicated" CNG fuel system layout is illustrated in Figure 10–7:

Technician A says that arrow X shows a fuel shut-off valve.

Technician B says that arrow Y shows a fuel shut-off valve.

Who is right?

a. A only

b. B only

c. Both A and B

d. Neither A nor B

35. CNG cylinders are being installed below the frame and between the axles of a vehicle having a wheelbase greater than 127 inches.

Technician A says that the minimum clearance from the road to the cylinder, its housing and fittings, with the vehicle loaded to its gross weight rating shall not be less than 9 inches.

Technician B says that no portion of a cylinder shall be located behind the rear bumper mounting face.

Who is right?

a. A only

b. B only

c. Both A and B

d. Neither A nor B

36. A vehicle equipped with a CNG fuel system shall bear which of the following?

a. A label showing the installer's name or company.

b. A label showing the cylinder retest date or expiration date.

c. Both a and b

d. Neither a nor b

37. A driver says that his bi-fuel vehicle has a loss of power at WOT on natural gas. There are no stored fault codes and heated oxygen sensor voltage is toggling between 300 and 600 millivolts at idle.

Technician A says that this could be caused by low fuel level.

Technician B says that this could be caused by a dirty fuel filter.

Who is right?

a. A only

b. B only

c. Both A and B

d. Neither A nor B

38. Oil is present in a CNG fuel system mixer and regulator.

Technician A says that this can cause driveability problems.

Technician B says that this can cause diaphragms to deteriorate.

Who is right?

a. A only

b. B only

c. Both A and B

d. Neither A nor B

39. All of the following would produce a rich mixture on a bi-fuel vehicle being driven on CNG, EXCEPT a:

a. restricted fuel filter.

b. leaking secondary pressure regulator.

c. high regulator pressure.

d. leaking gasoline injector.

40. Technician A says that NFPA 52 standards require that the refueling connection be located under the hood.

Technician B says that NFPA 52 standards require that a backflow valve be installed between the refueling connection and the remainder of the fuel storage system.

Who is right?

a. A only   **c.** Both A and B
b. B only   **d.** Neither A nor B

41. A pre-conversion evaluation is being made on a vehicle.

Technician A says that this is a good time to assess the driver's habits and expectations. If the vehicle is underpowered on gasoline, because of transmission/differential gear ratio, performance on natural gas may not be acceptable.

Technician B says that an engine that does not run well on gasoline may run worse on natural gas. Compression and ignition must also be in top condition for an engine to run well on natural gas.

Who is right?

a. A only   **c.** Both A and B
b. B only   **d.** Neither A nor B

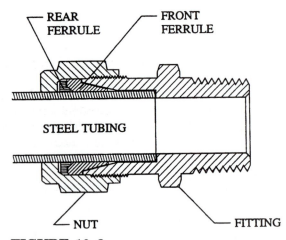

FIGURE 10–8

42. Technician A says that the fitting in Figure 10–8 may be assembled and disassembled repeatedly.

Technician B says that the fitting is a Gyrolok fitting.

Who is right?

a. A only
b. B only
c. Both A and B
d. Neither A nor B

43. A GFI system is being installed on a vehicle.

Technician A says to install the compuvalve so that the high-flow injector solenoids are pointing down.

Technician B says that the fuel filter used with the GFI system is not interchangeable with gasoline filters.

Who is right?

a. A only   **c.** Both A and B
b. B only   **d.** Neither A nor B

FIGURE 10–9

44. A vehicle equipped with a natural gas fuel system must be identified with the label in Figure 10–9 placed on the:

a. right side of the rear bumper.
b. upper surface of the radiator core support.
c. Either a or b
d. Neither a nor b

45. The adaptive digital processor (ADP) on an IMPCO natural gas system is being checked.

Technician A says that normal duty cycling of the ADP should range from 30–70%.

Technician B says to use a tachometer attached to the white wire in the ADP harness to read engine rpm.

Who is right?

a. A only
b. B only
c. Both A and B
d. Neither A nor B

46. The gas engine management (GEM) control system by MESA environmental is:

a. applicable to both bi-fuel and dedicated vehicle conversions.
b. a speed-density control strategy system.
c. compatible with OEM diagnostics.
d. All of the above

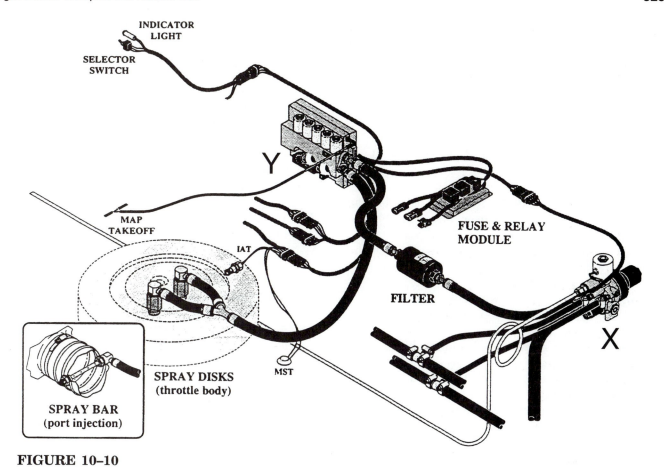

INDICATOR LIGHT

SELECTOR SWITCH

Y

MAP TAKEOFF

IAT

FUSE & RELAY MODULE

X

FILTER

MST

SPRAY DISKS (throttle body)

SPRAY BAR (port injection)

FIGURE 10–10

47. A generalized layout of a GFI system is pictured in Figure 10–10.

Technician A says that part X provides a consistent operating fuel pressure (100 psi) for the system.

Technician B says that part Y controls spark advance when running on natural gas.

Who is right?
a. A only
b. B only
c. Both A and B
d. Neither A nor B

48. Technician A says that MOGAS fuel systems use a lift plate type mixer.

Technician B says that an in-line type mixer is used.

Who is right?
a. A only
b. B only
c. Both A and B
d. Neither A nor B

49. Air-fuel ratios and emissions are being interpreted on an analyzer.

Technician A says that O_2 levels are highest when air–fuel ratios are near stoichiometric.

Technician B says that CO_2 levels are near zero when air–fuel ratios are near stoichiometric.

Who is right?
a. A only
b. B only
c. Both A and B
d. Neither A nor B

50. The natural gas fuel injection kit by BAYTECH has:
a. application for dedicated CNG light- and medium-duty vehicles only.
b. adaptive learning capability.
c. Both a and b
d. Neither a nor b

51. Technician A says that all CNG fill and fuel lines must be insulated when going through body panels.

Technician B says all CNG fill and fuel lines must have line clamps installed at least every 24 inches.

Who is right?

a. A only   **c.** Both A and B
b. B only   **d.** Neither A nor B

52. A CNG mixer is being installed.

Technician A says to install it between the mass airflow (MAF) sensor and the throttle body.

Technician B says to install it in front of the MAF sensor.

Who is right?

a. A only   **c.** Both A and B
b. B only   **d.** Neither A nor B

53. For best CNG engine performance, block learn should be:

a. 175   **b.** 130 to 110   **c.** 128   **d.** 115 to 150

54. Which of the following statements DOES NOT apply to a typical in-line fuel filter?

a. Has an arrow stamped on it
b. Is mounted on the in-board side of the regulator
c. Has a 65 micron rating
d. Is self-cleaning and does not require service

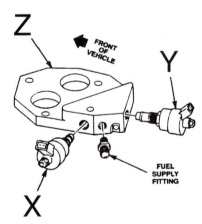

FIGURE 10–11

55. Parts X and Y in Figure 10–11 are slightly "cross-threaded."

Technician A says to use Teflon tape and reinstall them.

Technician B says to replace part Z.

Who is right?

a. A only   **c.** Both A and B
b. B only   **d.** Neither A nor B

56. Fuel management on a particular CNG system accomplishes fuel control by changing fuel pressure at the secondary regulator.

Technician A says that a vacuum leak in the line between the regulator and the fuel control valve will shut off the fuel at high speed.

Technician B says that it will decrease the fuel pressure at idle.

Who is right?

a. A only   **c.** Both A and B
b. B only   **d.** Neither A nor B

57. The fuel lockoff solenoid ground wire is shorted to ground. This will:

a. Cause the solenoid to stay open.
b. Cause the solenoid to stay closed.
c. Not affect the operation of the solenoid.
d. Cause a fuse to blow.

58. A hoop-wrapped composite cylinder has a 1″ long, 3/16″ deep cut near its top head. Which of the following is recommended?

a. Discard the cylinder
b. Fill the cut with epoxy resin and rehydrostatic test
c. Use the cylinder (provided there is no evidence of delamination)
d. Install a new overwrap

59. A CNG cylinder shows discoloration caused by fire damage and the manufacturer's label is missing.

Technician A says that the cylinder can be returned to service if the protective coating is still intact.

Technician B says that if the label is missing, the cylinder must be condemned.

Who is right?

a. A only   **c.** Both A and B
b. B only   **d.** Neither A nor B

60. The neck of a cylinder is stamped with these markings:

DOT-3AA 2400
2-96

Technician A says that the date of the next required hydrostatic test is indicated.

Technician B says the exemption number is indicated.

Who is right?

a. A only   **c.** Both A and B
b. B only   **d.** Neither A nor B

61. A five-year-old pick-up truck with 115,000 miles showing on the odometer is being considered for a bi-fuel conversion.

Technician A says that new suspension system springs must be installed.

Technician B says that a new rebuilt engine must be installed.

Who is right?
a. A only
b. B only
c. Both A and B
d. Neither A nor B

62. Technician A says that metal clamping bands (brackets) and their supports shall not be in direct contact with a cylinder.

Technician B says that 1″ diameter bolts (grade 8) are the minimum size to be used when attaching the brackets.

Who is right?
a. A only   **c.** Both A and B
b. B only   **d.** Neither A nor B

63. A vacuum gauge shows a 17″ Hg reading at idle. However, it slowly drops to 8″ Hg as the throttle is suddenly opened and held at 2000 rpm. Which of these is most likely indicated?
a. Retarded ignition timing
b. Restricted exhaust system
c. Stuck open EGR valve
d. Vacuum leak

64. A system is being leak tested using natural gas.

Technician A says that an electronic leak detection instrument can be used.

Technician B says that a non–ammonia-based soap and water solution can be used.

Who is right?
a. A only   **c.** Both A and B
b. B only   **d.** Neither A nor B

65. It has just been determined that a CNG fuel system has a leak at the primary regulator inlet fitting.

Technician A says to try tightening the fitting.

Technician B says to test drive it to see if the leak has stopped.

Who is right?
a. A only   **c.** Both A and B
b. B only   **d.** Neither A nor B

66. A bi-fuel vehicle has been sitting for several weeks. It runs okay on natural gas, but rough on gasoline.

Technician A says that the CAT could be plugged.

Technician B says that the injectors could be clogged.

Who is right?
a. A only   **c.** Both A and B
b. B only   **d.** Neither A nor B

67. Technician A says that fabricated mounting brackets must be allowed to flex in six principle directions.

Technician B says that all connections must be able to freely breakaway in the event of a collision.

Who is right?
a. A only   **c.** Both A and B
b. B only   **d.** Neither A nor B

68. Technician A says to use Teflon paste when installing high pressure lines and fittings.

Technician B says to use Teflon tape when installing high pressure lines and fittings.

Who is right?
a. A only   **c.** Both A and B
b. B only   **d.** Neither A nor B

69. A CNG vehicle misses (cuts-out) when turning sharp corners.

Technician A says that a cylinder could be incorrectly oriented.

Technician B says that a regulator could be incorrectly oriented.

Who is right?
a. A only   **c.** Both A and B
b. B only   **d.** Neither A nor B

70. A dual timing ignition curve on a CNG vehicle is BEST CHECKED by using a:
a. scope
b. dyno
c. timing light
d. four-gas analyzer

71. Technician A says that it's OK to mount cylinders in the bed of a pick-up truck.

Technician B says that it's OK to mount cylinders to the frame of a small school bus.

Who is right?
a. A only   **c.** Both A and B
b. B only   **d.** Neither A nor B

72. Technician A says that the CNG secondary regulator should be installed in the orientation prescribed by the manufacturer.

Technician B says that it should be installed in a location that will minimize the risk of the damage in the event of a collision.

Who is right?
a. A only
b. B only
c. Both A and B
d. Neither A nor B

73. A bi-fuel conversion kit has been installed on a vehicle. The original timing tag attached to the vehicle reads 8° BTDC. Where should the base spark timing be set?
a. 6° BTDC
b. 8° BTDC
c. 10° BTDC
d. None of the above

74. Technician A says that a fuel temperature gauge can be tested with an ohmmeter.

Technician B says that fuel gauge can be tested with an ammeter.

Who is right?
a. A only
b. B only
c. Both A and B
d. Neither A nor B

75. Tubing, valves, and fittings in a CNG system must all be capable of withstanding a hydrostatic test of at least _____ times their rated service pressure.
a. 1½
b. 2
c. 3
d. 4

76. The cylinder on a bi-fuel vehicle has reached its re-test date and must be removed.

Technician A says that the gas in the cylinder can be transferred to another CNG vehicle.

Technician B says that the gas in the cylinder can be vented to the atmosphere.

Who is right?
a. A only
b. B only
c. Both A and B
d. Neither A nor B

77. A "hiss" is heard when refueling a CNG vehicle.

Technician A says that this could be caused by a damaged o-ring in the inside of the refueling receptacle.

Technician B says that this could be caused by normal wear on the refueling nozzle.

Who is right?
a. A only
b. B only
c. Both A and B
d. Neither A nor B

78. A vehicle has a no-start condition on CNG, but starts normally on gasoline.

Technician A says that this could be caused by an air leak between the mixer and the air filter.

Technician B says that this could be caused by an air leak between the mixer and the throttle.

Who is right?
a. A only
b. B only
c. Both A and B
d. Neither A nor B

79. A gasoline fuel injected engine is running overly rich.

Technician A says that this could be caused by a stuck open EGR valve.

Technician B says that this could be caused by a bad oxygen sensor.

Who is right?
a. A only
b. B only
c. Both A and B
d. Neither A nor B

80. During a post-conversion road test, a slight "buzzing" noise can be heard in the driver's compartment.

Technician A says that this can be caused by conversion equipment mounted to a body panel.

Technician B says that this can be caused by CNG going into the engine, and is often considered normal depending on the type of conversion.

Who is right?
a. A only
b. B only
c. Both A and B
d. Neither A nor B

81. A gasoline engine is being converted to also run on CNG.

Technician A says to install spark plugs one heat range hotter.

Technician B says to gap the plugs 0.010″ wider.

Who is right?
a. A only
b. B only
c. Both A and B
d. Neither A nor B

82. Technician A says that if engine coolant level is low, the primary regulator can malfunction.

Technician B says that this can cause the regulator to freeze up.

Who is right?
a. A only
b. B only
c. Both A and B
d. Neither A nor B

Section 11

ENGINE MACHINIST

STUDY OUTLINE

The Engine Machinist Test Series consists of three tests. They are as follows:

- Cylinder Head Specialist
- Cylinder Block Specialist
- Assembly Specialist

This study outline includes content material for each test.

I. Cylinder Head Specialist
   A. Disassembly and Cleaning
      1. Inspect for damage (valve seat looseness, coolant erosion, and cracks)
      2. Remove external components
         a. Studs
         b. ID tags
         c. Fittings and adapters
         d. Core and gallery plugs
         e. Housings and covers
         f. Sensors
         g. Precombustion chambers and injector assemblies
         h. Manifolds
      3. Inspect and remove valve train components
         a. Camshaft carrier, camshaft bearing caps, and camshaft
         b. Valve springs, rotators, retainers, and locks
         c. Valves/seals
         d. Oil pump and distributor drive
         e. Camshaft drive and retaining mechanisms
      4. Clean head and related components using proper method/correct waste disposal
         a. Hand cleaning
         b. High-pressure spraying
         c. Cold soaking
         d. Hot-tank immersion
         e. Steam cleaning
         f. Glass bead cleaning
         g. Airless shot blasting
         h. Pyrolytic oven cleaning
      5. Identify location
         a. Camshaft bearings
         b. Valves
         c. Valve springs (position)
         d. Rotators
         e. Casting numbers

      6. Teardown measurement
         a. Installed valve stem height
         b. Valve head protrusion/recession
         c. Lash adjustment shims
         d. Valve guide installed height
   B. Crack Repair
      1. Determine extent of crack and evaluate for repair
         a. Magnetic inspection
         b. Dye penetrant inspection
         c. Magnetic fluorescent inspection
         d. Pressure testing
      2. Understand accepted industry procedures
         a. Pinning
         b. Welding (cast iron and aluminum)
         c. Epoxy repair
         d. Heli-coil repair of damaged threads
   C. Inspection and Machining
      1. Evaluate visually
         a. Structural integrity and porosity
         b. Mating surfaces
         c. Deck finish
         d. Valve seat condition
         e. Injector area
         f. Precombustion chamber fit
         g. Fire ring grooves
         h. Valve condition
         i. Other valve train components (rocker arms, cam followers, studs, and so on)
      2. Measure/repair or adjust as needed
         a. Cylinder head warpage
         b. Valve guide wear
         c. Injector tip location
         d. Lifter bores
         e. Valve lash
         f. Valve stem installed height
         g. Valve spring installed height
         h. Deck finish
         i. Valve seat width
   D. Assembly
      1. Install related parts
         a. Camshaft bearings (check fit)
         b. Valves (check for seating)
         c. Seals
         d. Camshaft (including drive mechanisms)

II. Cylinder Block Specialist
  A. Disassembly and Cleaning
    1. Inspect for major damage (foreign material in pan, detonation, burn-through between cylinders, and deck surface cracks)
    2. Remove external components
        a. Crankshaft pulley/vibration damper
        b. Studs/dowel pins
        c. Fittings and adapters
        d. Core and gallery plugs
        e. Housings and covers
    3. Visual inspection of removed external components
        a. Pin-holed front covers (electrolysis damage)
        b. Vibration damper hub wear/keyway wear
        c. Crankshaft oil slinger
        d. Flywheel/flexplate
    4. Remove internal components
        a. Check all connecting rod and main bearing caps for correct position and numbering
        b. Oil pump, screen, and driveshaft
        c. Cut cylinder wall ring ridge
        d. Connecting rod and piston assemblies (include use of protective boots)
        e. Piston pins/bushings
        f. Main bearing caps/lower bearings
        g. Crankshaft/rear seal assembly
        h. Upper bearings
        i. Cylinder liners/seals/fire deck inspection
        j. Cam bearings/bushings
    5. Visual inspection of removed internal components
        a. Bearing distress patterns (radius ride, fatigue, lack of oil, and tapered journal)
        b. Piston skirt diagonal wear
        c. Thrust bearing/washer wear
        d. Crankshaft snout wear
    6. Cleaning block and related components using proper method (refer to Section I.4 of this outline)
  B. Crack Repair
    1. Determine extent of crack and evaluate for repair (refer to Section I-B of this outline)
  C. Block Machining Procedures
    1. Chamfering head bolt holes
    2. Removing all burrs and casting slag
    3. Tapping main oil galleries for pipe plug installation
    4. Align boring/align honing
    5. Deck surfacing
    6. Honing lifter bores
    7. Boring/honing cylinders (include using a torque plate)
    8. Cutting liner (wet-sleeve) counterbores
    9. Bell-housing mounting surface
  D. Crankshaft Inspection/Machining
    1. Keyways and threads
    2. Flywheel flange runout/snout trueness/and bend (include correction procedures)
    3. Rear main oil seal surface
    4. Journals (size and wear)
    5. Magnetic inspection
    6. Thrust wall runout
    7. Grinding between centers versus holding in two universal chucks
    8. Checking crankpin width
    9. Restoring fillets
    10. Re-radius and polish all oil hole edges
    11. Micro-finishing journals
    12. Identification markings
  E. Crankshaft Rebuilding
    1. Hard chroming
    2. "Submerged arc" welding
    3. Metal spraying
    4. Oxyacetylene welding
    5. Tuftriding
    6. Shot peening
    7. Cross-drilling
  F. Crankshaft Failure Analysis
    1. Torsional stress failure
    2. Bending stress failure
  G. Connecting Rod and Piston Inspection
    1. Measuring big-end bore
    2. Checking alignment (bend, twist, and offset)
    3. Checking pin hole in piston and rod (roundness, alignment, taper, and surface finish)
    4. Measuring piston diameter
    5. Measuring ring groove wear
  H. Connecting Rod Failure Analysis
    1. Improper rod bolt tightening
    2. Rod beam failure (bending stress)
    3. Pressed-in pin seizure
    4. Breakage due to bearing failure
    5. Stress raiser failure (nicks)
  I. Piston Failure Analysis
    1. Abnormal combustion (preignition and detonation)
    2. Scuffing/scoring
    3. Breakage from insufficient pin clearance
    4. Overheating
    5. Skirt cracking
  J. Connecting Rod and Piston Machining/Assembling
    1. Rod reconditioning steps
    2. Honing versus boring
    3. Center-to-center length
    4. Pin bushing installation/expanding
    5. Pin attachment methods (recommended clearances for each)
    6. Installing pressed-in pins (hydraulic press, electric pin furnace, and gas-fired heater)
    7. Piston head installation position
    8. Spurt hole/bleed hole position
  K. Balancing Procedures
    1. Weighing rod big-ends
    2. Determine total weight of each rod
    3. Grind rod small-end balance pads

4. Determine bob weight totals
5. Internal/external balanced engines
L. Cylinder Block Preparation
1. Sleeving
2. Chamfering the bore
3. Glaze breaking
4. Cleaning the block after machining
5. Painting the block
   a. Glyptal
III. Assembly Specialist
A. Engine Disassembly, Inspection, and Cleaning (refer to Sections I and II of this outline)
B. Short Block Assembly Procedures (refer to Section I-D of this outline)
1. Blow dry compressed air through all oil holes in block
2. Determine rod and main bearing oil clearance using the crown wall thickness method
3. Break any sharp edges at the main cap parting surfaces with a fine file
4. Install all plugs and bushings where applicable
5. Draw or drive in each cam bearing
6. Install camshaft—lubricate lobes and bearing journals (mushroom-type lifters must be installed beforehand)

7. Install crankshaft and bearings (including rear main seal) and auxiliary shafts
8. Align thrust bearing
9. Measure crankshaft end play
10. Install valve timing components
11. Install rings on pistons (understand markings)
12. Stagger ring gaps
13. Install piston assemblies/rod bearings (prelubricate)
14. Rotate engine and measure rod side clearance
15. Install oil pump/front cover
16. Install vibration damper
C. Long Block Assembly Procedures
1. Install cylinder head(s)
2. Install manifold(s)
3. Install all related tinware
4. Install water pump
5. Install carburetor/fuel injection assembly
6. Bell housing alignment
D. Final Assembly
1. Adjust valves
2. Set static ignition timing
3. Prelubricate (prime) engine prior to starting
E. Break-In Procedure

---

1. Machinist A says that when camshaft lobes are reground, valve lift is reduced.

   Machinist B says that when camshaft lobes are reground, valve duration is reduced.

   Who is right?
   a. A only   c. Both A and B
   b. B only   d. Neither A nor B

2. A crankshaft grinding machine has a tendency to grind out-of-round journals.

   Machinist A says that this could be caused by insufficient pressure on the steady rest blocks.

   Machinist B says that this could be caused by loose throwhead clamps.

   Who is right?
   a. A only   c. Both A and B
   b. B only   d. Neither A nor B

3. A pair of high performance (HP) cylinder heads are being assembled. When the valves are in full open position, clearance between the spring retainer and the valve guide upper end is as shown in Figure 11–1.

   Assembler A says to use longer stem valves.
   Assembler B says to use longer valve springs.
   Who is right?
   a. A only   c. Both A and B
   b. B only   d. Neither A nor B

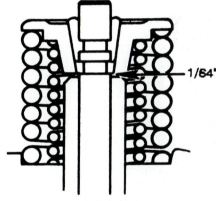

FIGURE 11–1

FIGURE 11–2

4. In the illustration in Figure 11–2, the boring bar mike is set to bore the cylinder at:
   a. 3 ⅛″ plus 0.030″.   c. 3.105″.
   b. 3.745″.   d. 3.150″.

5. Excessive connecting rod side clearance is generally corrected by:
   a. replacing the rods.
   b. installing oversize (O/S) rod bearings.
   c. grinding the crankshaft.
   d. re-sizing the rods.

6. A grinding wheel has just been installed on a valve refacing machine.

   Machinist A says to dress the wheel.

   Machinist B says to have coolant flowing over the wheel when dressing.

   Who is right?
   a. A only   c. Both A and B
   b. B only   d. Neither A nor B

7. A ⅛″ wall thickness cylinder sleeve is going to be installed in a passenger car block.

   Machinist A says that boring for the sleeve will require going 0.1875″ over the standard cylinder bore.

   Machinist B says that the sleeve should have a 0.002″ to 0.003″ press-fit in the block.

   Who is right?
   a. A only   c. Both A and B
   b. B only   d. Neither A nor B

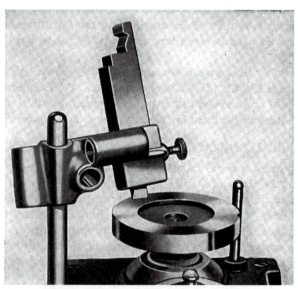

FIGURE 11–3

8. Machinist A says to use no hand pressure when performing the operation in Figure 11–3.

   Machinist B says to use no lubricant when performing the operation.

   Who is right?
   a. A only   c. Both A and B
   b. B only   d. Neither A nor B

9. A new bushing has been precision fit (honed) in the "eye" of a connecting rod. The pin enters easily from either end, but becomes tight in the center of the bushing.

   Machinist A says to burnish the bushing.

   Machinist B says that the bushing is bell-mouthed.

   Who is right?
   a. A only
   b. B only
   c. Both A and B
   d. Neither A nor B

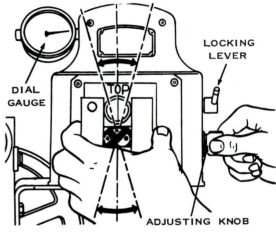

FIGURE 11–4

10. Refer to Figure 11–4.

    Machinist A says that the dial gauge is being calibrated (set).

    Machinist B says that turning the adjusting knob counterclockwise expands the gauging fingers.

    Who is right?
    a. A only
    b. B only
    c. Both A and B
    d. Neither A nor B

FIGURE 11–5

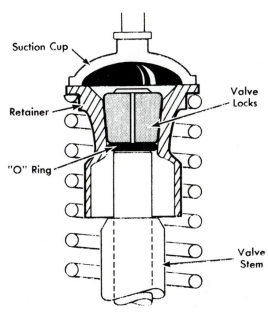

FIGURE 11–7

11. During a cylinder honing operation, the load meter needle swings more than 10 points, and the amber light flashes when the needle swings to the right (see Figure 11–5).

Machinist A says to keep the hone working longer in the top of the cylinder.

Machinist B says that this indicates taper in the cylinder.

Who is right?

a. A only
b. B only
c. Both A and B
d. Neither A nor B

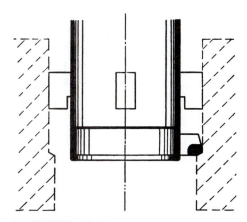

FIGURE 11–6

12. The "catspaws" pictured in Figure 11–6 are used to:
a. center the boring bar in the cylinder bore.
b. support the cutter head during the boring process.
c. Both a and b
d. Neither a nor b

13. What is being done in Figure 11–7?
a. Checking retainer clearance
b. Checking valve lock fit
c. Checking valve stem wear
d. Testing o-ring seal effectiveness

14. A wet-type cylinder sleeve is being installed in a Cummins engine. Which of the following is correct?
a. Remove scale or rust from the counterbore with a wire brush.
b. Measure flatness of the counterbore.
c. Both a and b
d. Neither a nor b

15. Two machinists are discussing ways to help minimize wet sleeve cavitation.

Machinist A says to fit sleeves in the block without excess clearance.

Machinist B says to make sure that pistons are not fit too loosely in the sleeves.

Who is right?

a. A only
b. B only
c. Both A and B
d. Neither A nor B

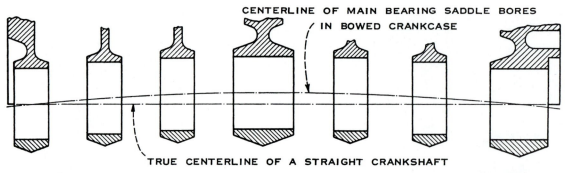

CENTERLINE OF MAIN BEARING SADDLE BORES IN BOWED CRANKCASE

TRUE CENTERLINE OF A STRAIGHT CRANKSHAFT

FIGURE 11–8

16. A crankcase is bowed as shown in Figure 11–8.

Machinist A says that correction can be made by line-boring semifinished inserts installed in the crankcase.

Machinist B says that correction can be made by line-honing the crankcase, then installing precision inserts.

Who is right?

a. A only   **c.** Both A and B
b. B only   **d.** Neither A nor B

FIGURE 11–9

17. Machinist A says that the piston in Figure 11–9 has been expanded by knurling.

Machinist B says that knurled pistons can be fitted to a tighter wall clearance than recommended by the factory.

Who is right?

a. A only
b. B only
c. Both A and B
d. Neither A nor B

X

FIGURE 11–10

18. Tool X in Figure 11–10 is used to:
a. burnish the bushing in the rod.
b. decrease pin clearance.
c. Both a and b
d. Neither a nor b

19. All of the following are recommended when installing a wet-type cylinder sleeve EXCEPT:
a. shimming the sleeve when the counterbore is too deep.
b. measuring the depth of the counterbore.
c. measuring the OD of the counterbore.
d. lubricating the sealing rings.

FIGURE 11–11

20. Machinist A says that the picture in Figure 11–11 shows setting the depth stop.
    Machinist B says that the picture above shows chamfering the corner of the insert.
    Who is right?
    a. A only
    b. B only
    c. Both A and B
    d. Neither A nor B

21. An engine is going to be rebuilt that uses a viscous damper. Which of the following statements is true?
    a. Replace the damper if a slight fluid leak is noticed.
    b. Replace the damper if the OD appears swelled.
    c. Both a and b
    d. Neither a nor b

22. A valve seat ring needs to be removed from an aluminum cylinder head.
    Machinist A says to pry the ring out with a hooked tool.
    Machinist B says to cut the ring out on a seat and guide machine.
    Who is right?
    a. A only
    b. B only
    c. Both A and B
    d. Neither A nor B

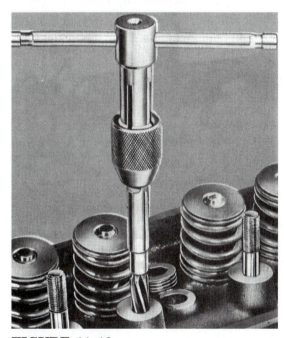

FIGURE 11–12

23. Refer to Figure 11–12.
    Machinist A says that a broken stud is being removed.
    Machinist B says that the stud bore is being reamed.
    Who is right?
    a. A only   **c.** Both A and B
    b. B only   **d.** Neither A nor B

FIGURE 11–13

24. Pictured in Figure 11–13 is a piston from an engine that failed after an overhaul. This could have been caused by:
   a. not following the CPL.
   b. using the wrong injectors.
   c. Both a and b
   d. Neither a nor b

25. A GM V-8 diesel engine has had repeat head gasket failure at 5,000-mile intervals. This could be caused by:
   a. missing dowel pins in the block.
   b. bolt holes in the block not being drilled deep enough.
   c. Both a and b
   d. Neither a nor b

26. A post valve job leak test is being performed on a cylinder head fitted with aluminized valves.

   Machinist A says that the valve faces will leak vacuum.

   Machinist B says that these valves do not seat in and seal until the engine has run a short time.

   Who is right?
   a. A only   c. Both A and B
   b. B only   d. Neither A nor B

27. An automobile engine that uses wrist pin clips is being assembled.

   Assembler A says to install the wrist pin clips with the sharp edged side facing towards the wrist pin.

   Assembler B says that if the pistons are being reused, discard the old wrist pin clips.

   Who is right?
   a. A only   c. Both A and B
   b. B only   d. Neither A nor B

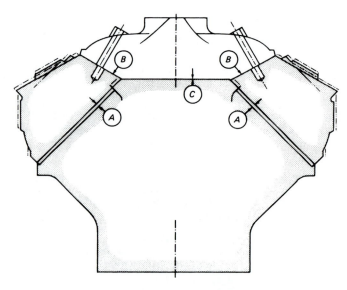

After machining the head at surface *A*, material should be machined from surface *B* for proper intake manifold alignment. Note how the bolt holes in the intake manifold do not line up after machining the head gasket surface *A*.

THE AMOUNT OF CORRECTIVE MACHINING REQUIRED VARIES WITH THE ANGLE AT WHICH THE HEAD IS MADE. HEAD ANGLE IS THE VARIANCE FROM 90°. FOR INSTANCE, A HEAD THAT HAS THE HEAD GASKET AND THE INTAKE MANIFOLD SURFACE MADE AT A RIGHT ANGLE (90°) TO EACH OTHER WOULD BE CLASSIFIED AS A 0° HEAD.

0°	Head angle (Big Block Ford) Amount removed at *A* × 1.0 = Amount to be removed at *B*
5°	Head angle Amount removed at *A* × 1.1 = Amount to be removed at *B*
10°	Head angle (Small Block Chevy and Ford) Amount removed at *A* × 1.2 = Amount to be removed at *B*
15°	Head angle (Chrysler, Y Block Ford) Amount removed at *A* × 1.4 = Amount to be removed at *B*
20°	Head angle (Oldsmobile) Amount removed at *A* × 1.7 = Amount to be removed at *B*
25°	Head angle (Cadillac, Dodge, Plymouth) Amount removed at *A* × 2.0 = Amount to be removed at *B*
30°	Head angle Amount removed at *A* × 3.0 = Amount to be removed at *B*

FIGURE 11–14

28. A pair of Chevrolet small block cylinder heads have had .015″ removed from surface "A" in Figure 11–14. How much material should be machined from the intake manifold side of each head for proper port alignment?
   a. .015″   b. .030″   c. .036″   d. .018″

29. Machinist A says that cast iron guides should be reamed wet for best results in both size and finish.

   Machinist B says that phosphor bronze guides should be reamed dry for best results in both size and finish.

   Who is right?
   a. A only   c. Both A and B
   b. B only   d. Neither A nor B

FIGURE 11–15

30. The clearance measurement in Figure 11–15 is too tight.

Machinist A says to replace the camshaft.

Machinist B says to install an oversize sprocket.

Who is right?
a. A only
b. B only
c. Both A and B
d. Neither A nor B

31. A crankshaft grinding wheel is being mounted on its hub.

Machinist A says to never mount a grinding wheel using paper shims or gaskets.

Machinist B says to use a cheater bar or pipe to tighten mounting bolts.

Who is right?
a. A only
b. B only
c. Both A and B
d. Neither A nor B

32. Rod throws are going to be ground on a crankshaft grinding machine.

Machinist A says to use the cross-slide adjustment to center the throws.

Machinist B says to dress a radius on the wheel.

Who is right?
a. A only
b. B only
c. Both A and B
d. Neither A nor B

33. Rod-reconditioning requires two steps. They are:
a. cleaning the rod bore and replacing bolts and nuts.
b. installing new inserts and tightening bolts to proper torque.
c. reducing the rod bore and swedging it back to original size.
d. reducing the rod bore and honing it back to original size.

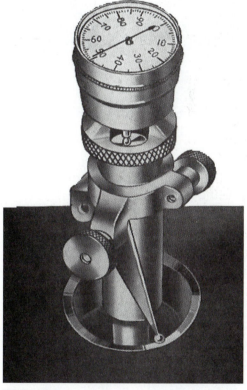

FIGURE 11–16

34. The tool in Figure 11–16 is used to measure:
a. valve stem height.
b. valve seat depth.
c. Both a and b
d. Neither a nor b

35. Machinist A says that too much clearance between the crankshaft and crankshaft bearings can cause low oil pressure.

Machinist B says that too much clearance between the camshaft and camshaft bearings can cause low oil pressure.

Who is right?
a. A only
b. B only
c. Both A and B
d. Neither A nor B

FIGURE 11–17

36. Refer to the picture in Figure 11–17.

Machinist A says that valve guide rub area is being reduced.

Machinist B says that inner valve spring seats are being cut.

Who is right?

a. A only
b. B only
c. Both A and B
d. Neither A nor B

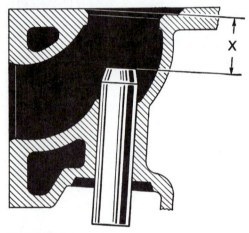

FIGURE 11–18

37. Measurement X in Figure 11–18 is incorrect. This could cause:
a. the spring retainer to bottom out on top of the guide when the valve fully opens.
b. air flow in the port to be restricted.
c. Both a and b
d. Neither a nor b

38. Connecting rod bearing "crush" is essential for:
a. preventing the bearings from turning in the big-end bore.
b. good heat dissipation.
c. Both a and b
d. Neither a nor b

FIGURE 11–19

39. The tool in Figure 11–19 is used for:
a. removing rocker arm studs.
b. pressing in rocker arm studs.
c. Both a and b
d. Neither a nor b

40. A camshaft binds when installed in new cam bearings. This could be caused by:
a. a bent camshaft.
b. high spots on bearings.
c. Both a and b
d. Neither a nor b

41. Valve timing is set during engine assembly by:
a. using a timing light.
b. adjusting valve opening on the intake stroke.
c. Both a and b
d. Neither a nor b

42. Machinist A says that compression leakage can result if liner height is too low.

Machinist B says that too much lube oil consumption can result if liner height is too low.

Who is right?

a. A only   **c.** Both A and B
b. B only   **d.** Neither A nor B

43. A diesel engine blows white smoke and is hard to start. Teardown inspection shows that the compression rings and their lands are broken. This could be caused by:

a. using too much starting fluid (ether).
b. overfueling.
c. Both a and b
d. Neither a nor b

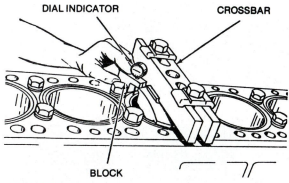

FIGURE 11–20

44. What is the machinist measuring in Figure 11–20?

a. Liner height projection
b. Counterbore depth
c. Both a and b
d. Neither a nor b

45. A heavy-duty diesel engine head gasket has failed three times in a row in the same place. What could be causing this?

a. Incorrect tightening sequence
b. Improper torque
c. High spots on the cylinder block top face
d. Any of the above

46. A diesel engine with 6,000 miles on a major overhaul has several burned valves and seats. This could be caused by:

a. overadvanced fuel system timing.
b. valves being set too tight.
c. Both a and b
d. Neither a nor b

FIGURE 11–21

47. Refer to Figure 11–21.

Assembler A says that this type of oil seal should be soaked in oil prior to installation.

Assembler B says that when the oil seal is fully seated, trim the ends.

Who is right?

a. A only   **c.** Both A and B
b. B only   **d.** Neither A nor B

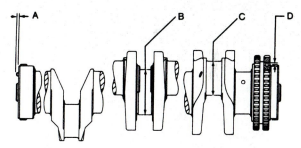

FIGURE 11–22

48. In the drawing in Figure 11–22, main bearing journal size would be measured at point:
a. A. **b.** B. **c.** C. **d.** D.

49. Assembler A says that the oil pump pickup should fit tight in the pump body.

Assembler B says that the oil pump pickup should be within 1/4″ from the bottom of the pan.

Who is right?

a. A only   **c.** Both A and B
b. B only   **d.** Neither A nor B

50. An engine assembler is setting the required clearance between rotor lobes on a Detroit blower. This is done by:

a. adding or removing shims.
b. changing the end cover thrust plate.
c. using oversize or undersize gears.
d. indexing the lobes.

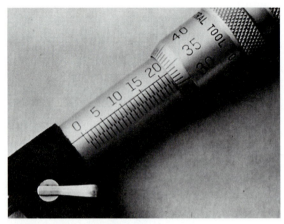

FIGURE 11–23

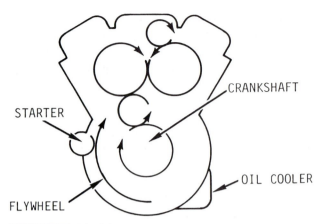

FIGURE 11–24

51. What is the reading on the micrometer shown in Figure 11–23?
    a. 21.84 mm
    b. 20.34 mm
    c. 23.34 mm
    d. None of the above

52. Valve adjustment on an OHV engine with adjustable hydraulic valve lifters is being made.

    Assembler A says to tighten the adjusting nuts to zero clearance, then set preload by backing off one-half to three-quarters of a turn.

    Assembler B says that the engine must be running.

    Who is right?
    a. A only
    b. B only
    c. Both A and B
    d. Neither A nor B

53. Assembler A says that rocker arm assemblies should be checked for plugs in the ends of rocker shafts.

    Assembler B says that rocker arm assemblies should be checked for the direction of oil holes in rocker shafts.

    Who is right?
    a. A only
    b. B only
    c. Both A and B
    d. Neither A nor B

54. The gear train in Figure 11–24 is on a series 71 Detroit engine. Which of these statements is true?
    a. A right-hand rotation engine is shown.
    b. The blower would turn clockwise as viewed from the rear of the engine.
    c. Both a and b
    d. Neither a nor b

FIGURE 11–25

55. A "Jake" brake is being installed on a rebuilt Mack engine.

    Assembler A says that the adjustment in Figure 11–25 must be made with the engine running.

    Assembler B says that the adjustment must be made with the engine hot.

    Who is right?
    a. A only
    b. B only
    c. Both A and B
    d. Neither A nor B

56. Assembler A says that on automobile engines, the rear main bearing is used as the thrust bearing.

Assembler B says that on automobile engines, the center main bearing is used as the thrust bearing.

Who is right?

a. A only
c. Both A and B
b. B only
d. Neither A nor B

57. A machinist fails to allow a grinding machine to "spark out" while surfacing a cylinder head. This can cause the:

a. surface finish to be too smooth.
b. grinding wheel to overheat.
c. grinding wheel to become glazed.
d. surface finish not to be flat.

58. An engine requires line boring, and it is found that housing bore specs are not available. Using the following information, mathematically determine the correct housing bore diameter.

```
Shaft diameter (2.3750")
Bearing wall thickness (.0615")
Oil clearance (.002")
```

a. 2.500"   **b.** 2.436"   **c.** 2.434"   **d.** 2.438"

59. A flywheel ring gear requires replacement.

Machinist A says to heat one spot on the old gear with a torch, then drive the gear off with a hammer and punch.

Machinist B says to heat the replacement gear with a torch, then quickly drop it into position.

Who is right?

a. A only
c. Both A and B
b. B only
d. Neither A nor B

60. A recessed (stepped) flywheel needs to be refaced.

Machinist A says that the clutch surface should be refaced parallel to the crankshaft flange.

Machinist B says that the pressure plate attachment surface should be refaced the same amount as the clutch surface.

Who is right?

a. A only
c. Both A and B
b. B only
d. Neither A nor B

61. Machinist A says that when line honing, all main bearing bores cannot be machined at the same time.

Machinist B says that when align boring, the thrust surfaces on a bearing cannot be faced.

Who is right?

a. A only
c. Both A and B
b. B only
d. Neither A nor B

62. Main caps are being prepared prior to line honing.

Machinist A says that the parting face of the thrust cap should be ground so that the cap will tilt slightly when installed.

Machinist B says that caps are ground at the parting face to reduce housing bore diameter.

Who is right?

a. A only
c. Both A and B
b. B only
d. Neither A nor B

63. Machinist A says that main bearing bore alignment can be checked with a precision ground arbor.

Machinist B says that main bearing bore alignment can be checked with a straightedge and feeler gauge.

Who is right?

a. A only
c. Both A and B
b. B only
d. Neither A nor B

64. It is recommended that a valve seat insert be installed if:

a. it is recessed.
b. it is loose.
c. installed spring height exceeds specs by over .060".
d. Any of the above exist

65. A typical automotive valve seat is being ground at 45°.

Machinist A says that a 30° stone will narrow the seat and move it away from the valve margin.

Machinist B says that a 60° stone will widen the seat and move it closer to the valve margin.

Who is right?

a. A only
c. Both A and B
b. B only
d. Neither A nor B

66. A cylinder head with mushroomed valve stem tips needs to be disassembled. Which of the following is the correct procedure?

a. Drive the valve through the valve guide.
b. Drive out the valve guide with the valve installed.
c. Both a and b
d. Neither a nor b

67. A cylinder head has a repeated history of stud "pullout."

Machinist A recommends modifying the head for installation of threaded studs.

Machinist B recommends pinning the studs. Who is right?

a. A only   c. Both A and B
b. B only   d. Neither A nor B

68. Machinist A says that a crankshaft should be micro-finished (polished) after grinding.

Machinist B says that nodular cast iron crankshafts should be final polished in the same direction as engine rotation.

Who is right?

a. A only   c. Both A and B
b. B only   d. Neither A nor B

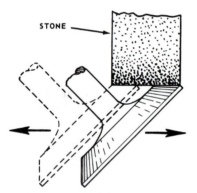

FIGURE 11–26

69. When performing the machine operation in Figure 11–26:

a. move the valve face back and forth off the stone.

b. have coolant flowing on the valve face.

c. Both a and b

d. Neither a nor b

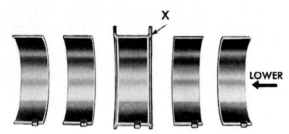

FIGURE 11–27

70. Assembler A says that a set of upper main bearing insert halves are shown in Figure 11–27.

Assembler B says that bearing insert X is a thrust bearing.

Who is right?

a. A only   c. Both A and B
b. B only   d. Neither A nor B

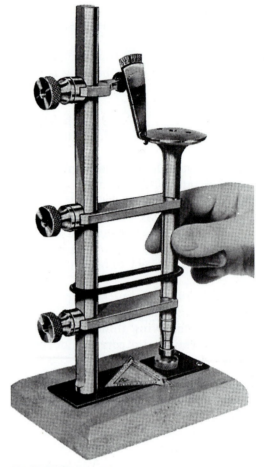

FIGURE 11–28

71. What is being measured in Figure 11–28?

a. Valve face runout

b. Valve height

c. Both a and b

d. Neither a nor b

72. Small cracks can be seen on the face of a Caterpillar head at the injector hole area.

Machinist A says that plugs are available for making this repair on heads that have the precombustion chamber perpendicular to the surface of the head.

Machinist B says that plugs are available for making this repair on heads that have the precombustion chamber at a compound angle to the surface of the head.

Who is right?

a. A only

b. B only

c. Both A and B

d. Neither A nor B

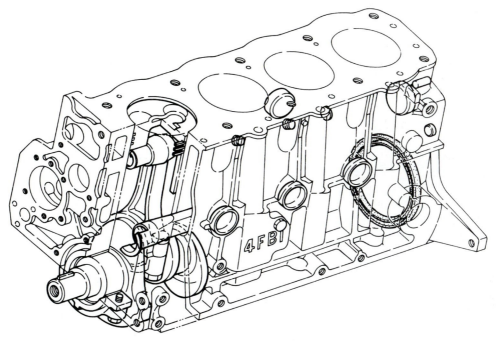

FIGURE 11–29

73. Assembler A says that the rear seal lip in Figure 11–29 is positioned backwards.

    Assembler B says that the rear seal lip above should be lubricated for break-in when installing.

    Who is right?

  a. A only   **c.** Both A and B

  b. B only   **d.** Neither A nor B

74. All of the following should be done when installing a cup-type core plug, EXCEPT:

  a. using emery paper to clean the inside edge of the plug hole.

  b. making sure the plug is free of bent edges.

  c. coating the plug OD with sealer.

  d. driving the plug slightly above the top edge of the hole.

75. An engine that has the oil pump as an integral part of the timing gear cover is being assembled.

    Assembler A says to pack the oil pump screen with petroleum jelly.

    Assembler B says that the pumps for these engines are not self-priming.

    Who is right?

  a. A only

  b. B only

  c. Both A and B

  d. Neither A nor B

76. On certain engines, what often gets into the oil pump and causes the intermediate shaft to twist and break?

  a. Camshaft sprocket material

  b. Umbrella valve stem seal material

  c. Either a or b

  d. Neither a nor b

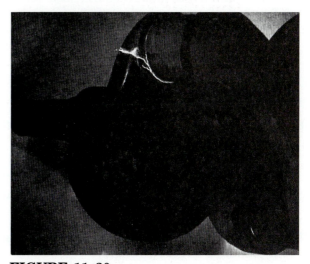

FIGURE 11–30

77. Machinist A says that the crankshaft in Figure 11–30 can be used again if the journals are ground to a smaller diameter.

    Machinist B says that the crankshaft above can be used again if it is cold welded.

    Who is right?

  a. A only   **c.** Both A and B

  b. B only   **d.** Neither A nor B

FIGURE 11–31

78. The damage in Figure 11–31 could have been caused by:
   a. wrong spark plug application.
   b. preignition.
   c. Both a and b
   d. Neither a nor b

79. New connecting rod bolts are going to be installed in an engine that is being rebuilt.
   Machinist A says to recondition the rods before installing the new bolts.
   Machinist B says to tighten the new bolts using the stretch method or a torque wrench.
   Who is right?
   a. A only   **c.** Both A and B
   b. B only   **d.** Neither A nor B

80. Cast iron cylinder heads can be checked for cracks by:
   a. pressure testing.
   b. dye penetrant inspection.
   c. Both a and b
   d. Neither a nor b

81. Worn injector sleeves need to be removed from a Cummins 250 series engine.
   Machinist A says to drive them out.
   Machinist B says to press them out.
   Who is right?
   a. A only   **c.** Both A and B
   b. B only   **d.** Neither A nor B

82. Assembler A says that a cam follower roller with a smooth glossy finish should be replaced.
   Assembler B says that a cam follower roller with a spalled finish should be replaced.
   Who is right?
   a. A only   **c.** Both A and B
   b. B only   **d.** Neither A nor B

83. Head gaskets are being installed on a small block Chevrolet.
   Assembler A says that all head bolt threads should be wire brushed.
   Assembler B says that sealer should be applied to the threads on all head bolts.
   Who is right?
   a. A only   **c.** Both A and B
   b. B only   **d.** Neither A nor B

84. Bronze-wall spiral bushings are going to be installed in a cylinder head equipped with integral guides.
   Machinist A says that a tap and reamer are used.
   Machinist B says that a broach and cutoff tool are used.
   Who is right?
   a. A only
   b. B only
   c. Both A and B
   d. Neither A nor B

85. Machinist A says that worn integral valve guides can be repaired by knurling.
   Machinist B says that worn integral valve guides can be repaired by reaming to fit over-sized stems.
   Who is right?
   a. A only
   b. B only
   c. Both A and B
   d. Neither A nor B

86. A counterbore is being machined into a head in order to install a new valve seat.
   Machinist A says to check the counterbore; it must be free of waves.
   Machinist B says to check the counterbore for roundness.
   Who is right?
   a. A only
   b. B only
   c. Both A and B
   d. Neither A nor B

87. A cylinder head is factory equipped with removable valve guides. All of the guides are worn and need to be replaced.

Machinist A says that all valve seats must be ground prior to installing the guides.

Machinist B says that intake and exhaust guides installed height must be the same.

Who is right?

a. A only   **c.** Both A and B
b. B only   **d.** Neither A nor B

88. A new injector sleeve is going to be installed into a GMC Series 53 engine.

Machinist A says to flare the tip of the sleeve.

Machinist B says to cut the seat in the bottom of the sleeve.

Who is right?

a. A only   **c.** Both A and B
b. B only   **d.** Neither A nor B

FIGURE 11–32

89. Machinist A says that the condition in Figure 11–32 shows face-to-seat interference.

Machinist B says that the condition above will lead to preignition and premature valve burning.

Who is right?

a. A only   **c.** Both A and B
b. B only   **d.** Neither A nor B

90. A 90° V-type block is being machined for a racer.

Machinist A says to bore the cylinders using the pan rails as the reference point.

Machinist B says that deck clearance should vary between right bank and left bank pistons.

Who is right?

a. A only   **c.** Both A and B
b. B only   **d.** Neither A nor B

91. Incorrectly machined lifter bores can cause:
a. camshaft "walk."
b. camshaft lobe scuffing.
c. Both a and b
d. Neither a nor b

92. A race engine is being built that uses angle milled heads and aftermarket pistons.

Builder A says that the relationship of valve head angle to piston relief must be checked during assembly.

Builder B says that molding clay is an often used item when assembling such engines.

Who is right?

a. A only   **c.** Both A and B
b. B only   **d.** Neither A nor B

FIGURE 11–33

93. Refer to the machining tool in Figure 11–33.

Machinist A says that this type tool is used prior to installing certain press-on valve stem seals.

Machinist B says that this type tool is used to chamfer the valve guide top.

Who is right?

a. A only   **c.** Both A and B
b. B only   **d.** Neither A nor B

94. Machinist A says to chamfer the ends of the connecting rod "eye" before pressing in a replacement pin bushing.

Machinist B says that when boring a pin bushing to finished size, keep the centerline parallel to the centerline of the connecting rod "big-end."

Who is right?

a. A only   **c.** Both A and B
b. B only   **d.** Neither A nor B

95. A crankshaft is being preheated prior to welding.

Welder A says to quickly warm the surface with a propane torch.

Welder B says to avoid deep preheating penetration, because this can lead to breakage problems on welded crankshafts.

Who is right?

a. A only
c. Both A and B
b. B only
d. Neither A nor B

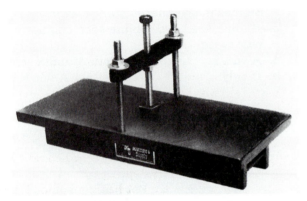

FIGURE 11–34

96. The fixture in Figure 11–34 is used to:
  a. straighten heads.
  b. pressure test heads.
  c. Both a and b
  d. Neither a nor b

97. In order to properly check connecting rod bearing thickness:
  a. use a ball-anvil micrometer.
  b. measure at the parting line.
  c. Both a and b
  d. Neither a nor b

98. Valve seats are being installed in an aluminum cylinder head (import).

Machinist A says to use a lubricant when cutting the counterbore.

Machinist B says to set the cutter 0.060″ below the size on the seat ring box.

Who is right?

a. A only
c. Both A and B
b. B only
d. Neither A nor B

99. A valve guide hone can be used to size:
  a. bronze replacement guides.
  b. knurled guides.
  c. integral guides.
  d. All of the above

100. An engine equipped with a full round rear main seal is being assembled.

Assembler A says to install the flywheel with an impact wrench in order to ensure no rear main seal leakage.

Assembler B says to slightly overtorque the flywheel mounting bolts in order to ensure no rear main seal leakage.

Who is right?

  a. A only
  b. B only
  c. Both A and B
  d. Neither A nor B

101. A crankshaft is going to be Tufftrided®. Which statement below is true regarding this process?
  a. A molten salt bath is used.
  b. Nitrogen is diffused into the metal.
  c. Fillets are hardened.
  d. All of the above

102. Assembler A says that rod inserts are designed to be slightly longer than the circumference length of the rod bore. This additional length is to give a tight seating in the rod bore and is referred to as "crush."

Assembler B says that "crush" is what determines the rod bearing oil clearance.

Who is right?

  a. A only
  b. B only
  c. Both A and B
  d. Neither A nor B

103. A crankshaft is going to be balanced. Which of these statements is true?
  a. Bob weights are used to simulate total rod-piston weight.
  b. Material can be removed from counterweights by drilling holes.
  c. Both a and b
  d. Neither a nor b

104. A knurling tool has broken off inside a valve guide.

Machinist A says that the tool can be removed with an EDM machine.

Machinist B says that the tool can be removed with a masonry drill.

Who is right?

  a. A only
  b. B only
  c. Both A and B
  d. Neither A nor B

105. A General Motors 140 CID engine has stripped main bearing threads.

Machinist A says that this condition can be repaired by installing Heli-Coil® inserts.

Machinist B says that this condition can be repaired by installing new main bearing bolts coated with J-B Weld®.

Who is right?

a. A only   c. Both A and B
b. B only   d. Neither A nor B

106. An International V-8 head shows cracking between a spark plug hole and the intake port.

Machinist A says that this can be repaired with anaerobic sealer.

Machinist B says that this can be repaired by heat welding.

Who is right?

a. A only   c. Both A and B
b. B only   d. Neither A nor B

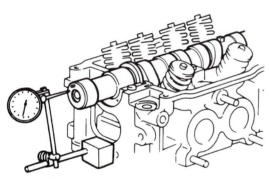

FIGURE 11–35

107. What is being checked in Figure 11–35?

a. Thrust   c. Both a and b
b. Journal runout   d. Neither a nor b

108. A cylinder head with pressed-in studs is being modified for the installation of threaded jam nut studs.

Machinist A says that this will require machining material from each stud boss.

Machinist B says that this will require tapping each stud hole.

Who is right?

a. A only   c. Both A and B
b. B only   d. Neither A nor B

109. "Tipping" small-block Ford valves more than .030″ may:

a. remove the heat-treating hardness.
b. cause the valve keepers to pop out.
c. Both a and b
d. Neither a nor b

110. Correcting rocker arm geometry can be accomplished by:

a. using a longer or shorter valve stem.
b. adding shims under the rocker arm stands.
c. Both a and b
d. Neither a nor b

111. Incorrect rocker arm geometry can be caused by:

a. installing a high-lift camshaft.
b. excessive block surfacing.
c. worn push rods.
d. All of the above

112. A valve head is excessively cupped. This can:

a. take-up valve clearance.
b. hold the valve open.
c. Both a and b
d. Neither a nor b

113. Premature valve guide wear can be caused by:

a. out-of-square valve springs.
b. valve spring seats not being machined perpendicular to the guides.
c. Both a and b
d. Neither a nor b

114. A new camshaft goes "flat" after several thousand miles. This could be caused by:

a. excessive valve spring pressure.
b. reinstalling used lifters.
c. dilution of the oil by fuel or coolant.
d. All of the above

115. All the water-cooled valve guides in a GMC 454 engine have excessive oil clearance.

Machinist A says to remove all carbon buildup from the valve pockets prior to driving out the old guides; then install new guides using sealer.

Machinist B says that these guides may be repaired in place by installing threaded liners.

Who is right?

a. A only
b. B only
c. Both A and B
d. Neither A nor B

116. A set of diesel engine connecting rods are being reconditioned.

Machinist A says to place a feeler gauge under one side of the cap and rod when grinding parting surfaces.

Machinist B says that center-to-center distance can be controlled by boring the bushings.

Who is right?

a. A only
c. Both A and B
b. B only
d. Neither A nor B

117. A crankshaft fractures (breaks) at a 45° angle across a rod bearing journal and through the oil hole. This could be caused by:

a. the wrong vibration damper.
b. the wrong torque converter.
c. excessive gear train backlash.
d. All of the above

118. Assembler A says that certain engines require the torque angle method of head bolt tightening.

Assembler B says that certain engines require the torque-to-yield method of head bolt tightening.

Who is right?

a. A only
c. Both A and B
b. B only
d. Neither A nor B

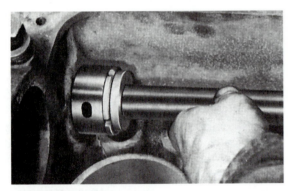

FIGURE 11–36

119. The tool in Figure 11–36 is being used to install cam bearings into a block.

Assembler A says to register oil holes.

Assembler B says to back off on the driving bar about ⅛-turn; this will allow for the 0.003″ to 0.006″ press fit.

Who is right?

a. A only
b. B only
c. Both A and B
d. Neither A nor B

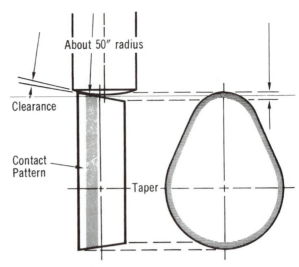

FIGURE 11–37

120. Refer to Figure 11–37.

Machinist A says that cam lobes should never be ground on a taper as shown.

Machinist B says that lifters should never be ground to a radius as shown.

Who is right?

a. A only
c. Both A and B
b. B only
d. Neither A nor B

FIGURE 11–38

121. The cylinder head in Figure 11–38 is being set up for:

a. pressure testing.
c. Both a and b
b. magna-fluxing.
d. Neither a nor b

122. A machinist complains of "chatter" when rigid honing cylinders. This could be caused by:

a. the wrong type of coolant.
b. the stone guides being too tight.
c. Both a and b
d. Neither a nor b

FIGURE 11–39

123. A piston has a mottled greyish pitted appearance on its skirt (see Figure 11–39).

Machinist A says that coolant leakage into the crankcase could be the cause.

Machinist B says that boring the cylinder at the wrong angle to the crankshaft could be the cause.

Who is right?

a. A only
b. B only
c. Both A and B
d. Neither A nor B

FIGURE 11–40

124. The machinist in Figure 11–40 is:
a. using a manulathe.
b. regrooving a piston.
c. Both a and b
d. Neither a nor b

FIGURE 11–41

125. A shop rebuilt a VW engine for a customer. After 700 miles of driving, all of the pistons were badly damaged as shown in Figure 11–41.

Machinist A says that too high of a compression ratio could be the cause.

Machinist B says that too low of a fuel octane could be the cause.

Who is right?

a. A only
b. B only
c. Both A and B
d. Neither A nor B

126. A just rebuilt engine is losing coolant through an internal leak. This could be caused by:
a. a damaged transmission oil cooler.
b. a "pin-holed" timing chain cover.
c. Both a and b
d. Neither a nor b

127. Rounded corners result on an aluminum cylinder head after finishing on a belt surfacer.

Machinist A says that this could be caused by using a worn or improperly tightened belt.

Machinist B says that this could be caused by holding the head against the restraint rail.

Who is right?

a. A only
b. B only
c. Both A and B
d. Neither A nor B

FIGURE 11–42

128. Refer to the chamfer in Figure 11–42.

Machinist A says that this is done primarily as an aid when installing the piston assembly into the cylinder.

Machinist B says that this can be put in freehand with an abrasive cone.

Who is right?
a. A only
b. B only
c. Both A and B
d. Neither A nor B

129. Machinist A says to remove all threaded front and rear oil gallery plugs prior to cleaning a block.

Machinist B says that these plugs can be easily removed by using a block of paraffin.

Who is right?
a. A only
b. B only
c. Both A and B
d. Neither A nor B

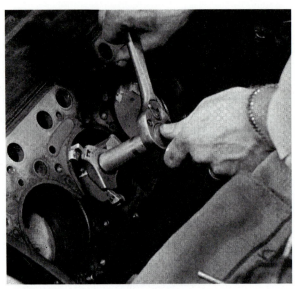

FIGURE 11–43

130. What is being done in Figure 11–43?
a. Cutting a chamfer
b. Removing a ridge
c. Dressing a sleeve counterbore
d. Deglazing a cylinder

FIGURE 11–44

131. What operation is being performed in Figure 11–44?
a. Measuring center-to-center length
b. Checking alignment
c. Straightening
d. Re-sizing

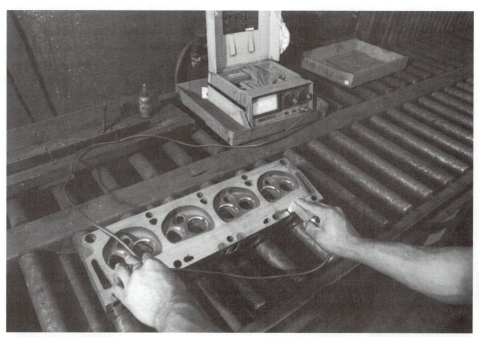

FIGURE 11–45

132. The tool in Figure 11–45 is used to:
a. measure surface roughness.
b. measure head thickness.
c. Both a and b
d. Neither a nor b

133. The tool in Figure 11–46 is used to
a. measure hardness
b. measure magnetism
c. Both a and b
d. Neither a nor b

134. Which of the following is true regarding the dye penetrant method of crack detection?
a. Can be used on nonmagnetic materials
b. Usually consists of a 3-step spray system
c. Defects show up as bright red traces
d. All of the above

135. Assembler A says to add a dab of RTV at the intake manifold gasket and endstrip seal intersections to assure a positive seal on small block Chevrolet engines.

Assembler B says to sparingly apply sealer to intake manifold gaskets on small block Ford engines. Too much sealer can plug coolant drain slots.

Who is right?
a. A only
b. B only
c. Both A and B
d. Neither A nor B

FIGURE 11–46

FIGURE 11-47

136. The machine in Figure 11–47 is used to:
   a. clean small parts.
   b. degrease cylinder heads.
   c. Both a and b
   d. Neither a nor b

137. A set of piston rings are being installed.
   Assembler A says to be sure expander-spacer ends are overlapped.
   Assembler B says to stagger the ring ends.
   Who is right?
   a. A only
   b. B only
   c. Both A and B
   d. Neither A nor B

138. A head gasket is being installed on an engine that has an aluminum head.
   Assembler A says to install the head gasket armor flange against the block if possible.
   Assembler B says that it may be necessary to torque the head bolts with a torque angle/meter.
   Who is right?
   a. A only
   b. B only
   c. Both A and B
   d. Neither A nor B

139. New valve stem o-ring seals have been installed on a set of Chevrolet heads.
   Assembler A says to test for leakage by using a rubber suction cup bulb.
   Assembler B says to test for leakage by filling the recess around the hole in the center of the spring retainer with oil.
   Who is right?
   a. A only
   b. B only
   c. Both A and B
   d. Neither A nor B

140. A customer complains that his newly rebuilt engine has lifter "pump-up." This could be caused by:
   a. weak valve springs.
   b. excessive no-load reving.
   c. Both a and b
   d. Neither a nor b

141. After surfacing an OHC head, the camshaft will not turn.
   Machinist A says to true the camshaft tunnel.
   Machinist B says to install an undersize camshaft.
   Who is right?
   a. A only
   b. B only
   c. Both A and B
   d. Neither A nor B

FIGURE 11-48

FIGURE 11-49

142. Machinist A says to use lubricant when performing the operation in Figure 11-48.

Machinist B says to remove dowel pins when performing the operation above.

Who is right?
a. A only
b. B only
c. Both A and B
d. Neither A nor B

143. Some crankshafts have threaded-in plugs.

Machinist A says that these plugs can be removed in order to clean oil holes.

Machinist B says to punch mark these plugs prior to removal in order to maintain balance.

Who is right?
a. A only
b. B only
c. Both A and B
d. Neither A nor B

144. A crankshaft snout has a torn keyway.

Machinist A says that the crankshaft must be "junked."

Machinist B says that this is often the result of lower-than-specified vibration damper bolt torque.

Who is right?
a. A only
b. B only
c. Both A and B
d. Neither A nor B

145. The shim in Figure 11-49 (see arrow) is being added in order to:
a. correct valve spring height.
b. correct valve spring tension.
c. Both a and b
d. Neither a nor b

FIGURE 11-50

146. Machinist A says that the machine in Figure 11-50 can be used to bore main bearings.

Machinist B says that the machine can be used to bore cam bearings.

Who is right?
a. A only
b. B only
c. Both A and B
d. Neither A nor B

147. An engine with a cylinder bore of 3 13/16″ is bored eighty-thousandths oversize. What will the new diameter be?
a. 3.8205″   **c.** 3.8750″
b. 3.8650″   **d.** 3.8925″

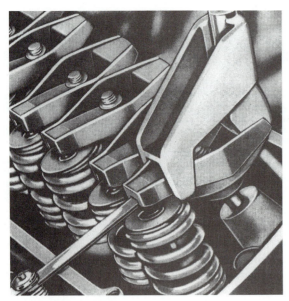

FIGURE 11–51

148. Refer to Figure 11–51.

Assembler A says that valve clearance with the lifter bottomed out is being checked.

Assembler B says that adjustment can be made by using a different length push rod.

Who is right?

a. A only   c. Both A and B
b. B only   d. Neither A nor B

FIGURE 11–52

149. The cylinder in Figure 11–52 is being checked for:

a. glazing.   c. Both a and b
b. scuffing.   d. Neither a nor b

150. Valve guide wear can be measured by using:

a. a split-ball gauge.
b. a new valve and dial indicator.
c. Both a and b
d. Neither a nor b

FIGURE 11–53

151. The cylinder head measurement in Figure 11–53 is incorrect.

Machinist A says that this can cause the lifters to bottom out.

Machinist B says that it may be necessary to grind the end of the valve stems.

Who is right?

a. A only
b. B only
c. Both A and B
d. Neither A nor B

152. A crankshaft is ground undersize by a machinist. However, he fails to properly relieve the fillets. This can cause:

a. bearing distress.
b. overheating and cracking.
c. Both a and b
d. Neither a nor b

153. A crankshaft thrust bearing has just been installed.

Assembler A says to seat (align) the thrust bearing.

Assembler B says if crankshaft end play is too great, replace the thrust bearing.

Who is right?

a. A only
b. B only
c. Both A and B
d. Neither A nor B

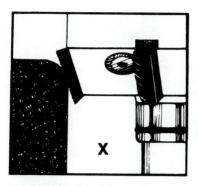
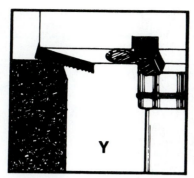
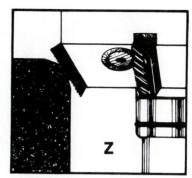

FIGURE 11-54

154. Machinist A says that Figures X and Y in Figure 11–54 show a valve seat being narrowed.

Machinist B says that Figure Z shows cutting a valve seat.

Who is right?
a. A only
b. B only
c. Both A and B
d. Neither A nor B

155. When installing a piston assembly:
a. position the crankshaft rod journal at BDC.
b. slip boots over the rod bolts.
c. make sure the rings are installed right side up.
d. do all the above

156. Machinist A says that there must be a slight amount of free play in the driving dog setup when grinding master cams.

Machinist B says that a camshaft should be checked for runout and recentered before grinding it.

Who is right?
a. A only
b. B only
c. Both A and B
d. Neither A nor B

157. Two machinists are discussing crankshaft grinding.

Machinist A says that when grinding main bearing journals, the shaft need only be centralized.

Machinist B says that when grinding crankpin journals, offset the centers one-half the stroke.

Who is right?
a. A only   c. Both A and B
b. B only   d. Neither A nor B

158. Machinist A says that when using threaded crack repair pins, the pins are generally interlocked.

Machinist B says that when using threaded crack repair pins, the pins are generally installed with sealer.

Who is right?
a. A only   c. Both A and B
b. B only   d. Neither A nor B

159. Cracks in an iron head are going to be repaired by heat welding.

Welder A says to preheat the entire casting to about 1,400°F.

Welder B says to use an acetylene torch adjusted to a neutral flame.

Who is right?
a. A only   c. Both A and B
b. B only   d. Neither A nor B

160. A cracked aluminum head is going to be repaired by TIG welding.

Welder A says do not preheat the head.

Welder B says to remove all carbon, oil, and dirt from the surrounding crack area.

Who is right?
a. A only   c. Both A and B
b. B only   d. Neither A nor B

161. Machinist A says that repairing damaged threads using Keenserts® does not require an inserting tool.

Machinist B says that repairing damaged threads using a Heli-Coil® requires a special tap.

Who is right?
a. A only
b. B only
c. Both A and B
d. Neither A nor B

FIGURE 11–55

162. The piece of equipment in Figure 11–55 is used for:
   a. heating the pistons for rod removal.
   b. heating the rods for piston assembly.
   c. Both a and b
   d. Neither a nor b

163. Machinist A says that a warped aluminum head can be straightened by clamping it against a flat steel plate and placing it in an oven for 4 hours at 500°F, followed by a slow cool-down.

   Machinist B says that a warped aluminum head can be straightened by heating the head in an oven to 600°. After reaching this temperature, place the head in a hydraulic press and press into straightness.

   Who is right?
   a. A only
   b. B only
   c. Both A and B
   d. Neither A nor B

164. Machinist A says that piston diameter is often measured with a telescoping gauge.

   Machinist B says that cylinder bore diameter is often measured with a telescoping gauge and an outside micrometer.

   Who is right?
   a. A only   c. Both A and B
   b. B only   d. Neither A nor B

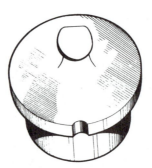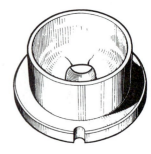

FIGURE 11–56

165. Machinist A says that the parts in Figure 11–56 must fit tight when installed.

   Machinist B says that the parts must be replaced if any cracks appear around the gas outlet.

   Who is right?
   a. A only   c. Both A and B
   b. B only   d. Neither A nor B

166. A valve seat has a .001″ runout (TIR) after grinding.

   Machinist A says to regrind the seat.

   Machinist B says to replace the grinding pilots.

   Who is right?
   a. A only
   b. B only
   c. Both A and B
   d. Neither A nor B

167. When installing a camshaft, you accidentally knock out the block plug at the rear. What would result when the engine was started?
   a. Engine coolant would get into the oil.
   b. An oil pressure loss would occur.
   c. Both a and b
   d. Neither a nor b

168. Which of the measurements below is MOST LIKELY not within specifications for a typical passenger car gasoline engine?
   a. Valve-stem-to-guide clearance—.002″
   b. Cylinder head warpage—.004″
   c. Intake valve seat width—.125″
   d. Exhaust valve margin—1/32″

169. Machinist A says that the rod center-to-center distance can be compensated for when using the machine in Figure 11–57.
   Machinist B says that the rod small end will automatically be bored parallel to the big end when using the machine.
   Who is right?
   a. A only   c. Both A and B
   b. B only   d. Neither A nor B

170. When installing a new set of piston rings, you discover that all the top compression rings have a side clearance varying from .012″ to .018″. What would you do?
   a. Install ring expanders.
   b. Increase the ring groove width.
   c. Replace the pistons.
   d. Nothing—this is an acceptable specification.

171. Machinist A says that a hydraulic lifter is designed to maintain zero lash.
   Machinist B says that a hydraulic lifter camshaft has clearance ramps ground into the lobes.
   Who is right?
   a. A only   c. Both A and B
   b. B only   d. Neither A nor B

FIGURE 11–58

172. Assembler A says that the setup in Figure 11–58 is used to prime the lubrication system.
   Assembler B says that the setup is used to turn the oil pump drive.
   Who is right?
   a. A only
   b. B only
   c. Both A and B
   d. Neither A nor B

173. You are installing a set of new hydraulic valve lifters (non-roller) in an engine. What should be the contour of the new lifter bottom?
   a. Dished (concaved)
   b. Crowned (convexed)
   c. Flat
   d. Tapered

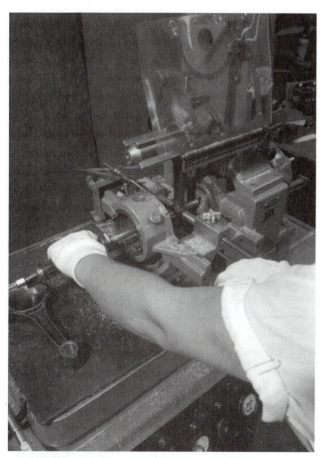

FIGURE 11–57

FIGURE 11–59

174. What operation is being performed in Figure 11–59?
   a. Knurling
   b. Thin walling
   c. Reaming
   d. None of the above

FIGURE 11–60

175. What is being done in Figure 11–60?
   a. Removing the ridge
   b. Installing a liner
   c. Pulling a wet sleeve
   d. Boring the cylinder

176. You are about to assemble a cylinder head. You notice that the valve springs have the coils closer together at one end. How should the springs be installed?
   Assembler A says that the closed coil end of the spring should go toward the head of the valve.
   Assembler B says that the closed coil end goes toward the valve tip.
   Who is right?
   a. A only
   b. B only
   c. Both A and B
   d. Neither A nor B

177. Assembler A says that umbrella valve stem seals are installed with the cup side up (toward the retainer).
   Assembler B says that o-ring valve stem seals are generally installed after the valve spring is compressed.
   Who is right?
   a. A only
   b. B only
   c. Both A and B
   d. Neither A nor B

178. A "cam" ground piston will have its largest diameter:
   a. across the thrust face, 90° from the pin.
   b. across the skirt parallel to the pin.
   c. at 45° from the pin centerline.
   d. at 45° from the pin bosses.

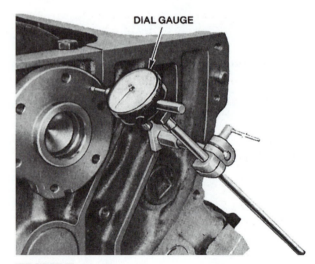

FIGURE 11–61

179. The dial gauge in Figure 11–61 is positioned to check:
   a. crankshaft end play.
   b. crankshaft flange runout.
   c. Both a and b
   d. Neither a nor b

180. A valve seat is being installed in an aluminum head. Which of the following would be considered the MOST NORMAL interference fit?
a. .001–.002″
b. 1/64″
c. .006–.008″
d. .004–.006″

181. All the exhaust valve seats (inserts) in an engine are cracked. This could be caused by:
a. a loose intake manifold.
b. high exhaust back pressure.
c. Both a and b
d. Neither a nor b

182. Machinist A says that a loose valve seat can be fixed by staking it.
   Machinist B says that a loose seat can be detected by tapping on it with a hammer.
   Who is right?
a. A only
b. B only
c. Both A and B
d. Neither A nor B

183. Valves being considered for reuse should be checked for:
a. stem wear.
b. keeper groove wear.
c. margin.
d. All of the above

184. The valves need to be adjusted on an air-cooled engine. Which of these methods is used?
a. Grinding the stems
b. Grinding the lifters
c. Both a and b
d. Neither a nor b

185. Which of the stones in Figure 11–62 would be used for "throating" a 45° valve seat?
a. Stone A
b. Stone B
c. Stone C
d. None of them

FIGURE 11–63

186. The damage in Figure 11–63 was MOST LIKELY caused by:
a. stems cut too short.
b. overreving.
c. worn keepers.
d. bad rotaters.

187. Which of the following surface finishes would be the MOST ACCEPTABLE for the deck on a late-model cast iron cylinder head?
a. 12 Ra (arithmetic average)
b. 25 Ra (arithmetic average)
c. 80 Ra (arithmetic average)
d. 150 Ra (arithmetic average)

188. Before installing a new exhaust manifold gasket, what must be done?
a. Check for warping of the manifold; surfaces must be straight within 0.010″.
b. Make sure manifold gasket surfaces are free of pits and erosion.
c. Both a and b
d. Neither a nor b

A   B   C

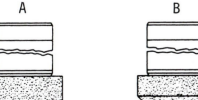
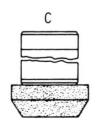

FIGURE 11–62

189. An OHC aluminum head is going to be rebuilt. Which of the following sequences would be correct?
  a. Straighten head, surface deck, align cam bores.
  b. Surface deck, straighten head, align cam bores.
  c. Align cam bores, straighten head, surface deck.
  d. Surface deck, align cam bores, straighten head.

190. An aluminum cylinder head is badly corroded. This could be caused by:
  a. electrolysis.
  b. combustion gas entering the cooling system.
  c. use of improper coolant.
  d. All of the above

191. An OHC cylinder head is being disassembled. Several lash adjusters (lifters) are stuck in their bores. Which of these methods can be used to remove them?
  a. Heat the bore and use a slide hammer.
  b. Install a zerk fitting and use a grease gun.
  c. Both a and b
  d. Neither a nor b

192. Valve lash adjustment on the engine in Figure 11–64 involves:
  a. changing selective thickness shims.
  b. placing a feeler gauge between the tappet and shim.
  c. Both a and b
  d. Neither a nor b

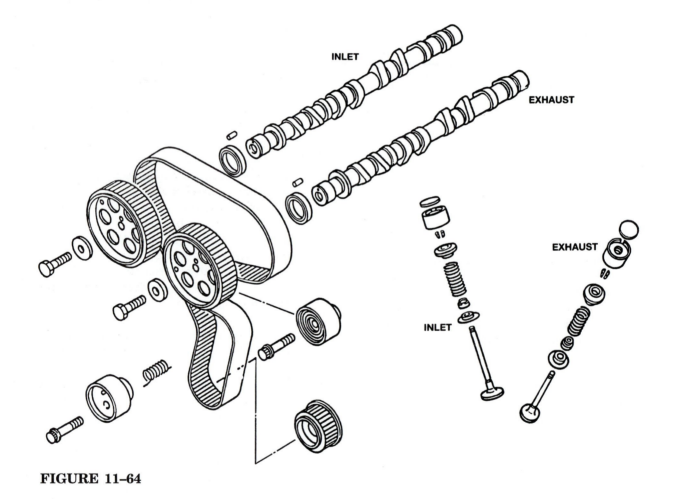

FIGURE 11–64

193. A head has had its combustion chambers reduced from 87 cc to 78 cc.

Machinist A says that this will raise the compression ratio.

Machinist B says that the valves will have to be sunk.

Who is right?
a. A only
b. B only
c. Both A and B
d. Neither A nor B

194. All the machining has just been completed on an aluminum head casting. It is ready for final assembly.

Assembler A says to place the head in a final rinse of caustic soda.

Assembler B says to clean the head with compressed air.

Who is right?
a. A only
b. B only
c. Both A and B
d. Neither A nor B

195. Pressure testing is ideal for detecting leaks around:
a. rocker arm studs.
b. valve guides.
c. injector tubes.
d. All of the above

196. Machinist A says that cracks in an aluminum head can often be detected by passing on oxyacetylene flame over the casting. Carbon in the flame is trapped in the crack, thus highlighting it.

Machinist B says that cracks in an aluminum head can often be repaired by using an electric arc and nickel rod.

Who is right?
a. A only
b. B only
c. Both A and B
d. Neither A nor B

197. An OHC cylinder head is being assembled. Which of the following would most likely be performed last?
a. Checking dry valve lash
b. Placing a vacuum cup over each combustion chamber
c. Measuring valve tip height
d. Determining deck clearance

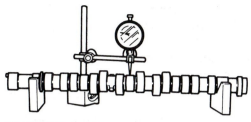

FIGURE 11–65

198. Machinist A says that the setup in Figure 11–65 can be used to measure cam timing.

Machinist B says that the setup can be used to measure cam TIR.

Who is right?
a. A only
b. B only
c. Both A and B
d. Neither A nor B

199. Machinist A says that some valve guides have a tapered OD, and must be driven out from the valve seat side.

Machinist B says that some valve guides are flanged (stepped), and must be driven out from the valve seat side.

Who is right?
a. A only
b. B only
c. Both A and B
d. Neither A nor B

200. Valve stem "metal pickup" (scoring) can:
a. be caused by lack of lubrication.
b. lead to valve breakage.
c. Both a and b
d. Neither a nor b

201. Machinist A says that binding valve rotators can be repaired by brazing.

Machinist B says that binding rotators should be replaced.

Who is right?
a. A only
b. B only
c. Both A and B
d. Neither A nor B

202. Machinist A says that valve rotation used in conjunction with LPG can cause accelerated seat recession.

Machinist B says that valve rotation helps to wipe the seat clean of deposit buildup.

Who is right?
a. A only
b. B only
c. Both A and B
d. Neither A nor B

203. A 4-valve diesel head has excessive stem pitting. This could be caused by:
   a. valve leakage.
   b. a worn crosshead.
   c. Both a and b
   d. Neither a nor b

204. Broken rocker arms can be caused by:
   a. excessive valve spring tension.
   b. improper valve clearance.
   c. valve spring coil bind.
   d. All of the above

205. A valve has a v-shaped channel burned into its face. This could be caused by:
   a. poor seating.
   b. combustion deposits.
   c. Both a and b
   d. Neither a nor b

206. Which of the following would provide the most precise valve guide sizing and best wall finish?
   a. 4-fluted reamer
   b. Spiral reamer
   c. Roller knurler
   d. Guide hone

207. Machinist A says that pushrods can be checked for straightness by using a flat surface and feeler gauge.
   Machinist B says that tightening down rocker arm assemblies too fast can bend pushrods.
   Who is right?
   a. A only   **c.** Both A and B
   b. B only   **d.** Neither A nor B

208. After disassembling a cylinder head, the valve springs are being visually inspected.
   Machinist A says that spring ends should show shine or polish.
   Machinist B says to bead blast rusty springs and reuse them.
   Who is right?
   a. A only   **c.** Both A and B
   b. B only   **d.** Neither A nor B

209. A badly warped OHC head is being belt surfaced into flatness. What may be the result?
   a. A broken camshaft
   b. Unequal combustion chamber volume
   c. Both a and b
   d. Neither a nor b

210. Camshaft bind can be caused by:
   a. excessive runout.
   b. an improperly installed bearing.
   c. bore misalignment.
   d. All of the above

211. All of the following are generally true when installing press-fit cam bearings EXCEPT:
   a. determining the correct location for each bearing.
   b. deburring the lead-in edge of each bearing bore.
   c. indexing the bearing oil holes.
   d. allowing the driver to "bounce" against the bearing.

212. When magnafluxing an iron cylinder head,
   a. dust on the powder before applying the magnet.
   b. make sure surfaces are clean and dry.
   c. keep the magnet in one position only when inspecting an area.
   d. All of the above

213. Tapered cast iron plugs are being used to pin a combustion chamber crack. All of the following should be done EXCEPT:
   a. using sealer.
   b. applying minimum torque.
   c. peening the pins.
   d. allowing 1/4″ spacing between the pins.

214. Machinist A says that valve margin helps the valve withstand pressure and control heat.
   Machinist B says that valve margin, as a general rule, should not be less than 1/8″.
   Who is right?
   a. A only   **c.** Both A and B
   b. B only   **d.** Neither A nor B

215. On an engine that has a gear-driven camshaft, the top of the front cam bearing is worn and the bottom of the back cam bearing is worn. What is the cause?
   Machinist A says that the timing gear lash could be incorrect.
   Machinist B says that the timing gear installation marks could be incorrect.
   Who is right?
   a. A only
   b. B only
   c. Both A and B
   d. Neither A nor B

216. Which of the following would generally be considered the LEAST acceptable way to repair worn crankshaft journals?
a. Submerged arc welding
b. Metal spraying
c. Hard chroming
d. Oxyacetylene welding

217. A block is going to be thermal cleaned in an oven.
Machinist A says to remove the cam bearings.
Machinist B says to make sure the main bearing caps are numbered before removing.
Who is right?
a. A only
b. B only
c. Both A and B
d. Neither A nor B

218. All the top ring grooves in a set of pistons are badly worn.
Machinist A says to discard the pistons.
Machinist B says to install tapered (keystone) rings.
Who is right?
a. A only
b. B only
c. Both A and B
d. Neither A nor B

219. Piston diameter is measured at all of the following locations, EXCEPT:
a. bottom of skirt.
b. center of skirt.
c. below oil ring groove.
d. above top ring groove.

220. The size of a crankshaft journal is made correct by:
a. sweep grinding.
b. plunge grinding.
c. Either a or b
d. Neither a nor b

221. Machinist A says that valve guide bell-mouthing can be measured with a valve grinding pilot.
Machinist B says that valve guide bell-mouthing can be measured with a used valve.
Who is right?
a. A only
b. B only
c. Both A and B
d. Neither A nor B

222. During the boring of a block, the cutter chatters.
Machinist A says to increase the rpm of the cutter and increase the nose radius of the tool bit.
Machinist B says that the tool bit is ground with too fine a tip.
Who is right?
a. A only
b. B only
c. Both A and B
d. Neither A nor B

223. Which of the following would be used to measure lifter bore size?
a. An outside micrometer
b. A dial indicator
c. A diddle gauge
d. A cam bore plug gauge

224. Why would dowels need to be removed from the end of a crankshaft?
a. To true the flange
b. To surface the thrust
c. Either a or b
d. Neither a nor b

225. All of the following are related to the internal balance of an engine EXCEPT:
a. the damper.
b. the balance shafts.
c. pressed-on (clipped-on) weights.
d. the flywheel.

226. A 3/32″ sleeve is being installed in a 4.000 bore. What will the approximate OD size of the sleeve be?
a. 4.0469″
b. 4.0937″
c. 4.1875″
d. 4.1895″

227. A sleeve needs to be installed in a block.
Machinist A says to install the sleeve before boring the other cylinders.
Machinist B says to leave a step in the bottom of the bore to help retain the sleeve.
Who is right?
a. A only
b. B only
c. Both A and B
d. Neither A nor B

228. Machinist A says that the main bearing caps should be torqued in place before boring a block.
Machinist B says that the oil pump should be torqued in place before boring a block.
Who is right?
a. A only
b. B only
c. Both A and B
d. Neither A nor B

229. Machinist A says that a crankshaft can be identified by the casting number.

Machinist B says that a crankshaft can be identified by measuring the main and rod journal diameter.

Who is right?
- **a.** A only
- **b.** B only
- **c.** Both A and B
- **d.** Neither A nor B

230. An engine has a "spun" cam bearing and the oil supply passage under it is badly cracked. What should be done?
- **a.** Sleeve the cam bearing bore and pin the crack.
- **b.** Install an oversize cam bearing and weld the crack.
- **c.** Line bore the cam tunnel.
- **d.** Discard the block.

231. On an engine that has the oil pump driven off the crankshaft, what should be done after align boring?
- **a.** Shim the bearing caps
- **b.** Grind the pump gears
- **c.** Either a or b
- **d.** Neither a nor b

232. There is a groove in the deck of a block between two adjacent cylinders. What could be the cause?
- **a.** A blown head gasket
- **b.** Incorrect piston-to-deck clearance
- **c.** Either a or b
- **d.** Neither a nor b

233. What size radius gauge is used when grinding a radius to a specification of .103–.112″?
- **a.** 5/64″ **b.** 3/32″ **c.** 7/64″ **d.** 1/8″

234. An engine that is designed to be run on leaded gas is run on unleaded gas.

Machinist A says that excessive valve seat wear may be the result in this situation.

Machinist B says that installing replaceable hard seats will help prevent seat and valve wear in this situation.

Who is right?
- **a.** A only
- **b.** B only
- **c.** Both A and B
- **d.** Neither A nor B

235. A connecting rod has a large deep scratch in its eye (small end). What should be done?
- **a.** Install a bushing
- **b.** Measure it
- **c.** Discard it
- **d.** Hone it

236. A block has a crack that runs between two adjacent freeze plug holes. This is MOST LIKELY due to:
- **a.** installing plugs that were oversize.
- **b.** frozen coolant.
- **c.** overheating.
- **d.** fatigue.

237. Machinist A says that shims are installed on aluminum heads to protect the spring pad from wear.

Machinist B says that guides can be removed from aluminum heads by counterboring the guide and driving it out.

Who is right?
- **a.** A only
- **b.** B only
- **c.** Both A and B
- **d.** Neither A nor B

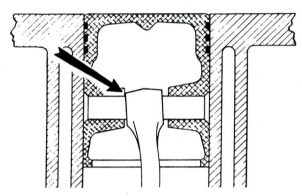

FIGURE 11–66

238. The pressure area shown in Figure 11–66 (see arrow) is caused by:
- **a.** a misaligned rod.
- **b.** a cracked skirt.
- **c.** excessive thrust wear.
- **d.** a missing pin clip.

239. Engine assembler A says that RTV sealer cures in the presence of air.

Engine assembler B says that anaerobic sealer cures in the absence of air.

Who is right?
- **a.** A only
- **b.** B only
- **c.** Both A and B
- **d.** Neither A nor B

240. A block has main caps that fit loose. What should be done in this situation?
- **a.** Replace the caps
- **b.** Knurl the caps
- **c.** Weld the caps
- **d.** Shim the caps

241. What tool should be used when installing an oxygen sensor?
   a. A pipe wrench
   b. An 8-point socket
   c. A 12-point socket
   d. A special wrench

242. When completely machining a V-8 block, which of the following should be done first?
   a. True the cam bores
   b. Bore the cylinders
   c. Surface the decks
   d. Align bore the crank tunnel

243. A just assembled engine is being prepared for starting. Which of the following is accepted procedure?
   a. Install the distributor with the rotor facing toward the rear of the engine
   b. Charge the lubrication system by spinning the oil pump drive
   c. Both a and b
   d. Neither a nor b

244. A new turbocharger is being installed. Which of the following should be done?
   a. Block the compressor wheel so that it will not turn when the engine is first started
   b. Fill the center cartridge with grease
   c. Both a and b
   d. Neither a nor b

245. Assembler A says that heat tabs should be fastened with rivets.
   Assembler B says that heat tabs should be installed as close as possible to the exhaust manifold.
   Who is right?
   a. A only   c. Both A and B
   b. B only   d. Neither A nor B

246. Using a 1/2″ drill in cast iron would require a cutting speed of:
   a. 400 rpm.   c. 720 rpm.
   b. 560 rpm.   d. 2,400 rpm.

247. A piston ring has a stamped dot marking on it.
   Assembler A says this mark indicates that the ring is to be installed in the second piston groove.
   Assembler B says this mark should face the combustion chamber when installed.
   Who is right?
   a. A only   c. Both A and B
   b. B only   d. Neither A nor B

248. A set of mushroom-type lifters is being installed.
   Assembler A says to coat the lifter bottoms with EP lubricant.
   Assembler B says to insert the camshaft after installing the lifters.
   Who is right?
   a. A only   c. Both A and B
   b. B only   d. Neither A nor B

249. When installing a timing chain cover:
   a. make sure the woodruff key is in place.
   b. make sure the oil slinger is not bent.
   c. Both a and b
   d. Neither a nor b

250. Machinist A says that cylinder block identification can be determined by the bore spacing.
   Machinist B says that cylinder block identification can be determined by the casting clock numbers.
   Who is right?
   a. A only   c. Both A and B
   b. B only   d. Neither A nor B

251. Assembler A says that cup-type core plugs can be removed by driving them in with a punch, and then pulling them out with a pair of channel lock pliers.
   Assembler B says that flat (disc-type) core plugs are installed by driving them in until the crown is just over center.
   Who is right?
   a. A only   c. Both A and B
   b. B only   d. Neither A nor B

252. Lifter bores can be flex-honed in order to:
   a. Remove rust.
   b. Size the diameter.
   c. Both a and b
   d. Neither a nor b

253. Which of the following statements is the LEAST LIKELY cause of a bent pushrod?
   a. Overspeeding
   b. Sticking valve
   c. Worn rocker stud
   d. Excessive valve guide clearance

ANSWERS

1. Engine Repair

1. c	41. c	81. b	121. c	161. c
2. c	42. c	82. b	122. c	162. d
3. a	43. a	83. b	123. d	163. c
4. b	44. c	84. a	124. a	164. c
5. c	45. a	85. c	125. a	165. c
6. c	46. d	86. b	126. b	166. d
7. a	47. d	87. c	127. d	167. d
8. c	48. a	88. a	128. b	168. c
9. d	49. c	89. c	129. c	169. b
10. c	50. d	90. c	130. a	170. c
11. c	51. c	91. c	131. d	171. d
12. b	52. c	92. c	132. b	172. d
13. c	53. a	93. b	133. b	173. c
14. c	54. a	94. b	134. c	174. d
15. d	55. d	95. c	135. d	175. d
16. d	56. c	96. a	136. c	176. c
17. b	57. a	97. d	137. d	177. d
18. b	58. a	98. b	138. a	178. d
19. c	59. d	99. b	139. c	179. d
20. d	60. a	100. c	140. c	180. d
21. c	61. b	101. a	141. c	181. b
22. c	62. c	102. d	142. c	182. b
23. a	63. c	103. b	143. c	183. b
24. c	64. d	104. d	144. c	184. b
25. d	65. c	105. a	145. c	185. b
26. b	66. d	106. a	146. d	186. b
27. c	67. d	107. b	147. d	187. a
28. a	68. c	108. b	148. c	188. c
29. a	69. b	109. c	149. c	189. d
30. c	70. b	110. d	150. c	190. c
31. b	71. c	111. a	151. c	191. a
32. b	72. c	112. a	152. a	192. b
33. a	73. c	113. c	153. c	193. c
34. d	74. d	114. c	154. a	194. a
35. c	75. b	115. c	155. d	195. d
36. c	76. d	116. a	156. d	196. b
37. d	77. c	117. a	157. d	197. c
38. c	78. d	118. a	158. c	
39. b	79. a	119. d	159. a	
40. c	80. b	120. d	160. c	

2. Automatic Transmission/Transaxle

1. c	5. b	9. c	13. d	17. b
2. c	6. d	10. a	14. c	18. c
3. c	7. c	11. b	15. d	19. a
4. d	8. a	12. a	16. c	20. c

21. c	56. b	91. a	126. c	161. c
22. d	57. b	92. b	127. b	162. d
23. a	58. c	93. b	128. c	163. c
24. a	59. c	94. a	129. b	164. c
25. d	60. a	95. c	130. c	165. c
26. d	61. a	96. d	131. d	166. c
27. c	62. c	97. a	132. a	167. d
28. c	63. c	98. c	133. b	168. c
29. c	64. a	99. a	134. c	169. c
30. b	65. c	100. b	135. c	170. d
31. d	66. b	101. c	136. c	171. b
32. a	67. c	102. d	137. c	172. c
33. d	68. b	103. c	138. c	173. d
34. d	69. c	104. a	139. d	174. d
35. d	70. c	105. b	140. c	175. c
36. d	71. c	106. a	141. b	176. a
37. d	72. d	107. c	142. d	177. c
38. d	73. a	108. b	143. c	178. b
39. b	74. d	109. a	144. d	179. d
40. d	75. a	110. c	145. d	180. a
41. c	76. c	111. b	146. a	181. b
42. b	77. a	112. c	147. d	182. b
43. c	78. b	113. a	148. b	183. c
44. a	79. c	114. c	149. a	184. c
45. c	80. c	115. a	150. a	185. b
46. a	81. b	116. a	151. c	186. a
47. d	82. b	117. c	152. c	187. d
48. c	83. c	118. d	153. a	188. c
49. c	84. d	119. c	154. c	189. d
50. d	85. d	120. b	155. c	190. a
51. d	86. a	121. d	156. c	191. a
52. b	87. a	122. d	157. c	
53. c	88. d	123. a	158. a	
54. c	89. c	124. a	159. c	
55. a	90. b	125. c	160. a	

3. Manual Drive Train and Axles

1. c	26. a	51. c	76. d	101. a
2. d	27. a	52. a	77. a	102. a
3. b	28. b	53. a	78. b	103. a
4. d	29. a	54. a	79. c	104. c
5. d	30. c	55. c	80. c	105. d
6. d	31. c	56. d	81. b	106. b
7. b	32. c	57. b	82. b	107. c
8. c	33. d	58. c	83. a	108. c
9. a	34. d	59. c	84. c	109. c
10. c	35. b	60. c	85. a	110. a
11. a	36. c	61. b	86. c	111. c
12. c	37. c	62. c	87. b	112. b
13. c	38. b	63. b	88. b	113. d
14. b	39. b	64. c	89. d	114. d
15. c	40. c	65. b	90. b	115. c
16. c	41. c	66. d	91. a	116. d
17. c	42. a	67. a	92. c	117. b
18. a	43. c	68. c	93. b	118. c
19. a	44. c	69. c	94. c	119. d
20. c	45. d	70. d	95. c	120. b
21. b	46. d	71. c	96. c	121. c
22. c	47. a	72. c	97. c	122. a
23. d	48. d	73. d	98. c	123. c
24. b	49. b	74. b	99. b	124. d
25. a	50. d	75. b	100. c	125. d

126. a   140. a   154. b   168. d   182. b
127. b   141. b   155. a   169. c   183. b
128. a   142. b   156. a   170. d   184. c
129. d   143. c   157. d   171. c   185. d
130. c   144. a   158. d   172. c   186. c
131. b   145. d   159. b   173. d   187. b
132. c   146. d   160. c   174. b   188. d
133. a   147. d   161. b   175. c   189. d
134. c   148. a   162. d   176. a   190. b
135. d   149. c   163. b   177. d   191. a
136. b   150. b   164. d   178. a   192. c
137. a   151. d   165. c   179. a   193. d
138. c   152. d   166. a   180. a   194. d
139. b   153. a   167. b   181. b   195. a

4. Suspension and Steering

1. d   45. b   89. c   133. a   177. c
2. c   46. b   90. d   134. d   178. c
3. c   47. c   91. d   135. c   179. c
4. d   48. d   92. d   136. b   180. d
5. d   49. c   93. c   137. c   181. c
6. a   50. a   94. d   138. b   182. a
7. a   51. c   95. a   139. c   183. c
8. a   52. c   96. c   140. a   184. c
9. d   53. a   97. c   141. d   185. a
10. b   54. d   98. c   142. c   186. c
11. a   55. c   99. d   143. a   187. d
12. b   56. b   100. c   144. b   188. d
13. b   57. c   101. a   145. d   189. c
14. c   58. c   102. a   146. c   190. d
15. a   59. b   103. c   147. d   191. c
16. c   60. c   104. b   148. a   192. c
17. a   61. b   105. d   149. b   193. c
18. c   62. c   106. a   150. c   194. d
19. a   63. d   107. d   151. a   195. c
20. c   64. d   108. b   152. b   196. c
21. c   65. b   109. c   153. b   197. b
22. d   66. a   110. c   154. d   198. c
23. b   67. d   111. d   155. a   199. c
24. c   68. a   112. d   156. d   200. c
25. c   69. c   113. d   157. a   201. c
26. a   70. c   114. b   158. c   202. d
27. b   71. c   115. b   159. c   203. c
28. b   72. b   116. d   160. a   204. c
29. c   73. b   117. c   161. a   205. a
30. b   74. a   118. b   162. c   206. a
31. c   75. b   119. d   163. c   207. a
32. d   76. a   120. a   164. d   208. a
33. a   77. a   121. b   165. b   209. c
34. c   78. c   122. c   166. b   210. c
35. b   79. c   123. c   167. c   211. c
36. d   80. c   124. d   168. d   212. d
37. c   81. b   125. b   169. c   213. a
38. b   82. a   126. c   170. c   214. d
39. a   83. a   127. a   171. a   215. d
40. b   84. d   128. d   172. c   216. a
41. c   85. b   129. c   173. d   217. a
42. c   86. c   130. c   174. a
43. d   87. a   131. d   175. d
44. a   88. a   132. c   176. b

5. Brakes

1. d	41. a	81. d	121. b	161. c
2. d	42. a	82. d	122. c	162. c
3. c	43. a	83. c	123. b	163. d
4. c	44. d	84. c	124. c	164. c
5. c	45. b	85. b	125. d	165. d
6. b	46. d	86. d	126. c	166. b
7. b	47. d	87. d	127. d	167. b
8. b	48. b	88. c	128. d	168. d
9. b	49. c	89. b	129. b	169. d
10. c	50. c	90. c	130. b	170. d
11. c	51. c	91. c	131. d	171. c
12. b	52. d	92. b	132. c	172. c
13. d	53. b	93. d	133. c	173. b
14. c	54. a	94. c	134. b	174. b
15. d	55. b	95. b	135. b	175. d
16. d	56. b	96. d	136. c	176. d
17. b	57. c	97. d	137. d	177. c
18. a	58. d	98. b	138. c	178. d
19. d	59. c	99. b	139. a	179. d
20. c	60. a	100. d	140. b	180. c
21. d	61. d	101. d	141. b	181. c
22. b	62. a	102. d	142. c	182. b
23. c	63. d	103. d	143. a	183. c
24. b	64. c	104. d	144. d	184. a
25. b	65. d	105. a	145. d	185. b
26. a	66. a	106. c	146. c	186. b
27. b	67. c	107. c	147. d	187. b
28. d	68. c	108. b	148. b	188. c
29. d	69. c	109. c	149. d	189. c
30. c	70. c	110. a	150. b	190. b
31. c	71. a	111. b	151. d	191. c
32. d	72. a	112. b	152. c	192. c
33. c	73. d	113. d	153. d	193. b
34. a	74. c	114. c	154. a	194. b
35. a	75. b	115. c	155. c	195. a
36. d	76. b	116. c	156. b	196. b
37. c	77. a	117. d	157. d	197. a
38. a	78. d	118. c	158. c	198. d
39. d	79. c	119. b	159. a	199. d
40. b	80. d	120. a	160. d	200. b

6. Electrical/Electronic Systems

1. c	17. d	33. c	49. d	65. c
2. d	18. c	34. c	50. c	66. c
3. c	19. b	35. b	51. c	67. d
4. b	20. c	36. a	52. a	68. a
5. a	21. d	37. d	53. c	69. a
6. c	22. a	38. c	54. d	70. d
7. b	23. d	39. c	55. d	71. b
8. b	24. d	40. c	56. c	72. d
9. d	25. d	41. c	57. d	73. c
10. c	26. c	42. d	58. c	74. c
11. d	27. b	43. b	59. d	75. c
12. a	28. c	44. c	60. c	76. d
13. a	29. a	45. c	61. b	77. c
14. c	30. c	46. c	62. d	78. c
15. a	31. c	47. b	63. c	79. a
16. c	32. d	48. d	64. c	80. c

81. b	104. d	127. c	150. b	173. a
82. c	105. b	128. b	151. c	174. a
83. b	106. a	129. c	152. c	175. c
84. d	107. c	130. c	153. b	176. a
85. c	108. c	131. a	154. d	177. c
86. b	109. c	132. a	155. b	178. c
87. a	110. a	133. b	156. c	179. b
88. c	111. a	134. c	157. b	180. a
89. a	112. d	135. c	158. d	181. a
90. a	113. b	136. c	159. d	182. d
91. b	114. a	137. d	160. d	183. d
92. c	115. d	138. b	161. c	184. c
93. c	116. d	139. b	162. b	185. d
94. c	117. c	140. d	163. a	186. b
95. b	118. b	141. d	164. d	187. a
96. c	119. c	142. d	165. c	188. b
97. a	120. a	143. d	166. c	189. d
98. d	121. c	144. c	167. d	190. d
99. d	122. b	145. c	168. d	191. c
100. a	123. d	146. a	169. c	
101. a	124. c	147. b	170. d	
102. c	125. b	148. b	171. c	
103. a	126. b	149. d	172. a	

7. Heating and Air Conditioning

1. a	35. c	69. c	103. c	137. b
2. d	36. a	70. a	104. c	138. c
3. b	37. a	71. a	105. b	139. c
4. c	38. d	72. d	106. a	140. c
5. b	39. a	73. c	107. c	141. a
6. a	40. b	74. c	108. d	142. b
7. a	41. c	75. a	109. c	143. d
8. c	42. d	76. a	110. c	144. c
9. d	43. b	77. d	111. a	145. d
10. c	44. a	78. c	112. d	146. a
11. c	45. c	79. d	113. c	147. c
12. c	46. a	80. d	114. d	148. b
13. b	47. a	81. a	115. c	149. c
14. b	48. b	82. c	116. b	150. c
15. a	49. b	83. d	117. b	151. c
16. c	50. d	84. a	118. c	152. c
17. c	51. b	85. d	119. b	153. c
18. a	52. c	86. b	120. b	154. c
19. a	53. b	87. c	121. a	155. a
20. d	54. c	88. a	122. a	156. a
21. a	55. a	89. c	123. b	157. a
22. b	56. a	90. c	124. b	158. c
23. a	57. a	91. c	125. b	159. b
24. a	58. c	92. c	126. c	160. b
25. c	59. a	93. c	127. a	161. d
26. c	60. d	94. d	128. d	162. c
27. c	61. c	95. d	129. a	163. a
28. d	62. d	96. c	130. c	164. b
29. c	63. b	97. d	131. c	165. d
30. c	64. b	98. c	132. a	166. d
31. a	65. a	99. c	133. c	167. a
32. c	66. c	100. c	134. c	168. d
33. c	67. d	101. d	135. c	169. c
34. d	68. d	102. c	136. c	170. d

8. Engine Performance

1. c	46. b	91. a	136. c	181. a
2. c	47. a	92. d	137. b	182. d
3. d	48. c	93. b	138. c	183. c
4. a	49. b	94. a	139. b	184. d
5. b	50. d	95. d	140. a	185. c
6. c	51. b	96. c	141. c	186. c
7. c	52. d	97. c	142. c	187. c
8. a	53. c	98. b	143. d	188. c
9. a	54. b	99. b	144. c	189. a
10. b	55. a	100. c	145. b	190. a
11. c	56. b	101. c	146. d	191. c
12. d	57. c	102. c	147. d	192. a
13. d	58. a	103. d	148. a	193. c
14. d	59. a	104. c	149. b	194. d
15. d	60. b	105. b	150. a	195. d
16. c	61. a	106. a	151. c	196. d
17. a	62. d	107. c	152. c	197. d
18. b	63. c	108. b	153. b	198. c
19. b	64. d	109. c	154. c	199. b
20. c	65. c	110. c	155. c	200. c
21. c	66. d	111. c	156. b	201. d
22. b	67. d	112. b	157. a	202. c
23. a	68. c	113. c	158. c	203. c
24. a	69. b	114. c	159. c	204. c
25. c	70. c	115. c	160. c	205. c
26. b	71. c	116. a	161. c	206. b
27. b	72. c	117. c	162. c	207. b
28. c	73. a	118. a	163. c	208. d
29. a	74. c	119. c	164. d	209. c
30. c	75. c	120. c	165. c	210. b
31. c	76. c	121. b	166. d	211. b
32. d	77. b	122. b	167. b	212. d
33. c	78. c	123. a	168. c	213. c
34. c	79. d	124. a	169. b	214. d
35. d	80. c	125. c	170. d	215. d
36. b	81. c	126. c	171. d	216. a
37. a	82. a	127. c	172. d	217. c
38. d	83. c	128. d	173. d	218. d
39. c	84. b	129. c	174. a	219. a
40. b	85. c	130. d	175. b	220. d
41. d	86. c	131. d	176. b	221. c
42. c	87. d	132. a	177. d	222. b
43. a	88. b	133. c	178. c	223. a
44. c	89. d	134. d	179. c	224. a
45. a	90. b	135. a	180. c	

9. Advanced Engine Performance Specialist

1. b	12. b	23. c	34. c	45. b
2. d	13. a	24. c	35. c	46. d
3. d	14. c	25. d	36. b	47. a
4. c	15. b	26. b	37. c	48. d
5. b	16. d	27. c	38. d	49. c
6. c	17. a	28. d	39. c	50. d
7. d	18. d	29. d	40. a	51. c
8. c	19. a	30. a	41. c	52. c
9. a	20. a	31. d	42. d	53. c
10. b	21. c	32. c	43. a	54. c
11. a	22. b	33. b	44. b	55. a

56. b	68. b	80. d	92. b	104. c
57. a	69. a	81. b	93. b	105. c
58. d	70. a	82. c	94. a	106. b
59. a	71. c	83. d	95. a	107. d
60. a	72. b	84. a	96. c	108. a
61. b	73. c	85. c	97. a	109. c
62. b	74. c	86. c	98. d	110. d
63. d	75. b	87. d	99. c	111. d
64. a	76. a	88. c	100. b	112. d
65. d	77. b	89. c	101. b	
66. d	78. c	90. c	102. d	
67. b	79. a	91. a	103. d	

10. Light Vehicle Compressed Natural Gas

1. d	18. a	35. c	52. a	69. c
2. d	19. a	36. c	53. d	70. c
3. c	20. a	37. c	54. d	71. c
4. b	21. d	38. c	55. b	72. c
5. d	22. a	39. a	56. d	73. b
6. c	23. c	40. b	57. c	74. a
7. a	24. c	41. c	58. a	75. d
8. a	25. d	42. c	59. b	76. b
9. c	26. c	43. b	60. b	77. a
10. c	27. d	44. d	61. d	78. b
11. a	28. d	45. c	62. a	79. b
12. b	29. d	46. d	63. b	80. c
13. d	30. c	47. c	64. c	81. d
14. c	31. a	48. c	65. d	82. c
15. a	32. d	49. d	66. d	
16. d	33. b	50. b	67. d	
17. d	34. c	51. c	68. a	

11. Engine Machinist

1. d	25. c	49. c	73. b	97. a
2. c	26. c	50. a	74. d	98. a
3. d	27. b	51. a	75. c	99. d
4. a	28. d	52. d	76. d	100. d
5. a	29. d	53. c	77. d	101. d
6. c	30. d	54. b	78. c	102. a
7. b	31. d	55. d	79. b	103. c
8. a	32. b	56. c	80. c	104. c
9. b	33. d	57. d	81. c	105. a
10. c	34. d	58. a	82. b	106. b
11. b	35. c	59. c	83. c	107. a
12. c	36. d	60. c	84. c	108. c
13. d	37. c	61. d	85. c	109. c
14. c	38. c	62. b	86. c	110. c
15. c	39. a	63. c	87. d	111. d
16. c	40. c	64. d	88. c	112. c
17. c	41. d	65. a	89. a	113. c
18. a	42. a	66. d	90. d	114. d
19. a	43. c	67. c	91. c	115. c
20. a	44. a	68. c	92. c	116. b
21. c	45. d	69. b	93. c	117. c
22. c	46. b	70. b	94. c	118. c
23. b	47. c	71. a	95. d	119. c
24. c	48. b	72. c	96. a	120. d

121. a	148. c	175. a	202. c	229. a
122. c	149. d	176. a	203. a	230. d
123. a	150. c	177. d	204. d	231. d
124. c	151. c	178. a	205. c	232. a
125. c	152. c	179. c	206. d	233. c
126. c	153. c	180. d	207. c	234. c
127. c	154. c	181. c	208. d	235. c
128. c	155. d	182. b	209. c	236. a
129. c	156. b	183. d	210. d	237. c
130. b	157. c	184. a	211. d	238. a
131. b	158. c	185. c	212. b	239. c
132. a	159. c	186. a	213. d	240. b
133. a	160. b	187. c	214. a	241. d
134. d	161. c	188. c	215. a	242. d
135. c	162. b	189. a	216. d	243. b
136. a	163. c	190. d	217. c	244. d
137. b	164. b	191. c	218. a	245. d
138. b	165. a	192. a	219. d	246. b
139. c	166. d	193. a	220. c	247. b
140. c	167. b	194. d	221. d	248. c
141. a	168. c	195. d	222. d	249. c
142. b	169. c	196. a	223. b	250. d
143. c	170. c	197. d	224. a	251. c
144. b	171. a	198. b	225. a	252. a
145. a	172. c	199. c	226. c	253. d
146. c	173. b	200. c	227. c	
147. d	174. c	201. b	228. a	